MYTHS AND FOLK-TALES

MYTHS AND FOLK-TALES

OF THE

RUSSIANS, WESTERN SLAVS, AND MAGYARS

By JEREMIAH CURTIN

BENJAMIN BLOM, INC.
Publishers, New York 1971

First published Boston, 1890
Reissued 1971 by
Benjamin Blom, Inc.
New York, N.Y. 10025

Library of Congress
Catalog Card Number 74-160611

Reprinted from a copy in
the collection of
The New York Public Library

Printed in the
United States of America

To FRANCIS JAMES CHILD, PH. D., LL. D.

Professor of English in Harvard University,
Cambridge, Mass.

MY DEAR PROFESSOR CHILD, —

It is more than a quarter of a century since you began for Harvard that collection of myths, folk-tales, and ballads, in all European languages, which has grown under your hand to such proportions that it is now, perhaps, the most complete of its kind in either hemisphere.

This work was begun by you through a clear perception of what was needed for laborers in a most important field of inquiry, and achieved by tireless and patient care in seeking and finding.

Your labors as a scholar are honored abroad as at home, and your work on English and Scottish ballads will endure as a monument of skill and devotion.

During your career as Professor you have been true to the ideals of Harvard scholarship and life, adding to them meanwhile something of your own.

Whoso adds to or freshens the spirit of our revered Alma Mater deserves well of the country; for Harvard, now in the second half of the third century of her existence, is the oldest witness and, so far, the most eloquent that we have to the collective and continuous striving of Americans towards a higher life.

To you, — the distinguished Professor, the earnest scholar, the faithful friend, — I, one of thousands who have listened to your instruction, dedicate this volume, gathered from a field in which you take so much delight.

JEREMIAH CURTIN.

SMITHSONIAN INSTITUTION,
BUREAU OF ETHNOLOGY.
WASHINGTON D. C. October 23, 1890.

CONTENTS.

CHEKH MYTHS AND FOLK-TALES.

MAGYAR MYTHS AND FOLK-TALES.

INTRODUCTION.

———◆———

A FEW tens of years ago it was all-important to understand and explain the brotherhood and blood-bond
of Aryan nations, and their relation to the Semitic race ; to
discover and set forth the meaning of that which in mental
work, historic strivings, and spiritual ideals ties the historic
nations to one another. At the present time this work is
done, if not completely, at least measurably well, and a new
work awaits us, to demonstrate that there is a higher and a
mightier bond, — the relationship of created things with one
another, and their inseverable connection with That which
some men reverence as God, but which other men call the
Unknowable, the Unseen.

This new work, which is the necessary continuation of
the first, and which alone can give it completeness and
significance, will be achieved when we have established the
science of mythology.

Of course all that may be attempted in a volume like the
present is to throw out a few hints, and to mention some of
the uses of mythology as a science.

There is a large body of myths and folk-tales already
published in Europe, and still a great number as yet un-
collected. Many of these tales are of remarkable beauty.
They are of deep interest both to young and old, and
nowhere do they enjoy more delicate appreciation than
among educated people in America and England. The

delight in a beautiful and wonderful story is the very highest mental pleasure for a child, and great even for a grown man; but the explanation of it (if explanation there be) and the nature of its heroes (if that can be discovered) are dear to the mind of a mature person of culture. Much has been written touching the heroes of folk-tales, as well as the characters in Aryan mythology, but it appears to have produced small effect; for to most readers it seems unproven, and founded mainly on the views of each writer. This is the reason why the chief, almost the only, value found in folk-tales, as yet, is the story itself, with its simple beauty, incomparable grotesqueness, and marvellous adventures.

The great majority even of the least modified tales of Europe have mainly substituted heroes, — sons of kings, tsars, merchants, poor men, soldiers, — so that in most cases the birth, occupation, or name of the present hero gives no clew to the original hero of the tale; but incidents do. The incidents are often an indication of what kind of person the original hero must have been.

A few of the tales in this volume have preserved elemental heroes; and this is a fact of great value, for it points to a similarity with the American system of mythology.

We have in the present volume Raven, — not the common bird, but that elemental power which, after having been overcome, turned into the common raven of to-day, and flew off to the mountains; Whirlwind and South Wind are both heroes, — one as a leading, the other as an important secondary, character in two of the Russian stories. We have two brothers Wind, in "The Cuirassier and the Horned Princess," in whom the personal character of Wind is well maintained. The steed, fire-eating and wise, of the Magyars, which appears also in Russian and other Slav tales, always mangy and miserable except in action, is a very significant character, whose real nature one may hope to demonstrate. But we have no tale in which it is clear who all the characters are; the modifying influences were too great and long-continued to permit that. Though myth-tales are, perhaps, more interesting for the majority of modern readers in their present form, they will not have their full interest for science till it is shown who most of the actors are under their disguises.

This is the nearest task of mythology.

There are masterpieces in literature filled with myths, inspired with myth conceptions of many kinds, simply colored by the life of the time and the nations among which these masterpieces were written and moulded to shape by artists, made strong from the spirit of great, simple people, as unknown to us as the nameless heroes who perished before Agamemnon. How much mythology is there in the Iliad and the Odyssey, in the Æneid, in the Divine Comedy of Dante, in the works of the other three great Italian poets? How much in Paradise Lost? How could "King Lear" and "Midsummer Night's Dream," or the "Idylls of the King" have been written without Keltic mythology? Many of these literary masterpieces have not merely myths in their composition as a sentence has words, but the earlier ones are enlarged or modified myth-tales of those periods, while the later ones are largely modelled on and inspired by the earlier.

The early chronicles of nations are as strikingly associated with mythology as are the masterpieces of literature. Omitting others, one case may be noted here, — that of the voluminous Gaelic chronicles and the so-called historical tales of Ireland, which, in the guise of history, give mythology, and preserve for coming investigators a whole buried Pantheon.

The service of the science of mythology will be great in connection with the myth-tales of nations, with literature, and with early history; but its weightiest service will be rendered in the domain of religion, for without mythology there can be no thorough understanding of any religion on earth, either in its inception or its growth.

But how is this science from which men may receive such service to be founded?

In one way alone : by obtaining from races outside of the Aryan and Semitic their myths, their beliefs, their view of the world ; this done, the rest will follow as a result of intelligent labor. But the great battle is in the first part of the work, for the inherent difficulty of the task has been increased by Europeans, who have exterminated great numbers among the best primitive races, partially civilized or rather degraded others, and rendered the remainder distrustful and not easily approached on the subject of their myths and ethnic beliefs.

As to the collection of these myths and beliefs, the following may be stated : —

There is everywhere a sort of selvage of short tales and anecdotes, small information about ghosts and snakes, among all these races, which are easily obtained ; and most Europeans seem to think that when they have collected some of these trivial things they have all that the given people possess. But they are greatly mistaken. All these people have something better. There was not a single stock of Indians in America which did not possess, in beautiful forms, the elements of an extensive literature, with a religion and philosophy which would have thrown light on many beginnings of Aryan and Semitic thought, a knowledge of which in so many cases is now lost to us, but which we hope to recover in time. The same may be said of other primitive races, still unbroken, unmodified ; and though much has been lost, still enough remains to serve our purpose fully, if civilized men instead of slaying " savages," directly and indirectly, will treat them as human beings, and not add to the labor of those workers who in the near future will surely endeavor, singly or in small groups, to study the chief primitive races of the earth, and win from them, not short insignificant odds and ends of information, but great masses of material ; for the educated world may rest assured that these races possess in large volume some of the most beautiful productions of the human mind, and facts that are not merely of great, but of unique, value.

In the introduction to my volume, " Myths and Folk-lore of Ireland," I endeavored to explain in brief what the myths of America are, especially the Creation-myths, referring only to those which I myself have collected. I stated that, " All myths have the same origin, and that all run parallel up to a certain point, which may be taken as the point to which the least developed peoples have risen " (page 27). I do not know any better way of illustrating this than to bring into evidence myths of the Morning-star. The Indians have a great many myths in which the Morning-star figures as the Light-bringer, — the same office as that indicated by the Latin word *Lucifer ;* and here I may be permitted to present a short chapter of my personal experience with reference to that word and the Morning-star.

I remember well the feelings roused in my mind at mention or sight of the name Lucifer during the earlier years of my life. It stood for me as the name of a being stupendous, dreadful in moral deformity, lurid, hideous, and mighty. I remember also the surprise with which when I had grown somewhat older and begun to study Latin, I came upon the name in Virgil, where it means the Light-bringer, or Morning-star, — the herald of the sun. Many years after I had found the name in Virgil, I spent a night at the house of a friend in Milwaukee, Wisconsin, right at the shore of Lake Michigan. The night was clear but without a moon, — a night of stars, which is the most impressive of all nights, vast, brooding, majestic. At three o'clock in the morning I woke, and being near an uncurtained window, rose and looked out. Rather low in the east was the Morning-star, shining like silver, with a bluish tinge of steel. I looked towards the west; the great infinity was filled with the hosts of heaven, ranged behind this Morning-star. I saw at once the origin of the myth which grew to have such tremendous moral meaning, because the Morning-star was not in this case the usher of the day but the chieftain of night, the Prince of Darkness, the mortal enemy of the Lord of Light. I returned to bed knowing that the battle in heaven would soon begin. I rose when the sun was high next morning. All the world was bright, shining and active, gladsome and fresh, from the rays of the sun; the kingdom of light was established; but the Prince of Darkness and all his confederates had vanished, cast down from the sky, and to the endless eternity of God their places will know them no more in *that* night again. They are lost beyond hope or redemption, beyond penance or prayer.

I have in mind at this moment two Indian stories of the Morning-star, — one Modoc, the other Delaware. The Modoc story is very long, and contains much valuable matter; but the group of incidents that I wish to refer to here are the daily adventures and exploits of a personage who seems to be no other than the sky with the sun in it. This personage is destroyed every evening. He always gets into trouble, and is burned up ; but in his back is a golden disk, which neither fire nor anything in the world can destroy. From this disk his body is reconstituted every morning ; and all that is needed for the resurrection is the summons of the Morning-star, who calls out, " It is time to rise, old man ; you have slept long enough." Then the old man springs new again from his ashes through virtue of the immortal disk and the compelling word of the star.

Now, the Morning-star is the attendant spirit or " medicine " of the personage with the disk, and cannot escape the performance of his office ; he has to work at it forever. So the old man cannot fail to rise every morning. As the golden disk is no other than the sun, the Morning-star of the Modocs is the same character as the Lucifer of the Latins.

The Delaware story, also a long one, has many grotesque and striking elements. I will tell it in a closely compressed form. The person who is the hero of this tale has a wife, who, while he is absent hunting, turns into a man-eater, — becomes a devouring agency with a mania to swallow all flesh, but has a special and craving mania to eat up her own husband first of all ; so she runs to the woods to find him. Informed by a wise, talking dog, a species of brother of his, who had sprung out to anticipate the woman, the man rushes off southward, runs with all speed till he reaches a deep mighty river, where is an old man who makes a bridge by stretching his neck across the water. The hunted husband speaks kindly, and implores for means to cross or his wife will devour him. The old man lies down with his shoulder on one bank, stretches his neck, makes it flat like a horse's neck, to give safe passage ; soon his head is on the other bank, and the man walks over. The old bridge-maker promises to delay the woman, and then throw her into the river, where she will be eaten by monsters, — all save her stomach, in which her life resides; that will float down with the current, come to life, and the woman will be as well and furious as ever, unless the stomach is dragged out, cut to pieces, and burned.

The hunted man hastens, runs westward by the bank of the river, runs till he comes to two aunts who are witches. They promise to help him and kill the pursuer. Soon after, when the old man has shortened his neck and is sitting on his own side of the river, the wife comes up in hot pursuit, talks roughly, tries to hurry the old pontifex; but he will not hurry, waits, and then stretches his neck, putting the narrow side upward; it is no wider than the woman's feet. She storms, but he says that being old he might break his neck were he to give the broad side as a path; she must walk on the narrow side, and carefully too. She begins to cross, but in the middle of the river grows restive and angry. The old man jerks his neck to one side; she falls to the water and is eaten right away, all save her stomach, which floats with the current. But the aunts, the two witches, are watching; they see and pull out the stomach, cut it up, and burn the life of that man-eater.

The man travels westward till he sees a young woman gathering branches for fuel. He speaks to her, is pleased; she is mild-eyed, kind-looking. He asks her to marry him; she says she is willing if he can live with her grandmother, who is very thick, very ugly, and malicious. He goes home with the young woman; they are married.

Soon after the marriage the old woman took her son-in-law to hunt on an island in a lake. They landed. She said, "Go down there," pointing to a place; "I will drive the game." He started, and when half way, looked back; the old woman was in the canoe paddling to the other shore. He called; she would not listen, and left him alone on the island. There was no escape. When the sun had gone down and darkness came, the water of the lake began to rise, and flooded the place. He selected the highest tree, and began to climb, — the water all the time rising; he climbed, and continued to climb. About three o'clock in the morning all the trees on the island, except that tree, were covered. Around on every side were great hungry savage-eyed creatures, rising with the water, waiting to eat the man. He looked, saw the Morning-star, and cried out: "When I was young the Morning-star appeared to me in a dream, and said that if ever I should be in distress he would save me."

The star heard the call, turned to a small boy standing sentry at his door, and said, "Who is that shouting on the island?"

"That," said the boy, "is the old woman's son-in-law. She put him there. He says you appeared to him in a dream and promised to save him."

"I did, and I will." The Morning-star came forth from his house and called: "Let daylight come!"

Dawn came that moment; the water began to fall, and at sunrise the island was dry. The man was saved, came down, went to the landing-place, and hid in the bushes. Soon the old woman's canoe struck the shore; the man heard her say: "Well, I suppose the larger bones of my son-in-law are under the tree. I must go and eat the marrow." When she had gone far enough, he sprang into the canoe and paddled away. The old woman turned, saw the escape of her son-in-law, and cried: "Come back! I 'll play no more tricks."

The man paddled to the other shore, and went to his wife. The old woman was alone, not able to escape.

When darkness came, the lake began to rise. She climbed the highest tree, climbed till the water was nearing the top, and the hungry, terrible creatures were waiting to eat her. Then she called out towards the east : " When J was young the Morning-star appeared to me in a dream, and said he would help me out of distress."

The Morning-star heard, and asked his boy : " Is that man on the island yet ? "

" Oh," said the boy, " the man is at home ; the old woman herself is on the island now. She says that you appeared to her in a dream, and promised to save her from distress."

" I never appeared to that old woman," said the star. " I will not hurry daylight to-day."

The water rose till the old woman was on the highest point of the tree that would bear her. The water raised all the crowd of hungry, terrible creatures. They tore her to pieces, devoured her.

So the Delawares on the Atlantic, who enjoy seniority among the Algonkin, — the most widely-extended Indian stock of America, — agree with the Modocs, near the Pacific, in the theory of the Morning-star, which for them, as for the Latins, was the Light-bearer. The opposite view, to which I refer in the night-scene at Milwaukee, gave birth to the myth of the struggle of the stars with the sun for possession of the sky. Now, a combination of these two myths — the one in which the Morning-star is the Light-bearer being the earlier — gives us a third, in which the Morning-star is not merely an opponent, but a rebel. This third myth, after it had increased in age, came to be used in describing, not an event in the sky, looked at variously by primitive men, but an event in the moral world ; and the stories of the Morning-star and the sun were transferred from the fields of heaven to the kingdom of the soul. This done, Milton had at hand the splendid mythologic material and accessories which he used with such power in Paradise Lost.

I know no American myth in which the Morning-star is represented as hostile to the sun; the discovery of one would be very interesting and valuable, as showing that the primitive people of this continent might possibly have worked out a physical myth like that made in the Eastern hemisphere, and afterwards spiritualized till it was given the meaning which we find in the pages of Milton.

But whatever the future may bring, the present American Morning-star myth is interesting; for it shows a complete parallelism with Aryan mythology as far as it goes, — that is, to the highest point reached by the non-Aryan tribes of America.

It should be remembered that whatever be the names of the myth-tale heroes at present, the original heroes were not human. They were not men and women, though in most cases the present heroes or heroines bear the names of men and women, or children; they perform deeds which no man could perform, which only one of the forces of Nature could perform, if it had the volition and desires of a person. This is the great cause of wonderful deeds in myth-tales.

The following Indian myth, in which we know exactly who the actors were, illustrates this fact very well. I give the myth from memory, and in a compressed form, making first the statement that in a part of eastern Oregon and Washington, where I found it, there are two winds, as the Indians informed me, which are all, or practically all, that blow in that region. One of these is a northeast, the other a southwest wind. The Indians subdivide each one of them into five. Each of these five is a little different from the other, — that

is, there are five kinds of southwest winds, and five kinds
of northeast winds. Each has a proper name describing
its character ; and in telling the myth these names are used,
just as the name Ivan the Fool, and Mirko the king's son are
used in Russia and Hungary. The Northeast brothers have
a sister more harassing and cruel than they, — cold, damp,
fitful. She also has a name describing her character. The
five Southwest winds have grandparents very old, who live
in a hut by themselves. They have no sister ; but the eldest
has a wife, brought by him to Oregon from her birthplace
in the Southern seas.

One time the Northeast winds challenged the others to a
wrestling-match, in which whoever should be thrown would
have his head cut off. The Southwest brothers were not
free to refuse ; they had to accept. All the details of this
match are described precisely as if the opponents were men
and not winds. The Southwest brothers were thrown, every
one, and each had his head cut off; all were killed, and
now the Northeast brothers were lords of that region. The
old feeble grandparents were all of the family left in Oregon.
The young wife went home to her parents and people in
the Southern seas. The victorious brothers did as they
pleased, — when they wished to knock any one down they
did so ; but the crowning wickedness of the victorious
family was the malice of the sister against the aged grandparents. She came every morning to their hut and insulted
them in a manner that will not bear recital. Weeping and
helpless, they endured the foulest abuse. The evil sister rejoiced, the wicked brothers rejoiced, and all men besides
were suffering. Some time after the widow had returned to
her home in the Southern seas a son was born to the late
eldest brother, — a wonderful boy. This posthumous child
grew not by years but by days ; and when he was three

weeks old he had attained full growth. He was a hero of awful strength ; nothing could resist him. He asked about his father ; his mother told how his fathers had perished (the brothers of a father are fathers too in the Indian system) at the hands of the Northeast brothers. " I will go to avenge my fathers," said he, and started.

He reached the coast near the Columbia River, which he ascended ; when at the Cascades he began to try his strength. He pulled out the greatest trees with their roots, overturned cliffs, and went on his way with delight. At last he arrived at the land where his fathers had ruled, and went first in the early morning to the hut of his great grandparents. They were very weak and wretched, but still they were able to tell of what they had suffered from the sister. " She will soon be here," said they ; so he lay in waiting.

She came, and was preparing to begin her insults when he seized her and put her to a painful death. Then he challenged the five wicked brothers to a wrestling-match, threw them all, and cut their heads off. The whole country rejoiced. No one felt pain. The young hero ruled that land to the delight of all. This hero was not a month old, and since we know the characters in the story, we know that the story is true.

When, in Gaelic, we find heroes like the son of Fin Mac-Cumhail, Fialan, who at the age of three years slew whole armies, with their champion leaders,[1] and the Shee an Gannon, who was born in the morning, named at noon, and went in the evening to ask his daughter of the King of Erin ; or in Russian, Ivan Tsarevich,[2] nine days old, who

----

[1] See in *Myths and Folk-Lore of Ireland*, "Fin MacCumhail and the Fenians of Erin in the Castle of Fear Dubh," p. 221, and "The Shee an Gannon and the Gruagach Gaire," p. 114.

[2] See Koshchéi Without-Death, p. 106.

after three sleeps of three days' and nights' duration each, went in search of Peerless Beauty, his bride, — we may feel sure that we are dealing mediately or immediately with that category of powers to which old-time divinities belong, the same race of personages as the Wind brothers of Oregon.

Now we may leave American myths and say a few words of the nations to whom the three groups of myth-tales belong, — the Russians, the Chekhs, and the Magyars. It is not easy to describe any one of them in a brief space, for each is remarkable in character and history.

The Russians are difficult to describe, not only because they are many, but because of their position. The key-note of this position has sounded through their whole history, from the time of Olga and Vladimir, in the Kieff period, to the present day. Listening to this note, Russian leaders have gained political skill, while the people have confirmed their national instinct and endured burdens which they would endure only for the thing which that key-note describes. To tell what it is we must make a digression.

The first political work of the world soundly done, as men of this age, with minds of modern situation, are able to see, was the work of Rome. Rome was the first power to assimilate peoples, to destroy provincialism, to make a State, in the great modern sense of the word. After the fall of Rome as a political power, with its work done and delivered, there followed a still greater, — a new Rome, with a wider ambition, and with plans further reaching than those of its predecessor. This new Rome saw standing before its face, in the East of Europe, the youngest brothers of the Aryan race — the Slavs — still unconverted. The new Rome was as different from the old as two things may be, save in this, that both had strong will to rule. The difference was that old Rome ruled in the name of man and better social order, while new Rome ruled in the name of God and morality ; but new Rome was as firmly fixed in purpose to rule by all the weapons that strong men may use in the world, as was old Rome.

It happened in history that the Teutonic branch of the Aryans fell heir to the Roman civilization of the West, and acquired the administrative experience and pride of power personal to lords of the earth. These Teutons, or Germans, became the agents through whom for a long period the Catholic Church acted most frequently in dealing with Eastern Europeans ; and the Germans were determined to be the exclusive dispensers and extenders of Christianity in that quarter, acquiring at the same time temporal lordship and lands for themselves. This produced a conflict along the whole eastern line, — on one side a defensive struggle of Slav against German ; on the other, that incursive and attacking movement of the Germans, continued age after age under various forms and guises, but which is as real to-day and as active as in times of its greatest intensity, though veiled in official circles with diplomatic tact. On the northern, or left wing of their advance, the Germans destroyed ethnologically ; that is, they conquered and Germanized the Slavs from places not far from Hamburg to a considerable distance east of Berlin. Next they destroyed Poland ; for they gained possession of the original lands of the Commonwealth on the Baltic, and pushed the Poles eastward to make good their losses at the expense of the Russians. The loss to the Slavs of the Polish lands on the Baltic was immense ; and to make the catastrophe more sorrowful for a man of that stock, the Slavs failed on the south, in the kingdom of Great Moravia, which with the present Moravia included the dominions of Hungary, and later on failed from the Danube everywhere southward as far as Slavs had a dwelling.

When all the Western Slavs had fallen, — not because they were less worthy individually, less brave, or less wise as separate persons than their invaders, but because they were younger and greener in political growth, — there remained in the East still two Slav nations (Poland and Russia) ; and the opposition of these forms the great tragic story of modern ages. And the most remarkable concomitant of this tragedy is, that the cause of it is misunderstood by most of us. It is thought, not only widely but well-nigh universally, in Western Europe and America that the first cause of the downfall of Poland was Russia; while the real causes were first and mightiest the peculiar make-up of Polish society, coupled with the unceasing activity of Germans in conquering and subjecting everything east of them by all the weapons that can be used either in peace or in war.

If Russia and Poland had both received Christianity from the same source, there would have been strong reasons for them to grow into one political body ; and they might have been able to do so. If both had received Christianity from the East, as Russia did, they might have stood shoulder to shoulder in brotherly defence against the Germanic West. If both had received Christianity directly from the West, they might have prevented the Germans from crusading to Christianize the East at the expense of its land and independence.

When one thinks of the enthusiastic and kindly labor of the Irish missionaries in the West, and of Cyril and Methodius among the Slavs, it seems hard . to believe that the Irish and Greeks had the same Master in mind as the ironclad monks on the Baltic. And they had not; for the Germans took the lands and persons of the converts, while the Irish and the Slav missionaries had no thought for themselves.

Poland fell, and Russia remains the one Slav State really independent; and Russia remains because, as I have just stated, the Russian people have in all centuries listened to and understood the key-note of their position, — which is : No foreign influence shall exist in Russia under any form whatever. To maintain this position the Russians have sacrificed more than any people in Europe ; and in many senses they have accomplished more.

The corollary to the above sentence, and which with it completes the abstract statement of Russia's whole policy, is : The West of Europe shall not dominate the East.

To the Russian people belong the myth-tales in the first division of this volume. I had hoped to include specimens from Little and White Russia, — that is, from those parts of Russia that were once under the dominion of Poland ; but lack of space has confined me to tales from Great Russia, — that portion of the Empire which first formed around Moscow.

The Chekhs of Bohemia are Slavs more nearly related in speech to the Poles than to the Russians. Twice have the Chekhs been very prominent in history, — once in the wars which followed the death of John Huss ; and again during the Thirty Years' War, in which they suffered beyond any other people. Reduced from three million to eight hundred thousand in number, they were supposed to be extinguished as Slavs ; but in spite of all emigration they have regained more than their old numbers, and are to-day if possible more determined than ever to preserve their historical identity. Take them all in all, there is not a people of more marked character, nor one whose history has greater claims on the student. In fact, the fifteenth and sixteenth centuries cannot be studied at all, in any true sense, without faithful attention to the Chekhs. To them belong our second group of tales.

The tales of the third group belong to the Magyars (the ruling race of Hungary), who exert more influence than any people of four times their numbers in Europe. Though forming not more, or in any case little more, than one third of the population of Hungary, — say five and a half to six millions, — they rule the other peoples of the kingdom, and possess preponderant power in the Empire of Austria-Hungary. They have directed its foreign policy for the last twenty years, — a fact of great significance. For though foreign affairs have at all times been more important for Austria than perhaps any State in Europe, they have never been more important than at present; and still they are intrusted to the Magyars, — a race forming little more than one sixth of the people of the Empire. The reason is not far to seek.

The Magyars, a non-Aryan people from the Ural-Altai regions, arrived in the places they now occupy about one thousand years ago, at the period of a desperate struggle between the Germans and the Slav kingdom of Great Moravia, — a struggle as envenomed as that between Carthage and Rome, but in which the Slavs seemed to be holding their own very well. At this juncture the Magyars struck Great Moravia in the rear with all their force, secured victory for the Germans, and inserted themselves as a dividing wedge between the Southern and the Northern Slavs.

The fall of Great Moravia closed the way to the political independence of the Western Slavs; after them, there remained in the whole Slav world but the Poles and the Russians with the possibility of political power.

There are no people so well qualified by their history and hopes to carry out the policy of Austria, and stand against Russia, as the Magyars. Politicians by genius and training, lords of the land by position, their whole existence depends on managing and balancing various forces. Having no personal sympathy for the Germans, looking down on the Slavs, they are a bitter necessity to the first, and they divide, rule, and dominate the second within the kingdom ; outside the kingdom it is their policy not to permit the Slavs to develop, unless as satellites of Austria-Hungary.

I regret my inability to include Polish myth-tales in this collection, owing to want of space. Should the present volume meet with favor, it will be followed during the coming year by another, in which a good deal of attention will be given the Poles, — a most interesting and, in very truth, a little known people.

JEREMIAH CURTIN.

Smithsonian Institution, Bureau of Ethnology.
Washington, D. C., *October* 29, 1890.

RUSSIAN MYTHS AND FOLK-TALES.

The Tsar dissuaded and dissuaded, but could not convince him. "Well, there is no help for it, go; God be with thee!"

Ivan saddled his good steed and set out. He rode and rode, whether it was long or short: a tale is soon told, but a deed is not soon done; he came to a forest. In that forest was the richest of castles. Ivan Tsarevich entered a broad court, saw an old man, and said, "Many years' health to thee!"

"We beg the favor of thy presence. Who art thou, gallant youth?"

"I am Ivan Tsarevich, the son of Tsar Bail Bailyanyin and of Tsaritsa Nastasya, Golden Tress."

"Oh, my own nephew! Whither is God bearing thee?"

"For this cause and that," said he, "I am in search of my mother. Canst thou not tell me, uncle, where to find her?"

"No, nephew, I cannot; with what I am able, with that I do service. But here is a ball; throw it ahead, it will roll on before thee and lead thee to steep, rugged mountains. In those mountains is a cave, enter it; take there iron claws, put them on thy hands and thy feet, and climb up the mountains. Perhaps thou wilt find there thy mother, Nastasya, Golden Tress."

That was good aid. Ivan Tsarevich took leave of his uncle, and threw the ball before him; the ball rolled and rolled on, he rode behind it. Whether it

RUSSIAN MYTHS AND FOLK-TALES.

———◆———

THE THREE KINGDOMS, — THE COPPER, THE SILVER, AND THE GOLDEN.

IN a certain kingdom in a certain land lived a Tsar, — Bail Bailyanyin. He had a wife, Nastasya, Golden Tress, and three sons, — Pyotr Tsarevich, Vassili Tsarevich, and Ivan Tsarevich. The Tsaritsa went with her maidens and nurses to walk in the garden. All at once such a mighty Whirlwind rose that, God save us! it caught the Tsaritsa and bore her it was unknown whither.

The Tsar was grieved and distressed, and knew not what to do. His sons grew up, and he said to them: "My dear children, which of you will go to seek your mother?"

The two elder brothers made ready and went. After they had gone, the youngest begged permission of his father. "No," said the Tsar, "go not, my dear son; do not leave me an old man in loneliness."

"Let me go, father; I want awfully to wander over the white world and find my mother."

was long or short, he saw his brothers, Pyotr Tsarevich and Vassili Tsarevich. They were encamped in
the open field with thousands of troops. His brothers were surprised, and asked, " Where art thou
going, Ivan Tsarevich? "

" Oh! " said he, " I grew weary at home, and I
thought of going to look for my mother. Send your
army home, and let us go on together."

They sent home the army, and the three went
on together after the ball. While yet at a distance
they saw the mountains, — such steep and lofty
mountains that, God save us ! they touched the
heavens with their heads. The ball rolled straight
to a cave. Ivan Tsarevich slipped down from his
horse and said to his brothers, " Here, brothers, is
my good steed; I will go up on the mountains to
look for my mother, and ye remain here. Wait for
me just three months. If I am not here in three
months, there will be no use in waiting longer."

The brothers thought, but how could a man
climb these mountains? He would break his head
there.

"Well," said they, " go, with God; we will wait
for thee here."

Ivan approached the cave; he saw that the door
was of iron. He struck it with all his strength. It
opened, he entered; iron claws went on to his feet
and hands of themselves. He began to climb the
mountains, — climb, climb; he toiled a whole month,

reaching the top with difficulty. "Well," said he, "glory be to God!" He rested a little, and walked along on the mountain; walked and walked, walked and walked, saw a copper castle, at the gate terrible serpents fastened with copper chains, crowds of them; and right there was a well, and at the well a copper bucket hung by a copper chain. Ivan Tsarevich drew water and gave the serpents to drink. They became quiet, lay down, and he passed into the court.

The Tsaritsa of the Copper Kingdom ran out to meet him. "Who art thou, gallant youth?"

"I am Ivan Tsarevich."

"Well, hast thou come of thy own will, or against thy will?"

"Of my own will; I am in search of my mother, Nastasya, Golden Tress. A certain Whirlwind bore her away out of the garden. Dost thou know where she is?"

"No; but not far from here lives my second sister, the Tsaritsa of the Silver kingdom, — maybe she will tell thee."

She gave him a copper ball and a copper ring. "The ball," said she, "will lead thee to my second sister, and in this ring is the whole Copper Kingdom. When thou overcomest Whirlwind, who keeps me here and flies to me once in three months, forget me not, poor woman, rescue me from this place, and take me with thee to the free world."

"I will," said Ivan Tsarevich. He threw the copper ball before him; the ball rolled ahead, and he followed after. He came to the Silver Kingdom and saw a castle finer than the first, all silver; at the gate were terrible serpents fastened to silver chains, and at the side of them was a well with a silver bucket. Ivan Tsarevich drew water and gave the serpents to drink. They lay down then, and let him enter the castle. The Tsaritsa of the Silver Kingdom came out.

"It will soon be three years," said she, "since mighty Whirlwind confined me here, and no Russian have I heard with hearing, or seen with sight; but now a Russian I see. Who art thou, good youth?"

"I am Ivan Tsarevich."

"How didst thou happen hither, — with thy own will, or against thy will?"

"With my own will; I am in search of my mother. She went in the green garden to walk, Whirlwind came and bore her away, it is unknown whither. Canst thou not tell me where to find her?"

"No, I cannot; but not far from here lives my eldest sister, the Tsaritsa of the Golden Kingdom, Yelena the Beautiful, — maybe she will tell thee. Here is a silver ball, roll it ahead and follow; it will lead thee to the Golden Kingdom. But see, when thou hast killed Whirlwind, forget me not, poor woman; rescue me from this place, and take me to the free world. Whirlwind holds me captive, and flies hither once in two months." Then she gave him a silver ring, saying, "In this ring is the whole Silver Kingdom."

Ivan rolled the ball; wherever it went he followed. Whether it was long or short, he saw a golden castle gleaming like fire; at the gate was a crowd of terrible serpents fastened to golden chains, and right there a well, at the well a golden bucket on a golden chain. Ivan Tsarevich drew water, and gave the serpents to drink; they lay down and were soothed. He entered the palace; Yelena the Beautiful met him.

"Who art thou, gallant youth?"

"I am Ivan Tsarevich."

"How hast thou come hither,—of thy own will, or against thy will?"

"I came of my own will; I am in search of my mother, Nastasya, Golden Tress. Knowest thou not where to find her?"

"Why should n't I know? She lives not far from here, Whirlwind flies to her once a week, and to me once a month. Here is a golden ball for thee: throw it ahead and follow, — it will lead thee to thy mother. And take besides this golden ring; in this ring is the whole Golden Kingdom. And be careful when thou hast conquered Whirlwind. Forget me not, poor woman; take me with thee to the free world."

"I will take thee," said he.

Ivan Tsarevich rolled the ball and followed after; he went and went till he came to such a palace that,

Lord save us! it was just blazing with diamonds and precious stones. At the gate six-headed serpents were hissing. Ivan Tsarevich gave them to drink; the serpents were soothed, and let him pass to the castle. He went through the great chambers, and in the most distant found his own mother. She was sitting on a lofty throne arrayed in Tsaritsa's robes and crowned with a costly crown. She looked at the stranger and cried: " Ah! is that thou, my dear son? How hast thou come hither? "

" So and so," said Ivan; " I have come for thee."

" Well, dear son, 't will be hard for thee. Here in these mountains reigns Whirlwind, the evil and mighty, all spirits obey him; he is the one that bore me away. Thou wilt have to fight him; come quickly to the cellar."

They went to the cellar; there were two tubs of water, one on the right, the other on the left hand. " Drink," said the Tsaritsa, " from the right-hand tub."

Ivan drank.

" Well, what strength is in thee? "

" I am so strong that I could turn the whole castle over with one hand."

" Then drink more."

Ivan drank again.

" What strength is in thee now? "

" If I wished, I could turn the whole world over."

" That is very great strength. Move these tubs

from one place to the other: put that on the right
to the left, that on the left take to the right."

Ivan interchanged the tubs.

"Thou seest, my dear son, in one tub is water of
strength, in the other water of weakness.   Whoso
drinks from the first will be a strong, mighty hero;
whoso drinks from the second will grow weak altogether.   Whirlwind always drinks the water of
strength and puts it on the right side; so we
must deceive him, or thou canst never overcome
him."

They returned to the castle.

"Soon Whirlwind will fly home," said the Tsaritsa
to Ivan Tsarevich.   "Sit under my purple robe, so
that he may not see thee; and when he comes and
runs to embrace and kiss me, do thou seize his club.
He will rise high, high; he will bear thee over seas,
over precipices: but see to it, let not the club go out
of thy hand.   Whirlwind will grow tired, will want
to drink the water of strength, will come down to the
cellar and rush to the tub placed on the right hand;
but do thou drink from the tub on the left.   Then he
will grow weak; wrest his sword from him, and with
one blow hew off his head.   When his head is off,
that moment there will be voices behind thee crying,
'Strike again, strike again.'   Strike not, my son, but
say in answer, 'A hero's hand strikes not twice, but
always once.'"

Ivan Tsarevich had barely hidden under the robe

when the court grew dark and everything trembled. Whirlwind flew home, struck the earth, became a brave hero, and entered the castle, in his hands a club.

"Tfu, tfu, tfu! somehow it smells of Russia here. Was any one visiting?"

"I don't know why it seems so to thee," said the Tsaritsa.

Whirlwind rushed to embrace her; but Ivan that moment seized the club.

"I'll eat thee!" shouted Whirlwind.

"Well, grandmother spoke double; either thou wilt eat, or thou wilt not."

Whirlwind tore out through the window and up to the sky; he bore Ivan Tsarevich away. Over mountains he said, "I will smash thee;" over seas he said, "I will drown thee." But Ivan did not let the club out of his hands. Whirlwind flew over the whole world, wearied himself out, and began to sink. He came down straight into the cellar, rushed to the tub on the right hand, and fell to drinking the water of weakness; but Ivan ran to the left, drank his fill of the water of strength, and became the first mighty hero in the whole world. He saw that Whirlwind had become utterly weak, wrested the sharp sword from him, and cut off his head with a blow. Voices cried behind, "Strike again, strike again, or he will come to life!" "No," said Ivan; "a hero's hand strikes not twice, but always finishes at a blow."

Straightway he made a fire, burned the body and the head, scattered the ashes to the wind.

The mother of Ivan Tsarevich was glad. " Now, my dear son," said she, " let us rejoice. We will eat; and then for home with all speed, for it is wearisome here, — there are no people."

" But who serves thee? "

" Thou wilt see directly."

They had barely thought of eating, when a table set itself, and various meats and wines appeared on the table of themselves. The Tsaritsa and the Tsarevich dined. Meanwhile unseen musicians played wonderful songs for them. They ate and drank, and when they had rested, Ivan said, —

" Let us go, mother, it is time; for under the mountains my brothers are waiting. And on the road I must save three Tsaritsas who are living in Whirlwind's castles."

They took everything needful and set out on the journey. They went first to the Tsaritsa of the Golden Kingdom, then to her sisters of the Silver and Copper Kingdoms. They took them, and brought linen and all kinds of stuffs. In a short time they reached the place where they had to go down the mountain.

Ivan Tsarevich let his mother down first on the linen, then Yelena the Beautiful and her two sisters. The brothers were standing below waiting, and they thought to themselves, " Let us leave Ivan Tsarevich

up there; we will take our mother and the three
Tsaritsas to our father, and say that we found them."
"I'll take Yelena the Beautiful for myself," said
Pyotr Tsarevich; "thou, Vassili, wilt have the
Tsaritsa of the Silver Kingdom; and we will
give the Tsaritsa of the Copper Kingdom to some
general."

When it was time for Ivan Tsarevich to come
down from the mountain, his elder brothers seized
the linen, pulled and tore it away. Ivan remained
on the mountain. What could he do? He wept
bitterly; then turned back, walked and walked over
the Copper Kingdom, over the Silver Kingdom and
the Golden Kingdom, — not a soul did he see. He
came to the Diamond Kingdom, — no one there
either. What was he to do alone, — deathly weariness! He looked around; on the window of the
castle a whistle was lying. He took it in his hand.
"Let me play from weariness," said he. He had
barely blown when out sprang Lame and Crooked.

"What is thy pleasure?"

Said Ivan Tsarevich, "I want to eat." That moment, from wherever it came, a table was set, and
on the table the very best food. Ivan Tsarevich ate
and thought, "Now it would not be bad to rest."
He blew on the whistle. Lame and Crooked
appeared.

"What is thy pleasure, Ivan Tsarevich?"

"That a bed be ready." The word was n't out of

his mouth when the bed was ready. He lay down, slept splendidly, then whistled again.

"What is thy pleasure?" asked Lame and Crooked.

"Everything can be done, then?"

"Everything is possible, Ivan Tsarevich. Whoever blows that whistle, we will do everything for him. As we served Whirlwind before, so we are glad to serve thee now; it is only necessary to keep the whistle by thee at all times."

"Well," said Ivan, "let me be in my own kingdom this minute."

He had barely spoken when he appeared in his own kingdom, in the middle of the market square. He was walking along the square, when a shoemaker came toward him, — such a jolly fellow! The Tsarevich asked: "Whither art thou going, good man?"

"I am taking shoes to sell; I am a shoemaker."

"Take me into thy service," said Ivan.

"Dost thou know how to make shoes?"

"Yes, I can do everything. I can make not only shoes, but clothes."

"Well, come on."

They went to his house. The shoemaker said: "Go to work; here is leather for thee, — the best kind; I 'll see what skill thou hast."

Ivan Tsarevich went to his own room, and took out the whistle. Lame and Crooked came. "What is thy pleasure, Ivan Tsarevich?"

"To have shoes ready by to-morrow."

" Oh, that is not work, that is play ! "

" Here is the leather."

" What sort of leather is that? That's trash, nothing more; that should go out of the window."

Next morning Ivan Tsarevich woke up; on the table were beautiful shoes, the very best.

The shoemaker rose. " Well, young man, hast thou made the shoes? "

" They are finished."

" Well, show them." He looked at the shoes and was astonished. " See what a man I have got for myself, — not a shoemaker, but a wonder! " He took the shoes and carried them to the market to sell.

At that same time three weddings were in preparation at the palace. Pyotr Tsarevich was to marry Yelena the Beautiful, Vassili Tsarevich the Tsaritsa of the Silver Kingdom, and they were giving the Tsaritsa of the Copper Kingdom to a general. They were making dresses for those weddings. Yelena the Beautiful wanted shoes. Our shoemaker's shoes were better than all the others brought to the palace.

When Yelena looked at them she said, " What does this mean? They make shoes like these only in the mountains." She paid the shoemaker a large price and said, " Make me without measure another pair wonderfully sewed, ornamented with precious stones, and studded with diamonds. They must be ready by to-morrow; if not, to the gallows with thee."

The shoemaker took the precious stones and money and went home, — such a gloomy man! "Misery," said he, "what am I to do now? How can I make shoes by to-morrow, and besides without measure? It is clear that they will hang me to-morrow; let me have at least a last frolic with my friends."

He went to the inn. These friends of his were numerous; they asked, "Why art thou so gloomy, brother?"

"Oh, my dear friends," answered he, "they are going to hang me to-morrow!"

"Why so?"

The shoemaker told his trouble. "How think of work in such a position? Better I'll frolic to-night for the last time."

So they drank and drank, frolicked and frolicked; the shoemaker was staggering already.

"Well," said he, "I'll take home a keg of spirits, lie down to sleep; and to-morrow when they come to hang me, I'll drink a gallon and a half right away. Let them hang me without my senses."

He came home. "Well, thou reprobate!" said he to Ivan Tsarevich, "see what thy shoes have done . . . so and so. . . . When they come in the morning for me, wake me up."

In the night Ivan Tsarevich took out the whistle and blew. Lame and Crooked appeared. "What is thy pleasure, Ivan Tsarevich?"

"That shoes of such a kind be ready."

" We obey ! "

Ivan lay down to sleep. Next morning he woke up; the shoes were on the table shining like fire. He went to rouse his master.

" It is time to rise, master."

" What ! have they come for me ? Bring the keg quickly ! Here is a cup, pour the spirits in ; let them hang me drunk."

" But the shoes are made."

" How made ? Where are they ? "

The master ran and saw them. " But when did we make them ? "

" In the night. Is it possible that thou dost not remember when we cut and sewed ? "

" Oh, I 've slept so long, brother ! I barely, barely remember."

He took the shoes, wrapped them up, and ran to the palace.

Yelena the Beautiful saw the shoes and knew what had happened. " Surely," she thought, " the spirits made these for Ivan Tsarevich. — How didst thou make these ? " asked she of the shoemaker.

" Oh ! I know how to do everything."

" If that is the case, make me a wedding robe embroidered with gold, ornamented with diamonds and precious stones ; let it be ready to-morrow morning : if not, off with thy head ! "

The shoemaker went home again gloomy, and his friends were long waiting for him. " Well, what is it ? "

"Nothing but cursedness. The destroyer of Christian people has come; she commanded me to make her a robe with gold and precious stones by to-morrow morning: and what sort of a tailor am I? They will take my head surely to-morrow."

"Ah! brother, the morning is wiser than the evening; let us go and frolic."

They went to the inn, they drank and frolicked; the shoemaker got tipsy again, brought home a whole keg of spirits, and said to Ivan Tsarevich: "Now, young fellow, when thou wilt rouse me in the morning I'll toss off three gallons; let them cut the head off me drunk. I could n't make such a robe in a lifetime." The shoemaker lay down to sleep and snored.

Ivan Tsarevich blew on the whistle, and Lame and Crooked appeared. "What is thy pleasure, Tsarevich?"

"That a robe be ready by to-morrow morning exactly such as Yelena the Beautiful wore in Whirlwind's house."

"We obey; it will be ready."

Ivan Tsarevich woke at daylight; the robe was on the table, shining like fire, so that the whole chamber was lighted up. Then he roused his master, who rubbed his eyes and asked, "What! have they come to cut my head off? Give the spirits here this minute."

"But the robe is ready."

"Is that true ? When did we make it?"

" In the night, of course; dost thou not remember cutting it thyself?"

" Ah, brother, I just remember, — see it as in a dream!"

The shoemaker took the robe and ran to the palace.

Yelena the Beautiful gave him much money and the command, " See that to-morrow by daylight the Golden Kingdom be on the sea, seven versts from shore, and from it to our palace let there be a golden bridge with costly velvet spread upon it, and at the railings on both sides let wonderful trees be growing, and let there be wonderful song-birds singing, with various voices. If thou wilt not have it done by morning, I'll give orders to quarter thee."

The shoemaker went from Yelena the Beautiful with drooping head. His friends met him. " Well, brother?"

" What well! I am lost; to-morrow I shall be quartered. She gave me such a task that no devil could do it."

" Oh, never mind! the morning is wiser than the evening; let us go to the inn."

" Well, let us go; at the last parting we must have a carousal at least."

They drank and drank; and towards evening the shoemaker drank so much they had to lead him home. " Farewell, young fellow," said he to Ivan; " to-morrow they will put me to death."

" But has a new task been given?"

2

"Yes, so and so, so and so." He lay down and snored; but Ivan Tsarevich went straight to his room, and blew on the whistle. Lame and Crooked appeared.

"What is thy pleasure, Ivan Tsarevich?"

"Can ye do me such a work as this?"

"Ivan Tsarevich, this is a work indeed. But there is no avoiding it; toward morning all will be ready."

When daylight began to come, Ivan woke up, looked out of the window. Fathers! everything was ready as asked for. A golden castle was gleaming like fire. He roused his master, who sprang up. "Well, have they come for me? Give the keg here this minute!"

"But the palace is ready."

"What dost thou say?"

The shoemaker looked through the window and said, "Ah!" in astonishment, "how was that done?"

"Dost thou not remember how thou and I fixed it?"

"Yes, it is clear that I have slept too soundly; I barely, barely remember."

They ran to the golden castle; in it was wealth untold, unseen.

Said Ivan Tsarevich: "Here, master, is a wing, go and dust the railing of the bridge; and if they come and ask who lives in the palace, say thou nothing, but give this letter."

"Very well."

The shoemaker went to dust the railing of the bridge.

In the morning Yelena the Beautiful woke up; she saw the golden castle, and ran straight to the Tsar. "See what is done in our place! There is a golden palace on the sea, and from that palace a golden bridge seven versts long; and on both sides of the bridge wonderful trees are growing, and song-birds are singing in various voices."

The Tsar sent immediately to ask what that meant? Had not some hero come to his kingdom? The messengers came to the shoemaker, asked him. "I know not, but there is a letter to thy Tsar." In that letter Ivan Tsarevich related everything to his father as it was, — how he had liberated his mother, won Yelena the Beautiful, and how his elder brothers had deceived him. With the letter Ivan Tsarevich sent golden carriages, and begged the Tsar and Tsaritsa to come to him. Let Yelena the Beautiful and her sisters and his brothers be brought behind in simple wagons.

All assembled at once and started. Ivan Tsarevich met them with joy. The Tsar wished to put his elder sons to death for their untruths; but Ivan Tsarevich implored his father, and they were forgiven. Then began a mountain of a feast. Ivan Tsarevich married Yelena the Beautiful. They gave the Tsaritsa of the Silver Kingdom to Pyotr Tsarevich, the Tsaritsa of the Copper Kingdom to Vassili Tsarevich, and made the shoemaker a general.

IVAN TSAREVICH, THE FIRE–BIRD, AND THE GRAY WOLF.

IN a certain kingdom, in a certain land, lived Tsar Vwislav Andronovich; he had three sons, — Dmitri Tsarevich, Vassili Tsarevich, and Ivan Tsarevich. Tsar Vwislav had a garden so rich that in no land was there better. In the garden grew many precious trees, with fruit and without fruit.

Tsar Vwislav had one favorite apple-tree, and on that tree grew apples all golden. The Fire-bird used to fly to the garden of Tsar Vwislav. She had wings of gold, and eyes like crystals of the East; and she used to fly to that garden every night, sit on the favorite apple-tree, pluck from it golden apples, and then fly away.

The Tsar grieved greatly over that apple-tree because the Fire-bird plucked from it many apples. Therefore he called his three sons and said: " My dear children, whichever one of you can catch the Fire-bird in my garden and take her alive, to him will I give during my life one half of the kingdom, and at my death I will give it all."

Then the sons cried out in one voice: " Gracious sovereign, our father, we will try with great pleasure to take the Fire-bird alive."

The first night Dmitri Tsarevich went to watch in the garden, and sat under the apple-tree from which the Fire-bird had been plucking the apples. He fell asleep, and did not hear the Fire-bird when she came, nor when she plucked many apples.

Next morning Tsar Vwislav called his son Dmitri Tsarevich, and asked, " Well, my dear son, hast thou seen the Fire-bird? "

" No, gracious sovereign, my father, she came not last night."

The next night Vassili Tsarevich went to the garden to watch the Fire-bird. He sat under the same apple-tree, and in a couple of hours fell asleep so soundly that he did not hear the Fire-bird when she came nor when she plucked apples.

Next morning Tsar Vwislav called him and asked, " Well, my dear son, hast thou seen the Fire-bird? "

" Gracious sovereign, my father, she came not last night."

The third night Ivan Tsarevich went to watch in the garden, and sat under the same apple-tree. He sat an hour, a second, and a third. All at once the whole garden was lighted up as if by many fires. The Fire-bird flew hither, perched on the apple-tree, and began to pluck apples. Ivan stole up to her so warily that he caught her tail, but could not hold the bird, she tore off, flew away; and there remained in the hand of Ivan Tsarevich but one feather of the tail, which he held very firmly.

Next morning, the moment Tsar Vwislav woke from his sleep, Ivan Tsarevich went to him and gave him the feather of the Fire-bird. The Tsar was greatly delighted that his youngest son had been able to get even one feather of the Fire-bird. This feather was so wonderful and bright that when carried into a dark chamber it shone as if a great multitude of tapers were lighted in that place. Tsar Vwislav put the feather in his cabinet as a thing to be guarded forever. From that time forth the Fire-bird flew to the garden no more.

Tsar Vwislav again called his sons, and said: " My dear children, I give you my blessing. Set out, find the Fire-bird, and bring her to me alive; and what I promised at first he will surely receive who brings me the bird."

Dmitri and Vassili Tsarevich began to cherish hatred against their youngest brother because he had pulled the feather from the tail of the Fire-bird. They took their father's blessing, and both went to find the Fire-bird. Ivan Tsarevich too began to beg his father's blessing. The Tsar said to him: " My dear son, my darling child, thou art still young, unused to such a long and difficult journey: why shouldst thou part from me? Thy brothers have gone; now, if thou goest too, and all three of you fail to return for a long time (I am old, and walk under God), and if during your absence the Lord takes my life, who would rule in my place? There might be rebellion too, or disagreement among our people, — there would be no one to stop it; or if an enemy should invade our land, there would be no one to command our men."

But no matter how the Tsar tried to detain Ivan Tsarevich, he could not avoid letting him go at his urgent prayer. Ivan Tsarevich took a blessing of his father, chose a horse, and rode away; he rode on, not knowing himself whither.

Riding by the path by the road, whether it was near or far, high or low, a tale is soon told, but a deed's not soon done. At last he came to the green meadows. In the open field a pillar stands, and on the pillar these words are written: "Whoever goes from the pillar straight forward will be hungry and cold; whoever goes to the right hand will be healthy and well, but his horse will be dead; whoever goes to the left hand will be killed himself, but his horse will be living and well." Ivan read the inscription, and went to the right hand, holding in mind that though his horse might be killed, he would remain alive, and might in time get another horse.

He rode one day, a second, and a third. All at once an enormous gray wolf came out against him and said: "Oh! is that thou, tender youth, Ivan Tsarevich? Thou hast read on the pillar that thy horse will be dead: why hast thou come hither, then?" The wolf said these words, tore Ivan Tsarevich's horse in two, and went to one side.

Ivan grieved greatly for his horse. He cried bitterly, and went forward on foot. He walked all day, and was unspeakably tired. He was going to sit down and rest, when all at once the Gray Wolf caught up with him and said: " I am sorry for thee, Ivan Tsarevich, thou art tired from walking; I am sorry that I ate thy good steed. Well, sit on me, the old wolf, and tell me whither to bear thee, and why."

Ivan Tsarevich told the Gray Wolf whither he had to go, and the Gray Wolf shot ahead with him swifter than a horse. After a time, just at nightfall, he brought Ivan Tsarevich to a stone wall not very high, halted, and said: " Now, Ivan Tsarevich, come down from the Gray Wolf, climb over that stone wall; on the other side is a garden, and in the garden the Fire-bird, in a golden cage. Take the Fire-bird, but touch not the cage. If thou takest the cage, thou 'lt not escape; they will seize thee straightway."

Ivan Tsarevich climbed over the wall into the garden, saw the Fire-bird in the golden cage, and was greatly tempted by the cage. He took the bird out, and was going back; but changed his mind, and thought, " Why have I taken the bird without the cage? Where can I put her? " He returned; but had barely taken down the cage when there was a hammering and thundering throughout the whole garden, for there were wires attached to the cage. The

watchmen woke up at that moment, ran to the garden, caught Ivan Tsarevich with the Fire-bird, and
took him to the Tsar, who was called Dolmat. Tsar
Dolmat was terribly enraged at Ivan, and shouted
at him in loud, angry tones: "Is it not a shame for
thee, young man, to steal? But who art thou, of
what land, of what father a son, and how do they
call thee by name?"

Ivan Tsarevich replied: "I am from Vwislav's
kingdom, the son of Tsar Vwislav Andronovich, and
they call me Ivan Tsarevich. Thy Fire-bird used to
fly to our garden each night and pluck golden apples
from my father's favorite apple-tree, and destroyed
almost the whole tree. Therefore my father has sent
me to find the Fire-bird and bring it to him."

"Oh, youthful young man, Ivan Tsarevich," said
Tsar Dolmat, "is it fitting to do as thou hast done?
Thou shouldst have come to me, and I would have
given thee the Fire-bird with honor; but now will it
be well for thee when I send to all lands to declare
how dishonorably thou hast acted in my kingdom?
Listen, however, Ivan Tsarevich. If thou wilt do me
a service, — if thou wilt go beyond the thrice ninth
land to the thirtieth kingdom and get for me from
Tsar Afron the golden-maned steed, I will forgive
thy offence and give thee the Fire-bird with great
honor; if not, I will publish in all kingdoms that
thou art a dishonorable thief."

Ivan Tsarevich went away from Tsar Dolmat in

great grief, promising to obtain for him the golden-maned steed.

He came to the Gray Wolf, and told him all that Tsar Dolmat had said.

"Oh! is that thou, youthful young man, Ivan Tsarevich? Why didst thou disobey my words and take the golden cage?"

"I have offended in thy sight," said Ivan to the Gray Wolf.

"Well, let that go; sit on me, and I will take thee wherever thou wilt."

Ivan Tsarevich sat on the back of the Gray Wolf. The wolf was as swift as an arrow, and ran, whether it was long or short, till he came at last to the kingdom of Tsar Afron in the night-time. Coming to the white-walled stables, the Gray Wolf said: "Go, Ivan Tsarevich, into these white-walled stables (the grooms on guard are sleeping soundly), and take the golden-maned steed. On the wall hangs a golden bridle; but take not the bridle, or it will go ill with thee."

Ivan Tsarevich entered the white-walled stables, took the steed, and was coming back; but he saw on the walls the golden bridle, and was so tempted that he took it from the nail. That moment there went a thunder and a noise throughout the stables, because strings were tied to the bridle. The grooms on guard woke up that moment, rushed in, seized Ivan Tsarevich, and took him to Tsar Afron. Tsar Afron began to question him. "Oh, youthful young man, tell me from what land thou art, of what father a son, and how do they call thee by name?"

To this Ivan Tsarevich replied : "I am from Vwislav's kingdom, the son of Tsar Vwislav, and they call me Ivan Tsarevich."

"Oh, youthful young man, Ivan Tsarevich!" said Tsar Afron, "was that which thou hast done the deed of an honorable knight? I would have given thee the golden-maned steed with honor. But now will it be well for thee when I send to all lands a declaration of how dishonorably thou hast acted in my kingdom? Hear me, however, Ivan Tsarevich: if thou wilt do me a service and go beyond the thrice ninth land to the thirtieth kingdom and bring to me Princess Yelena the Beautiful, with whom I am in love heart and soul for a long time, but whom I cannot obtain, I will pardon thy offence and give thee the golden-maned steed with honor. And if thou wilt not do me this service, I will declare in all lands that thou art a dishonorable thief.

Ivan Tsarevich promised Tsar Afron to bring Yelena the Beautiful, left the palace, and fell to crying bitterly.

He came to the Gray Wolf and told him all that had happened.

"Oh, Ivan Tsarevich, thou youthful young man," said the Gray Wolf, " why didst thou disobey me and take the golden bridle?"

"I have offended in thy sight," said Ivan Tsarevich.

"Well, let that go," replied the Wolf.   " Sit on me;
I will take thee wherever need be."

Ivan Tsarevich sat on the back of the Gray Wolf,
who ran as swiftly as an arrow flies, and he ran in
such fashion as to be told in a tale no long time;
and at last he came to the kingdom of Yelena the
Beautiful.   Coming to the golden fence which sur-
rounded her wonderful garden, the Wolf said : " Now,
Ivan Tsarevich, come down from me and go back by
the same road along which we came and wait in the
field, under the green oak."

Ivan Tsarevich went where he was commanded.
But the Gray Wolf sat near the golden fence, and
waited till Yelena the Beautiful should walk in the
garden.

Toward evening, when the sun was sinking low in
the west, therefore, it was not very warm in the air,
Princess Yelena went to walk in the garden with her
maidens and court ladies.   When she entered the
garden and approached the place where the Gray
Wolf was sitting behind the fence, he jumped out
suddenly, caught the princess, sprang back again, and
bore her away with all his power and might.   He
came to the green oak in the open field where Ivan
Tsarevich was waiting, and said, "Ivan Tsarevich, sit on
me quickly."   Ivan sat on him, and the Gray Wolf bore
them both along swiftly to the kingdom of Tsar Afron.

The nurses and maidens and all the court ladies
who had been walking in the garden with the prin-

cess Yelena the Beautiful ran straightway to the palace and sent pursuers to overtake the Gray Wolf; but no matter how they ran, they could not overtake him, and turned back.

Ivan Tsarevich while sitting on the Gray Wolf with princess Yelena the Beautiful came to love her with his heart, and she Ivan Tsarevich; and when the Gray Wolf arrived at the kingdom of Tsar Afron, and Ivan Tsarevich had to take Yelena the Beautiful to the palace and give her to Tsar Afron, he grew very sad, and began to weep tearfully.

" What art thou weeping for, Ivan Tsarevich? " asked the Gray Wolf.

" My friend, why should I, good youth, not weep? I have formed a heartfelt love for Yelena the Beautiful, and now I must give her to Tsar Afron for the golden-maned steed; and if I yield her not, then Tsar Afron will dishonor me in all lands."

" I have served thee much, Ivan Tsarevich," said the Gray Wolf, " and I will do yet this service. Listen to me. I will turn myself into a princess, Yelena the Beautiful. Do thou give me to Tsar Afron and take from him the golden-maned steed; he will think me the real princess. And when thou art sitting on the steed and riding far away, I will beg of Tsar Afron permission to walk in the open field. When he lets me go with the maidens and nurses and all the court ladies, and I am with them in the open field, remember me, and I will come to thee."

The Gray Wolf spoke these words, struck the damp earth, and became a princess, Yelena the Beautiful, so that it was not possible in any way to know that the wolf was not the princess. Ivan Tsarevich told Yelena the Beautiful to wait outside the town, and took the Gray Wolf to the palace of Tsar Afron.

When Ivan Tsarevich came with the pretended Yelena the Beautiful, Tsar Afron was greatly delighted in his heart that he had received a treasure which he had long desired. He took the false maiden, and gave Ivan Tsarevich the golden-maned steed.

Ivan Tsarevich mounted the steed and rode out of the town, seated Yelena the Beautiful with him, and rode on, holding his way toward the kingdom of Tsar Dolmat.

The Gray Wolf lived with Tsar Afron a day, a second, and a third, instead of Yelena the Beautiful. On the fourth day he went to Tsar Afron, begging to go out in the open field to walk, to drive away cruel grief and sorrow. Then Tsar Afron said: " Oh, my beautiful princess Yelena, I will do everything for thee; I will let thee go to the open field to walk!" And straightway he commanded the nurses, the maidens, and all the court ladies to go to the open field and walk with the beautiful princess.

Ivan Tsarevich was riding along his road and path with Yelena the Beautiful, talking with her; and he

had forgotten about the Gray Wolf, but afterward remembered. "Oh, where is my Gray Wolf?"

All at once, from wherever he came, the wolf
stood before Ivan, and said: "Ivan Tsarevich, sit on
me, the Gray Wolf, and let the beautiful princess ride
on the golden-maned steed."

Ivan Tsarevich sat on the Gray Wolf, and they
went toward the kingdom of Tsar Dolmat. Whether
they journeyed long or short, when they had come
to the kingdom they stopped about three versts from
the capital town; and Ivan Tsarevich began to implore: "Listen to me, Gray Wolf, my dear friend.
Thou hast shown me many a service, show me the
last one now; and the last one is this: Couldst thou
not turn to a golden-maned steed instead of this one?
for I do not like to part with this horse."

Suddenly the Gray Wolf struck the damp earth
and became a golden-maned steed. Ivan Tsarevich,
leaving princess Yelena in the green meadow, sat on
the Gray Wolf and went to the palace of Tsar Dolmat. The moment he came, Tsar Dolmat saw that
Ivan Tsarevich was riding on the golden-maned
steed, and he rejoiced greatly. Straightway he went
out of the palace, met the Tsarevich in the broad
court, kissed him, took him by the right hand, and
led him into the white stone chambers. Tsar Dolmat
on the occasion of such joy gave orders for a feast,
and they sat at the oaken table at the spread cloth.
They ate, they drank, they amused themselves, and

rejoiced exactly two days; and on the third day Tsar
Dolmat gave Ivan Tsarevich the Fire-bird together
with the golden cage.   Ivan took the Fire-bird, went
outside the town, sat on the golden-maned steed
together with Yelena the Beautiful, and went toward
his own native place, toward the kingdom of Tsar
Vwislav.

Tsar Dolmat the next day thought to take a ride
through the open field on his golden-maned steed.
He ordered them to saddle him; he sat on the horse,
and rode to the open field.   The moment he urged
the horse, the horse threw Tsar Dolmat off his back,
became the Gray Wolf as before, ran off, and came
up with Ivan Tsarevich.   "Ivan Tsarevich," said he,
"sit on me, the Gray Wolf, and let Yelena the Beautiful ride on the golden-maned steed."

Ivan sat on the Gray Wolf, and they went their
way.   When the Gray Wolf had brought Ivan to the
place where he had torn his horse, he stopped and
said: "I have served thee sufficiently, with faith and
truth.   On this spot I tore thy horse in two; to this
spot I have brought thee.   Come down from me, the
Gray Wolf: thou hast a golden-maned steed; sit on
him, and go wherever thou hast need.   I am no
longer thy servant."

The Gray Wolf said these words and ran to one
side.   Ivan wept bitterly for the Gray Wolf, and
went on with the beautiful princess.

Whether he rode long or short with the beautiful

princess, when he was within twenty versts of his own kingdom he stopped, dismounted, and he and the beautiful princess rested from the heat of the sun under a tree; he tied the golden-maned steed to the same tree, and put the cage of the Fire-bird by his side. Lying on the soft grass, they talked pleasantly, and fell soundly asleep.

At that time the brothers of Ivan Tsarevich, Dmitri and Vassili Tsarevich, after travelling through many lands without finding the Fire-bird, were on their way home with empty hands, and came unexpectedly upon their brother with the beautiful princess. Seeing the golden-maned steed and the Fire-bird in the cage, they were greatly tempted, and thought of killing their brother Ivan. Dmitri took his own sword out of the scabbard, stabbed Ivan Tsarevich, and cut him to pieces; then he roused the beautiful princess and asked: " Beautiful maiden, of what land art thou, of what father a daughter, and how do they call thee by name?"

The beautiful princess, seeing Ivan Tsarevich dead, was terribly frightened; she began to shed bitter tears, and in her tears she said: " I am Princess Yelena the Beautiful; Ivan Tsarevich, whom ye have given to a cruel death, got me. If ye were good knights, ye would have gone with him into the open field and conquered him there; but ye killed him when asleep; and what fame will ye receive for yourselves? A sleeping man is the same as a dead one."

Then Dmitri Tsarevich put his sword to the heart of Yelena the Beautiful and said: " Hear me, Yelena the Beautiful, thou art now in our hands; we will take thee to our father, Tsar Vwislav, thou wilt tell him that we got thee and the Fire-bird and the golden-maned steed. If not, we will give thee to death this minute." The princess, afraid of death, promised them, and swore by everything sacred that she would speak as commanded. Then they began to cast lots who should have Yelena the Beautiful, and who the golden-maned steed; and the lot fell that the princess should go to Vassili, and the golden-maned steed to Dmitri.

Then Vassili Tsarevich took the princess, and placed her on his horse; Dmitri sat on the golden-maned steed, and took the Fire-bird to give to their father, Tsar Vwislav; and they went their way.

Ivan Tsarevich lay dead on that spot exactly thirty days; then the Gray Wolf ran up, knew Ivan by his odor, wanted to aid him, to bring him to life, but knew not how. Just then the Gray Wolf saw a raven with two young ones who were flying above the body and wanted to eat the flesh of Ivan Tsarevich. The wolf hid behind a bush; and when the young ravens had come down and were ready to eat the body, he sprang out, caught one, and was going to tear it in two. Then the raven came down, sat a little way from the Gray Wolf, and said: " Oh, Gray Wolf, touch not my young child; it has done nothing to thee ! "

"Listen to me, raven," said the Gray Wolf. "I will not touch thy child; I will let it go unharmed and well if thou wilt do me a service. Fly beyond the thrice ninth land to the thirtieth kingdom, and bring me the water of death and the water of life."

"I will do that, but touch not my son." Having said these words, the raven flew away and soon disappeared from sight. On the third day the raven returned, bringing two vials, in one the water of life, in the other the water of death, and gave them both to the Gray Wolf. The wolf took the vials, tore the young raven in two, sprinkled it with the water of death; the little raven grew together, he sprinkled it with the water of life, and the raven sprang up and flew away.

The Gray Wolf sprinkled Ivan Tsarevich with the water of death: the body grew together; he sprinkled it with the water of life: Ivan Tsarevich stood up and exclaimed, "Oh, how long I have slept!"

"Thou wouldst have slept forever, had it not been for me. Thy brothers cut thee to pieces and carried off Princess Yelena with the golden-maned steed and the Fire-bird. Now hurry with all speed to thy own country; Vassili Tsarevich will marry thy bride to-day. To reach home quickly, sit on me; I will bear thee."

Ivan sat on the Gray Wolf; the wolf ran with him to the kingdom of Tsar Vwislav, and whether it was long or short, he ran to the edge of the town.

Ivan sprang from the Gray Wolf, walked into the town, and found that his brother Vassili had married Yelena the Beautiful, had returned with her from the ceremony, and was sitting with her at the feast.

Ivan Tsarevich entered the palace; and when Yelena the Beautiful saw him, she sprang up from the table, kissed him, and cried out: "This is my dear bridegroom, Ivan Tsarevich, and not that scoundrel at the table."

Then Tsar Vwislav rose from his place and asked the meaning of these words. Yelena the Beautiful told the whole truth, — told how Ivan Tsarevich had won her, the golden-maned steed, and the Fire-bird; how his elder brother had killed him while asleep; and how they had terrified her into saying that they had won everything.

Tsar Vwislav was terribly enraged at Dmitri and Vassili, and cast them into prison; but Ivan Tsarevich married Yelena the Beautiful, and lived with her in harmony and love, so that one of them could not exist a single minute without the other.

IVAN THE PEASANT'S SON AND THE LITTLE MAN HIMSELF ONE-FINGER TALL, HIS MUSTACHE SEVEN VERSTS IN LENGTH.

IN a certain kingdom in a certain land there lived a Tsar, and in the courtyard of the Tsar was a pillar, and in the pillar three rings, one gold, one silver, and the third copper. One night the Tsar dreamed that there was a horse tied to the gold ring, that every hair on him was silver, and the clear moon was on his forehead. In the morning the Tsar rose up and ordered it to be proclaimed that whoever could interpret the dream and get the horse for him, to that man would he give his daughter, and one half the kingdom in addition.

At the summons of the Tsar a multitude of princes, boyars, and all kinds of lords assembled. No man could explain the dream; no man would undertake to get the horse. At last they explained to the Tsar that such and such a poor man had a son Ivan, who could interpret the dream and get the horse.

The Tsar commanded them to summon Ivan. They summoned him. The Tsar asked, "Canst thou explain my dream and get the horse?"

"Tell me first," answered Ivan, "what the dream was, and what horse thou dost need."

The Tsar said: " Last night I dreamed that a horse was tied to the gold ring in my courtyard; every hair on him was silver, and on his forehead the clear moon."

" That is not a dream, but a reality; for last night the twelve-headed serpent came to thee on that horse and wanted to steal thy daughter."

" Is it possible to get that horse?"

" It is," answered Ivan; " but only when my fifteenth year is passed."

Ivan was then but twelve years old. The Tsar took him to his court, gave him food and drink till his fifteenth year.

When his fifteenth year had passed, Ivan said to the Tsar: " Now give me a horse on which I can ride to the place where the serpent is."

The Tsar led him to his stables and showed him all his horses; but he could not find a single one, by reason of his strength and weight. When he placed his hero's hand on any horse, that horse fell to the ground; and he said to the Tsar: " Let me go to the open country to seek a horse of sufficient strength."

The Tsar let him go. Ivan the peasant's son looked for three years; nowhere could he find a horse. He was returning to the Tsar in tears, when an old man happened to meet him, and asked, "Why dost thou weep, young man?"

To this question Ivan answered rudely; just chased the old man away.

The old man said: " Look out, young fellow; do not speak ill."

Ivan went away a little from the old man, and thought, " Why have I offended the old man? Old people know much."

He returned, caught up with the old man, fell down before him, and said: " Grandfather, forgive me! I offended thee through grief. This is what I am crying about: three years have I travelled through the open country among many herds; nowhere can I find a horse to suit me."

The old man said: " Go to such a village; there in the stable of a poor peasant is a mare; that mare has a mangy colt; take the colt and feed him, — he will be strong enough for thee."

Ivan bowed down to the old man, and went to the village; went straight to the peasant's stable; saw the mare with the mangy colt, on which he put his hands. The colt did not quiver in the least. Ivan took him from the peasant, fed him some time, came to the Tsar, and said that he had a horse. Then he began to make ready to visit the serpent.

The Tsar asked: " How many men dost thou need, Ivan? "

" I need no men," replied Ivan; " I can get the horse alone. Thou mightest give me perhaps half a dozen to send on messages."

The Tsar gave him six men; they made ready and set out. Whether they travelled long or short it is unknown to any man; only this is known, — that they came to a fiery river. Over the river was a bridge; near the river an enormous forest. In that forest they pitched a tent, got many things to drink, and began to eat and make merry.

Ivan the peasant's son said to his comrades: " Let us stand guard every night in turn, and see if any man passes the river."

It happened that when any of Ivan's comrades went on guard, each one of them got drunk in the evening and could see nothing. At last Ivan himself went on guard; and just at midnight he saw that a three-headed serpent was crossing the river, and the serpent called, " I have no enemy, no calumniator, unless one enemy and one calumniator, Ivan the peasant's son; but the raven has n't brought his bones in a bladder yet."

Ivan the peasant's son sprang from under the bridge. " Thou liest; I am here ! "

" If thou art here, then let us make trial; " and the serpent on horseback advanced against Ivan. But Ivan went forth on foot, gave a blow with his sabre, and cut off the three heads of the serpent, took the horse for himself, and tied him to the tent.

The next night Ivan the peasant's son killed the six-headed serpent, the third night the nine-headed one, and threw them into the fiery river. When he went on guard the fourth night the twelve-headed serpent came, and began to speak wrathfully. " Who

art thou, Ivan the peasant's son? Come out this minute to me! Why didst thou kill my sons?"

Ivan the peasant's son slipped out and said: " Let
me go first to my tent, and then I will fight with
thee."

"Well, go on."

Ivan ran to his comrades. " Here, boys, is a bowl,
look into it; when it shall be filled with blood, come
to me."

He returned and stood against the serpent; they
rushed and struck each other. Ivan at the first blow
cut four heads off the serpent, but went himself to
his knees in the earth; when they met the second
time, Ivan cut three heads off and sank to his waist
in the earth; the third time they met he cut off three
more heads, and sank to his breast in the earth; at
last he cut off one head, and sank to his neck in
the earth. Then only did his comrades think of
him; they looked, and saw that the blood was running over the edge of the bowl. They hastened out,
cut off the last head of the serpent, and pulled Ivan
out of the earth. Ivan took the serpent's horse and
led him to the tent.

Night passed, morning came; the good youth
began to eat, drink, and be merry. Ivan the peasant's son rose up from the merry-making and said to
his comrades, "Do ye wait here." He turned into
a cat, and went along the bridge over the fiery river,
came to the house where the serpents used to live,

and began to make friends with the cats there. In the house there remained alive only the old mother of the serpents and her three daughters-in-law; they were sitting in the chamber talking to one another. "How could we destroy that scoundrel, that Ivan the peasant's son?"

The youngest daughter-in-law said: "I'll bring hunger on the road, and turn myself into an apple-tree, so that when he eats an apple it will tear him to pieces in a moment."

The second daughter-in-law said: "I will bring thirst on the road, and turn myself into a well; let him try to drink."

The eldest said: "I'll bring sleep and make a bed of myself; let Ivan try to lie down, he'll die in a minute."

At last the old woman said: "I'll open my mouth from earth to sky and swallow them all."

Ivan heard what they said, went out of the chamber, turned into a man, and went back to his comrades. "Now, boys, make ready for the road."

They made ready, went their way, and to begin with a terrible hunger appeared on the road, so that they had nothing to eat. They saw an apple-tree. Ivan's comrades wanted to pluck the apples, but Ivan would not let them. "That is not an apple-tree," said he; and began to slash at it: blood came out. Another time thirst came upon them. Ivan saw a well; he would not let them drink from it; he began to slash at it: blood came forth. Then sleep came on them; there was a bed on the road. Ivan cut it to pieces. They came to the jaws stretched from the earth to the sky. What was to be done? They thought of jumping through on a run. No man was able to jump through save Ivan; and he was borne out of the trouble by his wonderful steed, every hair of which was silver, and the bright moon on his forehead.

He came to a river; at the river was a hut; there he was met by a little man, himself one finger tall, his mustache seven versts in length, who said: " Give me the horse; and if thou wilt not give him quietly, I 'll take him by force."

Ivan answered: " Leave me, cursed reptile, or I 'll crush thee under the horse."

The little man himself, one finger tall, his mustache seven versts in length, knocked him on to the ground, sat on the horse, and rode away. Ivan went into the hut and grieved greatly for his horse. In the hut was lying on the stove a footless, handless man, and he said to Ivan: " Listen, good hero, — I know not how to call thee by name. Why didst thou try to fight with him? I was something more of a hero than thou, and still he gnawed my hands and feet off."

" Why? "

" Because I ate bread on his table."

Ivan began to ask how he could win his horse back. The footless, handless said, —

" Go to such a river and take the ferry, ferry for

three years, take money from no man: then thou mayest win the horse back."

Ivan bowed down to him, went to the river, took the ferry, and ferried three whole years for nothing. Once it happened to him to ferry over three old men; they offered him money, he would not take it.

" Tell me, good hero, why thou takest no money?"

He said, " According to a promise."

"What promise?"

"A malicious man took my horse, and good people told me to take the ferry for three years, and receive money from no man."

The old men said: " If thou choosest, Ivan, we are ready to help thee to get back thy horse."

"Help me, my friends."

The old men were not common people; they were the Freezer, the Devourer, and the Wizard. The Wizard went out on the shore, made the picture of a boat in the sand and said: "Well, brothers, you see this boat?"

"We see it."

"Sit in it."

All four sat in the boat.

The Wizard said: " Now, light little boat, do me a service as thou didst do before."

Straightway the boat rose in the air, and in a flash, just like an arrow sent from a bow, it brought them to a great stony mountain. At that mountain stood a house, and in the house lived the little man,—

himself one finger tall, his mustache seven versts in length. The old men sent Ivan to ask for the horse. Ivan began to ask.

The little man said: " Steal the Tsar's daughter and bring her to me; then I 'll give thee the horse."

Ivan told this to his comrades. They left him at once and went to the Tsar. The Tsar knew what they had come for, and commanded his servants to heat the bath red hot. " Let them suffocate there," said he. Then he asked his guests to the bath. They thanked him and went. The Wizard commanded the Freezer to go first. The Freezer went into the bath and made it cool. Then they washed and steamed themselves, and came to the Tsar. He ordered a great dinner to be given, and a multitude of all kinds of food was on the table. The Devourer began and ate everything. In the night they came together, stole the Tsar's daughter, and brought her to the little man himself, one finger tall, his mustache seven versts in length. They gave him the Tsar's daughter and got the horse.

Ivan bowed down to the old men, sat on the horse, and went to the Tsar. He travelled and travelled, stopped in an open field to rest, put up his tent, and lay down. He woke up, threw out his hand, the Tsar's daughter was by him; he was delighted, and asked, " How didst thou come here? "

"I turned into a pin, and stuck myself into thy collar."

That moment she turned into a pin again. Ivan stuck her into his collar and travelled on; came to the Tsar. The Tsar saw the wondrous horse, received the good hero with honor, and told how his daughter had been stolen.

Ivan said: " Do not grieve, I have brought her back."

He went into the next chamber; the Tsarevna turned into a fair maiden. Ivan took her by the hand and brought her to the Tsar.

The Tsar was still more rejoiced. He took the horse for himself, and gave his daughter to Ivan. Ivan is living yet with his young wife.

THE FEATHER OF BRIGHT FINIST THE
FALCON.

THERE lived an old man with his old wife. They had three daughters. The youngest was such a beauty that she could neither be told of in a tale nor described with a pen. Once the old man was going to town to the fair, and he said: " My dear daughters, say what ye want; I will buy all ye wish at the fair."

The eldest said, "Father, buy me a new dress." The second said, " Father, buy me a shawl kerchief." But the youngest said, " Buy me a red flower."

The old man laughed at his youngest daughter. "Oh, little dunce! what dost thou want of a red flower? Great good in it for thee; better I 'll buy thee clothes."

No matter what he said, he could not persuade her. " Buy me a little red flower, nothing but that." The old man went to the fair, bought the eldest daughter a dress, the second a shawl kerchief; but in the whole town he could not find a red flower. Only as he was coming home did an unknown old man happen in his way. The old man had a red flower in his hand. " Sell me thy flower, old man."

"It is not for sale, it is reserved. If thy youngest daughter will marry my son, Bright Finist the Falcon, I will give the flower as a gift."

The father grew thoughtful. Not to take the flower was to grieve his daughter, and to take it was to give her in marriage, God knows to whom! He thought and thought; still he took the flower. "What harm?" said he to himself; "they will come with proposals by and by. If he is not the right man, why, we can refuse." He came home, gave the eldest daughter her dress, the second her shawl, and to the youngest he gave the flower, saying, "I like not thy flower, my dear daughter; greatly I like it not." And then he whispered in her ear: "The flower was reserved, and not for sale. I took it from a strange man for the promise to give thee in marriage to his son, Bright Finist the Falcon."

"Be not troubled, father, he is so good and kind; he flies as a bright falcon in the sky, and when he strikes the damp earth he is a hero of heroes."

"But dost thou know him?"

"I know him, father. Last Sunday he was at Mass, and looked at me all the time. I talked to him — he loves me, father."

The old man shook his head, looked at his daughter very sharply, made the sign of the cross on her, and said: "Go to thy room, my dear daughter, it is time to sleep. The morning is wiser than the evening; we will talk this matter over hereafter."

The daughter shut herself up in her room, put the red flower in water, opened the window, and looked into the blue distance. Wherever he came from, Bright Finist the Falcon of Flowery Feathers wheeled before her, sprang in through the window, struck the floor, and became a young man. The maiden was frightened; but when he spoke it became one knows not how joyous and pleasant at her heart. They talked till dawn, — I know not indeed of what; I know only that when day began to break, Bright Finist the Falcon of Flowery Feathers kissed her and said: "Every night as soon as the bright little flower is placed on the window I will fly to thee, my dear. But here is a feather from my wing. Shouldst thou wish for robes, go out on the balcony and wave it on the right side; in a moment all that thy soul desires will appear before thee." He kissed her once more, turned into a bright falcon, and flew away beyond the dark forest.

The maiden looked after her fated one, closed the window, and lay down to sleep. From that time every night, as soon as she placed the little red flower at the window, the good youth, Bright Finist the Falcon, flew to her.

Well, Sunday came. The elder sisters began to dress for Mass. "But what art thou going to wear? Thou hast nothing new," said they to the youngest one.

She answered, "Never mind; I can pray even at home." 4

The elder sisters went to church, and the youngest sat at the window in an old dress and looked at the orthodox people going to church. She bided her time, went out on the porch, waved her colored feather on the right; and from wherever they came there appeared before her a crystal carriage, blooded horses, servants in gold, robes, and every ornament of precious stones. In one moment the beautiful maiden was dressed, sat in the carriage, and dashed off to church. The people look, admire her beauty. "It is clear that some Tsar's daughter has come," said they among themselves.

As soon as "Dostoino" was sung, she went out of the church, sat in the carriage, and was whirled back home. The orthodox people went out to look at her, to see where she would go; but nothing of the sort, — her trace had grown cold long ago.

Our beauty had barely come to the court when she waved her bright feather on the left side; in a moment the maidens undressed her and the carriage vanished. She was sitting as if nothing had happened, looking out through the window to see how the orthodox people go home from church.

The sisters too came home. "Well, sister," said they, "what a beauty was at church to-day! Just a sight, neither to be told in a tale nor described with a pen. It must be that she is some Tsar's daughter from another land, so splendidly dressed, wonderfully!"

The second and third Sundays came; the beautiful
maiden mystified the orthodox people, and her sisters, her father, and her mother.   But the last time
when she undressed she forgot to take out of her
hair the diamond pin.   The elder sisters came from
the church and told her of the Tsar's daughter; but
when they looked at the youngest sister the diamonds
were blazing in her hair.

"Oh, sister, what is this?" cried they; "why just
such a pin was in the hair of the Tsar's daughter to-
day.   Where didst thou get it?"

The beautiful maiden was confused, and ran to her
chamber.   There was no end of guesses and whis-
pers, but the youngest sister said nothing and
laughed in secret.   The elder sisters began to watch
her and to listen in the night at her chamber; and
they overheard one time her conversation with Bright
Finist the Falcon, and saw with their own eyes at
daybreak how he sprang from the window and flew
off beyond the dark forest.

The elder sisters were clearly malicious.   They
planned to put hidden knives for the evening on
the window of their sister's room, so that Bright
Finist the Falcon might cut his colored wings.   They
did this straightway; the youngest sister knew nothing of the matter.   She put her red flower on the
window, lay down on the couch, and fell asleep
soundly.   Bright Finist the Falcon flew to the
window, and as he was springing in cut his left foot;

but the beautiful maiden knew nothing of this; she was sleeping so sweetly, so calmly. Angrily did Bright Finist the Falcon rise to the sky and fly beyond the dark forest.

In the morning the maiden woke up. She looked on every side; it was daylight already, and the good youth was not there. She looked at the window, and on the window were two sharp knives across each other, and red blood was dripping from them to the flower. Long did the maiden shed bitter tears, many sleepless nights did she pass by the window of her chamber. She waved the bright feather in vain; Bright Finist the Falcon flies no longer himself, and sends not his servants.

At last she went to her father with tears in her eyes and begged his blessing, gave orders to forge three pairs of iron shoes, three iron staves, three iron caps, and three iron Easter cakes; she put a pair of shoes on her feet, the cap on her head, took a staff in her hand, and went toward that point from which Bright Finist the Falcon had flown to her. She goes through slumbering forests, she goes over stumps, over logs. One pair of iron shoes are trodden out, one iron cap is worn off, one staff is breaking up, one cake is gnawed away, and the beautiful maiden walks on, walks all the time, and the forest grows darker, grows denser.

All at once she sees standing before her an iron hut on hen's legs, and it turns without ceasing.

"Hut, hut!" said she, "stand with thy back to the forest, thy front to me."

The hut turned its front to her. She entered the hut, and in it was lying a Baba-Yaga from corner to corner, her lips on the crosspiece, her nose in the loft.

"Tfu-tfu-tfu! in former days nothing of Russia was seen with sight nor heard with hearing; but now the odor of Russia goes through the wide world in visible seeming, runs to one's nose. Where dost thou hold thy way, beautiful maiden? Art flying from labor, or seekest labor?"

"Oh, grandmother dear, I had Bright Finist the Falcon of Flowery Feathers; my sisters did harm him! Now I am seeking for Bright Finist the Falcon."

"Oh, my child, thou hast far to go; thrice nine lands must yet be passed! Bright Finist the Falcon of Flowery Feathers lives in the fiftieth kingdom in the eightieth land, and is now betrothed to the daughter of a Tsar."

The Baba-Yaga nourished and fed the maiden with what God had sent, and put her to bed. Next morning, when the light was just coming, she roused her, gave her a present for the road, — a small golden hammer and ten little diamond nails, — and said: "When thou comest to the blue sea, the bride of Bright Finist the Falcon will come out on the shore to walk; take the golden hammer and drive the diamond nails. She will try to buy them of thee; but, beautiful maiden, take no pay, only ask to see Bright

Finist the Falcon.   Now go, with God, to my second sister."

Again the fair maiden goes through the dark forest, goes farther and farther; the forest is darker and deeper, the tree-tops wind up to the sky.   Now almost the second pair of shoes are trodden out, the second cap worn away, the second iron staff breaking, the iron cake gnawed away; before the maiden is an iron hut on hen's legs, and it turns without ceasing.

" Hut, oh, hut! " said she, " stop with thy back to the trees and thy front to me, so that I may creep in and eat."

The hut turned its back to the trees and its front to the maiden.   She entered.   In the hut lay a Baba-Yaga from corner to corner, her lips on the cross-piece, her nose in the loft.

" Tfu-tfu-tfu ! in former days nothing of Russia was seen with sight or heard with hearing; but now the odor of Russia goes through the wide world.   Whither dost hold thy way, fair maiden? "

" Grandmother, dear, I am seeking Bright Finist the Falcon."

" Oh ! he is going to marry; they have the maiden's party to-night," said the Baba-Yaga.

She gave her to eat and drink, and put the maiden to sleep.   At daybreak next morning she roused her, gave her a golden plate with a diamond ball, and enjoined on her most firmly, " When thou comest to the shore of the blue sea, roll the diamond ball on the golden plate. The bride of Bright Finist the Falcon of Flowery Feathers will try to buy the plate and ball; but take nothing for it, only ask to see Bright Finist the Falcon. Now go, with God, to my eldest sister."

Again the fair maiden goes through the dark forest, goes farther and farther; the forest grows darker and deeper. Now are the third pair of shoes almost trodden out, the third cap is wearing off, the third staff is breaking, and the last cake is gnawed away. On hen's legs stands an iron hut and turns about.

" Hut, oh, hut! " cried she, " stand with thy back to the trees and thy face to me; I must creep in and eat bread."

The hut turned. In the hut lay another Baba-Yaga from corner to corner, her lips on the cross-piece, her nose in the loft.

" Tfu-tfu-tfu ! in former times nothing of Russia was seen with sight nor heard with hearing; but now the odor of Russia goes through the wide world. Where, beautiful maiden, dost thou hold thy way? "

" Grandmother, dear, I am seeking Bright Finist the Falcon."

" Oh, fair maiden, hè has married a Tsar's daughter! Here is my swift steed; sit on him, and go, with God."

The maiden sat on the steed and shot away farther. The forest grew thinner and thinner.

Behold, the blue sea is before her; broad and roomy is it spread, and there in the distance, like fire, burn the golden summits above the lofty, white-walled chambers.   That is the kingdom of Bright Finist the Falcon.   She sat then on the movable sand of the shore, and hammered with hammer the diamond nails.   All at once the Tsar's daughter goes with her nurses and maidens and trusty serving-women along the shore; she stops, and wants to buy the diamond nails and the golden hammer.

"Tsar's daughter, let me but look at Bright Finist the Falcon, I will give them for nothing," answered the maiden.

"Bright Finist the Falcon is sleeping at present, and has ordered that none be admitted; but give me thy beautiful nails and hammer, I will show him to thee."

She took the hammer and nails, ran to the palace, stuck into the clothes of Bright Finist the Falcon a magic pin, so that he should sleep more soundly and not wake; then she commanded her nurses to con-duct the beautiful maiden through the palace to her husband, and went herself to walk.

Long did the maiden struggle, long did she weep over her dear one; she could not wake him in any way.   When she had walked to her pleasure, the Tsar's daughter came home, drove her away, and pulled out the pin.

Bright Finist the Falcon woke.   " Oh, how long I

have slept! Some one was here," said he, " and wept over me all the time, talking the while; but I could not open my eyes, I felt so heavy."

"Thou wast only dreaming," said the Tsar's daughter; "no one was here."

Next day the beautiful maiden sat again on the shore of the blue sea, and was rolling a diamond ball on a golden plate.

The Tsar's daughter went out to walk; she saw them, and said, " Sell them to me."

" Let me look at Bright Finist the Falcon, and I will give them for nothing."

The Tsar's daughter agreed, and again she pierced the clothes of Bright Finist the Falcon with a magic ,pin. Again the fair maiden wept bitterly over her dear one, but could not rouse him.

The third day she sat on the shore of the blue sea, so sad and sorrowful, she was feeding her steed with glowing coals. The Tsar's daughter, seeing that the steed was eating fire, wanted to buy him.

" Let me look on Bright Finist the Falcon, and I 'll give the steed for nothing."

The Tsar's daughter agreed, ran to the palace, and said to her husband, " Let me look in thy head." She sat down to look in his head, and stuck the pin in his hair; straightway he was in a deep sleep. Then she sent her nurses for the beautiful maiden.

The fair maiden came, tried to wake her dear, embraced him and kissed him, crying bitterly, bitterly herself; he wakes not. Then she began to look in his head, and out fell the magic pin.

Bright Finist the Falcon woke all at once; he saw the fair maiden and was glad. She told him every-thing as it was, — how her malicious sisters had envied her, how she had wandered, and how she had ex-changed with the Tsar's daughter. He loved her more than before, kissed her on the sweet lips, and gave command to call without delay boyars, princes, and people of every degree. Then he asked: "What is your judgment: with which wife should I spend my life, — with her who sold me, or her who bought me?"

All the boyars, princes, and people of each degree decided in one voice to take the woman who had bought him; but the one who had sold him, to hang on the gate and shoot her. Bright Finist the Falcon of Flowery Feathers did this.

THE PIG WITH GOLD BRISTLES, THE DEER WITH GOLDEN HORNS, AND THE GOLDEN-MANED STEED WITH GOLDEN TAIL.

THERE lived a Tsar, and he had a daughter, Tsarevna, Priceless Beauty, not to be told of in a tale nor described with a pen. The Tsar issued a call throughout all towns that whoever would kiss the Tsarevna through twelve windows, no matter of what stock he might be, he would get the Tsarevna for wife, and receive half the kingdom.

In this kingdom lived a merchant, and he had three sons; the two elder were crafty, and the third, the youngest, was a simpleton. Well, the elder brothers said, " Father, we will go to get the Tsarevna."

" Go, with God," said the merchant.

They took the very best horses and began to make ready for the road. The fool also was preparing.

" Where art thou going, fool? How couldst thou kiss the Tsarevna?" and they laughed at him in every manner.

They went away, and the simpleton dragged along after them on a poor mangy little horse. He went into the field, and he cried with a shrill voice: " Oh, blue-brown, cunning bay, stand before me as leaf before stem ! "

Wherever he came from, a splendid steed rushed up; the ground trembled. The simpleton crept into one ear of the steed and out of the other, and became such a beauty as had never been seen nor heard of. He sat on the horse, and rode to the Tsar's palace; and when he rushed up he broke six panes of glass.

All were astonished, and cried, " Who is that? Seize him, hold him ! "

But his trace was cold. He rode away into the field, crept into one ear of his steed, out of the other, and became just such a simpleton as before; he sat on his wretched horse, rode home, and lay on the stove.

His brothers came back and said: " Well, father, there was a hero, — such a hero ! He broke through six glasses at once."

The simpleton from the stove cried out: " Ah, brothers, was not that I ? "

" Thou dunce ! how couldst thou do it; how couldst thou get the Tsarevna? Thou art not worth her finger nail."

Next day the brothers prepared again to go to the Tsar's palace; the simpleton also prepared. " What art thou going for, thou dunce ? " laughed the brothers; " thou art needed there, I suppose ! "

The simpleton went again on his mangy, wretched little horse to the field, and cried in a shrill voice:

" Oh, blue-brown, cunning bay, stand before me as leaf before stem ! "

The steed rushed, the ground trembled, the simpleton crept into one ear of the steed and out of the other, and became such a beauty as had never been seen or heard of before. He rushed through the Tsar's court, broke all the twelve windows, and kissed the Tsarevna, Priceless Beauty. She put a mark straight on his forehead.

All were astonished, and cried: " Stop him, hold him ! Who is he ? "

But his trace was cold. He rode out to the field, crept into one ear and out of the other, became just such a simpleton as before, came home, tied a rag around his forehead, pretended that his head was aching, and lay down on the stove.

His brothers returned and said : " Oh, father, there was a hero, such a hero ! At once he broke all twelve windows and kissed the Tsarevna."

The simpleton cried out from the stove : " Ah, brothers, was it not I ? "

" Oh, thou dunce, how could it be ? "

Meanwhile the Tsarevna was thinking who her bridegroom could be. She went to the Tsar and said : " Father, let me bring together all the Tsars' sons, kings' sons, nobles, merchants, and peasants to a feast, to a talk, and find out who kissed me." The Tsar permitted her.

Well, the whole Christian world met. The Tsarevna

herself went among them all, entertained all with wine, examined to see if she could find the mark on any man's forehead. She went to each; at last she brought wine to the simpleton.

"What hast thou bound up there?" asked the Tsarevna.

"So, nothing; my head aches," said the simpleton.

"Well, then, untie it." The Tsarevna unbound his head, recognized the mark, and grew faint.

The Tsar said to her, "It is impossible to change the word now; it has to be so, — be his wife."

They married the simpleton and the Tsarevna. She was weeping bitterly; her two sisters, who had married Tsars' sons, were laughing at her, and said: "There it is; she has married a fool!"

Once the Tsar called all his sons-in-law and said: "I have heard that in such a state, in such a kingdom, there is a wonder, — a pig with gold bristles. Is it not possible in some way to get this pig? Try."

Well, the two crafty sons-in-law saddled the very best horses, sat on them, and rode away.

The fool took from the stable the very last miserable horse, and followed his brothers. He came out into an open field, and cried with a shrill voice: "Come, blue-brown, cunning bay, stand before me as leaf before stem!" Wherever he came from, the wondrous horse was snorting and tearing the ground with his hoof. The simpleton crawled into one ear and out of the other.

Wherever they came from, there stood before him two youths, and they asked, "What dost thou wish, what is thy pleasure?"

"To have a tent here, and in the tent a bed; beside the tent to have the pig with gold bristles walking."

All was done in a moment. The tent was there, in the tent a bed; on the bed lay the simpleton, but such a hero that no one could know him. The pig with gold bristles was walking by the side of the tent in the meadow.

The other brothers-in-law travelled and travelled; nowhere could they see a pig with gold bristles. On their way home they approached the tent and saw the wonder. "Oh! here is where the pig with gold bristles is walking; let us go," said they, "and whatever must be given we will give, we will buy the pig and please our father-in-law."

They went to the tent and saluted the owner. The simpleton asked: "Where are ye travelling? what are ye looking for?"

"Wilt thou sell us the pig with gold bristles? we are looking for this pig a long time."

"No, I want it myself."

"Ask what will please thee, but sell."

They offered him a thousand for the pig, and two and three and more; but the simpleton would not consent. "I will not take a hundred thousand," said he.

"Oh, let us have him, please; take what seems good to thee!"

" Well, ye need him so greatly, I will give him, and will not take much, — the middle toe of each man's foot."

They thought and thought, took off their boots, and each man cut off the middle toe of his foot. The simpleton took the toes, hid them, and gave the pig with gold bristles. The brothers-in-law went home, taking the pig with them.

The Tsar was so glad that he knew not what to call them, where to seat them, or what to give them to eat.

" Have ye seen the fool? " asked the Tsar.

" With seeing we have not seen him, with hearing we have not heard."

The simpleton crept into one ear of his horse, out of the other, and became just such a fool as before. He killed his horse, took off his skin, and put it on; then he caught magpies, crows, jackdaws, and sparrows, tied them around himself, and went home. He came into the palace and let all his birds loose; they flew around on every side, and broke nearly all the windows of the palace.

The Tsarevna, Priceless Beauty, covered herself with tears, and her sisters were screaming with laughter.   " Our husbands," said they, " brought home the pig with gold bristles, and thy fool — look, if it please thee, how he has dressed himself as a monster ! "

The Tsar shouted: "What a clown ! I 'll fix him."

Again the Tsar called his sons-in-law.   " My dear

sons-in-law, I have heard that in such a kingdom, in such a land, there is a wonder, — a deer with golden horns and a golden tail. Can ye not get him in any way?"

"We can, your Majesty."

Now the two crafty sons-in-law saddled the very best horses and set out.

" Well," said the Tsar to the simpleton, "go thou with the others."

The simpleton took from the stable the very last miserable horse and followed his brothers. He went out in the open field and cried with a shrill voice: "Oh, blue-brown, cunning bay, stand before me as leaf before stem." Wherever he came from, the wonderful horse was there, snorting and tearing the ground with his hoofs. The simpleton crept in one of his ears and out of the other. Wherever they came from, two young men stood before him and asked: "What dost thou want?"

" I want a tent here, in the tent a bed, and at the side of the tent a deer with golden horns and a golden tail."

That moment the tent was there, in the tent a bed, on the bed the simpleton stretched himself, — such a beauty that no man could know him; at the side of the tent walked a deer with golden horns and a golden tail.

The crafty brothers travelled and travelled. Nowhere did they see such a deer, and they turned

5

to come home. They came near the tent and saw the wonder. "Oh, this is where the deer with golden horns and a golden tail is! Let us go," said they; "whatever must be given we'll give, buy that deer, and please our father-in-law."

They came up and saluted. The simpleton asked: "Why are ye travelling; what are ye seeking?"

"Wilt thou sell us the deer with golden horns and a golden tail?"

"No, it is not for sale; I want it myself."

"Ask what will please thee, but sell." They offered one, two, three thousand, and more. The simpleton would n't listen to the offers, would not take money.

"But if my deer has pleased you, I'll sell him, if ye like, at a cheap price,— the middle finger of each man's hand."

They thought and thought, and agreed. They took off their gloves and cut off the middle finger. The simpleton put the fingers away and gave the deer.

The sons-in-law came home, and brought the deer with golden horns and a golden tail. The Tsar from joy knew not what to call them, where to seat them, or with what to entertain them.

"Have ye seen the fool anywhere?" asked the Tsar.

"With seeing we have not seen him, with hearing we have not heard."

The simpleton crept into one ear of the horse and out of the other, and became just such a simpleton as he had been before. He killed his wretched horse, skinned him, and put on the skin; then caught a lot of jackdaws, crows, magpies, and sparrows, tied them around himself, and went home. He came again to the palace, and let out the birds in different directions; his wife was sobbing, and her sisters were laughing. " Our husbands," said they, " brought home the deer with golden horns and a golden tail, and thy fool — look at him ! "

The Tsar shouted at the fool: " What an ignorant lout ! " and he gave half the kingdom to his crafty sons-in-law.

The third time the Tsar called his crafty sons-in-law, and said : " My dear sons-in-law, I will give you the whole kingdom if ye will get for me the golden-maned steed with golden tail; I have heard that he is in such a kingdom and such a land."

The crafty sons-in-law saddled the very best horses and went on their journey.

The Tsar sent also the fool. " Well, go thou too."

The simpleton took the very last wretched horse from the stable and followed his crafty brothers. He came to the open field and cried with a shrill voice : " Oh, blue-brown, cunning bay, stand before me as leaf before stem ! " Wherever he came from, the marvellous steed was snorting, and tearing the earth with his hoof. Behold, the simpleton crept into one ear and out of the other, and became such a beauty that it was not in the power of man to recognize him.

Then, wherever they came from, there stood before him two youths, and they asked, "What dost thou wish; what dost thou want?"

"I want a tent here, in the tent a bed, and at the side of the tent the golden-maned steed with golden tail."

That minute the tent was made, in the tent a bed. The simpleton stretched himself on the bed; at the side of the tent the golden-maned steed with golden tail was walking.

The crafty sons-in-law travelled and travelled; nowhere did they see that kind of steed, and were on their way home. They drew near the tent, and saw the wonder.

"Oh, here is the place where the golden-maned steed with golden tail is walking. Let us go in," said they; "we will give whatever they ask, and buy him to please our father-in-law."

The simpleton asked: "Whither are ye travelling; what are ye seeking?"

"Sell us the golden-maned steed with golden tail."

"He is not for sale; I want him myself."

"Ask what may please thee, only sell him;" and they offered one, two, three thousand and more.

"I would not take a hundred thousand," said the simpleton.

"Sell him to us; take what will please thee."

"Well, if ye need him greatly, I will give him to you; I will not take a high price. Let me cut a strap from the back of each one of you."

They thought and thought, struggled and struggled, wanted the horse very badly, were sorry for themselves, but decided at last, undressed, and took off their shirts. The simpleton cut from the back of each one of them a strap, took the straps, put them away, and delivered the steed.

The sons-in-law came home bringing the golden-maned steed with golden tail. The Tsar from delight knew not what to call them, where to seat them, or how to entertain them, and gave them the remaining half of the kingdom. The simpleton crept into one ear of the steed and out of the other, and became what he had been before. He killed his wretched horse, took off the skin, put it on himself, caught magpies, crows, jackdaws, and sparrows, tied them around himself, came to the palace, and let out the birds; they flew in different directions, and broke nearly all the windows. The Tsarevna, his wife, was crying, and her sisters were laughing at her. "Our husbands have brought the golden-maned steed with golden tail; but look at thy fool going around such a fright!"

The Tsar shouted at the fool: "What an ignorant lout! I'll have thee shot."

And the simpleton asked: "With what wilt thou reward me?"

"What reward shouldst thou have?" asked the Tsar.

"If the truth must be told, I got for thee the pig

with gold bristles, the deer with golden horns and a golden tail, and the golden-maned steed with golden tail."

" How canst thou prove that? " asked the Tsar.

" Command thy sons-in-law, Gosudár, to take off their boots."

The sons-in-law began to make excuses; they didn't want to take off their boots.

" Take off your boots," urged the Tsar; " there is no harm in that."

They took off their boots. The Tsar looks: one toe is missing.

" Here are their toes," said the simpleton. " Order them now to take off their gloves."

They removed their gloves, and the Tsar saw there was a finger missing.

" Here are their fingers," said the simpleton. " Order them now to take off their shirts."

The Tsar saw that the affair was coming true, and ordered them to undress. They took off their shirts, and the Tsar saw that each one of them had a strap cut from his back the width of two fingers.

" Here are the straps," said the simpleton; and told the whole story as it was.

The Tsar didn't know how to entertain him, nor how to reward him. He gave him the whole kingdom, and the other sons-in-law, because they had deceived him, he had shot.

The simpleton went to the open field and cried

with a shrill voice: "Oh, blue-brown, cunning bay, stand before me as leaf before stem!" The horse ran, the ground trembled, the simpleton crept into one ear of the steed and out of the other, and became a hero and a beauty.

He came home, began to live with his Tsarevna and win wealth.

WATER OF YOUTH, WATER OF LIFE, AND WATER OF DEATH.

IN a certain kingdom in a certain land there lived a Tsar; that Tsar had three sons, — two crafty, and the third simple. Somehow the Tsar had a dream that beyond the thrice ninth land, in the thirtieth kingdom, there was a beautiful maiden, from whose hands and feet water was flowing, that whoever would drink that water would become thirty years younger. The Tsar was very old. He summoned his sons and counsellors, and asked: "Can any one explain my dream?"

The counsellors answered the Tsar: "We have not seen with sight nor heard with hearing of such a beautiful maiden, and how to go to her is unknown to us."

Now the eldest son, Dmitri Tsarevich, spoke up: "Father, give me thy blessing to go in all four directions, look at people, show myself, and make search for the beautiful maiden."

The Tsar gave his parental blessing. "Take," said he, "treasure as much as thou wishest, and all kinds of troops as many as are necessary."

Dmitri Tsarevich took one hundred thousand men and set out on the road, on the journey. He rode a day, he rode a week, he rode a month, and two and three months. No matter whom he asked, no one knew of the beautiful maiden, and he came to such desert places that there were only heaven and earth. He urged his horse on, and behold before him is a lofty mountain; he could not see the top with his eyes. Somehow he climbed the mountain and found there an ancient, a gray old man.

" Hail, grandfather ! "

" Hail, brave youth ! Art fleeing from labor, or seekest thou labor ? "

" I am seeking labor."

" What dost thou need ? "

" I have heard that beyond the thrice ninth land, in the thirtieth kingdom, is a beautiful maiden, from whose hands and feet healing water flows, and that whoever gets and drinks this water will grow thirty years younger."

" Well, brother, thou canst not go there."

" Why not ? "

" Because there are three broad rivers on the road, and on these rivers three ferries: at the first ferry they will cut off thy right hand, at the second thy left foot, at the third they will take thy head."

Dmitri Tsarevich was grieved; he hung his stormy head below his shoulders, and thought: " Must I spare my father's head ? Must I spare my own ? I'll turn back."

He came down from the mountain, went back to

his father, and said: "No, father, I have not been able to find her; there is nothing to be heard of that maiden."

The second son, Vassili Tsarevich, began to beg: "Father, give me thy blessing; perhaps I can find her."

"Go, my son."

Vassili Tsarevich took one hundred thousand men, and set out on his road, on his journey. He rode a day, he rode a week, he rode a month, and two, and three, and entered such places that there was nothing but forests and swamps. He found there Baba-Yaga, boneleg. "Hail, Baba-Yaga, boneleg!"

"Hail, brave youth! Art thou fleeing from labor, or seekest labor?"

"I am seeking labor. I have heard that beyond the thrice ninth land, in the thirtieth kingdom, is a beautiful maiden, from whose feet and hands healing water flows."

"There is, father; only thou canst not go there."

"Why not?"

"Because on the road there are three ferries: at the first ferry they will cut off thy right hand, at the second thy left foot, at the third off with thy head."

"It is not a question of saving my father's head, but sparing my own."

He returned, and said to his father: "No, father, I could not find her; there is nothing to be heard of that maiden."

The youngest son, Ivan Tsarevich, began to beg: "Give me thy blessing, father; maybe I shall find her."

The father gave him his blessing. "Go, my dear son; take troops and treasure all that are needed."

"I need nothing, only give me a good steed and the sword Kládyenets."

Ivan Tsarevich mounted his steed, took the sword Kládyenets, and set out on his way, on his journey. He rode a day, he rode a week, he rode a month, and two and three; and rode into such places that his horse was to the knees in water, to the breast in grass, and he, good youth, had nothing to eat. He saw a cabin on hen's feet, and entered: inside sat Baba-Yaga, boneleg.

"Hail, grandmother!"

"Hail, Ivan Tsarevich! Art flying from labor, or seekest labor?"

"What labor? I am going to the thirtieth kingdom; there, it is said, lives a beautiful maiden, from whose hands and feet healing water flows."

"There is, father; though with sight I have not seen her, with hearing I have heard of her: but to her it is not for thee to go."

"Why so?"

"Because there are three ferries on the way: at the first ferry they will cut off thy right hand, at the second thy left foot, at the third off with thy head."

"Well, grandmother, one head is not much; I will go, whatever God gives."

"Ah! Ivan Tsarevich, better turn back; thou art still a green youth, hast never been in places of danger, hast not seen great terror."

"No," said Ivan; "if thou seizest the rope, don't say thou art not strong." He took farewell of Baba-Yaga and went farther.

He rode a day, a second, and a third, and came to the first ferry: the ferrymen were sleeping on the opposite bank. "What is to be done?" thought Ivan. "If I shout, they 'll be deaf for the rest of their lives; if I whistle, I shall sink the ferry-boat." He whistled a half whistle. The ferrymen sprang up that minute and ferried him across the river.

"What is the price of your work, brothers?"

"Give us thy right hand."

"Oh, I want that for myself!" Then Ivan Tsarevich struck with his sword on the right, and on the left. He cut down all the ferrymen, mounted his horse, and galloped ahead. At the two other ferries he got away in the same fashion. He was drawing near the thirtieth kingdom. On the boundary stood a wild man, in stature tall as a forest, in thickness the equal of a great stack of hay; he held in his hands an enormous oak-tree.

"Oh, worm!" said the giant to Ivan Tsarevich, "whither art thou riding?"

"I am going to the thirtieth kingdom; I want to see the beautiful maiden from whose hands and feet healing water flows."

"How couldst thou, little pigmy, go there? I am

a hundred years guarding her kingdom, great, mighty heroes came here, — not the like of thee, — and they fell from my strong hand. What art thou? Just a little worm!"

Ivan Tsarevich saw that he could not manage the giant, and he turned aside. He travelled and travelled till he came to a sleeping forest; in the forest was a cabin, and in the cabin an old, ancient woman was sitting. She saw the good youth, and said: "Hail, Ivan Tsarevich! Why has God brought thee hither?"

He told her all without concealment. The old woman gave him magic herbs and a ball.

"Go out," said she, "into the open field, make a fire, and throw these herbs on it; but take care to stand on the windward. From these magic herbs the giant will sleep a deep sleep; cut his head off, then let the ball roll, and follow. The ball will take thee to those regions where the beautiful maiden reigns. She lives in a great golden castle, and often rides out with her army to the green meadows to amuse herself. Nine days does she stay there; then sleeps a hero's sleep nine days and nine nights."

Ivan Tsarevich thanked the old woman and went to the open field, where he made a fire and threw into it the magic herbs. The stormy wind bore the smoke to where the wild man was standing on guard. It grew dim in his eyes; he lay on the damp earth and fell soundly asleep. Ivan Tsarevich cut off his head, let the ball roll, and rode on. He travelled and travelled till the golden palace was visible; then he turned from the road, let his horse out to feed, and crept into a thicket himself. He had just hidden, when dust was rising in a column from the front of the palace: the beautiful maiden rode out with her army to amuse herself in the green meadows. The Tsarevich saw that the whole army was formed of maidens alone. One was beautiful, the next surpassed that one; fairer than all, and beyond admiration was the Tsarevna herself.

Nine days was she sporting in the green meadows, and the Tsarevich did not take his eyes from her, still he could not gaze his fill. On the tenth day he went to the golden palace. The beautiful maiden was lying on a couch of down, sleeping a hero's sleep; from her hands and feet healing water was flowing. At the same time her trusty army was sleeping as well.

Ivan Tsarevich took a flask of the healing water. His heroic heart could not withstand her maiden beauty. He tarried awhile, then left the palace, mounted his good steed, and rushed toward home.

Nine days slept the beautiful maiden, and when she woke her rage was dreadful. She stamped, she screamed with a piercing voice: " What wretch has been here?" she sprang on to her fleet-flying mare, and struck into a chase after Ivan Tsarevich. The mare races, the ground trembles; she caught up with the good hero, struck him with her sword, and straight in the breast did she strike. The Tsarevich fell on the damp earth: his bright eyes close, his red blood stiffens. The fair maiden looked at him, and great pity seized her; through the whole world might she search, and not find such a beauty. She placed her white hand on his wound, moistened it with healing water. All at once the wound closed, and Ivan Tsarevich rose up unharmed.

"Wilt thou take me as wife?" asked she.

"I will, beautiful maiden."

"Well, go home, and wait three years."

Ivan Tsarevich took farewell of his betrothed bride and continued his journey. He was drawing near his own kingdom; but his elder brothers had put guards everywhere, so as not to let him come near his father. The guards gave notice at once that Ivan Tsarevich was coming. The elder brothers met him on the road, drugged him, took the flask of healing water, and threw him into a deep pit. Ivan Tsarevich came out in the underground kingdom.

He travelled and travelled in the underground kingdom. When he came to a certain place, a great storm rose up, lightning flashed, thunder roared, rain fell. He went to a tree to find shelter; looked up, and saw young birds in that tree all wet. He took off his coat, covered them, and sat himself under the tree.

When the old bird flew to the tree, she was so large that she hid the light, and it grew dark as if night were near. When she saw her young covered, she asked: "Who has protected my little birds?" Then, seeing the Tsarevich, she said: "It is thou who didst this; God save thee! Whatever thou wishest, ask of me; I will do everything for thee."

He said, "Bear me out into the upper world."

"Make ready," said the bird, "a double box. Fill one half of it with every kind of game, and in the other half put water, so as to have something with which to nourish me."

The Tsarevich did all that was asked. The bird took the box on her back, and the Tsarevich sat in the middle. She flew up; and whether it was long or short, she bore him to this upper world, took farewell of him, and flew home.

Ivan Tsarevich went to his father; but the old Tsar did not like him by reason of the lies which his brothers had told, and sent him into exile. For three whole years Ivan wandered from place to place. When three years had passed, the beautiful maiden sailed in a ship to the capital town of Ivan Tsarevich's father. She sent a letter to the Tsar, demanding the man who had stolen the water, and if he refused she would burn and destroy his kingdom utterly.

The Tsar sent his eldest son; he went to the ship. Two little boys, grandsons of the Tsar, saw him, and asked their mother: "Is that our father?"

"No, that is your uncle."

" How shall we meet him? "

" Take each one a whip and flog him back home."

The eldest Tsarevich returned, looking as if he had eaten something unsalted.

The maiden continued her threats, demanded the guilty man. The Tsar sent his second son, and the same thing happened to him as to the eldest. Now the Tsar gave command to find the youngest Tsarevich.

When the Tsarevich was found, his father wished him to go on the ship to the maiden. But he said: " I will go when a crystal bridge is built to the ship, and on the bridge there shall be many kinds of food and wine set out."

There was no help for it; they built the bridge, prepared the food, brought wines and meat.

The Tsarevich collected his comrades. "Come with me, attend me," said he; "eat ye and drink, spare nothing."

While he was walking on the bridge the little boys cried out: " Mother, who is that? "

" That is your father."

" How shall we meet him? "

" Take him by the hands and lead him to me."

They did so; there was kissing and embracing. After that they went to the Tsar, told him all just as it had been. The Tsar drove his eldest sons from the castle, and lived with Ivan, — lived on and gained wealth.

6

FOOTLESS AND BLIND CHAMPIONS.

IN a certain kingdom, in a certain land, there lived a Tsar with his Tsaritsa. They had a son, Ivan Tsarevich, and Katoma of the Oaken Cap was appointed tutor to care for and guard Ivan.

The Tsar and Tsaritsa attained to ancient years, fell ill, and had no thought to recover. They summoned Ivan Tsarevich and said: "When we die, do thou obey in all things Katoma of the Oaken Cap and honor him. If thou obeyest him, thou 'lt be happy; but if disobedient, thou wilt perish like a fly."

Next day the Tsar and Tsaritsa died. Ivan buried his parents and lived according to their command: whatever he did, he always held counsel with his tutor. Whether it was long or short, the Tsarevich grew to years of manhood and thought of marrying. He came to Katoma of the Oaken Cap and said: " I feel dreary alone; I wish to marry."

" Well, Tsarevich, where is the halt? Thy years are such that it is time to think of a bride. Go to the great chamber, — there the portraits of all Tsars' daughters and all kings' daughters are collected. Look at them and choose; if any please thee, propose for that one."

Ivan Tsarevich went to the great chamber, examined the portraits; and Princess Anna the Beautiful suited his mind, — such a beauty that in the whole world there was not her equal. Under her portrait was written that if any man gave her a riddle and she could not solve it, she would marry the man; and whose riddle she solved, off went his head. Ivan Tsarevich read this inscription, grew very sorrowful, and went to his uncle. " I have been," said he, " in the great chamber, and have found for myself a bride, — Anna the Beautiful; but I know not how to get her."

" Yes, Tsarevich, it is difficult to win her. If thou go alone, thou wilt never succeed; but if thou take me and will do what I say, perhaps the affair may be settled."

Ivan Tsarevich begged Katoma of the Oaken Cap to go with him, and gave his faithful word to obey him in sorrow and in joy.

They prepared for the road and the journey, and went to ask Princess Anna the Beautiful in marriage. They travelled one year, travelled a second, then a third, and passed over many lands. Ivan Tsarevich said: " Uncle, we are travelling now so long a time, are nearing the land of Anna the Beautiful, and we know not what riddle to give her."

" Oh, we will think of one yet."

They went farther. Uncle Katoma looked on the road, and there was lying a purse with gold. He took it up, poured all the money out of it into his own purse, and said: " Here is the riddle, Ivan Tsarevich. When thou comest to the princess, give her the riddle in these words: 'We were travelling along, and we saw good lying on the road. We took good with good and put it in our good.' She'll not solve that riddle all her life; and every other one she would know in a moment,— she would just look into her magic book, and as soon as she knew the riddle she would have thy head cut off."

Well, Ivan Tsarevich with his uncle came at last to the lofty palace where the beautiful princess was living. At that very time she was on the balcony, saw the travellers, and sent out to know whence they were, and what they had come for.

Ivan Tsarevich replied: " I have come from such and such a kingdom, and I wish to ask Anna the Beautiful in marriage."

They reported this to the princess. She gave answer that the Tsarevich should come to the palace and give, in the presence of all her counselling princes and boyars, a riddle. " With me," said she, " this order is established, that if I solve not the riddle of a man, I will marry him; but if I solve any man's riddle, I give him to a cruel death."

" Hear my riddle, beautiful princess," said Ivan. " We were going along, we saw good lying on the road, we took good with good and put it in our good."

Anna the Beautiful took her magic book, began to examine it and look for riddles; she went through the whole volume and found nothing. Then the counselling princes and boyars decided that the princess must marry Ivan Tsarevich. Though sorry, she had to give way, and began to prepare for the wedding; but plotting to win time and get rid of the bridegroom, she thought, " I will trouble him with difficult tasks." She called Ivan Tsarevich and said : " Oh, my dear Ivan Tsarevich, my betrothed husband, we must prepare for the wedding; do me a small service. In my kingdom in such a place stands a great iron pillar; bring it to the palace kitchen and cut it into small pieces as fuel for the cook."

" My princess, is it possible that I have come here to cut fuel? Is that my business? I have a servant for that, — Uncle Katoma of the Oaken Cap."

The Tsarevich called Uncle Katoma straightway, and commanded him to bring the iron pillar to the kitchen and cut it into small pieces as fuel for the cook.

Uncle Katoma went to the place mentioned, took the pillar in his arms, brought it to the palace kitchen, and cut it into small pieces. Four pieces of iron did he put in his pocket, saying, " They will be good in the future."

Next day the princess said to Ivan: " My dear Tsarevich, my betrothed husband, to-morrow we must go to the crown: I will go in a carriage, and thou on an heroic steed. Meanwhile thou shouldst try the steed."

"Shall I try a horse when I have a servant for that?" Ivan Tsarevich called Uncle Katoma of the Oaken Cap.

"Go," said he, "and order the stable-boys to lead forth the heroic steed; sit on him and ride him around. To-morrow I will go to the marriage on him."

Uncle Katoma saw through the cunning of the princess, without talking long. He went to the stable and ordered them to lead forth the heroic steed. Twelve men went: they opened twelve locks, opened twelve doors, and led out the magic horse by twelve iron chains.

Uncle Katoma went to the horse: the moment he sat on him the magic steed left the earth and rose higher than the standing forest, lower than the moving clouds. Katoma sat firmly; with one hand he held the mane, with the other he took from his pocket one of the iron bars and began to pound the horse between the ears with it. He broke one bar, took another, broke that, took a third, broke that. The fourth entered service; and Katoma so hammered the steed that he could not endure, but spoke with the voice of a man: "Father Katoma, let me even live in the white world; whatever thou wishest, command, — everything shall be as thou sayest."

"Listen, dog's meat!" answered Uncle Katoma. "To-morrow Ivan Tsarevich will ride thee to the marriage: see to it when they lead thee to the broad court, when the Tsarevich approaches and puts his hand on thee, that thou standest quietly, movest not an ear; and when he sits on thy back, sink to thy fetlocks, and walk under him with a heavy tread, as if an immeasurable burden were on thee."

The heroic steed heard the command and came down barely alive to the earth. Katoma took him by the tail and threw him to the side of the stable, saying, "Oh, coachmen and grooms, take this dog's meat to the stable!"

The next day rose, the hour of marriage came. They gave a carriage to the princess, and led out the heroic steed for Ivan Tsarevich. The people ran from every side in thousands. The bridegroom and the bride came forth from the white-walled palace. The princess sat in the carriage and waited for what would happen to Ivan Tsarevich. The magic steed, she thought, would scatter his hair to the wind and drag his bones over the field.

Ivan Tsarevich approached the steed, put his hand on his back, his foot in the stirrup; the horse stood as if fixed to the earth, moved not an ear. Ivan sat on his back; the horse sank in the ground to the fetlocks. They removed the twelve chains from him; the horse began to walk with a slow and heavy tread, the sweat rolled from him like rain.

"Oh, what a champion, what immeasurable strength!" said the people, looking at the Tsarevich.

They crowned the bridegroom with the bride.

They were coming out of the church, took each other by the hand, and the princess thought of testing once more the strength of Ivan Tsarevich. She pressed his hand with such force that he could not endure; the blood rushed to his face, his eyes went up under his forehead.

"So this is the kind of hero thou art!" thought the princess. " Thy uncle has deceived me grandly; but this will not go with thee for nothing."

Anna the Beautiful lived with Ivan Tsarevich as was befitting a wife with a God-given husband, and she in every way flattered him with words, but thought only of one thing, — how to destroy Uncle Katoma of the Oaken Cap. It was not difficult for her to manage the Tsarevich without the uncle. No matter how much calumny she invented, Ivan did not yield to her speeches; he had pity on his uncle. In a year's time he said to his wife: " My dear consort, beautiful princess, I should like to go with thee to my own kingdom."

" Very well, let us go; I have long wished to see thy kingdom."

They got ready and went, making Uncle Katoma coachman. They travelled and travelled. Ivan Tsarevich fell asleep on the way. All at once Anna the Beautiful began to rouse him and complain: " Now, Tsarevich, thou art sleeping all the time, hearest nothing. But thy uncle will not obey me; he drives the horses on purpose over hillocks and into holes, just as if trying to kill me. I spoke to him kindly, and he laughed at me. I will not live unless thou punish him."

Ivan in his drowsiness grew very angry at his uncle, and gave him over entirely to the princess. " Do with him as thou desirest." The princess gave orders to cut off his feet. Katoma allowed himself to be maltreated by her. " Let me endure," thought he ; " and the Tsarevich will know what it is to suffer sorrow." They cut off Katoma's feet. The princess looked around and saw a high stump on one side ; she called the servants and ordered them to seat him on that stump. Ivan Tsarevich she tied by a rope to the carriage, turned back, and went to her own kingdom. Uncle Katoma of the Oaken Cap was sitting on the stump, shedding bitter tears. " Farewell, Ivan Tsarevich," said he, " thou wilt remember me ; " and Ivan Tsarevich ran jumping behind the carriage. He knew himself that he had made a mistake, but he could not turn back.

Anna the Beautiful came to her own kingdom, and she made Ivan Tsarevich herd cows. Every morning he went with the herd into the open field, and in the evening he drove them back into the princess' yard ; and at that time she sat on the balcony and counted the cows, were they all there ? She counted them, and ordered the Tsarevich to kiss the last cow on the tail ; and the cow was so well trained that when she came to the gate she stopped and raised her tail.

Uncle Katoma was sitting on the stump one day, a second, a third, without food or drink. He could in no way slip down, and it was coming to him to die of hunger. Not far away was a thick wood, and in that wood lived a blind, mighty hero; and he nourished himself only with this, that when he knew by the smell that a beast was running past, — a hare, fox, or bear, — that moment he ran, caught it, and his dinner was ready. The hero was very swift of foot, and no running beast could escape him. Behold, it happened thus: a fox was slipping by; the hero heard it and pursued; the fox ran to the tall stump and turned aside. The blind champion hurried, and in the run struck his forehead against the stump so that he drove it out of the ground with its roots.

Katoma was thrown to the earth, and asked, " Who art thou ? "

" The blind hero; I live in this forest thirty years, and I nourish myself only in this way. If I seize a beast, I roast it on the fire; otherwise I should have died of hunger long since."

" Is it possible that thou art blind from birth ? "

" No, not from birth; Anna the Beautiful put out my eyes."

" Well, brother," said Uncle Katoma of the Oaken Cap, " and I through her am footless; she cut off my two feet, the cursed woman."

The two heroes talked to each other, and agreed to

live together and find food in common. The blind
said to the footless: "Sit on me and show the way; I
will serve thee with my feet, and thou shalt serve
me with thy eyes."

He took the footless and carried him. Katoma
sat, looked on both sides, and cried out: "To the
right; to the left; straight ahead." They lived in
this way some time in the forest and caught food, —
hares, foxes, and bears.

Once the footless asked: "Is it possible that we
shall live all our lives without company? I have
heard that in a certain town there is a rich merchant
with his daughter, and the daughter is very chari-
table to poor people and cripples, and gives alms
herself to all. Let us carry her off, brother; let her
live with us as a housekeeper."

The blind man took a wagon, put the footless in it,
and drew him to the town. They went straight to
the house of the rich merchant. The merchant's
daughter saw them through the window. Straightway she sprang up and went to give them something.
She went to the footless: "Take this, poor man, for
Christ's sake." While taking the gift he seized her
by the hand and into the wagon with her. He called
to the blind man, who ran so swiftly that no horse-
man could come up with him.

The merchant sent a party in pursuit, but no one
could overtake the two men. The heroes brought
the merchant's daughter to their hut in the forest, and

said to her: "Be to us in the place of our own sister; live with us, keep the house, for we have no one to cook a meal for us or to wash our shirts. God will not forget thee for doing this."

The maiden remained with them. The heroes respected and loved her, and considered her as their own sister. The way was, they used to go hunting, and she was always at home, took care of the housekeeping, cooked for them, washed for them. Now a Baba-Yaga, boneleg, began to come to the hut and suck the blood of the merchant's daughter. The moment the heroes went to hunt, Baba-Yaga was there. Whether it was long or short, the fair maiden's face fell away; she grew thin and poor.

The blind man saw nothing, but Uncle Katoma of the Oaken Cap noticed that something was wrong. He spoke of it to the blind man, and they questioned their adopted sister. They began to urge her to answer. The Baba-Yaga had strictly forbidden her to confess. For a long time she was afraid to tell of her trouble; long she resisted. At last they persuaded her, and she confessed everything. "Whenever ye go away to hunt, an ancient old woman comes, evil-faced, long-haired, gray; she makes me search in her head, and then sucks my blood."

"Ah!" said the blind man, "that is Baba-Yaga. Wait, we must settle with her in our own fashion; to-morrow we will not go to hunt, we will try to come upon her and catch her."

Next morning they did not go to hunt.

"Well, footless uncle," said the blind man, "crawl thou under the bench; sit quietly. I will go outside and stay under the window. And thou, sister, when Baba-Yaga comes, sit right here in this window, search in her head, separate her hair gradually, and let it out of the window. I will catch her by the gray locks."

It was said and done. The blind man caught the Baba-Yaga by the gray locks and cried, "Ei! Uncle Katoma, crawl from under the bench and hold the viperous old hag till I go into the house."

Baba-Yaga heard trouble, wanted to jump up, and raised her head. What could she do? She had no chance; she tore and tore, — no use.

Then Katoma crawled from under the bench, threw himself on her like a stone mountain, and began to smother Baba-Yaga. She was frightened out of her wits.

The blind man sprang into the house, and said to the footless: "We must make a big fire now, burn the old outcast, and scatter her ashes to the wind."

Baba-Yaga implored. "Father, dove, forgive me; whatever thou wishest I 'll do."

"Well, old witch," said the heroes, "show us the well of living and healing water."

"Only don't beat me, and I 'll show you this moment."

Uncle Katoma sat on the blind man, the blind man took Baba-Yaga by the hair, and she led them to the forest depth, brought them to a well, and said: " Here is the healing and living water."

" See to it, Uncle Katoma," said the blind man, " make no mistake; if she deceives us now, we cannot mend matters while we live."

Uncle Katoma of the Oaken Cap broke from a tree a green branch and threw it into the well; the branch had not reached the water when it burst into a blaze.

" Ah, thou hast turned to deceit ! "

They began to choke the old woman, and wanted to throw her into the fiery well. She implored more than before, and gave an awful oath that now she would play no tricks. " 'Pon my true word, I will lead you now to good water."

They agreed to try once more, and the old woman brought them to another well.

Uncle Katoma broke a dry branch from a tree, and threw it into the well; the branch had not reached the water when it gave out buds, grew green, and blossomed.

" Oh, this is good water ! " said Uncle Katoma.

The blind man moistened his eyes with it, and in a moment he saw. He let the footless down into the water, and his feet grew out.

Both were rejoiced, and said: " Now we will restore everything; but first we must settle with Baba-Yaga. If we forgive her now, we shall not see good ourselves; she will plot evil against us all our lives."

They returned to the fiery well and threw Baba-

Yaga into it, so that she perished. Then Uncle Katoma married the merchant's daughter, and all three went to the kingdom of Anna the Beautiful to liberate Ivan Tsarevich.

They were approaching the capital town. They looked, Ivan Tsarevich was driving a herd of cows.

"Stop, herdsman!" said Uncle Katoma. "Whither art thou driving these cows?"

" I am driving them to the royal castle. The princess always counts them herself, to see if all the cows are there."

"Well, herdsman, here are my clothes; put them on. I'll put on thine, and drive the cows."

" No, brother, that is impossible; if the princess should know it, woe to me."

" Never fear, nothing will come of it; Uncle Katoma is security for thee in that."

Ivan Tsarevich sighed, and said: " Oh, kind man, if Uncle Katoma were living I should not be herding cows in this field."

Then Uncle Katoma confessed to him who he was. Ivan Tsarevich embraced him firmly and shed tears. " I did not think to see thee."

They changed clothes. Uncle Katoma drove the cows to the princess's yard. Anna the Beautiful came out on the balcony, counted to see if all the cows were there, and gave command to drive them into the shed. All went in but the last one; she stopped at the gate. Katoma jumped up. " What art thou waiting for, dog's meat?" caught her by the tail, and pulled her skin off.

The princess saw this and cried: "What is that scoundrel of a herdsman doing? Seize him; bring him to me!"

Here the servants caught Katoma and dragged him to the palace. He made no excuse, for he was confident in himself. They brought him to the palace. She looked at him and asked: "Who art thou? Whence art thou here?"

"I am the man whose feet thou didst cut off, and thou didst seat me on a stump; they call me Uncle Katoma of the Oaken Cap."

"Well," thought the princess, "if he has brought back his feet, there is no use in playing tricks with him;" and she begged forgiveness of him, was sorry for her sins, and took an oath to love Ivan Tsarevich forever and obey him in all things.

Ivan Tsarevich forgave her, and began to live with her in peace and harmony. The blind hero lived with them, and Uncle Katoma went with his wife to the rich merchant and lived in his house.

THE THREE KINGDOMS.

IN that ancient time when God's world was full of wood-demons, witches, and river-maidens, when rivers of milk were flowing between banks of jelly, when over the fields roast partridges were flying, there lived a Tsar, Goroh by name, with his Tsaritsa, Anastasia the Beautiful; and they had three sons. A misfortune not small happened, — an unclean spirit carried away the Tsaritsa.

Said the eldest son to the Tsar: "Father, give me thy blessing; I will go in search of my mother."

He went away and vanished ; for three years there were neither tidings nor report of him.

The second son began to ask: "Father, give me thy blessing for the road, for the journey. Perhaps I may have the luck to find my brother and my mother."

The Tsar gave his blessing. The Tsarevich rode off and also disappeared as if he had sunk in water.

Ivan, the youngest son, came to the Tsar. "My dear father, give me thy blessing for the road, for the journey; perhaps I shall find my brothers and mother."

"Go thy way, my dear son."

Ivan Tsarevich set out for a strange, distant region. He travelled and travelled, and reached the blue sea. He stopped on the shore and thought: "Whither can I hold my way now?" All at once there flew to sea three and thirty spoonbills, struck the earth, and became fair maidens, — all beautiful, but one was better than all the rest. They undressed and rushed into the water. Whether they were bathing a long or short time, Ivan Tsarevich stole up and took the girdle of that maiden who was better than all the rest and hid it in his bosom. When they had finished bathing they came out on shore and began to dress. One girdle was gone.

"Ah! Ivan Tsarevich," said the beauty, "give me my girdle."

"Tell me first where my mother is."

"Thy mother is at the house of my father, Raven son of Raven (Voron Voronovich). Go up along the sea, thou wilt meet a silver bird with a golden crest; wherever it flies do thou follow."

Ivan Tsarevich gave her the girdle and went along the sea; there he met his brothers, exchanged greetings, and took them with him. They went together along the shore, saw the golden-tufted silver bird, and ran after it. The bird flew and flew till it rushed under an iron plate into an opening.

"Well, brothers," said Ivan Tsarevich, "give me your blessing in the place of father and mother. I will let myself down into this opening and discover what a land of strange faith is like, — perhaps our mother is there."

His brothers gave him their blessing. He sat on a rope swing, crawled into that deep opening, and went down no short distance. Just three years was he letting himself down, and then went on his road and way. He went and went, went and went. He saw the Copper Kingdom. In the castle were sitting three and thirty spoonbill maidens. They were embroidering towels with cunning designs, with towns and suburbs.

" Hail, Ivan Tsarevich ! " said the Tsaritsa of the Copper Kingdom. " Whither dost thou hold thy way ? "

" I am going in search of my mother."

" Thy mother is with my father, Raven son of Raven. He is cunning and wise; over mountains and valleys, over caves and clouds, has he flown. He will slay thee, good youth. Here is a ball for thee. Go to my second sister; hear what she will tell thee. If thou comest back, forget me not."

Ivan rolled the ball and followed; he came to the Silver Kingdom. The Tsaritsa of the Silver Kingdom said : " Till now the Russian odor was not to be seen with sight nor heard with hearing; but now the Russian odor appears visibly. Well, Ivan Tsarevich, art fleeing from work, or seekest work ? "

" Ah, fair maiden ! I am in search of my mother."

" Thy mother is with my father, Raven son of

Raven. Cunning is he and wise; over mountains, over valleys has he flown, over caves, over clouds has he swept. Oh, Tsarevich, he will slay thee! Here is a ball. Go to my youngest sister; hear what she will say to thee, whether to go on or come back."

Ivan Tsarevich came to the Golden Kingdom; there three and thirty spoonbill maidens were sitting embroidering towels. Taller than all, fairer than all, was the Tsaritsa of the Golden kingdom, — a beauty that could not be told of in a tale or described with a pen.

"Hail, Ivan Tsarevich!" said she. "Whither dost thou hold thy way?"

"I am going to seek my mother."

"Thy mother is with my father, Raven son of Raven. Cunning is he and wise. Oh, Tsarevich, he will slay thee surely! Here is a ball for thee. Go now to the Pearl Kingdom; there thy mother lives. When she sees thee she will be rejoiced, and that moment will say, ' Nurses and maidens, bring my son green wine;' but take it not. Ask her to give thee wine three years old that is in the cupboard, and a burnt crust for lunch, and do not forget that my father has in the yard two jars of water, — one water of strength, the other of weakness; put each in the place of the other, and drink of the water of strength."

The Tsarevich talked a long time with the Tsaritsa, and they fell in love with each other to such a degree that they hated to part; but there was no help for them. Ivan Tsarevich took farewell of her and went on his journey. He travelled and travelled till he came to the Pearl Kingdom. His mother saw him, was delighted, and cried out, " Nurses and maidens, bring my son green wine."

" I drink no common wine; give me wine three years old, and for a bite a burnt crust." He drank wine three years old, ate the burnt crust, went out in the broad court, put each jar in the place of the other, and fell to drinking the water of strength.

All at once Raven son of Raven flew home, bright as the clear day; but when he saw Ivan Tsarevich he grew gloomier than the dark night. He stooped down to the jar, and began to drink the water of weakness. Then Ivan Tsarevich fell upon his wings, and Raven son of Raven soared high, high; he bore Ivan over mountains, over valleys, over caves, over clouds. " What dost thou need, Ivan Tsarevich? If thou wishest, I will give thee treasure."

" I want nothing but the feather staff."

" No, Ivan Tsarevich, thou wishest to sit in a very wide sleigh." And again Raven son of Raven bore him over mountains, over valleys, over caves, over clouds.

Ivan held firmly, bore down with all his weight, and nearly broke the wings of Raven son of Raven, who screamed, " Break not my wings; take the feather staff!" He gave Ivan the feather staff, became a common raven himself, and flew away to the steep mountains.

Ivan Tsarevich went back, came to the Pearl Kingdom, took his mother, and set out for home. He looked; the Pearl Kingdom had turned into a ball, and was rolling after him. He came to the Golden Kingdom, then to the Silver, and then to the Copper Kingdom. He took and brought with him the three beautiful Tsaritsas, and those kingdoms were wound into balls and rolled after him. He came to the rope swing and sounded a golden trumpet: "My own brothers, if ye are alive, do not betray me."

The brothers heard the call, and drew out into the white world the beautiful soul maiden, the Tsaritsa of the Copper Kingdom. They saw her, and began to fight among themselves; one would not yield to the other.

"Why fight, good youths?" said the maiden. "Down there are better than I."

They let down the rope swing and drew up the Tsaritsa of the Silver Kingdom. Again they began to dispute and fight; one said, "Let her be mine, and come to me;" the other said, "I won't let her be thine."

"Do not fight, good youths; down there is a maiden more beautiful than I."

They stopped fighting, put down the rope swing, and drew up the Tsaritsa of the Golden Kingdom. Again they began to fight; but the Tsaritsa, the

beauty, immediately stopped them, saying: " Your
mother is waiting for you." They drew out their
mother, and let down the rope swing for Ivan Tsarevich; they raised him half way, and cut the rope.
Ivan Tsarevich fell into the depth and was terribly
shocked; he lay half a year without senses, came to
himself, and looked around, remembered everything
that had happened to him, took out the feather staff,
and struck the earth with it. That moment twelve
youths appeared. " What is thy command, Ivan
Tsarevich? "

" Take me out into the free world."

The youths seized him under the arms and bore
him into the free world. Ivan Tsarevich inquired
about his brothers, and heard that they had married
long before. The Tsaritsa of the Copper Kingdom
married the second brother; the Tsaritsa of the
Silver Kingdom, his eldest brother; but his own
bride would not marry any man: his old father
wanted to marry her. He summoned a council, ac-
cused his wife of intimacy with evil spirits, and gave
command to cut her head off. After the execution
he said to the Tsaritsa of the Golden Kingdom:
" Wilt thou marry me? "

" I will when thou makest shoes for me without
measure."

The Tsar gave command to issue a call and ask
all and each, would any man make shoes for the
Tsaritsa without taking her measure. At this time

Ivan Tsarevich had come to his own kingdom, and hired as a workman with a certain old man; and he sent him to the Tsar: "Go, grandfather, take this affair on thyself, and I will make the shoes for thee; but do not tell about me."

The old man went to the Tsar. "I," said he, "am ready to undertake the work."

The Tsar gave him leather for a pair of shoes, and asked: "But canst thou do it, old man?"

"Never fear, Gosudár. I have a son who is a shoemaker."

When he came home the old man gave the leather to Ivan Tsarevich, who cut it into bits and threw it out of the window; then he opened the Golden Kingdom and took out shoes already made. "Here, grandfather, take these and carry them to the Tsar."

The Tsar was delighted, and urged the bride: "Shall we go to the crown soon?"

She answered: "I will marry thee if thou wilt make for me robes to fit without measure."

The Tsar again was in trouble; he assembled all the dressmakers, and offered them much money if they would only make robes to fit without measuring the Tsaritsa.

Ivan Tsarevich said to the old man: "Grandfather, go to the Tsar, get cloth; I will sew robes for thee, but do not tell of me."

The old man dragged himself off to the palace, took satin and velvet, came home, and gave it to the

Tsarevich. Ivan Tsarevich took scissors straightway, and cut all the satin and velvet to pieces and threw them out of the window. Then he opened the Golden Kingdom and took out the most beautiful robes and gave them to the old man, saying, "Take these to the palace."

The Tsar was delighted. "Well, my beloved bride, is it not time for us to go to the crown?"

The Tsaritsa answered: "I will marry thee when thou wilt take the son of that old man and command that he be boiled in milk."

The Tsar thought awhile, then gave the command; and that day they collected three gallons of milk from each house, filled a great caldron, and boiled it on a hot fire. They brought Ivan Tsarevich. He took farewell of all, bowed to the earth, then threw himself into the caldron, dived once, dived twice, sprang out such a beauty that it could neither be told of in a tale nor described with a pen.

Said the Tsaritsa: "Look, Tsar! Whom shall I marry, — thee, old man, or that gallant youth?"

The Tsar thought awhile. "If I bathe in the milk, I shall become just such a beauty as he." He sprang into the caldron, and was cooked in a minute. But Ivan Tsarevich went to be crowned with the Tsaritsa of the Golden Kingdom; they were crowned, and began to live and live on, gaining wealth.

KOSHCHÉI WITHOUT–DEATH.

IT happened that once there lived in a certain land a Tsar and a Tsaritsa. They had a son, Ivan Tsarevich. When an infant the maidens rocked him; but do what they might, they could not rock him to sleep. "Tsar, great Gosudár, come, rock thy own son." The Tsar went to rock the child: "Sleep, little son, sleep my own dear; thou wilt grow up a man. I will get thee Peerless Beauty as bride,— the daughter of three mothers, the granddaughter of three grandmothers, and the sister of nine brothers." The Tsarevich went to sleep and slept for three days and three nights; woke up, and cried more than before.

The maidens rock him, but they cannot rock him to sleep; they call his father: "Tsar, great Gosudár, come, rock thy own son."

The Tsar rocked him, saying, "Sleep, little son, sleep, my own dear; thou wilt grow up a man. I will get thee Peerless Beauty as bride, the daughter of three mothers, the granddaughter of three grand-mothers, and the sister of nine brothers." The Tsarevich fell asleep, and again slept three days and three nights. He woke up and cried more than ever.

The maidens rock him, they cannot rock him to

sleep. " Come, Tsar, great Gosudár," said they, " rock thy own son."

The Tsar rocked him, saying the while, " Sleep, little son, sleep, my own dear; thou wilt grow up a man. I will get thee Peerless Beauty as bride, the daughter of three mothers, the granddaughter of three grandmothers."

The Tsarevich fell asleep and slept again three days and three nights. He woke up and said, " Give thy blessing, father; I am going to marry."

" What dost thou mean, my dear little child? Whither canst thou go? Thou art but nine days of age in all."

" If thou wilt give me thy blessing, I 'll go; if not, I 'll go also."

" Well, the Lord guide thee."

Ivan Tsarevich arrayed himself, and went to find a horse. He went a short way from the house, and met an old man. " Where art thou going, young man," asked he, — " of thy own will, or against thy will? "

" I will not talk with thee," answered the Tsarevich. He went on a little, changed his mind. " Why did I not say something to the old man. Old people bring us to sense." Straightway he overtook the old man. " Stop, grandfather. Of what didst thou ask me? "

" I asked where art thou going, young man, — of thy own will, or against thy will? "

" I go so much of my own will, and twice that much

against my will. I was in early years; my father
rocked me in the cradle; he promised to get me
Peerless Beauty as bride."

"Thou art a good youth, thou art well spoken;
but thou canst not go on foot. Peerless Beauty dwells
far away."

"How far?"

"In the Golden Kingdom, at the end of the white
world, where the sun comes up."

"What am I to do? I, young man, have no saddle-
horse unridden, and silken whip unused that are fitting for me."

"Why hast thou not? Thy father has thirty
horses all alike. Go home, tell the grooms to water
them at the blue sea; and whichever horse shall
push ahead, enter the water to its neck, and when it
drinks, waves rise on the blue sea and roll from
shore to shore, that one take."

"God save thee for the good word, grandfather!"

As the old man taught him, so did the Tsarevich
do, — he chose for himself an heroic steed, passed
the night, rose next morning early, opened the gate,
and was preparing to go.

The horse spoke to him in the language of men:
"Ivan Tsarevich, drop to the earth; I will push thee
three times." He pushed him once, he pushed him
twice; but the third time he pushed not. "If thou
wert pushed a third time, the earth would not bear
thee and me."

Ivan Tsarevich took his horse from the chains, saddled him, sat on him. The Tsar barely sees his son. He rides far, far. The day is growing short, night is coming on. A house stood like a town, each room is a chamber. He came to the house, straight to the porch, tied his horse to the copper ring, went into the first chamber, then into the second, prayed to God, asked to spend the night.

" Stay the night, good youth," said an old woman. " Whither is God bearing thee? "

" Old woman, thou dost ask impolitely. First give me to eat and to drink, put me to rest, and then ask me for news."

She gave him food and drink, put him to bed, and then asked for news.

" I was, grandmother," said he, " in tender years; my father rocked me in the cradle, and promised me Peerless Beauty as bride, — the daughter of three mothers, the granddaughter of three grandmothers, and the sister of nine brothers."

" Thou art a good youth, and fair spoken. I am living to the end of the seventh ten of years, and of that beauty I have not heard. Farther on the road lives my elder sister; maybe she knows. But sleep now; the morning is wiser than the evening."

Ivan Tsarevich passed the night; next morning he rose early, washed himself white, led forth his steed, saddled him, put his foot in the stirrup. The old woman merely saw him. He rode far with distance, high with height; the day was shortening, coming toward night. There stood a house like a town, each room was a chamber. He rode to the porch, tied his horse to a silver ring, went to the entrance, and then to the chamber, prayed to God, asked a night's lodging. An old woman said: " Tfu, tfu! so far a Russian bone was not seen with sight nor heard with hearing; but now a Russian bone has come itself to the house. Where hast thou come from, Ivan Tsarevich?"

" Oh, thou old hag, how angry thou art! Thou dost not ask with politeness; thou shouldst first give me food and drink, put me to rest, then ask for news."

She seated him at the table, gave him food and drink, put him to rest, sat at the head of the bed, and inquired: " Where is God bearing thee?"

" I was in tender years, grandmother; my father rocked me in the cradle and promised me Peerless Beauty as bride, — the daughter of three mothers, the granddaughter of three grandmothers, and the sister of nine brothers."

" Thou art a good youth, of kind speech. I am living toward the end of the eighth ten of years, and of that beauty I have never heard. Before thee on the road lives my elder sister, — mayhap she knows; she has answer-givers. Her first answer-givers are the beasts of the forests, the second are the birds of the air, the third are the fish and creatures of the sea. Whatever is in the white world obeys her. Go to her in the morning, but sleep now; the morning is wiser than the evening."

Ivan Tsarevich passed the night, rose early, washed himself very white, sat on his steed, and vanished. He rode far with distance, high with height. The day was growing short, drawing near to the night; and there stood a house like a town, each room was a chamber. He came to the porch, tied his horse to a golden ring, then went to the entrance, and next to the chamber, prayed to God, and asked a night's lodging. An old woman screamed at him. "Oh, thou, this and that kind of man, thou art not worthy of an iron ring, and thou hast tied thy horse to a gold one!"

"Well, grandmother, scold not; the horse may be loosed and tied to another ring."

"Oh, good hero, have I given thee a fright? Be not afraid; sit on the bench, and I will ask from what stock, from what town, thou dost come."

"Oh, grandmother, thou shouldst first give me food and drink, then ask for the news! Thou seest I'm a wayfaring man; I've not eaten all day."

Straightway the old woman set the table, brought bread and salt, poured out a glass of *vodka*, and began to entertain Ivan Tsarevich. He ate and drank plenty, threw himself on the bed. The old woman made no inquiry; he told her himself: "I was in tender years, my father rocked me in the cradle, promised me Peerless Beauty as bride, — the daughter

of three mothers, the granddaughter of three grandmothers, and the sister of nine brothers. Do me a
kindness, grandmother; tell me where Peerless Beauty
is living, and how I may reach her."

"But, Ivan Tsarevich, I know not myself; I am
ending the ninth ten of years, and I have not heard of
that beauty.   But sleep now with God; in the morning I will summon my answer-givers, — maybe one
of them knows."

Next day the old woman rose early, washed herself very white, came out with Ivan Tsarevich on the
porch, cried with a champion's voice, whistled with a
hero's whistle.   She cried to the sea-fish and creatures of the water, "Come hither."

That instant the blue sea boiled up, the fish, great
and small, came together, all creatures assembled and
went toward the shore; they covered the water.

The old woman asked: "Where lives Peerless
Beauty, the daughter of three mothers, the granddaughter of three grandmothers, the sister of nine
brothers?"

All the fish and all the creatures answered in one
voice: "We have not seen her with sight, nor heard
of her with hearing."

The old woman shouted over the land: "Assemble,
ye beasts of the forest."

The beasts run; they hide the earth.   In one voice
they answer: "We have not seen her with sight, nor
heard her with hearing."

The old woman cried toward the sky: "Come hither, ye birds of the air!"

The birds fly, they hide the light of day. In one voice they answer: "We have not seen her with sight, we have not heard her with hearing."

"There is no one else to ask," said the old woman. She took Ivan Tsarevich by the hand and led him into the room. They had just come in when the Mogol bird arrived on the wing, fell to the ground. There was no light in the window.

"Oh, thou Mogol bird, where hast thou been flying; why art thou late?"

"I was arraying Peerless Beauty for mass."

"Thou hast the news I need. Now do me a service with faith and truth, — carry Ivan Tsarevich to her."

"Gladly would I serve, but much food is needed."

"How much?"

"Three forties of beef, and a vessel of water."

Ivan Tsarevich filled the vessel with water, brought oxen with beef. He put the kegs on the bird, ran to the forge, and had a long iron lance made for himself; he came back and took farewell of the old woman. "Good-by," said he. "Feed my good steed enough; I will pay thee for everything."

He sat on the Mogol bird, and that moment it rose up and flew; it flew and looked around continually. When it looked, Ivan Tsarevich immediately gave a piece of meat on the end of his lance. Now

8

it was flying and flying no short time. The Tsare-vich had already given two kegs of beef, and had begun on the third; and he said, "O Mogol bird, fall to the damp earth; small nourishment is left."

"What art thou saying, Ivan Tsarevich? Below us are sleeping forests and sticky morasses; we could not escape to the end of our lives."

Ivan Tsarevich gave out all the beef and threw down the kegs; but the Mogol bird flies, looks around. What can be done? Ivan Tsarevich thought a while, cut off the calves of his own legs, and gave them to the bird. It swallowed them, and flew out over the green meadow, silken grass, blue flowers, then dropped to the earth. Ivan Tsarevich stood on his feet, walked along the meadow, was lame of both legs.

"What is the matter, Ivan Tsarevich? Art thou lame?"

"I am lame, Mogol bird; a little while ago I cut off my calves to nourish thee."

The Mogol bird coughed up the calves, put them on the legs of Ivan Tsarevich, blew and spat; the calves grew to their places, and the Tsarevich went on in strength and activity. He came to a great town, and stopped to rest with a grandmother living in a backyard.

"Sleep, Ivan Tsarevich; in the morning, when the bell rings, I'll rouse thee."

Ivan Tsarevich lay down and slept that minute; he slept the day, slept the night. The bells rang for early prayers, the backyard grandmother ran to him, fell to beating him with whatever she found at hand, but could not rouse him. The morning prayers were over, they rang for mass; Peerless Beauty went to church. The old grandmother came again, and went to work again at Ivan Tsarevich, beat him with whatever came under her hands; with great effort she woke him. Ivan Tsarevich sprang up very quickly, washed himself very white, dressed, and went to mass. He came to the church, prayed before the images, bowed down on every side, and especially to Peerless Beauty. They stood side by side and prayed. At the end of mass she went first to the cross, then he went out on a platform, looked at the blue sea; ships are approaching, six champions came to offer marriage.

The champions saw Ivan Tsarevich and began to ridicule him: "Oh, thou country clown, is such a beauty as this for thee? Thou art not worth her middle finger!"

They said this once, they said it twice, they said it thrice. Ivan Tsarevich was offended. He swung his arm, there was a street; he swung it a second time, the place was clear and smooth all around. Then he went to the old grandmother.

"Well, Ivan Tsarevich, hast thou seen Peerless Beauty?"

"I have, and I shall not forget her for an age."

"Now lie down to sleep. To-morrow thou wilt go to mass again; I will wake thee the minute the bell rings."

The Tsarevich lay down; he slept the day, he slept the night. The bell rang for early prayers; the grandmother ran to him, began to rouse him; whatever happened under her hand, with that she beat him; but she could n't wake him. They rang the bell for mass; again she beat him and roused him. Ivan Tsarevich sprang up very quickly, washed very white, dressed, and to church. He entered, prayed to the images, bowed on all four sides, especially to Peerless Beauty. She looked at him and blushed. They stood side by side, prayed to God. At the end of mass she went to the cross first, he second. The Tsarevich went out on a platform, looked on the blue sea; ships were sailing, twelve champions came. They began to ask Peerless Beauty in marriage, and to make sport of Ivan Tsarevich: "Oh, thou country clown, is such a beauty for thee? Thou art not worth her middle finger!"

He was offended at these speeches. He swung his arm, there was a street; he swung the other, the place was clear and smooth around.

He went to the old grandmother. "Hast thou seen Peerless Beauty?" asked she.

"I have, and for an age I shall not forget her."

"Well, sleep now; in the morning I will wake thee."

Ivan Tsarevich slept the day, he slept the night; they rang the bell for morning prayers; the old woman ran in to wake him, beat him with whatever happened under her hand, did not spare, but could not rouse him. They rang the bell for mass, and she was working away all the time at the Tsarevich. At last she roused him. He rose up quickly, washed himself very white, prepared, dressed, and to church. When he came he prayed to the images, bowed on all four sides, and separately to Peerless Beauty. She saluted him, put him at her right hand, and she stood at the left. They stand there, pray to God. At the end of mass he went first to the cross, she after him. The Tsarevich went out on the platform, looked on the blue sea; ships are sailing, and twenty-four champions come to offer marriage to Peerless Beauty.

The champions saw Ivan Tsarevich and straightway began to make sport of him: "Oh, country clown, is such a beauty for thee? Thou art not worth her middle finger!"

They attacked him on every side to take away his bride. Ivan Tsarevich did not endure this. He swung his arm, there was a street; he swung the other, the place was smooth and clear around. He killed all to the last man. Peerless Beauty took him by the hand, led him to her chambers, seated him at the oaken tables, at the spread cloths, entertained him, called him her bridegroom. Soon after they prepared for the road and set out for the land of Ivan Tsarevich. They travelled and travelled, halted in the open field to rest. Peerless Beauty lay down to sleep, and Ivan Tsarevich guarded her slumber. When she had slept enough, and woke up, the Tsarevich said : " Peerless Beauty, guard my white body; I will lie down to sleep."

" But wilt thou sleep long? "

" Nine days and nights; and I shall not turn from one side to the other. If thou tryest to wake me, thou wilt not rouse me. When the time comes I shall wake myself."

" It is long, Ivan Tsarevich; I shall be wearied."

"Wearied or not, there is no help for it."

He lay down to sleep, and slept exactly nine days and nights. Meanwhile Koshchéi Without-Death bore away Peerless Beauty to his own kingdom. Ivan Tsarevich woke up; there was no Peerless Beauty. He began to weep, and went along neither by the road nor the way. Whether it was long or short, he came to the kingdom of Koshchéi Without-Death, and begged lodgings of an old woman.

" Well, Ivan Tsarevich, why art thou so sad looking? "

" Thus and thus, grandmother; I had everything, now I have nothing."

" Thy affair is a bad one, Ivan Tsarevich; thou canst not kill Koshchéi."

" Well, I will look on my bride at least."

" Lie down, sleep till morning; to-morrow Koshchéi will go to war."

Ivan Tsarevich lay down, but sleep did not come to his mind. In the morning Koshchéi went out of the house, and Ivan Tsarevich went in. He stood at the gate and knocked. Peerless Beauty opened it, looked at him, and fell to weeping. They went to the upper chamber, sat at the table, and talked. Ivan Tsarevich instructed her. " Ask Koshchéi where his death is."

" I will."

He had just left the house when Koshchéi came in. " Oh ! " said he, " it smells of the Russian bone; it must be that Ivan Tsarevich was with thee."

" What art thou thinking of, Koshchéi Without-Death ? Where could I see Ivan Tsarevich. He has remained in slumbering forests and in sticky quagmires ; wild beasts have destroyed him ere now."

They sat down to sup. At supper Peerless Beauty said: " Tell me, Koshchéi Without-Death, where is thy death ? "

" Why dost thou wish to know, silly woman ? My death is tied up in the broom."

Early next morning Koshchéi went to war. Ivan Tsarevich came to Peerless Beauty. She took the broom, gilded it brightly with pure gold. The Tsarevich had just departed when Koshchéi cam in. " Ah ! " said he, " it smells of the Russian bone ; Ivan Tsarevich has been with thee."

" What dost thou mean, Koshchéi Without-Death ? Thou hast been flying through Russia thyself and hast caught up the odor of Russia ; it is from thee. Where should I see Ivan Tsarevich ? "

At supper Peerless Beauty sat on a small bench and seated Koshchéi on a large one. He looked under the threshold ; the broom was lying there gilded. " What does this mean ? "

" Oh, Koshchéi Without-Death, thou seest thyself how I honor thee ! "

" Oh, simple woman, I was joking ! My death is out there, fastened in the oak fence."

Next day Koshchéi went away. Ivan Tsarevich came and gilded the whole fence. Towards evening Koshchéi came home. " Ah ! " said he, " it smells of the Russian bone. Ivan Tsarevich has been with thee."

" What dost thou mean, Koshchéi Without-Death ? It seems I have told thee times more than one, where am I to see Ivan Tsarevich ? He has remained in dark forests, in sticky quagmires ; the wild beasts have torn him to pieces ere now."

Supper-time came. Peerless Beauty sat on a bench herself, and seated him on a chair. Koshchéi looked through the window, saw the fence gilded, shining like fire. " What is that ? "

"" Thou seest thyself, Koshchéi, how I respect thee.

If thou art dear to me, of importance is thy death."

This speech pleased Koshchéi Without-Death. " Oh, simple woman, I was joking with thee! My death is in an egg, the egg is in a duck, and the duck is in a stump floating on the sea."

When Koshchéi went off to war, Peerless Beauty baked cakes for Ivan Tsarevich and told him where to look for the death of Koshchéi. Ivan Tsarevich went neither by road nor by way, came to the ocean sea broad, and knew not where to go farther. The cakes had long since given out, and he had nothing to eat. All at once a hawk flew up. Ivan Tsarevich aimed. "Well, hawk, I'll shoot thee and eat thee raw."

" Do not eat me, Ivan Tsarevich; I will serve thee in time of need."

A bear ran along. " Oh, bear, crooked paw, I'll kill thee and eat thee raw! "

" Do not eat me, Ivan Tsarevich; I'll serve in time of need."

Behold, a pike is struggling on the beach. " Oh, big-toothed pike, thou hast come to it! I'll eat thee raw."

" Eat me not, Ivan Tsarevich; better throw me into the sea. I will serve thee in time of need."

Ivan stood there thinking, " The time of need will come, it is unknown when. But now I must go hungry." All at once the blue sea boiled up, waves rose, began to cover the shore. Ivan Tsarevich ran up the hill, ran with all his might, and the water followed at his heels; chasing, he ran to the very highest place and climbed a tree. A little later the water began to fall, the sea grew calm, fell, and a great stump was left on land. The bear ran up, raised the stump, and when he had hurled it to the ground the stump opened; out flew a duck and soared high, high. That minute, from wherever he came, the hawk flew, caught the duck, and in a twinkle tore her in two. An egg fell out; then the pike caught it, swam to the beach, and gave the egg to Ivan Tsarévich, who put it in his bosom and went to Koshchéi Without-Death. He came to the house. Peerless Beauty met him, she kissed him on the lips and fell on his shoulder. Koshchéi Without-Death was sitting at the window cursing.

"Oh, Ivan Tsarevich, thou wishest to take Peerless Beauty from me; and so thou wilt not live."

"Thou didst take her from me thyself," answered Ivan Tsarevich, took the egg from his bosom, and showed it to Koshchéi. "What is this?"

The light grew dim in the eyes of Koshchéi; then he became mild and obedient. Ivan Tsarevich threw the egg from one hand to the other. Koshchéi Without-Death staggered from corner to corner. This seemed pleasant to the Tsarevich. He threw the egg more quickly from hand to hand, and broke it; then Koshchéi fell and died.

Ivan Tsarevich attached the horses to his golden

carriage, took whole bags filled with gold and silver, and went to his father. Whether it was long or short, he came to that old woman who had inquired of every creature, fish, bird, and beast. He found his steed. "Glory be to God," said he, "the raven (black steed) is alive;" and he poured forth gold freely for her care of the steed. Though she were to live ninety-nine years longer, she would have enough. Then the Tsarevich sent a swift courier to the Tsar with a letter, in which he wrote: "Father, meet thy son; I am coming with my bride, Peerless Beauty."

His father got the letter, read it, and had not belief. "How could that be? Ivan Tsarevich left home when nine days old!" After the courier came the Tsarevich himself. The Tsar saw that his son had written the real truth; he ran out to the porch, met him, and gave command to beat drums and sound music.

"Father, bless me for the wedding."

Tsars have not to brew beer nor make wine; they have much of all things. That same day there was a joyous feast and a wedding. They crowned Ivan Tsarevich and Peerless Beauty, and put out on all streets great jars of various drinks; every one could come and drink what his soul desired. I was there, drank mead and wine; it flowed on my mustaches, but was not in my mouth.

VASSILISSA GOLDEN TRESS, BAREHEADED BEAUTY.

THERE lived a Tsar Svaitozar. This Tsar had two sons and a beauty of a daughter. Twenty years did she live in her bright chamber. The Tsar and Tsaritsa admired her, and so did the nurses and maidens; but no one of the princes and champions had seen her face. And this beauty was called Vassilissa Golden Tress. She went nowhere out of her chamber; the Tsarevna did not breathe the free air. She had many bright dresses and jewels, but was wearied; it was oppressive for her in the chamber. Her robes were a burden, her thick golden silk hair, covered with nothing, bound in a tress, fell to her feet, and people called her Vassilissa Golden Tress, Bareheaded Beauty. The kingdom was filled with her fame. Many Tsars heard of her and sent envoys to Tsar Svaitozar to beat with the forehead and ask the Tsarevna in marriage.

The Tsar was in no hurry, but when the time came, he sent messengers to all lands with tidings that the Tsarevna would choose a bridegroom; and inviting Tsars and Tsareviches to assemble and collect at his palace to feast, he went himself to the lofty chamber to tell Vassilissa the Beautiful. It was gladsome in the heart of the Tsarevna. Looking out of the sloping window from behind the golden lattice on the green garden, the flowery meadow, she was eager to walk; she asked him to let her go forth to the garden to play with the maidens. " My sovereign father," said she, " I have not seen the world of God yet, I have not walked on the grass, on the flowers, I have not looked on thy palace; let me go with my nurses and maidens to walk in thy garden."

The Tsar permitted, and Vassilissa the Beautiful went down from the lofty chamber to the broad court. The plank gate was open, and she appeared in the green meadow. In front was a steep mountain; on that mountain grew curly trees; on the meadow were beautiful flowers of many kinds. The Tsarevna plucked blue flowers, stepped aside a little from her nurses; there was no caution in her young mind; her face was exposed, her beauty uncovered. Suddenly a mighty whirlwind rose, such as had not been seen, heard of, or remembered by old people; the whirlwind turned and twisted — behold, it seized the Tsarevna and carried her through the air.

The nurses screamed and shrieked: they ran and stumbled, threw themselves on every side; they saw nothing but how the whirlwind shot away with her. And Vassilissa Golden Tress was borne over many lands, across deep rivers, through three kingdoms into the fourth, into the dominions of the Savage Serpent.

The nurses hurry to the palace, covering themselves with tears, throw themselves at the feet of the Tsar. "Sovereign, we are not answerable for the misfortune, we are answerable to thee. Give not command to slay us, command us to speak. The whirlwind bore away our sun, Vassilissa Golden Tress, the Beauty, and it is unknown whither."

The Tsar was sad, he was angry; but in his anger he pardoned the poor women.

Next morning the princes and kings' sons came to the Tsar's palace, and seeing the sadness and seriousness of the Tsar they asked him what had happened.

"There is a sin to my account," said the Tsar. "My dear daughter, Vassilissa Golden Tress, has been borne away by the whirlwind, I know not whither;" and he told everything as it had happened.

Talk rose among the guests, and the princes and kings' sons thought and talked among themselves. "Is not the Tsar refusing us; is he not unwilling to let us see his daughter?" They rushed to the chamber of the Tsarevna; nowhere did they find her.

The Tsar made them presents, gave to each one from his treasure. They mounted their steeds, he conducted them with honor; the bright guests took farewell, and went to their own lands.

The two young Tsareviches, brave brothers of Vassilissa Golden Tress, seeing the tears of their father and mother, begged of their parents: "Let us go, our father, — bless us, our mother, — to find your daughter, our sister."

" My dear sons, my own children," said the Tsar, without joy, " where will ye go? "

" We will go, father, everywhere, — where a road lies, where a bird flies, where the eyes have vision; mayhap we shall find her."

The Tsar gave his blessing, the Tsaritsa prepared them for the journey; they wept, and they parted.

The two Tsareviches journeyed on. Whether the road was near or far, long in going or short, they did not know. They travelled a year, they travelled two. They passed three kingdoms, lofty mountains were visible and seemed blue; between these mountains were sandy plains, — the land of the Savage Serpent. And the Tsareviches inquired of those whom they met had they not heard, had they not seen, where Tsarevna Vassilissa Golden Tress was. And from all the answer was one: " We know not where she is, and we have not heard."

The Tsar's sons approach a great town; a decrepit old man stands on the road; crooked-eyed and lame, with a crutch and a bag, he begs alms. The Tsareviches stopped, threw him a silver coin, and asked had he not seen, had he not heard of the Tsarevna Vassilissa Golden Tress, Bareheaded Beauty?

" Ah! my friend," said the old man, " it is clear that thou art from a strange land. Our ruler, the

Savage Serpent, has forbidden strongly and sternly to speak with men from abroad. We are forbidden under penalty to tell or relate how a whirlwind bore past the town the beautiful princess."

Now the sons of the Tsar understood that their sister was near. They urged on their restive steeds and approached the castle of gold which stood on a single pillar of silver; over the castle was a curtain of diamonds; the stairways, mother-of-pearl, opened and closed like wings.

At this moment Vassilissa the Beautiful was looking in sadness through the golden lattice, and she screamed out for joy. She knew her brothers from a distance, just as if her heart had told her. And the Tsarevna sent down in silence to meet them, to bring them to the castle; the Savage Serpent was absent.

Vassilissa the Beautiful was wary; she feared the serpent might see them. They had barely entered when the silver pillar groaned, the stairways opened, all the roofs glittered; the whole castle began to turn and move. The Tsarevna was frightened, and said to her brothers: "The serpent is coming, the serpent is coming; that's why the castle goes round! Hide, brothers!"

She had barely said this when the Savage Serpent flew in, cried with a thundering voice, and whistled with a hero's whistle: "What living man is here?"

"We, Savage Serpent," answered the Tsar's sons,

without fear; "from our birthplace we've come for our sister."

"Oh, the young men are here!" shouted the serpent, clapping his wings. "Ye should not die here from me, nor seek your sister to free; her own brothers, champions, are ye, but champions puny I see." And the serpent caught one of them with his wing, struck him against the other, whistled and shouted. The castle guard ran to him, took the dead Tsareviches, threw them both down a deep ditch.

The Tsarevna Vassilissa Golden Tress covered herself with tears, took neither food nor drink, would not look on the world. Two days and three passed. It was not right she should die, she did not decide to die; she took pity on her beauty, took counsel of hunger. On the third day she ate, and was thinking how to free herself from the serpent, and began to gain knowledge by wheedling.

"Savage Serpent," said she, "great is thy power, mighty thy flight: is it possible that thou hast no foe?"

"Not yet," replied the serpent; "it was fated at my birth that my foe should be Ivan Goroh [John Pea]; and he will be born from a pea."

The serpent said this in jest; he expected no foe. The strong one relied on his strength; but the jest came true.

The mother of Vassilissa Golden Tress was grieving because she had no news of her children after the Tsarevna, the Tsareviches, were lost.

9

She went one day to walk in the garden with her ladies; the day was hot, she was thirsty. In that garden, from a foot-hill, spring water ran forth in a stream, and above it was a white marble well. They drew, with a golden cup, water pure as a tear. The Tsaritsa was eager to drink, and with the water she swallowed a pea. The pea burst, and the Tsaritsa became heavy; the pea increased and grew. In time the Tsaritsa gave birth to a son; they called him Ivan Goroh, and he grew, not by the year, but by the hour, smooth and plump; he is lively, laughs, jumps, springs on the sand, and his strength is growing in him all the time, so that at ten years he was a mighty champion. Then he asked the Tsar and Tsaritsa if he had had many brothers and sisters, and he heard how it happened that the whirlwind had borne away his sister, it was unknown whither, how his two brothers had begged to go in search of their sister, and were lost without tidings.

"Father, mother," begged Ivan Goroh, "let me go too; give me your blessing to find my brothers and sister."

"What art thou saying, my child?" asked the Tsar and Tsaritsa at once. "Thou art still green and young; thy brothers went, they were lost, thou wilt go too and be lost."

"Mayhap I shall not be lost," said Ivan Goroh. "I want to find my brothers and sister."

The Tsar and Tsaritsa persuaded and begged their

dear son, but he craved, cried, and entreated. They prepared him for the road, let him go with tears.

Ivan Goroh was free. He went out into the open field, travelled one day, travelled another. Toward night he came to a dark forest; in that forest was a cabin on hen's legs; from the wind it was shaking and turning. Ivan spoke from the old saying, from his nurse's tale. " Cabin, cabin," said he, " turn thy back to the forest, thy front to me; " and the cabin turned around to Ivan. Out of the window an old woman was looking, and she asked, " Whom is God bringing? "

Ivan bowed, and hastened to ask: " Hast thou not seen, grandmother, in what direction the passing whirlwind carries beautiful maidens? "

" Oh, young man," said she, coughing, and looking at Ivan, " that whirlwind has frightened me too, so that I sit in this cabin a hundred and twenty years, and I go out nowhere! Maybe he would fly up and sweep me away. That 's not a whirlwind, but the Savage Serpent."

" How could one go to him? " asked Ivan.

" What art thou thinking of, my world? The serpent will swallow thee."

" Maybe he will not swallow me."

" See to it, champion, or thou wilt not save thy head. But shouldst thou come back, give me thy word to bring from the serpent's castle water with which, if a man sprinkles himself, he will grow young," said she, moving her teeth beyond measure.

"I will get it, grandmother, I give thee my word."

"I believe thee, on conscience! Go straight to where the sun sets. In one year thou wilt reach the bald mountain there; ask for the road to the serpent's kingdom."

"God save thee, grandmother!"

"There is no reason for thanks, father."

Well, Ivan Goroh went to the land where the sun sets. A story is soon told, but a deed's not soon done. He passed three kingdoms, and went to the serpent's land; before the gates of the town he saw a beggar, — a lame, blind old man with a crutch, — and giving him charity, he asked if the young Tsarevna Vassilissa Golden Tress was in that town.

"She is, but it is forbidden to say so," answered the beggar.

Ivan knew that his sister was there; the good, bold hero became courageous, and went to the palace. At that time Vassilissa Golden Tress was looking out of the window to see if the Savage Serpent was coming; and she saw from afar the young champion, wished to know of him, sent quietly to learn from what land he had come, of what stock was he, was he sent by her father or by her own mother.

Hearing that Ivan, her youngest brother, had come (and she did not know him by sight), Vassilissa ran to him, wet him with tears. "Run, brother, quickly!" cried she. "The serpent will soon be here; he will see thee, destroy thee."

" My dear sister," answered Ivan, " if another had spoken, I should not have listened. I have no fear of the serpent, no fear of his strength."

" But art thou Goroh, " asked Vassilissa Golden Tress, " to manage him? "

" Wait, friend sister; first give me to drink. I have travelled under heat, I am tired from the road; I want a drink."

" What dost thou drink, brother? "

" Three gallons of sweet mead, dear sister."

Vassilissa gave command to bring a three-gallon measure of sweet mead, and Goroh drank it all at one breath. He asked for another; the Tsarevna gave orders to hurry, looked, and wondered.

" Well, brother, I did not know thee; but now I believe that thou art Ivan Goroh! "

" Let me sit down a moment to rest from the road."

Vassilissa gave command to bring a strong chair; but the chair broke under Ivan, flew into bits. They brought another all bound with iron, and that one cracked and bent. " Oh, brother," cried Vassilissa, " that is the chair of the Savage Serpent! "

" Now it is clear that I am heavier than he," said Goroh, laughing.

He rose and went on the street, went from the castle to the forge; there he ordered the old sage, the serpent's blacksmith, to forge him an iron club of nine tons weight. The blacksmith hastened the work.

They hammered the iron; night and day the hammers thundered, the sparks just flying. In forty hours the work was done. Fifty men were barely able to carry the club; but Ivan Goroh, seizing it in one hand, hurled the club to the sky: it flew, roared like a storm, whirled above the clouds, vanished from the eye. All the people ran trembling from terror, thinking if that club falls on the town, it will break the walls and crush the people; if it falls in the sea, it will raise the sea and flood the town. But Ivan Goroh went quietly to the castle, and gave command to tell when the club was coming. The people ran from the square, looked from under the gate, looked out of windows. "Is n't the club coming?" They waited an hour, they waited two; the third hour they ran to say that the club was coming. Goroh sprang to the square, put forth his hand, caught the club as it came, bent not himself, but the iron bent on the palm of his hand. Ivan took the club, pressed it against his knee, straightened it, went to the castle.

All at once a terrible whistling was heard, the Savage Serpent was racing; Whirlwind, his steed, flying like an arrow, breathes fire. The serpent in shape is a champion, but his head is the head of a serpent. When he flies, the whole castle quivers; when he is ten versts distant, it begins to whirl and dance. But now the castle moves not: it is clear that some one is sitting inside. The serpent grew thought-

ful, whistled, shouted; the whirlwind steed shook his
dark mane, opened his broad wings, reared and
roared.

The serpent flew up to the castle, but the castle
moves not. "Ho!" roared the Savage Serpent,
"it is plain there is a foe. Is not Goroh at my
house?" Soon came the champion. "I'll put thee
on the palm of one hand, and slap with the other:
they won't find thy bones."

"We shall see," said Ivan Goroh.

He went out with his club, and the serpent cried
from his whirlwind: "Take thy place in a hurry."

"Take thy own place, Savage Serpent," said Ivan,
and raised his club.

The Savage Serpent flew up to strike Ivan, to
pierce him with his spear, and missed. Goroh
sprang to one side, did not stagger.

"Now I'll finish thee!" roared Goroh. Raising his
club, he struck the serpent a blow that tore him to
pieces, scattered him; the club went across the earth,
went through two kingdoms into a third.

The people hurled up their caps and saluted Ivan
Tsar. But Ivan seeing the wise blacksmith, as a
reward for having made the club quickly, he called
up the old man and said to the people: "Here is
your head; obey him while doing good, as before ye
obeyed the Savage Serpent for evil."

Ivan got also the water of life and the water of
death, sprinkled his brothers; they rose up, rubbed

their eyes and thought, "We slept long; God knows what has happened."

"Without me you would have slept forever, my dear brothers," said Ivan Goroh, pressing them to his restive heart.

He did not forget to take the serpent's water; he made a ship, and on the Swan's river sailed with Vassilissa Golden Tress to his own land through three kingdoms into the fourth. He did not forget the old woman in the cabin; he let her wash in the serpent's water. She turned into a young woman, began to sing and dance, ran out after Goroh, and conducted him to the road.

His father and mother met him with joy and honor. They sent messengers to all lands with tidings that their daughter Vassilissa had returned. In the town there was ringing, and in the ears triple ringing; trumpets sounded, drums were beaten, guns thundered.

A bridegroom came to Vassilissa, and a bride was found for the Tsarevich; they had four crowns made, and celebrated two weddings. At the rejoicing, at the gladness, there was a feast as a mountain, and mead a river.

The grandfathers of grandfathers were there; they drank mead, and it came to us, flowed on our mustaches, but reached not our mouths. Only it became known that Ivan, after the death of his father, received the crown, and ruled the land with renown; and age after age the name of Goroh was famous.

THE RING WITH TWELVE SCREWS.

THERE lived in a village a son with his mother, and the mother was a very old woman. The son was called Ivan the Fool. They lived in a poor little cottage with one window, and in great poverty. Such was their poverty that besides dry bread they ate almost nothing, and sometimes they had not even the dry bread. The mother would sit and spin, and Ivan the Fool would lie on the stove, roll in the ashes, and never wipe his nose. His mother would say to him time and again: "Ivanushka, thou art sitting there with thy nose unwiped. Why not go somewhere, even to the public-house? Some kind man may come along and take thee to work. Thou wouldst have even a bit of bread, while at home here we have nothing to keep the life in us."

"Very well, I'll go," said Ivan. He rose up and went to the public-house. On the way a man met him.

"Where art thou going, Ivan?"

"I am going to hire out to work."

"Come, work for me; I'll give thee such and such wages, and other things too."

Ivan agreed. He went to work.

The man had a dog with whelps; one of the whelps pleased Ivan greatly, and he trained it. A year passed, and the time came to pay wages for the work. The man was giving Ivan money, but he answered: "I need not thy money; give me that whelp of thine that I trained."

The man was glad that he had not to pay money, and gave the whelp.

Ivan went home; and when his mother found what he had done, she began to cry, saying: "All people are people, but thou art a fool; we had nothing to eat, and now there is another life to support."

Ivan the Fool said nothing, sat on the stove with unwiped nose, rolling in the ashes, and the whelp with him. Some time passed; whether it was short or long, his mother said again: "Why art thou sitting there without sense; why not go to the public-house? Some good man may come along and hire thee."

"Very good, I'll go," said the Fool.

He took his dog and started. A man met him on the road.

"Where art thou going, Ivan?"

"To find service," said he; "to hire out."

"Come, work for me."

"Very well," said Ivan.

They agreed, and Ivan went again to work; and that man had a cat with kittens. One of the kittens pleased the Fool, and he trained it. The time came for payment.

Ivan the Fool said to this man: "I need not thy money, but give me that kitten."

"If thou wilt have it," said the man.

Now the Fool went home, and his mother cried more than before. "All people are people, but thou wert born a fool. We had nothing to eat, and now we must support two useless lives!"

It was bitter for Ivan to hear this. He took his dog and cat and went out into the field. He saw in the middle of the field a fire burning in a great pile of wood, — such an awful pile of wood! When he drew nearer he saw that a snake was squirming in it, burning on hot coals.

The snake screamed to him in a human voice: "Oh, Ivan the Fool, save me! I will give thee a great ransom for my life."

Ivan took a stick and raised the snake out of the fire.

When he had thrown it out, there stood before him, not a snake, but a beautiful maiden; and she said: "Thanks to thee, Ivanushka. Thou hast done me great service; I will do thee still greater. We will go," said she, "to my mother. She will offer thee copper money: do not take it, because it is coals, and not money; she will offer thee silver coin: do not take that either, for that will be chips, and not silver; she will bring out to thee gold: take not even that, because instead of gold it is potsherds and broken bricks. But ask of her in reward the ring with twelve screws. It will be hard for her to give it; but be firm, she will give it for my sake."

Behold, all took place as she said. Though the old woman grew very angry, she gave the ring. Ivan was going along through the field, thinking, "What shall I do with this ring?"

He was looking at it, when that same young girl caught up with him and said: "Ivan, whatever thou wishest, thou wilt have. Only stand in the evening on the threshold, loosen all the twelve screws, and before thee twelve thousand men will appear: whatever thou wishest, command; all will be done."

Ivan went home, said nothing to his mother, sat on the stove, lay in the ashes with unwiped nose. Evening came; they lay down to sleep.

Ivan waited for the hour, went on the threshold, unscrewed the twelve screws, and twelve thousand men stood before him. "Thou art our master, we are thy men: declare thy soul's desire."

Said Ivan to the men: "Have it made that on this very spot a castle shall stand such as there is not in the world, and that I sleep on a bedstead of gold, on down of swans, and that my mother sleep in like manner; that coachmen, outriders, servants, and all kinds of powerful people be walking in my court and serving me."

"Lie down for thyself in God's name," said the men; "all will be done at thy word."

Ivan the Fool woke up next morning, and was

frightened even himself. He looked around; he was sleeping on a golden bedstead on down of swans, and there were lofty chambers and so rich that even the Tsar had not such. In the courtyard were walking coachmen, outriders, servants, and all kinds of mighty and important people who were serving him. The Fool was amazed, and thought, " This is good." He looked in the mirror, and did not know his own self; he had become a beauty that could not be described with a pen or be told of in a tale. As was fitting, the lord was as fine as his chambers.

When the Tsar woke up at the same hour, — and the Tsar lived in that town, — he looked, and behold opposite his palace stood a castle just gleaming in gold.

The Tsar sent to learn whose it was. " Let the owner come to me," said he, " and show what sort of man he is."

They informed Ivan, and he said: " Tell him that this is the castle of Ivan Tsarevich; and if he wants to see me, he is not so great a lord, let him come himself."

There was no help for it. The Tsar had to go to Ivan the Fool's castle. They became acquainted, and after that Ivan the Fool went to the Tsar. The Tsar had a most beautiful young Tsarevna of a daughter, and she brought refreshments to Ivan; and right there she pleased him greatly, and straightway he begged the Tsar to give her in marriage to him. Now the Tsar in his turn began to put on airs.

"Give her, — why not give her? But thou, Ivan Tsarevich, perform a service for me. My daughter is not of common stock, and therefore she must marry only the very best among the whole people. Arrange this for me, that from thy castle to mine there be a golden road, and that I have a bridge over the river, — not a common one, but such a bridge that one side shall be of gold, and the other of silver; and let all kinds of rare birds be swimming on the river, — geese and swans; and on the other side of the river let there be a church, — not a simple one, but one all wax, — and let there grow around it wax apple-trees and bear ripe apples. If thou do this, my daughter shall be thine; and if not, blame thyself." ("Well," thought the Tsar, "I have joked enough with Ivan Tsarevich;" but he kept his own counsel.)

"Agreed," said Ivan. "Now do thou make ready the wedding to-morrow." With that he departed.

In the evening, when all had lain down to sleep, he stood on the threshold, unscrewed all the screws in the ring: twelve thousand men stood before him.

"Thou art our master, we are thy men: command what thy soul desires."

"Thus and thus," said he; "I want this and that."

"All right," said they; "lie down with God."

In the morning the Tsar woke up, went to the window; but his eyes were dazzled. He sprang back six paces. That meant that the bridge was there, one side silver, the other gold, just blazing and shining. On the river were geese and swans and every rare bird. On the opposite bank stood a church of white wax, and around the church apple-trees, but without leaves; the naked branches were sticking up.

"Well," thought the Tsar, "the trick has failed; we must prepare our daughter for the wedding."

They arrayed her and drove to the church. When they were driving from the palace, buds began to come out on the apple-trees; when they were crossing the bridge, the apple-trees were coming into leaf; when they were driving up to the church, white blossoms were bursting forth on the trees; and when the time came to go home from the marriage ceremony, the servants and all kinds of people met them, gave them ripe apples on a golden salver. Then they began to celebrate the wedding. Feasts and balls were given; they had a feast which lasted three days and three nights.

After that, whether it was a short time or a long one, the Tsarevna began to tease Ivan. "Tell me, my dear husband, how dost thou do all this? How dost thou build a bridge in one night, and a wax church?"

Ivan the Fool would not tell her for a long time; but as he loved her very much, and she begged very hard, he said: " I have a ring with twelve screws, and it must be handled in such and such fashion."

Well, they lived on. The misery of the matter was this: one of their servants pleased the Tsarevna, — he was a fine-looking, shapely, strong fellow, and she conspired with him to rob her husband, take away the ring, and the two would then go to live beyond the sea.

As soon as evening came she took out the ring quietly, stood on the threshold, and unscrewed the twelve screws: twelve thousand men stood before her.

" Thou art our mistress, we are thy men: command what thy soul desires."

She said: "Take this castle for me and bear it beyond the sea, with all that is in it; and on this spot let the old cabin stand, with my ragged husband, Ivan the Fool, inside."

" Lie down with God," said the men; " all will be done on thy word."

Next morning Ivan woke up, looked around. He was lying on a bark mat, covered with a ragged coat, and not a sign of his castle. He began to cry bitterly, and went to the Tsar, his father-in-law. He came to the palace, asked to announce to the Tsar that his son-in-law had come. When the Tsar saw him he said: " Oh, thou this and that kind of breechesless fellow, what son-in-law art thou to me? My sons-in-law live in golden chambers and ride in silver carriages. Take him and wall him up in a stone pillar."

It was commanded and done.   They took Ivan and walled him up in a stone pillar.   But the cat and the dog did not leave him, they were there too, and dug out a hole for themselves; through the hole they gave food to Ivan.   But one time they thought: "Why do we sit here, dog and cat, with folded hands? Let's run beyond the sea and get the ring."

As they decided to do that, they did it.   They swam through the sea, found their castle.   The Tsarevna was walking in the garden with the servant, laughing at her husband.

" Well, do thou remain here a while, and I'll go to the chamber and get the ring," said the cat; and she went her way, mi-au, mi-au, under the door.   The Tsarevna heard her, and said: " Ah, here is that scoundrel's cat; let her in and feed her."   They let her in and fed her.   The cat walked through the chambers all the time and looked for the ring. She saw on the stove a glass box, and in the box the ring.

The cat was delighted.   " Glory be to God!" thought she.   " Now only wait for night; I'll get the ring, and then for home ! "

When all had lain down, the cat sprang on to the stove and threw down the glass box; it fell, and was broken.   She caught the ring in her mouth and hid under the door.   All in the house were roused ; the Tsarevna herself got up, and saw that the box was broken.

"Oh!" said she, "it must be the cat of that scoundrel broke it. Drive her out; drive her out!"

They chased out the cat, and she was glad; she ran to the dog.

"Well, brother dog," said she, "I have the ring. Now if we could only get home quickly!"

They swam through the sea, were a long time swimming. When the dog was tired, he sat on the cat; when the cat was tired, she sat on the dog; and so they worked on and it was not far from land. But the dog was growing weak. The cat saw this, and said, "Sit thou on me; thou art tired." The minute she said this the ring fell out of her mouth into the water. What was to be done? They swam to shore and wept tears. Meanwhile they grew hungry. The dog ran through the field and caught sparrows for himself, and the cat ran along the shore catching little fish thrown up by the waves; that was how she fed herself.

But all at once the cat cried out: "Oh, thou dog, come here quickly to me; I have found the ring! I caught a fish, began to eat it, and in the fish was the ring."

Now they were both powerfully glad; they ran to Ivan and brought him the ring.

Ivan waited till evening, unscrewed all the twelve screws, and twelve thousand men stood before him.

"Thou art our master, we are thy men: tell us to do what thy soul desires."

"Break in a minute this stone pillar so that dust from it shall not remain; and from beyond the sea bring hither my castle with all who are in it, and every one as sleeping now, and put it in the old place."

Straightway all this was done. In the morning Ivan went to his father-in-law. The Tsar met him, seated him in the first place, and said: "Where hast thou been pleased to pass thy time, my dear son-in-law?"

" I was beyond the sea," said Ivan.

"That's it," said the Tsar, " beyond the sea. 'T is clear that thou hadst pressing business, for thou didst not come to take farewell of thy father-in-law. But while thou wert gone, some sort of bare-legged fellow came to me and called himself my son-in-law. I gave command to wall him up in a stone pillar; he has perished there, doubtless. Well, beloved son-in-law, where hast thou been pleased to spend thy time; what sights hast thou seen?"

" I have seen," said Ivan, " various sights; and beyond the sea there was an affair of such kind that no man knew how to settle it."

" What was the affair?"

" Well, this is the kind of affair it was; and if thou art a wise man, decide it according to thy wisdom of Tsar: A husband had a wife, and while he was living she found a sweetheart for herself; she robbed her husband, and went away with the sweetheart beyond the sea; and now she is with that man. What, to thy thinking, should be done with that wife?"

"According to my wisdom of Tsar I will utter the following sentence: Tie them both to the tails of horses, and let the horses loose in the open field, — let that be their punishment."

"If that is thy judgment, very well," said Ivan. "Come with me as a guest; I will show thee other sights and another wonder."

They went to Ivan's castle, and found there the Tsar's daughter and the servant. As Ivan had commanded, they were still asleep.

There was no help for it; according to the word of the Tsar they tied them both to the tails of horses and urged the horses into the open field, — that was their punishment. But Ivan afterwards married that beautiful, most beautiful maiden whom he had saved from the fire, and they began to live and win wealth.

THE FOOTLESS AND THE BLIND.

IN a certain kingdom, in a certain state, lived a terrible Tsar. He was famed through all lands, — a terror to kings and princes. The Tsar took a thought to marry, and published an order in every town and village that whoever would find him a bride ruddier than the sun, fairer than the moon, and whiter than snow, would be rewarded with countless wealth. The report of this went through the whole kingdom; and from small to great, all were talking and thinking, but no one offered to find such a beauty.

Not far from the king's castle was a large brewery. The working-men came together for some reason, and began to say that a man might get much money from the Tsar, but where could such a bride be found?

"Well, brothers," said a man, Nikita Koltoma by name, "no one can find a bride for the Tsar without my help; but if I undertake it, then he will find her without fail."

"What art thou boasting of, thou fool? How couldst thou do that deed? There are famous and rich people, not the like of us, and they are afraid.

Thou couldst not do it in a dream, much less in thy senses."

"Well, say what ye please; but I have faith in myself," said he, "and I 'll get her."

"Ah, Nikita, don't boast; thou knowest our Tsar is terrible, and for an empty boast he will put thee to death."

"He won't put me to death; he will reward me with money."

They reported these speeches to the Tsar himself. He was delighted, and gave command to bring Nikita before his bright eyes. The soldiers ran, seized Nikita Koltoma, and hurried him to the palace. His comrades called after him : "Well, brother, thou hast said it; thou thinkest to joke with the Tsar: go now and give answer."

They brought Nikita to the great palace, and the terrible Tsar said to him: "Thou, Nikita, dost boast that thou art able to find me a bride ruddier than the sun, fairer than the moon, and whiter than snow."

"I can, your Majesty."

"Very well, brother. If thou wilt do me that service, I will reward thee with countless treasure and make thee first minister; but if thou hast lied, I have a sword, and thy head leaves thy shoulders."

"I am glad to serve thee, Great Tsar; but command that I have a holiday for a whole month."

The Tsar consented, and gave over his own signature an open order to Nikita, commanding that in all eating-houses and inns they should give him gratis all kinds of food and drink.

Nikita went through the capital to enjoy himself. Whatever inn he entered, he showed the paper; immediately they brought him everything that his soul desired. He caroused one day, a second, a third; a week, a second, a third week. And now the term is passed; 't is time to go to the Tsar.

Nikita took farewell of his friends, went to the palace, and asked the Tsar to collect for him twelve brave youths, the same in stature, in hair, and in voice, and to prepare besides thirteen white woven tents with golden embroidery. Everything was soon ready; the young men were collected at once, and the tents made.

"Now, Great Tsar," said Nikita, "get ready, and we will go for the bride."

They saddled their good steeds, packed the tents on the horses. After that they had a prayer in the church, took leave of the people of the town, sat on their steeds, and galloped away; nothing but a pillar of dust behind them. They travelled one day, a second, and a third. In the open field was a forge. Said Nikita: "Go straight ahead with God, and I will run into the forge and smoke a pipe." He entered the forge; fifteen blacksmiths were forging iron inside, striking with their hammers.

"God aid you, brothers!"

" God save thee, good man ! "

" Make me a staff fifteen poods [1] weight."

" To make it we are not unwilling; but who will turn the iron? Fifteen poods are no joke."

" That is nothing, brothers; you beat with the hammers, and I 'll turn the iron."

The blacksmiths went to work and forged an iron staff of fifteen poods. Nikita took the rod, went out into the field, and threw it up ninety feet, held out his hand; the iron staff fell on his hand, but was not equal to the strength of the hero, it broke in two. Nikita Koltoma paid the blacksmiths for their work, threw the broken rod to them, and rode away. He caught up with his comrades. They travelled three days more; again there was a forge in the open field.

" Go on, I will enter this forge," said Nikita. He went into the forge. Twenty-five blacksmiths were working inside, forging iron, pounding with their hammers.

" God aid thee, boys ! "

" God save thee, good man ! "

" Make me a staff twenty-five poods in weight."

" To forge is no trouble; but where is the man with strength to turn so much iron? "

" I will turn it myself."

He took the twenty-five poods weight of iron, heated it red hot, and turned it on the anvil while the blacksmiths pounded with their hammers. They

---

[1] One pood = 36 pounds.

made a staff twenty-five poods in weight. Nikita took that staff, went out into the open field, threw it up one hundred and fifty feet, and held out his hand: the staff struck the hero's hand and broke in two.

"No, this will not do," said Nikita. He paid for the work, sat on his horse, and rode away. He overtook his comrades. They travelled a day, a second, and a third. Again there was a forge in the open field.

"Go on," said Nikita; "I will smoke a pipe in this forge."

He entered the forge, where fifty blacksmiths were tormenting an old man. A gray-haired old man was lying on the anvil; ten men were holding him with pincers by the beard, and forty men were pounding him on the sides with hammers.

"Have pity on me, brothers!" cried the old man, with all his strength. "Leave the life in me to do penance!"

"God aid you!" said Nikita.

"God aid thee, good man!" said the blacksmiths.

"Why are ye tormenting the old man?"

"Because he owes each one of us a rouble, and he will not pay it. Why should n't we beat him?"

"What an unfortunate man," thought Nikita; "for fifty roubles he suffers such torment!" And he said to the blacksmiths: "Listen, brothers: I 'll pay you for him; let the old man go."

"Agreed, good man; it is all the same to us from whom we get the money, so that we have it."

Nikita took out fifty roubles. The blacksmiths took the money, and the moment they freed the old man out of the iron pincers, he vanished from the eye. Nikita looked. " But where is the old man? "

" Oh, look for him now; he is a wizard! "

Nikita ordered them to forge an iron staff of fifty poods. He hurled it up three hundred feet, and held out his hand: the staff stood the test, did not break. " This will do," said Nikita, and rode off to overtake his comrades. All at once he heard a voice behind him. Nikita Koltoma stopped; he looked around, and saw the same old man running after him.

" Thanks to thee," said the old man, " for saving me from cruel torture; I suffered that misery for thirty years exactly. Here is a present to remember me by, — take it; it will be of use to thee; " and he gave him a cap of invisibility. " Just put it on thy head; no man will see thee."

Nikita took the cap, thanked the old man, and galloped on. He overtook his comrades, and all rode together. Whether it was long or short, near or far, they came to a castle; around the castle was a great iron paling; there was no way to enter, on foot or on horseback. The terrible Tsar said: " Well, brother Nikita, there is no passage farther."

Nikita Koltoma answered: " Why not, Great Tsar? I 'll go through the whole world but I 'll find thee a bride. This paling is no stop to us. Now, boys, break the paling; open the gate to the wide court! "

The good youths came down from their horses and went at the paling; but no matter what they did, they could not break it, it stood fast.

"Oh, brothers," said Nikita, "ye sail in shallow water! No use in my depending on you; I must work myself."

Nikita sprang from his horse, went to the paling, took it with his heroic hand, pulled once, — the whole paling was on the ground. The terrible Tsar and the young men rode in on the broad court, and there on the green meadow they put up their white woven, gold-embroidered tents, ate what God sent them, lay down, and from weariness slept a sound sleep. Each one had a tent, but there was none for Nikita Koltoma; he found three worn bark mats, made himself a little hut, lay down on the bare ground. As to sleeping, he slept not; he waited for what would be.

At the morning dawn Yelena the Beautiful woke up in her chamber, looked out through her lattice-window, and saw that thirteen white woven tents were standing on her green meadow, and in front of all a small hut of bark rugs.

"What is this?" thought the Tsarevna; "whence have these guests come? See, the iron paling is broken!"

Yelena the Beautiful was terribly enraged; she called her powerful, mighty hero, and said: "To horse this minute! Ride to the tents and give all those disobedient scoundrels to a cruel death; throw their bodies over the fence, and bring the tents to me."

The powerful, mighty hero saddled his good steed, put on his battle-armor, and went toward the un- bidden guests. Nikita Koltoma saw him. "Who goes?" asked he.

"And who art thou, rude fellow, that askest?"

These words did not please Nikita. He sprang out of his hut, caught the hero by the foot, dragged him from the horse to the damp earth, raised his iron staff of fifty poods, gave him one blow, and said: "Go now to thy Tsarevna, tell her to stop her pride, not to waste her men, but to marry our terrible Tsar."

The hero galloped back, glad that Nikita had left him alive, came to the castle, and said to the Tsa- revna: "Men of immeasurable strength have come to our place. They ask thee for their terrible Tsar in marriage, and commanded me to tell thee to put an end to thy pride, not to waste thy army in vain, and to marry their Tsar."

When Yelena the Beautiful heard such bold speeches she was roused. She summoned her great, mighty heroes, and began to command them all: "My trusty servants, assemble a countless army, take down these white tents, kill these unbidden guests, that the dust of them be not here."

The great, mighty heroes did not stop long. They collected a countless army, sat on their heroic steeds, and bore down on the white woven, gold-embroidered tents.

As soon as they came to the bark hut, Nikita Koltoma sprang out before them, took his iron staff of fifty poods, and began to wave it at them in different directions. In a little while he had killed the whole army, and of the great, mighty heroes he left but one alive. " Go," said he, " to thy Tsarevna, Yelena the Beautiful, and tell her not to waste her army further. She cannot frighten us with armies. Now I have fought with you alone; what will happen to your kingdom when my comrades wake? We will not leave a stone upon a stone; we will scatter everything over the open field."

The hero returned to the Tsarevna and said: " Thy whole army is slain; against such champions no power can avail." Yelena the Beautiful sent to invite the terrible Tsar to the castle, and then ordered that the sharp arrow be ready; went herself to meet the guests with grace, with honor. The Tsarevna moves on to meet them, and behind her fifty men are bearing the bow and the arrow. Nikita Koltoma saw that that was a hero's bow, and knew at once that it was intended to treat them to the arrow. He put on the cap of invisibility, drew the bow, and aimed the arrow at the Tsarevna's chamber. In one moment he knocked off the whole top of her castle.

There was no help for her now. Yelena the Beautiful took the terrible Tsar by the hand, led him to the white-walled chambers, seated him and his men at the oaken tables with the spread cloths. They began to drink, to eat and rejoice. In the chambers were wonderful ornaments; the whole world might be searched, and the like wouldst thou find nowhere.

After dinner Nikita said to the terrible Tsar: "Does the young woman please thee, or shall we go for another?"

"No, Nikita, there is no use in travelling for nothing; there is not a better than this in the whole world."

"Well, then, marry now she is in our hands. But look out, Great Tsar, don't be caught napping. The first three nights she will try thy strength; she will put her hand on thee and press mightily, mightily: thou canst not endure it in any way. At these times hurry out of the chamber; I'll take thy place and soon tame her."

They set about the wedding, and Tsars have not to make mead or wine; all was on hand. They had the wedding, and the terrible Tsar went to the chamber of Yelena the Beautiful. He reclined on a couch.

Yelena put her hand on his breast and asked: "Is my hand heavy?"

"It is as heavy as a feather on water," answered the terrible Tsar; but he could barely draw breath, so had she pressed his breast. "Wait, I have forgotten to give an order; I must give it now." He left the chamber.

Nikita was standing at the door outside. " Well, brother, thou didst speak truly; she came very near putting the breath out of me."

" Never mind, I'll settle the matter; stay here."

Nikita entered the dark chamber, lay on the couch. Yelena thought the Tsar had returned. She put her hand on his breast, pressed and pressed; could do nothing. She put on both hands, and pressed more than before. Nikita Koltoma, like a man in sleep, caught her and hurled her to the floor, so that the whole castle shook. The Tsarevna got up, went quietly to her bed, and fell asleep.

Now Nikita slipped out to the Tsar and said: " Go in boldly; she will do nothing till to-morrow."

With Nikita's aid the Tsar escaped the second and the third time, and then lived as was proper with Yelena the Beautiful. Neither a long nor a short time passed, but Yelena the Beautiful discovered that the terrible Tsar had deceived her, that his strength was not great, that people were laughing at her, that Nikita was the man who had conquered her. She was in a terrible rage, and hid in her heart a cruel revenge.

The Tsar had in mind to go to his own kingdom, and said: "We have stayed here long enough; it is time to go home. Make ready for the road."

They prepared to go by the sea, and had a ship

laden with various precious things. They went on
board, and sailed out on the sea; sailed one day,
sailed a second, then a third. The Tsar was delighted; he could not rejoice sufficiently that he was
taking home a Tsaritsa ruddier than the sun, fairer
than the moon, whiter than snow. But Yelena the
Beautiful was thinking her own thought, — thinking
how to pay for the insult.

At that time an heroic slumber overcame Nikita,
and he slept for twelve whole days and nights. When
the Tsaritsa saw Nikita in this sleep, she summoned
her trusty servants, commanded them to cut off his
legs to the knee, put him in a boat, and push him
out into the sea. Before her eyes they cut off the legs
of the sleeping Nikita, put him in a boat, and pushed
him out to sea.

On the thirteenth day poor Nikita woke. He
looked around, — water everywhere; he was lying
without feet, and no trace of the ship.

Meanwhile the ship sailed on, sailed on. At last the
harbor was before them. The cannon thundered, the
people ran together. The merchants and boyars met
the Tsar with bread and salt, and congratulated him
on his marriage. The Tsar called guests, gave feasts,
and forgot to think of Nikita. Little time had he left
to rejoice. Yelena the Beautiful soon seized his kingdom, took the management of all to herself, and forced
him to herd pigs. The wrath of the Tsaritsa was not
allayed with this; she gave command to make search

on every side for relatives of Nikita Koltoma, and if any were found to bring them to the palace.

Messengers galloped and searched everywhere. They found a brother of Nikita, — Timoféi Koltoma; they brought him to the palace. Yelena the Beautiful gave command to take out his eyes and drive him from the town,

When they had blinded Timoféi they led him outside the town and left him in the open field. The blind man dragged along, found his way by feeling; he went and went, till he came to the sea-shore, advanced a step or two, and felt water under his feet. He halted, stood on one spot, moved neither backward nor forward; he was afraid to go. All at once the boat with Nikita was borne toward the shore. Nikita saw a man, was rejoiced, and called to him: " Ei! good man; help me to land."

The blind man answered: " Gladly would I help thee, but I cannot. I am without eyes; I see nothing."

" But whence art thou, and what is thy name? "

" I am Timoféi Koltoma. The new Tsaritsa, Yelena the Beautiful, had my eyes put out, and drove me from her kingdom."

" Ah! but thou art my own brother; I am Nikita Koltoma. Go thou, Timoféi, to the right side, — there a tall oak is growing; pull out the oak, bring it here, and throw it from the shore into the water. I will creep out upon it to thee."

Timoféi turned to the right, stepped forward, and found the tall old oak, seized it with both hands, pulled it out by the roots, drew the oak, and threw it into the water. The tree lay with one end on land, the other came down near the boat. Nikita crept out on shore somehow, kissed his brother, and said: " How is our terrible Tsar living now? "

" Oh, brother," answered Timoféi, " our terrible Tsar is now in great straits, — he is herding pigs in the field! Every morning he gets a pound of bread, a jug of water, and three rods on his back."

Then they talked about how they were to live and how to support themselves. Said Nikita: " Hear, brother, my advice: thou wilt carry me, because I am footless, and I will sit on thee and tell thee where to go."

"Agreed; be it as thou sayest. Though we are both maimed, we shall serve for one sound man."

So Nikita sat on his brother's shoulders and showed him the way. Timoféi walked and walked, and came into a slumbering forest. In that forest stood the cabin of Baba-Yaga. The brothers entered the cabin; there was not a soul inside.

"Well, brother," said Nikita, " feel in the oven. Is n't there some food? "

Timoféi crawled to the oven, took out every kind of food, put it on the table, and they both began to put the food away; from hunger they ate everything clean. Then Nikita began to examine the cabin. He saw on the window a small whistle, placed it to his lips and began to whistle. He looks — what sort of wonder! His blind brother is dancing, the cabin is dancing, the table, the dishes are dancing, everything dancing; the pots were broken into bits.

"Enough, Nikita, stop playing," begged the blind man; "my strength can hold out no longer."

Nikita stopped whistling, and that moment everything was silent. All at once the door opened, in walked Baba-Yaga, and she screamed with a loud voice: "Oh, homeless vagrants, to this minute not a bird has flown past, nor a beast run by here; and ye have come, devoured my food, broken my pots! Very good; I'll settle with you!"

"Silence, old carrion! We shall be able to settle with thee ourselves. Here, brother Timoféi, hold the old witch firmly!"

Timoféi caught the Baba-Yaga in his arms, squeezed her hard, hard; but Nikita seized her that moment by the hair and dragged her through the cabin.

"Oh, fathers," begged Baba-Yaga, "I'll be of use to you myself; whatever ye want I'll get you!"

"Well, then, old woman, speak. Canst thou get us healing and living water? If thou gettest it, I'll let thee go alive into the white world; if not, then I'll give thee to a cruel death."

Baba-Yaga agreed, and led them to two springs. "Here are for you the healing and living water."

Nikita Koltoma took the healing water, poured it

on himself, and his legs grew out. They were quite healthy, but would n't move. He took living water, moistened his legs, and began to use them. The same happened to Timoféi Koltoma: he washed the hollows of his eyes with healing water, eyes came in his head just as if they had never been injured, but saw nothing; he washed them with the living water, and they began to see better than ever.

The brothers thanked the old woman, let her go home, and went to liberate the terrible Tsar from suffering and misfortune. They came to the capital town and saw that the Tsar was herding pigs in front of the castle. Nikita Koltoma began to blow on the whistle, and the herdsman with the pigs fell to dancing. Yelena the Beautiful saw this from the window; she was furious, and gave command to take a bunch of rods and flog the pigherd and the musicians.

The guard ran out, seized them, brought them to the castle to treat them to rods. When Nikita Koltoma came to Yelena the Beautiful he made no delay, but seized her white hands and said: "Dost know me, Yelena the Beautiful? I am Nikita Koltoma. Well, terrible Tsar, she is in thy power; what thou wishest, that do."

The Tsar gave command to shoot her, and he made Nikita his first minister; he honored him always, and obeyed him in all things.

KOSHCHÉI WITHOUT-DEATH.

THERE was a Tsar who had one son, and when the Tsarevich was an infant his nurses and maids used to sing to him, " Baiyú, baiyú, Ivan Tsarevich; when thou 'lt grow up a man thou 'lt find thee a bride in the thirtieth kingdom, beyond the thrice ninth land, Vassilissa Kirbítyevna, and her marrow flows from bone to bone."

Fifteen years had passed for the Tsarevich, and he went to ask leave to search for his bride. " Where wilt thou go?" asked his father. " Thou art still too small."

" No, father; when I was small the nurses and maids sang to me, and told where my bride lives; and now I am going to find her."

The Tsar gave his blessing and sent word to all kingdoms that his son, Ivan Tsarevich, was going for his bride.

Well, the Tsarevich came to a town, gave his horse to be cared for, and went himself to walk along the streets. He walked, and saw that on the square they were punishing a man with a whip. " Why," asked he, " do ye flog him?"

" Because," answered they, " he went in debt ten thousand to an eminent merchant, and did not pay in season. And whoso redeems him, that man's wife Koshchéi Without-Death will bear away."

Now the Tsarevich thought and thought, and then went off. As he was walking through the town he came out again on the square, and they were still beating that man. Ivan Tsarevich pitied him and resolved to redeem him.

"I have no wife," thought Ivan; "there is no one to take from me." He paid the ten thousand and went to his lodgings.

All at once the man whom he had redeemed ran after him and called: "God save thee, Ivan Tsarevich ! If thou hadst not redeemed me, thou couldest not have gained thy bride in a lifetime; but now I will help thee. Buy me a horse and saddle straightway."

The Tsarevich bought him a horse and saddle, and asked: "What is thy name ? "

"They call me Bulat the hero."

They sat on the horses, went their way and road. When they came to the thirtieth kingdom, Bulat said: "Well, Ivan Tsarevich, give orders to buy and roast chickens, ducks, and geese, so that there may be plenty of everything, and I will go to get thy bride. And see to it: every time I run to thee, cut the right wing of a bird, and hand it to me on a plate."

Bulat the hero went to the lofty tower where Vassilissa Kirbítyevna was sitting, threw a stone lightly, and broke the summit of the gilded tower. He ran to the Tsarevich and said to him: "What, art thou sleeping? Give me a hen."

Ivan Tsarevich cut off the right wing and gave it on a plate. Bulat took the plate, ran to the tower, and cried out: "Hail, Vassilissa Kirbítyevna! Ivan Tsarevich gave command to bow to thee, and asked me to give thee this hen."

Vassilissa was frightened, and sat in silence. Bulat gave answer to himself instead of her: "Hail, Bulat the hero! Is Ivan Tsarevich in good health?

"Glory be to God, in good health.

"But why stand there, Bulat the hero? Take the key, open the cupboard, drink a glass of *vodka*, and go with God."

Bulat the hero ran to Ivan Tsarevich and said: "Art sitting here? Give me a duck."

He cut off the wing, and gave it on a plate.

Bulat bore it to the tower and said: "Hail, Vassilissa Kirbítyevna! Ivan Tsarevich gave command to bow to thee, and sent thee this duck."

She sat there, said nothing; but he answered instead of her: "Hail, Bulat the hero! Is Ivan Tsarevich well?

"Glory be to God, he is well.

"But why stand there, Bulat the hero? Take the key, open the cupboard, drink a glass, and go with God."

Bulat ran again to Ivan Tsarevich. "Art thou sitting here? Give me a goose."

Ivan cut off the right wing and gave it on a plate. Bulat the hero bore it to the tower. " Hail, Vassilissa Kirbítyevna! Ivan Tsarevich gave command to bow to thee, and sent thee this goose."

Vassilissa Kirbítyevna took the key quickly, opened the cupboard, and reached a glass of *vodka*. Bulat the hero took not the glass, but seized the maiden by the right hand, drew her out of the tower, and seated her on the Tsarevich's steed. They galloped away, the good hero and the beautiful soul-maiden, with all horse-speed.

Next morning Tsar Kirbít woke and rose. He saw that the top of the tower was broken and his daughter stolen; he grew powerfully angry, and gave command to pursue over all roads and ways.

Whether our heroes travelled much or little, Bulat took the ring from his hand, hid it, and said: " Go on, Ivan Tsarevich; but I will turn back and look for my ring."

Vassilissa Kirbítyevna began to implore: " Do not leave us, Bulat the hero; if it please thee, thou shalt have my ring."

" Impossible, Vassilissa Kirbítyevna; my ring was priceless. My own mother gave it me, and when giving, she said: " Wear and lose it not; forget not thy mother."

Bulat the hero galloped back and met the pursuers on the road. He slew them all straightway, left but one man to take news to the Tsar, hurried back, and caught up with the Tsarevich.

Whether they went much or little, Bulat hid his handkerchief and said: "Oh, Ivan Tsarevich, I have lost my handkerchief! Ride on thy road and way; I will soon come up with thee."

He turned back, went some versts, and met pursurers twice as many; he slew them all, and returned to Ivan, who asked: "Hast found the handkerchief?"

"I have found it."

Dark night overtook them. They pitched a tent; Bulat lay down to sleep, left Ivan Tsarevich on guard, and said to him: "If need be, rouse me."

Ivan Tsarevich stood and stood, grew tired; sleep began to bend him; he sat down at the tent and fell asleep.

From wherever he came, Koshchéi Without-Death bore away Vassilissa Kirbítyevna. Ivan Tsarevich woke up at dawn, saw that his bride was gone, and began to weep bitterly. Bulat the hero woke up and asked: "Why art thou weeping?"

"Why should I not weep? Some one has borne away Vassilissa Kirbítyevna."

"I told thee to keep watch. That is the work of Koshchéi Without-Death. Let us set out in search of her."

Long and long did they ride, till they saw two shepherds herding a flock. "Whose herd is that?"

The herdsmen answered: "This is the herd of Koshchéi Without-Death."

Bulat and Ivan Tsarevich asked the herdsmen if

Koshchéi Without-Death lived far from there, how to go to his house, what time they went home with the flock, and how they shut it in. Then they came down from their horses, wrung the necks of the shepherds, dressed themselves in their clothes, drove the herd home, and stood at the gate.

Ivan Tsarevich had a gold ring on one of his fingers, Vassilissa had given it to him. Vassilissa had a goat, and she washed herself morning and evening with the milk of that goat. The maid ran with a vessel, milked the goat, and was carrying the milk. Bulat took the Tsarevich's ring and threw it into the vessel.

"Oh, my dove," said the maid, "thou art getting impudent!" She came to Vassilissa Kirbítyevna and complained. "Now," said she, "the herdsmen have begun to make sport of us, — they threw a ring into the milk."

"Leave the milk; I will strain it myself," said Vassilissa. She strained the milk, saw the ring, and gave command to send the herdsmen to her. The herdsmen came.

"Hail, Vassilissa Kirbítyevna!" said Bulat the hero.

"Hail, Bulat the hero! Be well, Tsarevich! How did God bring you?"

"We came for thee, Vassilissa Kirbítyevna; thou wilt hide from us nowhere. We should find thee even on the bottom of the sea."

She seated them at the table, gave them every sort of food and all kinds of wine.

Said Bulat the hero: " When Koshchéi comes home from hunting, ask him, Vassilissa Kirbítyevna, where his death is. And now it would not be amiss. for us to hide."

As soon as the guests had hidden, Koshchéi Without-Death was flying home from the hunt. " Tfu-tfu ! " said he; " of old there was n't a sign of Russia to be heard with hearing or seen with sight; but now Russia runs into one's eyes and mouth."

Said Vassilissa: " Thou hast been flying through Russia thyself, and art full of its odor; so to thy thinking dost find it here."

Koshchéi ate his dinner and lay down to rest. Vassilissa came to him, threw herself on his neck, fondled him, and kissed him, saying: " My dear love, hardly was I able to wait for thee. I did not expect to see thee alive; I feared that savage beasts had devoured thee."

Koshchéi laughed aloud. " Simple woman! her hair is long, but her wit is short. Could savage beasts eat me ? "

" But where is thy death, then ? "

" My death is in the broom which lies around at the threshold."

As soon as Koshchéi had flown away, Vassilissa Kirbítyevna ran to Ivan Tsarevich.

Bulat asked: " Well, where is Koshchéi's death ? "

" In a broom thrown around at the threshold."

" No, he lies with design; thou must ask him more cunningly."

Vassilissa Kirbítyevna formed a plan. She took the broom, gilded it, adorned it with various ribbons, and placed it on the table. When Koshchéi Without-Death flew home, he saw the broom on the table, and asked why that was done.

" How was it possible," answered Vassilissa Kirbítyevna, " that thy death should roll around at the threshold? Better let it lie on the table."

" Ha, ha, ha! The woman is simple; her hair is long, but her wit is short! Could my death be here?"

" Where is it, then?"

" My death is hidden in the goat."

As soon as Koshchéi went off to the hunt, Vassilissa Kirbítyevna took the goat and adorned it with ribbons and bells, and gilded its horns. Koshchéi saw the goat; again he laughed. " Oh, the woman is simple; her hair is long, but her wit is short!"

" My death is far from here. On the sea, on the ocean, is an island; on that island stands an oak; under the oak is buried a chest; in the chest is a hare, in the hare a duck, in the duck an egg, and in the egg my death," said he, and flew away.

Vassilissa Kirbítyevna told all this to Ivan Tsarevich. They took supplies and went to find Koshchéi's death. Whether they travelled long or short, they ate all their provisions and began to be hungry.

A dog with her whelps happened in their way. " I will kill her," said Bulat the hero; " there is nothing else to eat."

" Do not kill me," said the dog, " do not make my children orphans, and I will serve thee myself."

" Well, God be with thee."

They went farther. On an oak was an eagle with eaglets. Said Bulat the hero: "I will kill the eagle."

" Kill me not," said the eagle, " make not my children orphans; I will serve thee myself."

" Let it be so; live to thy health."

They came to the ocean sea wide; on the shore a lobster was crawling. Said Bulat the hero: "I will kill it with a blow."

" Strike me not, good hero; there is not much good in me. Wilt eat me, thou 'lt not be satisfied. The time will come when I will serve thee myself."

" Well, crawl off with God," said Bulat the hero. He looked on the sea, saw a fisherman in a boat, and shouted, " Come to shore." The fisherman brought the boat. Ivan Tsarevich and Bulat the hero sat in it and went to the island; they landed, and came to the oak. Bulat the hero caught the oak with his mighty hands and tore it out with the roots. They took the chest from under the oak, opened it; out of the chest sprang a hare, and ran with all its breath.

" Ah ! " said Ivan Tsarevich, " if the dog were here now, she would catch the hare."

Behold, the dog is bringing the hare. Bulat the

hero tore it open; out of the hare flew the duck and rose high in the air.

"Ah!" said Ivan Tsarevich, "if the eagle were here, she would catch the duck." And already the eagle was bringing the duck.

Bulat the hero tore open the duck; an egg rolled out and fell into the sea.

"Ah!" said Ivan Tsarevich, "if the lobster would pull it out." The lobster was crawling and bringing the egg. They took the egg, went to Koshchéi Without-Death, struck him with the egg on the forehead; that moment he stretched out and died.

Ivan Tsarevich took Vassilissa Kirbítyevna, and they went their way. They travelled and travelled; dark night overtook them; they pitched their tent. Vassilissa Kirbítyevna lay down to rest. Said Bulat the hero, "Lie down too, Tsarevich, and I will stand guard."

At dark midnight twelve doves appeared, struck wing against wing, and became maidens.

"Well, Bulat the hero and Ivan Tsarevich, ye killed our brother, Koshchéi Without-Death, ye carried away our sister-in-law, Vassilissa Kirbítyevna; but no good will come to you either. When Ivan Tsarevich comes home, he will give command to bring out his favorite dog, the dog will break away from the keeper and tear the Tsarevich into small pieces; but whoso hears this and tells Ivan what we have said will become stone to the knees."

In the morning Bulat the hero roused the Tsarevich and Vassilissa Kirbítyevna; they made ready and went their road and way. A second night overtook them; they pitched their tent in the open field. Again Bulat said: " Lie down to sleep, Ivan Tsarevich; I will stand guard." In the dark midnight twelve doves came flying, they struck wing against wing, and became maidens.

" Well, Bulat and Ivan Tsarevich, ye killed our brother, Koshchéi Without-Death, ye carried away our sister-in-law; but no good will come to you, for when Ivan Tsarevich comes home he will give command to bring out his favorite horse, on which he has ridden since childhood. The horse will tear away from the groom and beat the Tsarevich to death; and whoso hears this and tells him will become stone to the girdle."

Morning came, again they travelled on. A third night overtook them. They pitched their tent and stopped in the open field. Bulat said: " Lie down to sleep, Ivan Tsarevich; I will stand watch." Again at midnight twelve doves came flying, struck wing against wing, and became maidens.

"Well, Bulat and Ivan Tsarevich, ye killed our brother, Koshchéi Without-Death, and carried away our sister-in-law; but no good will come to you. When Ivan Tsarevich comes home he will give command to lead out his favorite cow, on whose milk he has been nourished since childhood. She will tear away from the herder and raise the Tsarevich on her horns. But whoso sees and hears us, and tells him this, will become altogether stone." They finished the sentence, turned into doves, and flew home.

In the morning Ivan Tsarevich and Vassilissa set out on the road. The Tsarevich came home, married Vassilissa Kirbítyevna; and in a day or two he said to her, " I will show thee my favorite dog, with which I played all the time when I was little."

Bulat the hero took his sword, ground it sharp, sharp, and stood at the porch. They were bringing the dog. It tore away from the keeper and ran straight to the porch; but Bulat drew his sword and cut the dog in two. Ivan Tsarevich was angry, but for Bulat's former service he was silent.

The next day he ordered them to bring out his favorite horse. The horse broke his halter, tore away from the groom, and galloped straight at Ivan Tsarevich. Bulat the hero cut off the horse's head.

Ivan Tsarevich was still more in anger, and gave command to seize Bulat and hang him; but Vassilissa Kirbítyevna interceded. " Had it not been for him," said she, " thou wouldst never have won me."

On the third day the Tsarevich gave command to lead out his favorite cow. She tore away from the herder and ran straight at the Tsarevich. Bulat cut off her head too.

Now Ivan Tsarevich was so enraged that he would

listen to no one, gave orders to call the headsman to put Bulat to death on the spot.

"Oh, Ivan Tsarevich, if 't is thy wish to put me to death by the executioner, better let me die of myself; only let me speak three speeches."

Bulat told about the first night, how twelve doves flew to them in the open field, and what they said. That moment he was stone to the knees; he told of the second night, and was stone to the girdle. Now Ivan Tsarevich begged him not to speak to the end. Bulat answered: "'T is all the same now, I am stone to the girdle; it is not worth while to live." He told of the third night, and was all stone.

Ivan Tsarevich put him in a chamber apart, went there each day with Vassilissa, and wept bitterly.

Years passed on. Once Ivan Tsarevich was weeping over the stone hero Bulat, and heard a voice coming out of the stone: "Why dost thou weep? It is hard for me even as I am."

"Why should I not weep? How can I help it? Thou knowest I destroyed thee."

"If thou wishest, thou canst save me. Thou hast two children,—a son and a daughter. Kill them, pour their blood into a vessel, and rub this stone with the blood."

Ivan Tsarevich told this to Vassilissa Kirbítyevna. They grieved and mourned; decided to kill their children. They killed them, gathered the blood, and rubbed the stone.

12

When Bulat the hero came to life he asked the Tsarevich and his wife, " Were ye grieved for the children? "

" We were grieved, Bulat."

" Well, let us go to their room."

They went, and behold, the children were alive! The father and mother were delighted, and in their delight gave a feast to all.

GO TO THE VERGE OF DESTRUCTION AND BRING BACK SHMAT–RAZUM.

IN a certain kingdom there lived a wifeless, un-
married king, who had a whole company of
sharpshooters. They went to the forests, shot
birds of passage, and furnished the king's table with
game. Among these sharpshooters was one named
Fedot, who hit the mark and almost never missed;
for this reason the king loved him beyond all his
comrades.

Once while shooting in the early morning, just at
dawn, Fedot went into a dark, dense forest, and saw a
blue dove sitting on a tree. He aimed, fired, struck
her wing, and she fell to the damp earth. The sharpshooter picked her up, was going to twist her neck
and put her in his bag, when the blue dove spoke:
"Oh, brave youth, do not tear off my stormy little
head, do not send me out of the white world! Better
take me alive, carry me home, put me on the window,
and watch. As soon as sleep comes upon me strike
me that moment with the back of thy right hand, and
thou wilt gain great fortune."

Fedot marvelled. "What can it mean?" thought
he; "in seeming a bird, but she speaks with a

human voice. Never has such a thing happened to me before."

He brought the bird home, placed her on the window, and stood waiting. After a short time the bird put her head under her wing and fell asleep. The sharpshooter struck her lightly with the back of his right hand. The blue dove fell to the floor, and became a soul-maiden so beautiful as not to be imagined nor described, but only told about in a tale. Such another beauty could not be found in the whole world.

Said she to the young man, the king's sharpshooter: "Thou hast known how to get me; now know how to live with me. Thou wilt be my wedded husband, and I thy God-given wife. I am not a blue dove, but a king's daughter."

They agreed. Fedot married her, and they lived together. He is happy with his young wife, but does not forget his service. Every morning at dawn he takes his gun, goes out into the forest, and shoots game, which he carries to the king's kitchen.

His wife sees that he is wearied from this hunting, and says: " Listen, my dear. I am sorry for thee. Every God-given day thou dost wander through forests and swamps, comest home wet and worn, and profit to us not a whit. What sort of a life is this? But I know something so that thou wilt not be without gain. Get of roubles two hundred, and we will correct the whole business."

Fedot rushed around to his friends, got a rouble from one, and two from another, till he had just two hundred. " Now," said his wife, " buy different kinds of silk for this money."

He bought the silk; she took it, and said: " Be not troubled; pray to God and lie down to sleep: the morning is wiser than the evening."

He lay down and fell asleep; his wife went out on the porch, opened her magic book, and two unknown youths appeared at once. ." What dost thou wish? Command us."

" Take this silk, and in one single hour make a piece of such wonderful tapestry as has not been seen in the world; let the whole kingdom be embroidered on it, with towns, villages, rivers, and lakes."

They went to work, and not only in an hour, but in ten minutes they had the tapestry finished, — a wonder for all. They gave it to the sharpshooter's wife, and vanished in an instant just as if they never had been. In the morning she gave the tapestry to her husband. " Here," said she, " take this to the merchants' rows, sell it, but see that thou ask no price of thy own; take what they give."

Fedot went to the merchants' rows; a trader saw him, came up, and asked: " Well, my good man, is this article for sale?"

" It is."

" What's the price?"

" Thou art a dealer, name the price."

The merchant thought and thought, but could not fix a price. Now a second, a third, and a fourth came; no one could set a price on the tapestry. At this time the mayor of the palace was passing by and saw the crowd; wishing to know what the merchants were talking about, he jumped out of his carriage, came up to them, and said: " Good morning, merchants, dealers, guests from beyond the sea; what is the question?"

" Here is a piece of tapestry that we cannot value."

The mayor looked at the tapestry and marvelled himself. " Look here, sharpshooter," said he, " tell me in truth and sincerity where didst thou get such glorious tapestry?"

" My wife made it."

" How much must one give for it?"

" I know not myself; my wife told me to set no price on it, but what people would give, that would be ours."

" Well here are ten thousand for thee."

Fedot took the money and gave up the tapestry. The mayor was always near the person of the king, ate and drank at his table. When he went to the king's to dine he took the tapestry. " Would it not please your Majesty to see what a glorious piece of work I have bought to-day?"

The king looked; he saw his whole kingdom as if on the palm of his hand. He opened his mouth in amazement.

"This is indeed work; in all my life I have never seen such cunning art. Well, mayor, say what thou pleasest, but I shall not give this back to thee." Straightway the king took twenty-five thousand out of his pocket, placed the money in the mayor's hand, and hung the tapestry in the palace.

"That's nothing," thought the mayor; "I will order another still better." Straightway he galloped to find the sharpshooter, found his cottage, went in; and the moment he saw Fedot's wife he forgot himself, his errand, knew not why he had come. Before him was such a beauty that he would not take his eyes off her all his life; he would have looked and looked. He gazes on another man's wife, and in his head thought follows thought: "Where has it been seen, where heard of, that a simple soldier possessed such a treasure? Though I serve the king's person and rank as a general I have never beheld such beauty!"

The mayor came to his mind with difficulty, and went home, gainst his will. From that hour, from that time, he was not his own. Sleeping or waking, he thought only of the beautiful woman; he could neither eat nor drink, she was ever before his eyes. The king noticed the change, and asked: "What has come upon thee, — some grief?"

"Oh, your Majesty, I have seen the sharpshooter's wife; there is not such a beauty in the whole world! I am thinking of her all the time; I can neither eat nor drink, with no herb can I charm away my sorrow."

The desire came to the king to admire the woman himself. He ordered his carriage and drove to the soldier's quarters. He entered the room and saw unspeakable beauty. No matter who looked on the woman, — an old man, a youth; each was in love, lost his wits, a heart-flame pinched him. "Why," thought the king, "am I wifeless and single? Let me marry this beauty, — that is the thing. Why is she a sharpshooter's wife? It is her fate to be queen."

The king returned to his palace and said to the mayor: "Listen to me! Thou hast known how to show me this unimaginable beauty, now find the way to get rid of her husband; I want to marry her myself. And if thou dost not put him out of the way, blame thyself; for though thou art my faithful servant, thou 'lt die on the gallows."

The mayor went his way sadder than before. How was he to "finish the sharpshooter?" he could not think. As he was going through back lanes and waste places, a Baba-Yaga met him.

"Stop," said she, "servant of the king! I know all thy thoughts. If thou wilt, I will aid thee in this unavoidable sorrow."

"Aid me, grandmother, and I 'll pay what thou wishest."

"The king has ordered thee to put an end to Fedot the sharpshooter. That would be easy enough, for he is simple, were it not for his wife, who is awfully cunning. Well, we 'll give them such a riddle that it will not soon be explained. Go back to the king and say: 'Beyond the thrice-ninth land, in the thirtieth kingdom, is an island, on that island a deer with golden horns.' Let the king bring together half a hundred sailors, — the most good-for-nothing fellows, all bitter drunkards, — and order that a rotten old ship which has been out of service for thirty years be fitted for the voyage. Let him send Fedot the sharpshooter on that ship to get the deer with golden horns. In order to go to the island it is necessary to sail neither more nor less than three years, and back from the island three more; six in all. Well, the ship will sail out on the sea, serve about a month, and sink right there; the sharpshooter and the sailors will go to the bottom, every man!'"

The mayor listened to these words, thanked the Baba-Yaga for her counsel, rewarded her with gold, and went off on a run to the king. "Your Majesty," said he, "Fedot can be finished in such and such fashion."

The king consented, and issued an order at once to the navy to prepare for a voyage an old rotten ship, to provision it for six years, and man it with fifty sailors, the most dissolute and bitter drunk-ards. Messengers ran to all the dram-shops and drinking-houses, collected such sailors that it was dear and precious to look at them. One had a black eye, another had his nose driven to one side.

As soon as it was reported to the king that the ship was ready, he sent for the sharpshooter and said: "Now, Fedot, thou art a hero of mine,—the first shot in the company. Do me a service. Go beyond the thrice-ninth land to the thirtieth kingdom. In that place is an island, on that island lives the deer with golden horns. Take it alive, and bring it to me."

Fedot became thoughtful, knew not what to answer.

"Think, think not," said the king; "but if thou do not the work, I have a sword, and thy head leaves thy shoulders!"

Fedot wheeled round to the left and went forth from the palace, came home in the evening powerfully sad, not wishing to utter one word.

"Why dost thou grieve, my dearest?" asked his wife. "Is there some mishap?"

He told her all.

"This is why thou art grieved. There is reason, indeed; for it is an exploit, not a service. Pray to God and lie down to sleep; the morning is wiser than the evening: everything will be done."

The sharpshooter lay down and slept. But his wife opened her magic-book, at once two unknown youths appeared before her and asked: "What dost thou wish? What dost thou need?"

"Go beyond the thrice-ninth land to the thirtieth kingdom, to an island; seize there the deer with golden horns, and bring it here."

"We obey; it will be done before dawn."

They rushed like a whirlwind to the island, caught the deer with golden horns, and brought it straight to Fedot's house. An hour before daybreak all was done, and they vanished as if they had never been. The beautiful wife roused her husband at dawn and said: "Look out; the deer with golden horns is walking in the yard. Take it with thee on board the ship, sail forward five days, on the sixth turn back."

The sharpshooter put the deer in a close, fastened cage, and had it carried on board the ship.

"What's there?" asked the sailors.

"Oh, supplies and medicine! It's a long voyage; we shall need many a thing."

The day for sailing came. A great crowd of people went to see the ship leave the wharf. The king went himself, made Fedot chief over all the sailors, and bade him farewell.

The vessel sailed five days on the sea; the shores had long vanished. Fedot ordered a hundred-and-twenty-gallon cask to be rolled on to the deck, and said to the sailors: "Drink, brothers; spare it not, your souls are your measure!"

They were delighted, rushed to the cask, began to drink, and got so drunk that they rolled down on the deck, and fell fast asleep at the side of the cask. Fedot took the helm, turned the ship around toward the harbor, and sailed home. So that the sailors should not know anything about it, he kept pouring liquor into them from morning till night; when they began to open their eyes after one drunken fit, a new cask was ready. On the eleventh day the ship drew up at the wharf; the flag was hoisted, and guns fired. The king heard the firing, and ran down to the landing. "What does all this mean?" He saw the sharpshooter, fell into a towering passion, and rushed at him furiously. "How hast thou dared to come back before time?"

"But where was I to go, your Majesty? Some fool might have spent ten years in sailing over the seas and got nothing; but I, instead of spending six years, did the work in ten days. Would you be pleased to look at the golden-horned deer?"

Straightway they brought the cage from the ship and let out the golden-horned deer. The king saw that the sharpshooter was right; he could not touch him, he let him go home. The sailors had a holiday for six years; no one could ask them to work during that time, for the voyage was counted as six years, and they had served their time.

Next day the king called the mayor into his presence and threatened him: "What meanest thou; art making sport of me? 'T is clear thy head is not dear to thee. Do what thou pleasest, but find means of putting Fedot to a cruel death."

"Let me think, your Majesty; we may mend matters." The mayor went his way, betook himself to back lanes and waste places, met the Baba-Yaga.

"Stop, servant of the king! I know thy thoughts: dost wish I will help thee in trouble?"

" Oh, help me, grandmother! Fedot has brought the deer with golden horns."

" Oh, I have heard that already. It would be as easy to put Fedot out of the way as to take a pinch of snuff, for he is simple; but his wife is terribly cunning. Well, we'll give them another riddle that they will not solve so quickly. Tell the king to send the sharpshooter to the verge of destruction and bring back Shmat-Razum, — that's a task he will not accomplish to all eternity; he will either be lost without tidings, or come back empty-handed."

The mayor rewarded the old witch with gold and hurried to the king, who heard him and summoned Fedot.

"Fedot," said the king, "thou art a hero, the best shot I have. Thou hast brought me the deer with golden horns, now thou must do me another service; and if thou wilt not do it, I have a sword, and thy head leaves thy shoulders. Thou must go to the verge of destruction and bring back Shmat-Razum."

Fedot turned to the left, walked out of the palace, went home sad and thoughtful.

" My dear," asked his wife, "why art thou sad, has some misfortune happened?"

" Ah," said he, " one woe has rolled from my neck and another rolled on! The king sends me to the

verge of destruction to bring back Shmat-Razum.
For thy beauty I bear all this trouble and care."

"That," said she, " is no small task,—nine years
to go there, and nine to come back, eighteen in all.
Will good come of it? God knows. But pray to the
Lord and lie down to sleep; the morning is wiser
than the evening. To-morrow thou 'lt know all."

After Fedot had lain down, his wife opened her
magic book and asked the two unknown youths if
they knew how to go to the verge of destruction and
bring back Shmat-Razum. They answered: " We
know not." In the morning she roused her husband and said, " Go to the king and ask for the road
golden treasure, — thou hast eighteen years to wander; when thou hast the money come home for the
parting."

Fedot got the money from the king and returned
to take farewell of his wife. She gave him a towel
and a ball, and said: " When thou goest out of the
town throw the ball down before thee, and wherever
it rolls do thou follow. Here is a towel of my own
work; no matter where thou art, wipe thy face with
it after washing."

Fedot took farewell of his wife and comrades,
bowed down on all four sides, and went beyond the
barrier. He threw down the ball before him; it
rolled, rolled on, and he followed after.

About a month had passed, when the king summoned the mayor and said: " The sharpshooter has

gone to wander over the white world for eighteen
years; it is evident that he will not come back alive.
Eighteen years, as thou knowest, are not two weeks;
many a thing may happen on the road. He has
much money, and robbers will fall upon him perhaps,
strip him, and give him to a savage death. I think we
can begin at his wife now. Take my carriage, drive to
the soldier's quarters, and bring her to the palace."

The mayor drove to Fedot's house, entered, saluted
the sharpshooter's wife, and said: "Hail, witty woman,
the king has ordered us to present thee at the palace."

She went. The king received her with gladness,
led her to a golden chamber, and spoke these words:
"Dost thou wish to be queen? I will take thee in
marriage."

"Where has it ever been seen or heard of," asked
she, "that a wife was taken from her living husband? Though he is a simple soldier he is my law-
ful husband."

"If thou wilt not yield of thy free will, I will take
thee by force."

The beautiful woman laughed, struck the floor, became a blue dove, and flew out through the window.

Fedot journeyed over many lands and kingdoms, the ball rolling ahead of him all the time.
When he came to a river the ball became a bridge;
whenever he wanted rest it became a soft couch.
Whether it is long or short, a story is soon told, but
a deed is not soon done; the sharpshooter arrived at

a splendid palace, the ball rolled to the gate and disappeared. Fedot went straight up the stairs into a
rich chamber, where he was met by three maidens of
unspeakable loveliness.

"Whence comest, good man, and for what?"

" Oh, beautiful maidens, ye have not let me rest
after the long journey, but have begun to inquire.
First ye should give me to eat and drink, put me to
rest, and then make inquiry."

Straightway they set the table. When he had eaten
and drunk and rested, they brought him water, a
basin, and an embroidered towel. He took not the
towel, but said, " I have one of my own." When
they saw it they asked: " Good man, where didst
thou get that towel? "

" My wife gave it me."

" Then thy wife is our own sister."

They called their aged mother. The moment she
saw the towel she recognized it. " Why, this is my
daughter's work." She asked the guest all sorts of
questions. He told her how he had married her
daughter, and how the king had sent him to the verge
of destruction to bring back Shmat-Razum.

" Oh, my dear son-in-law, of that wonder even
I have not heard! Wait a moment; maybe my
servants have."

She went out on the balcony and called in a loud
voice. Presently all kinds of beasts ran up, and all
kinds of birds flew to her. " Hail to you, beasts of

the wilderness, birds of the air! Ye beasts run
through all places, ye birds fly everywhere; have ye
never heard how to go to the verge of destruction,
where Shmat-Razum lives?"

All the beasts and birds answered in one voice:
"No; we have never heard!"

Then the old woman sent them all to their homes in
hidden places, forests, and thickets; went to her magic
book, opened it, and that instant two giants appeared.
"What is thy pleasure; what dost thou wish?"

"This, my faithful servants, — bear my son-in-law
and me to the ocean sea wide, and stop just in the
middle above the very abyss."

Immediately they seized the sharpshooter and the
old woman and bore them on like a stormy whirlwind till they stopped just in the middle above the
abyss. They stood up themselves like pillars, holding the old woman and the sharpshooter in their
arms. The old woman cried out with a loud voice,
and all the fishes and living things in the sea swam
to her in such multitudes that the blue sea could not
be seen for them: "Hail, fish and worms of the sea!
Ye swim in all places, ye pass by all islands; have
ye not heard how to go to the verge of destruction,
where lives Shmat-Razum?"

All worms and fishes answered in one voice, "No;
we've not heard!"

All at once an old limping frog, who had been
thirty years out of service, pushed her way to the

front and said, " Kwa-kwa! I know where to find such a wonder!"

"Well, then, my dear, thou art the person I need," said the old woman. She took the frog, and commanded the giants to bear them home. They were at the palace in a flash. The old woman asked the frog how her son was to go.

"Oh!" said the frog, "that place is at the rim of the world, — far, far away. I would conduct him myself, but I am very old; I can barely move my legs, — I couldn't jump there in fifty years."

The old woman took a bowl with some fresh milk, put the frog in it, gave the bowl to Fedot, and said: "Carry this in thy hand; she will show thee the way."

The sharpshooter took farewell of the old woman and her daughters, and went on his journey, the frog showing him the way. Whether it was near or distant, long or short, he came at last to a flaming river, beyond which was a lofty mountain with a door in the side.

"Kwa-kwa!" said the frog. "Put me down out of the bowl; we must cross the river."

He put her on the ground.

"Now, good youth, sit thou on my back; do not spare me."

He sat on her back and pressed her to the ground; she began to swell, and swelled until she was as big as a stack of hay. The sharpshooter's one care was to keep from falling. "If I fall," thought he, "I shall be crushed." The frog cleared the flaming river at a jump, became small as before, and said: "Now, good youth, I will wait here; but do thou enter that door in the mountain. Thou wilt find a cave, — hide thyself well. After a time two old men will come in: listen to what they say, and watch what they do; when they are gone, act as they did."

The sharpshooter entered the door of the mountain; it was so dark in the cave that if a man strained his eyes out he could not see a thing. Fedot felt around and found a cupboard, crept in. After a while two old men entered and said, "Shmat-Razum, feed us!"

That moment, however it happened, the lamps were lighted, the dishes and plates rattled, and various kinds of food and wine appeared on the table. The old men ate and drank, and then ordered Shmat-Razum to remove everything. Everything disappeared in a flash; neither table, nor food, nor wine, nor lights remained. The two old men went out.

The sharpshooter crawled from the cupboard and cried, "Hei, Shmat-Razum!"

"What dost thou wish?"

"Feed me!"

Again the lights, the table, the food and drink appeared as before. Fedot sat at the table and said: "Hei, Shmat-Razum, sit down brother, with me, we'll eat and drink together; it is irksome for me alone."

The voice of the unseen answered: "Oh, kind man!

whence has God brought thee? It is nearly thirty years that I serve these old men in faith and in truth, and all this time they have never once seated me with themselves."

The sharpshooter looked and wondered. He saw no one, but the food was swept from the plates as if with a broom; the bottles raised themselves and poured the wine into glasses, — behold, in a moment bottles and glasses are empty!

" Shmat-Razum, dost thou wish to serve me?" asked the sharpshooter. " I 'll give thee a pleasant life."

" Why not? I am sick of being here; and thou, I see, art a kind man."

" All right; pick up everything and come along." The sharpshooter went out of the cave, looked around, saw no one, and asked: " Art thou here, Shmat-Razum?"

" Here; I 'll not leave thee, never fear."

" Very well," said Fedot, and sat on the frog, — she swelled, jumped over the river, and became small. He put her in the bowl, and went on the homeward road, came to his mother-in-law, and made his new servant entertain the old woman and her daughters. Shmat-Razum gave them such a feast that the old woman came very near dancing from joy. She ordered that three bowls of milk be given to the frog every day in reward for her faithfulness. The sharpshooter bade good by to his friends and set out for home. He travelled and journeyed till he was almost wearied to death. " Oh, Shmat-Razum," said he, " if thou couldst only know how tired I am, I am just losing my legs."

" Why not tell me long ago? " asked the other; " I should have brought thee home quickly." With that he seized Fedot and bore him like a rushing whirlwind, so swiftly that his cap fell off.

"Hei, Shmat-Razum, wait a minute; my cap is gone."

" Late, my master; thy cap is now three thousand miles behind."

Towns and villages, rivers and forests, just flashed before the eye; as Fedot was flying over a deep sea Shmat-Razum said: " If thou wishest, I will make a summer-house in the midst of the sea; thou canst rest, and acquire great fortune."

" Well, make it."

They dropped down toward the sea, and behold, where a moment before the waves were rolling, an island rose up, and in the centre a golden pleasure-house.

" Now, my master, sit down in this house, rest, and look at the sea. Presently three merchant-ships will sail by and cast anchor. Invite the merchants, enter-tain them well, and exchange me for three wonder-ful things which they have. I 'll come to thee again in my own time."

Fedot looked; three merchant-ships were sailing

from the west.   The merchants saw the island and
wondered.

"What does this mean?" asked they.   "How
many times have we sailed by here and seen nothing.
but water, and now an island and a pleasure-house!
Let us stand up to the shore, brothers, let us look and
admire."

They stopped the ships, cast anchor; the three
merchants stepped into a light boat, went to the
island, landed, and saluted Fedot, —

"Hail, worthy man!"

"Good health to you, foreign merchants!   We
crave kindness.   Come in, rejoice, have a good time,
and rest yourselves.   This pleasure-house was made
on purpose for passing guests."   They went in and
sat down.

"Hei, Shmat-Razum, meat and drink!"   A table
appeared; on the table wines and meats, whatever
the soul could desire was at hand in a moment.   The
merchants opened their mouths in amazement.

"Let us exchange," said they.   "Give us thy
servant, and take any one of our wonders."

"What wonders have ye?"

"Look, and thou wilt see."

One merchant took a small box from his pocket
and opened it: that minute a glorious garden was
spread over the whole island with flowers and paths;
he closed the box, and the garden was gone.   The
second merchant took an axe from under his skirts

and began to hit, hit strike, a ship came out: hit strike — another ship. He struck a hundred times — a hundred ships. They moved around the island under full canvas, with sailors and cannon. The sailors run and fire guns. The commanders come to the merchant for orders. He amused himself, hid his axe: the ships vanished from the eye, were as if they had never been. The third merchant took a horn, blew into it at one end: that minute an army appeared, cavalry and infantry, with muskets and cannons and flags; from every regiment come reports to the merchant, and he gives them orders. The army marches, with music sounding and banners waving. The merchant took his horn, blew in at the other end: there is nothing. Where has all the power gone to?

"Your wonders are strange," said the sharpshooter; "but these are all playthings for kings, and I am a simple soldier. If ye will exchange, however, I agree to give you my unseen servant for all three of your wonders."

"Is not that rather too much?"

"Well, ye know your own business, I suppose; but I will not exchange on other conditions."

The merchants thought to themselves, "What good are these ships and soldiers and garden to us? Let us exchange, — at least we shall have enough to eat and drink all our lives without trouble."

They gave the sharpshooter their wonders, and asked: "Shmat-Razum, wilt thou come with us?"

"Why not? It's all the same to me where I live."

The merchants returned to their ships and said: "Now, Shmat-Razum, fly about; give us to eat and drink." They invited all the men, and had such a feast that every one got drunk and slept a sound sleep.

The sharpshooter was sitting in the golden summer-house; he fell to thinking, and said: "I am sorry; where art thou now, trusty servant?"

"Here, my master."

Fedot rejoiced. "Isn't it time for us to go home?" The moment he spoke he was borne through the air as if by a whirlwind.

The merchants woke up, and wishing to drink off the effects of their carousal, cried out: "Give us to drink, Shmat-Razum." No one answered, nothing was brought; no matter how much they screamed and commanded, no result. "Well, gentlemen, this scoundrel has swindled us. Now Satan himself could not find him; the island has vanished, the pleasure-house is gone." The merchants grieved and regretted; then hoisted their sails and went to where they had business.

The sharpshooter soon arrived at his own kingdom, came down by the seashore. "Shmat-Razum, canst thou build me a palace here?"

"Why not? — it will be ready directly."

The palace appeared so splendid that it could not be described, — twice as good as the king's. Now the box was opened, and all around the palace was a glorious garden, with rare trees and flowers.

The sharpshooter sat by the window admiring the garden when all at once a blue dove flew in through the open window, struck the floor, and became his young wife. They embraced and kissed each other; then made inquiries and gave answer. Said his wife to Fedot: " Since the time thou didst leave me I have lived a lone dove in the forests and thickets."

Next morning the king went out on the balcony, and saw by the shore of the blue sea a new palace, and a green garden around it. "What insolent fellow has built on my land without leave?" Couriers hastened, discovered, reported, that the palace was built by Fedot, who was living there then, and with him his wife.

The king's anger increased. He gave orders to collect troops and go to the sea-shore, destroy the garden, break the palace into small pieces, and give the sharpshooter and his wife to a cruel death.

Fedot saw the strong army approaching. He took his axe quickly, and struck; a ship came forth; he struck a hundred times, — a hundred ships were ready; he blew his horn once, infantry was marching; he blew it a second time, cavalry was galloping. The commanders rushed to him from the ships, from the army, for orders. He ordered them to give battle. The music sounded at once, the drums rattled, the regiments advanced. The hundred ships open a

cannonade on the king's capital. The army moves
on at the sound of music and beat of drum. The
infantry rout the king's soldiers, the cavalry take
them prisoners. The king sees that his army is
fleeing, hurries forward himself to stop it. But
what could he do? Half an hour had not passed
before he was killed.

When the battle was over, the people came together and begged the sharpshooter to take the
government of the kingdom into his hands. He
agreed, became king, and his wife queen.

MARYA MOREVNA.

IN a certain kingdom in a certain land lived Ivan Tsarevich. He had three sisters. The first was Marya Tsarevna; the second, Olga Tsarevna; the third, Anna Tsarevna. Their father and mother were dead. When dying they said to their son: "Whoever woos first a sister of thine, give her to him; keep not thy sisters with thee long."

The Tsarevich buried his parents, and from sorrow went with his sisters to walk in the green garden. Suddenly a black cloud rose in the sky; a fearful storm was coming. "Let us go home, sisters," said Ivan Tsarevich. They had barely entered the castle when thunder roared, the ceiling opened, and a bright falcon flew into the chamber. The falcon struck the floor, became a gallant youth, and said: "Hail, Ivan Tsarevich! Ere now I came as a guest, but now I'm a suitor. I wish to sue for thy sister, Marya Tsarevna."

"If thou art pleasing to my sister, I shall not restrain her. Let her go, with God."

Marya Tsarevna agreed, the Falcon married her, and bore her away to his own kingdom.

Days followed days, hours chased hours, a whole year was as if it had not been. Ivan Tsarevich went with his two sisters to walk in the green garden. Again a cloud rose with whirlwind, with lightning. "Let us go home, my sisters," said the Tsarevich. They had barely entered the castle when a thunderclap came, the roof fell apart, the ceiling opened, and in flew an eagle. The eagle struck the floor and became a gallant youth. "Hail, Ivan Tsarevich! Ere now I came as a guest, but now I'm a suitor." And he asked for Olga Tsarevna in marriage.

Ivan Tsarevich answered: "If thou art pleasing to Olga Tsarevna, then let her marry thee; I take not her will from her." Olga Tsarevna consented, and accepted the Eagle in marriage. The Eagle caught her up and bore her to his own kingdom.

Another year passed. Ivan Tsarevich said to his youngest sister: "Let us go to walk in the green garden." They walked a little; again a cloud rose with whirlwind, with lightning. "Come home, my sister, come!" They returned to the castle, but had not sat down when a thunderclap came, the ceiling opened, and in flew a raven. The raven struck the floor and became a gallant youth. The others were beautiful in person, but he was still better.

"Well, Ivan Tsarevich! Ere now I came as a guest, but now I'm a wooer. Give me Anna Tsarevna."

"I take not her will from my sister. If thou hast pleased her, take her in marriage."

Anna Tsarevna married the Raven, and he bore her away to his own kingdom.

Ivan Tsarevich remained alone. He lived a whole year without sisters, grew wearied. "I will go," said he, "to seek out my sisters."

He made ready for the road, travelled and travelled, saw an army, a power lying slain on the field. Said Ivan Tsarevich: "If there is a living man here, let him speak. Who killed this great army?"

A living man answered: "Marya Morevna, the fair Korolyevna, killed all this great army."

Ivan Tsarevich went farther; he came to white tents. Marya Morevna, the fair Korolyevna, came forth to meet him. "Hail, Tsarevich! Where does God bear thee? Of thy own will, or against thy will?"

Ivan Tsarevich gave answer: "Good heroes travel not against their will."

"Well, if thy work be not hasty be a guest in my tents."

Ivan Tsarevich was glad; he spent two nights in the tents, pleased Marya Morevna, and married her. Marya Morevna, the fair Korolyevna, took him with her to her own kingdom. They lived together a time, and then the Korolyevna had a thought to make war; she left to her husband her household, and said: "Go everywhere, see after all things, but look not in this closet."

Ivan Tsarevich could not endure this, but when Marya Morevna had gone he rushed to the closet, opened the door, looked, and there Koshchéi Without-Death was hanging inside, fastened with twelve chains. Koshchéi implored the Tsarevich: "Take pity on me, give me to drink. Twelve years do I sit here in torment; I have not eaten nor drunk; my throat is parched."

The Tsarevich gave him a whole three-gallon tub of water. He drank it, and begged, "With one tub my thirst cannot be quenched." The Tsarevich gave him another tub. Koshchéi drank that, and begged for a third; and when he had drunk the third tub he regained his former strength, shook his chains, and in one moment broke all twelve.

"God save thee, Ivan Tsarevich!" said Koshchéi Without-Death; "now thou wilt never see Marya Morevna any more than thy own ears;" and he went out a terrific whirlwind, flew through the window, overtook on the road Marya Morevna, the fair Korolyevna, seized her, and bore her away.

But Ivan Tsarevich cried bitterly, bitterly, made ready, and went on his road, on his way. "Whatever may happen, I will find Marya Morevna." He travelled one day, he travelled a second; at the dawn of the third day he saw a wonderful palace, near the palace an oak, on the oak a bright falcon. The falcon flew down from the tree, struck the earth, turned into a gallant youth, and shouted: "Ah! my dear brother-in-law, how does God favor thee?"

Marya Tsarevna ran out, met Ivan Tsarevich joyously, asked about his health, his life, and told about her own life and household.

The Tsarevich stayed three days with them, and said: "I cannot stay longer, I am in search of my wife, Marya Morevna, the fair Korolyevna."

"It is hard to find her," said the Falcon. "In any case leave thy silver spoon here; we will look at it and think of thee."

Ivan Tsarevich left his silver spoon and went his way. He travelled a day, he travelled a second; at the dawn of the third he saw a castle better than the first, at the side of the castle an oak, on the oak sits an eagle. The eagle flew from the tree, struck the ground, turned into a gallant youth, and shouted: "Rise up, Olga Tsarevna; our dear brother is coming." Olga Tsarevna ran out that moment to meet him; she began to kiss, to embrace her brother, to ask about his health, and to tell of her own life and household.

Ivan Tsarevich remained three days with them, and then said: "I have no time to visit longer; I am going to seek my wife, Marya Morevna, the fair Korolyevna."

Said the Eagle: "It is hard for thee to find her. Leave with us thy silver fork; we will look at it and remember thee."

He left the fork and went his way. He travelled a day, he travelled a second; and on the dawn of the third day he saw a castle better than the other two.

At the side of the castle was an oak, and on the oak a raven was perched. The raven flew down, struck the earth, turned into a gallant youth, and cried: "Anna Tsarevna, hurry out; our brother is coming."

Anna Tsarevna ran out, met him joyously, began to kiss and embrace her brother, to ask about his health, and to tell about her own life and household.

Ivan Tsarevich stayed with them three short days, and said: "Farewell, I am going to look for my wife, Marya Morevna, the fair Korolyevna."

The Raven said: "It is hard for thee to find her; but leave thy gold ring with us, we will look at it and remember thee. If the ring is bright, it means that thou art alive and well; if dim, then we shall know that evil has come on thee."

Ivan Tsarevich left his gold ring and went his way. He travelled a day, he travelled a second; and on the third he came to Marya Morevna. She saw her dear one, rushed on his neck, covered herself with tears, and said: "Ivan Tsarevich, why didst thou not obey me; why didst thou look in the closet and let out Koshchéi Without-Death?"

"Forgive me, Marya Morevna; remember not the past. Better go with me while Koshchéi is not here; mayhap he will not overtake us."

They made ready and went. Koshchéi was out hunting; toward evening he was coming home, his good steed stumbled under him. "Why stumble, hungry crowbait; or dost feel some misfortune?"

The horse answered: "Ivan Tsarevich came and took Marya Morevna away."

"Can we overtake them?"

"Thou mightest sow wheat, wait till it should ripen, reap it, thresh it, make flour, bake five ovens of bread, eat that bread, go in pursuit, and overtake them."

Koshchéi galloped on, overtook Ivan Tsarevich. "Well," said he, "I forgive thee the first time for thy kindness, because thou didst give me water to drink; and a second time I'll forgive thee: but for the third have a care; I will hew thee to pieces."

He took Marya Morevna and led her away. Ivan Tsarevich sat on a stone and wept; he cried and cried, went back for Marya Morevna. Koshchéi Without-Death did not happen to be at home.

"Let us go, Marya Morevna."

"Ah, Ivan Tsarevich, he will overtake us!"

"Let him overtake us; anyhow, we shall pass a couple of hours together." They made ready and started away.

Koshchéi Without-Death was coming home; his good steed stumbled under him. "Why dost thou stumble, hungry crowbait; or feelest thou evil?"

"Ivan Tsarevich came and carried Marya Morevna away."

"Can they be overtaken?"

"Barley might be sown, waited for till ripe, harvested, threshed, and beer made of it; we might drink the beer, sleep after drinking, then pursue and catch them."

Koshchéi galloped on, rode up, overtook Ivan Tsarevich. "But I have said that thou canst no more see Marya Morevna than look at thy own ears." He took her away and led her home.

Ivan Tsarevich remained alone; he cried and cried, and went back for Marya Morevna. That time Koshchéi was not at home.

"Let us go, Marya Morevna."

"Ah! Ivan Tsarevich, he will come up with us, will hew thee to pieces."

"Let him hew me; I cannot live without thee." They made ready and started.

Koshchéi Without-Death was coming home; his good steed stumbled under him. "Why dost thou stumble, hungry crowbait; or feelest thou evil?"

"Ivan Tsarevich came, and took Marya Morevna away."

Koshchéi galloped on, caught up with Ivan Tsarevich, hewed him into small pieces, put him in a pitched barrel, took that barrel, strengthened it with iron hoops, and cast it into the blue sea. Marya Morevna he took home.

Now the silver grew black at the houses of Ivan Tsarevich's brothers-in-law. "Oh," said they, "it is clear that some evil has happened!"

The Eagle rushed off to the blue sea, caught the barrel, and drew it to shore; the Falcon flew for the

living water, and the Raven for the dead water. All
flew together to the same place, broke the barrel,
took out the pieces of Ivan Tsarevich, washed them,
put them together in proper order. The Raven
sprinkled them with dead water, the body grew together and united; the Falcon sprinkled the body
with living water. Ivan Tsarevich trembled, rose up,
and said, " Oh, how long I have been sleeping ! "

" Thou wouldst have slept still longer without us,"
answered the brothers-in-law. " Come now to our
houses."

" No, brothers, I shall go to seek Marya Morevna."
He came to her and said, " Discover from Koshchéi
Without-Death where he found such a steed."

Behold, Marya Morevna seized a favorable moment, inquired of Koshchéi. Koshchéi said : " Beyond the thrice-ninth land, in the thirtieth kingdom,
beyond the fiery river, lives Baba-Yaga; and she has
a mare on which she flies round the world each
day; she has many other glorious mares. I was
her herdsman for three days. I let not one mare
stray from her, and for that service Baba-Yaga gave
me a colt."

" But how didst thou cross the river of fire ? "

" I have a kerchief of such sort that when I wave
it on the right side three times, a bridge is made, lofty
and high; the fire cannot reach it."

Marya Morevna listened, told all to Ivan Tsarevich, carried away the kerchief, and gave it to him.

Ivan Tsarevich crossed the fiery river, and went to Baga-Yaga. Long did he go without eating and drinking; a bird from beyond the sea, with her little children, happened in his way. "I'll eat one little chick," said Ivan Tsarevich.

"Eat it not, Ivan Tsarevich," begged the bird from beyond the sea; "in time I will serve thee."

He went farther, saw in the forest a swarm of bees. "I'll take some honey," said he.

The queen-bee called out, "Touch not my honey, Ivan Tsarevich; in time I will serve thee."

He left the honey and went on. Then a lioness and her whelp met him. "At least I'll eat this little lion; I feel such hunger that I am sick."

"Touch him not, Ivan Tsarevich; in time I will serve thee."

"Well, let it be as thou sayest."

He went on hungry; he travelled and travelled. There is the house of Baba-Yaga. Around the house stand twelve stakes; on eleven are heads of men, — only one stake is unoccupied.

"Hail to thee, grandmother!"

"Hail to thee, Ivan Tsarevich! Hast come of thy own good will, or from need?"

"I have come to earn of thee an heroic steed."

"Very well, Tsarevich; no need to serve a year with me, but three days in all. If thou wilt herd my mares, I'll give thee an heroic steed; but if not, be not angry, thy head will be on the last stake."

Ivan Tsarevich consented. Baba-Yaga gave him food with drink, and ordered him to begin the work. As soon as he had driven the mares afield, they raised their tails and all ran apart through the meadows. The Tsarevich could not cast his eyes round before they had vanished. Then he began to weep and grow sad; he sat on a stone and fell asleep. The sun was going down when the bird from beyond the sea flew up and roused him.

" Rise, Ivan Tsarevich; the mares are now home."

The Tsarevich stood up, came home, but Baba-Yaga was screaming and crying at her mares. " Why did ye come home? "

" How could we help it, when birds from the whole world flew together and almost picked our eyes out? "

"Well, to-morrow don't run in the meadows, but scatter through the sleeping forest."

Ivan Tsarevich slept the night; in the morning Baba-Yaga said: " See to it, Tsarevich. If thou dost not herd the mares, if thou losest even one of them, thy stormy head will be on the stake."

He drove the mares afield. That moment they raised their tails and ran through the sleeping forest. Again the Tsarevich sat down on a stone, cried and cried, then fell asleep. The sun had gone behind the forest when the lioness ran up. " Rise, Ivan Tsarevich; the mares are driven in."

Ivan Tsarevich stood up and went home. Baba-

Yaga was screaming and crying more than before at her mares. " Why did ye come home? "

" How could we help coming? Savage beasts ran at us from the whole world, came. near tearing us to pieces."

" Well, run to-morrow into the blue sea."

Ivan Tsarevich slept that night; next morning Baba-Yaga sent him to herd the mares. " If thou dost not guard them, thy stormy head will be on the stake."

He drove the mares to the field; that moment they raised their tails .and vanished from the eye, ran into the blue sea, and stood to their necks in the water.

Ivan Tsarevich sat on a stone, cried, and fell asleep. The sun had gone beyond the forest when a bee flew up and said: "Ivan Tsarevich, the mares are driven in. But when thou art home, do not show thyself before the eyes of Baba-Yaga; go to the stable and hide behind the manger. There is a mangy little colt lying on the dung-heap; steal him, and at dark midnight leave the place."

Ivan Tsarevich rose up, made his way to the stable, and lay down behind the manger. Baba-Yaga screamed and cried at her mares: " Why did ye come home? "

" How could we help coming home when bees, seen and unseen, flew from the whole world and began to sting us on every side till the blood came! "

Baba-Yaga went to sleep, and just at midnight Ivan

Tsarevich stole from her the mangy colt, saddled him, sat on his back, and galloped to the fiery river; when he came to the river he shook the kerchief three times on the right side, and suddenly, from wherever it came, a high, splendid bridge was hanging over the river. The Tsarevich crossed on the bridge, waved the kerchief on the left side only twice, and there remained above the river a bridge very, very slender.

In the morning Baba-Yaga woke up; the mangy colt is not to be seen with sight. Baba-Yaga, on an iron mortar, rushed off in pursuit with all her breath, urging forward with a pestle, and removing her trail with a broom. She galloped to the fiery river, looked and thought: "The bridge is good." She rode out on it, and the moment she reached the middle the bridge broke. Baba-Yaga went headlong into the river; there a savage death came to her.

Ivan Tsarevich fed his colt in the green meadows, and it became a marvellous steed. The Tsarevich came to Marya Morevna; she ran out to him, threw herself on his neck.

"How has God brought thee to life?"

"In this way and that way," said he; "come with me."

"I am afraid, Ivan Tsarevich. If Koshchéi overtakes us again, thou wilt be cut to pieces."

"No, he will not overtake us. I have a glorious, heroic steed now; he goes like a bird."

They sat on the horse and rode off. Koshchéi

Without-Death was coming home ; under him stumbled his steed.

" Why stumble, hungry crow-bait; or feelest thou evil? "

" Ivan Tsarevich came, took away Marya Morevna."

" Can we overtake him? "

" God knows ! Now Ivan Tsarevich has an heroic steed better than I."

" I cannot stand this," said Koshchéi the Deathless, " I'll give chase."

Whether it was long or short, he caught up with Ivan Tsarevich, sprang to the ground, and wanted to cut him with his sharp sword. That moment Ivan's horse struck, with all the sweep of his hoof, Koshchéi Without-Death, and smashed his skull. The Tsarevich finished him with his club. Then he raised a pile of wood, made a fire, burned Koshchéi Without-Death on the fire, and scattered the ashes to the wind.

Marya Morevna mounted Koshchéi's horse, and Ivan Tsarevich his own. They went to visit the Raven, then the Eagle, and last the Falcon; wherever they came they were met with joy.

" Oh, Ivan Tsarevich, we did not think to see thee ! It was not for nothing thou didst struggle; another such beauty as Marya Morevna could not be found if sought for in the whole world."

They visited and feasted, and set out for their own kingdom; arrived there, gained wealth, and drank mead.

VARIANT OF THE RESCUE OF IVAN TSAREVICH
AND THE WINNING OF THE COLT.

EAGLE son of Eagle flew to the sea and brought
mighty winds, the sea rose, and threw the barrel
on shore. Falcon son of Falcon grasped the barrel in his talons, bore it high, high in the air, and
dropped it thence to the ground. The barrel fell
and was broken in pieces; but Raven son of Raven
carried healing water and living water and sprinkled
Ivan Tsarevich with them. Then all three of them
caught him up and bore him to the thrice-ninth land,
to the thirtieth kingdom. They brought him to the
thirtieth kingdom and said: "Go now to the blue
sea, where lives a marvellous mare; in front of her
twelve men are mowing hay, and twelve rakers are
raking what they mow: she follows them and eats
the hay. When the mare drinks water, the blue sea
rises in waves and leaves fall from the trees; when
she scratches herself on hundred-year oaks, they fall
to the ground like bundles of oats. Every month
she has one colt; twelve wolves follow her and devour
these colts. Bide thy time; and the moment a colt is
born with a star on its forehead, seize it quickly,— that
colt will be an heroic steed for thee. On that colt
Koshchéi Without-Death will not overtake thee."
Ivan Tsarevich did as his brothers-in-law taught him.

YELENA THE WISE.

IN a certain kingdom, in a certain land, the Tsar had a golden company; in this company served a soldier, Ivan by name, a hero in appearance. The Tsar took him into favor and began to reward him with rank; in a short time he made him colonel. The superior officers envied him. "Why have we served for our rank as we have thirty years, and he has got every rank all at once? We must get rid of him, or he will go ahead of us."

The generals and counselling boyars arranged a trip on the sea, prepared the ship, invited Ivan the colonel to go with them. They sailed out into the open sea, and went around till late in the evening. Ivan grew tired, lay on a bed, and fell into a deep sleep. That was all the boyars and generals were waiting for. They seized him, put him in a boat, pushed him out to sea, and returned home themselves.

Soon dark clouds came up and a storm began to roar; the waves rose and carried the boat it is unknown whither; they carried it far, far away, and cast it out on an island. Here Ivan woke up, looked, saw a desert land, no trace of the ship, and the sea ran terribly high.

"It is clear," thought he, "that the ship has been wrecked by the storm, and all my comrades are drowned. Glory be to God that I am safe myself!"

He went to look at the island, walked and walked. Nowhere did he see a springing beast, a flying bird, or a dwelling of man. Whether it was long or short, Ivan wandered to an underground passage; through this he went down a deep precipice, and came to the underground kingdom, where the six-headed serpent lived and reigned. He saw a white-walled castle, entered. The first chamber was empty, in the second there was no one, in the third the six-headed serpent was sleeping a hero's sleep. At his side stood a table, on the table an enormous book was lying.

Ivan opened the book and read to the page where it was written that a Tsar had never a son, but always a Tsaritsa had sons. He took and scratched out these words with a knife, and in place of them wrote that a Tsaritsa had never a son, but always a Tsar had sons.

In an hour's time the serpent turned to his other side, woke up, opened his eyes, saw Ivan, and asked: "From what place hast thou come? I live so many years in the world and I have not seen one man in my kingdom."

"How from what place? But thou knowest I am thy son."

"How can that be?" asked the serpent. "I will

look in the book and see if a Tsar can have a son."

He opened the book, read in it what Ivan had written, and was convinced. " Thou art right, my son."

He took Ivan by the hand, led him through all his treasure-chambers, showed him his countless wealth, and they began to live and live on together.

Some time passed, and the six-headed serpent said : " My dear son, here are the keys of all the chambers; go wherever thy desire may lead thee, but do not dare to look into that chamber which is fastened with two locks, one of gold, the other of silver. I will fly around the world, will look at people, and amuse myself."

He gave the keys, and flew away out of the underground kingdom to wander through the white world. Ivan Tsarevich remained all alone. He lived a month, a second and a third month, and the year was coming to an end, when it became dreary for him, and he thought to examine the chambers; he walked and walked till he came straight in front of the forbidden chamber. The good youth could not restrain himself; he took out the keys, opened both locks, the gold and the silver, opened the oaken door.

In that chamber were sitting two maidens riveted in chains : one was Tsarevna Yelena the Wise, and the other her maid. The Tsarevna had golden wings, and her maid silver wings. Said Yelena the Wise :

" Hail, good hero! Do us a service not great: give us each of a glass of spring water to drink."

Ivan, looking at her unspeakable beauty, forgot all about the serpent, pited the poor prisoners, poured out two glasses of spring water, and gave them to the beautiful women. They drank, shook themselves; the iron rings were broken, and the heavy chains fell. The beautiful women clapped their wings and flew through the open window; then only did Ivan come to his mind. He shut the empty chamber, came out on the porch, sat on the step, hung his stormy head below his mighty shoulders, and grew powerfully, powerfully sad. How was he to give answer? Suddenly the wind began to whistle, a mighty storm rose up, the six-headed serpent flew home.

" Hail, my dear son! "

Ivan answered not a word.

"Why art thou silent; or has something happened?"

" Evil, father, — I did not obey thy command. I looked into that chamber where two maidens were sitting riveted in chains, I gave them spring water to drink, they drank, shook themselves, clapped their wings, and flew out through the open window."

The serpent was terribly enraged; he began to abuse and curse in every fashion. Then he took an iron rod, heated it red hot, and gave Ivan three blows on the back. " It is thy luck," said he, "that thou art my son; if thou wert not, I should eat thee alive."

As soon as Ivan's back had healed he began to

beg of the serpent: "Father, let me go out into the world to look for Yelena the Wise."

"What couldst thou do? I was thirty-three years getting her, and barely, barely had I the skill to catch her."

"Let me go, father; let me try my fortune."

"Well, after me if thou pleasest. Here is the carpet that flies of itself: wherever thou wishest, there will it bear thee; only I am sorry for thee, since Yelena the Wise is terribly cunning. If thou catch her she will still overreach and deceive thee."

Ivan sat on the carpet that flies of itself, flew out of the underground kingdom, and had n't time to wink before he found himself in a beautiful garden. He went to a pond, sat under a laburnum-bush, and began to look and admire the gold and silver fish swimming in the clear water. Before five minutes had passed, Yelena the Wise had flown to the pond with her maid. They took off their wings at once, put them near the bush, undressed, and ran into the water to bathe.

Ivan took the wings quietly, came from under the bush, and cried with a loud voice: "But now ye are in my hands!"

The beautiful women sprang out of the pond, put on their clothes, came to the good youth, and begged him to give back their wings. "No," said Ivan, "I will not give them for anything. Yelena the Wise, thou hast pleased me more than the bright sun; now

I will take thee to my father and my mother, I will marry thee, and thou shalt be my wife, and I will be thy husband."

The Tsarevna's maid said: " Hear me, good youth: 't is thy wish to marry Yelena the Wise, but why detain me. Better give me my wings; I will serve thee in time."

Ivan thought and thought, and gave her the silver wings. She tied them on quickly, sprang up, and flew far, far away. After that, Ivan made a box, put the golden wings into it, and closed it firmly with a lock. He sat on the self-flying carpet, placed Yelena the Wise at his side, and flew away to his own kingdom. He came to his father, to his mother, brought them his bride, and begged them to love and to favor her. Then there was rejoicing such as no one had seen.

Next day Ivan gave his mother the key of the box. " Take care of it for a time," said he, " give it to no one; and I will go to the Tsar and invite him to the wedding."

As soon as he had gone, Yelena the Wise ran in: " Mother, give me the key of the box; I must get clothes to dress for the wedding." The mother, knowing nothing, gave her the key without fear. Yelena the Wise ran to the box, raised the lid, took her wings, put them on, clapped them once and again; that was all they saw of her.

The bridegroom came home. " Mother, where is my bride. It is time to prepare for the crown."

" Oh, my dear son, she has flown away ! "

Deeply did the good youth sigh; he took farewell of his father and his mother, sat on his self-flying carpet, and flew to the underground kingdom, to the six-headed serpent, who saw him and said: " Well, daring head, did I speak in vain when I said that thou couldst not get Yelena the Wise; and if thou didst get her she would deceive thee?"

" Thou art right, father; but no matter what comes, I will try again, I will go to get her."

" Ah! thou irrestrainable fellow, knowest thou she has a rule that whoever wants to marry her must hide three times, and if she finds him she will have his head cut off? Many a hero has gone to her, but all to the last man have laid down their stormy heads; and the same is preparing for thee. But here is a flint and steel for thee: when Yelena the Wise makes thee hide, strike the flint with the steel, — strike out a spark, and set fire to the grass of the steppe. At that moment a blue-winged eagle will appear and raise thee above the third range of clouds; if that does not succeed, strike fire again, and let it into the blue sea. A giant pike will swim to land, will take thee and bear thee away to the depth of the sea; and if Yelena the Wise finds thee, then there is no place in which thou canst hide from her."

Ivan Tsarevich took the flint and steel, thanked the six-headed serpent, and flew off on the carpet. Whether it was long or short, near or far, he flew beyond the thrice-ninth land to the thirtieth kingdom, where lived Yelena the Wise. Her palace was flashing like fire; it was made of pure silver and gold. At her gate, on iron points, were the heads of eleven heroes. Ivan the good youth became thoughtful. "Eleven heads on the points, mine will surely be the twelfth." He came down in the broad court, went on the lofty porch, and straight to the chamber.

Yelena the Wise met him. "Thou!" said she, "why art thou here?"

"I want to take thee in marriage."

"Well, all right, try. If thou art able to hide from me, I will marry thee; if not, thou wilt pay with thy head."

Ivan went out in the open field, took his flint and steel, struck fire, and put it to the steppe grass. From wherever he came, a blue-winged eagle flew to him and said, with the voice of a man, "Good youth, sit on me quickly; hold firmly, or thou wilt fall."

Ivan sat on the eagle, grasped firmly with his hands. The eagle clapped his wings, and rose high beyond the third range of clouds. He is well hidden; it seems no one can find him. But Yelena the Wise had a mirror: all she had to do was to look in it, and the whole world was open to her. She knew in a moment where and what was going on in the white world. She stepped up to that mirror, looked in it, and knew every secret.

"Stop, cunning fellow," cried Yelena the Wise,

15

with a loud voice; " I see thou hast flown above the third range of clouds. The blue-winged eagle bore thee; it is time to come down to the earth."

Ivan came to the earth, slipped off the eagle, went to the sea-shore, struck fire, and put it to the blue sea. Suddenly, from wherever he came, a giant pike swam to shore. "Well, good youth, creep into my mouth; I'll hide thee in the bottom of the sea." He opened his jaws, took in the young man, sank with him in the abyss of the sea, and covered him with sand.

"Now," thought Ivan, " perhaps it will be all right." But the point was not there.

Yelena the Wise barely looked in the mirror, and saw everything at once. " Stop, cunning fellow, I see thou hast gone into the giant pike, and thou art sitting now in the abyss of the sea beneath rolling sands; it is time to come to shore." The pike swam to shore, threw out the good youth, and vanished in the sea.

Ivan returned to the broad court of Yelena the Wise, sat on the porch, and grew powerfully thoughtful and sad. At that moment the maid of Yelena the Wise ran up the stairway. " Why are thou sad, good youth? "

" How can I be glad? If I hide not the third time, I must part with the white world; so here I am sitting and waiting for death."

" Grieve not; foretell no evil on thy own stormy

head. Once I promised to serve thee; I spoke no empty word. Come, I will hide thee."

She took Ivan by the hand, led him in, and put him behind the mirror. A little later Yelena the Wise ran to the chamber, looked and looked in the mirror. She could not see her bridegroom; the appointed time had passed. She grew angry, and with vexation struck the glass; it fell into fragments, and before her stood Ivan the brave youth.

There was no help for it, — she had to yield this time. At the house of Yelena the Wise there was no need of waiting to make mead or wine; that day they had a noble feast and a wedding. They were crowned, and began to live, — to live on and win wealth.

THE SEVEN SIMEONS, FULL BROTHERS.

THERE lived an old man and his old wife; they lived many years, to a great age. Then they began to pray to God to give them a child who in their old age might help them to work. They prayed a year, they prayed a second, they prayed a third and fourth, they prayed a fifth and a sixth, and did not receive a child; but in the seventh year the Lord gave them seven sons, and they called them all Simeon. When the old man with the old woman died, the Simeons were left orphans all in their tenth year.

They ploughed their own land, and were not worse than their neighbors. It happened one time to Tsar Ador, the ruler of all that country, to pass their village, and he saw the Seven Simeons working in the field. He wondered greatly that such small boys were ploughing and harrowing. Therefore he sent his chief boyar to inquire whose children they were. When the boyar came to the Simeons he asked why they, such small children, were doing such heavy work?

The eldest Simeon answered that they were orphans, that there was no one to work for them, and said at the same time that they were all called Simeon. The boyar left them and told this to the Tsar, who wondered greatly that so many small boys, brothers, should be called by one name. Therefore he sent the same boyar to take them to the palace. The boyar carried out the command of the Tsar and took all the Simeons with him. When the Tsar came to the palace he assembled the boyars and men of counsel and asked advice in the following words:

"My boyars and men of counsel, ye see these seven orphans who have no relatives: I wish to make of them men who may be grateful to me hereafter; therefore I ask counsel of you. In what science or art should I have them instructed?"

To this all answered as follows: "Most Gracious Sovereign, as they are now grown somewhat and have reason, dost thou not think it well to ask each one of them separately with what science or art he would like to occupy himself?"

The Tsar accepted this advice gladly, and began by asking the eldest Simeon: "Listen to me, my friend: with whatever science or art thou wishest to occupy thyself, in that I will have thee instructed."

Simeon answered: "Your Majesty, I have no wish to occupy myself with any science or art; but if you would give command to build a forge in the middle of your court-yard, I would forge a pillar reaching to the sky."

The Tsar saw that there was no reason to teach

this Simeon, for he knew well enough the art of a blacksmith; still, he did not believe that the boy could forge a pillar to the very sky, therefore he gave command to build in quick time a forge in the middle of his court-yard. After the first he called the second Simeon. " And thou, my friend, whatever science or art thou wishest to study, in that will I give thee to be taught."

Then that Simeon answered: " Your Majesty, I do not wish to study any science or art; but if my eldest brother will forge a pillar to the sky, then I will climb that pillar to the top, and will look at all lands, and tell you what is going on in each one of them."

The Tsar considered that there was no need to teach this Simeon either, because he was wise already. Then he asked the third Simeon: " Thou, my friend, what science or art dost thou wish to learn? "

Simeon answered: " Your Majesty, I do not wish to learn any science or art; but if my eldest brother will make me an axe, with the axe I will strike once, twice; that moment there will be a ship."

Then the king answered: " I need shipwrights, and thou shouldst not be taught anything else." Next he asked the fourth: " Thou, Simeon, what science or art dost thou wish to know? "

" Your Majesty," answered he, " I do not wish to know any science; but if my third brother should make a ship, and if it should happen to that ship to be at sea, and an enemy should attack it, I would seize it by the prow and take the ship to the underground kingdom; and when the enemy had gone away I would bring it back to the surface of the sea."

The Tsar was astonished at these great wonders of the fourth Simeon, and he said: "There is no need to teach thee either." Then he asked the fifth Simeon: "And thou, Simeon, what science or art dost thou wish to learn?"

"I do not wish to learn any," said he; "but if my eldest brother will make me a gun, with that gun, if I see a bird, I will hit it, even one hundred versts distant."

"Well, thou wilt be a splendid sharpshooter for me," said the Tsar. Then he asked the sixth Simeon: "Thou, Simeon, what science dost thou wish to begin?"

"Your Majesty," said Simeon, "I have no wish to begin any science or art; but if my fifth brother will shoot a bird on the wing, I will not let it reach the earth, but will catch it and bring it to you."

"Thou 'rt very cunning," said the Tsar; "thou wilt take the place of a retriever for me in the field." Then the Tsar asked the last Simeon: "What art or science dost thou wish to learn?"

"Your Majesty," answered he, "I do not wish to learn any science or art, because I have a most precious craft."

"But what is thy craft? Tell me, if it please thee."

"I know how to steal dexterously," said Simeon, " so that no man can steal in comparison with me."

The Tsar became greatly enraged, hearing of such an evil art, and said to his boyars and men of counsel: " Gentlemen, how do ye advise me to punish this thief Simeon? Tell me what death should he die ? "

"Your Majesty," said they all to him, "why put him to death? He is a thief in name, but a thief who may be needed on an occasion."

" For what reason ? " asked the Tsar.

"For this reason: your Majesty is trying now these ten years to get Tsarevna Yelena the Beautiful, and you have not been able to get her; and besides, have lost great forces and armies, and spent much treasure and other things. Mayhap this Simeon the thief may in some way be able to steal Yelena the Beautiful for your Majesty."

The Tsar said in answer: " My friends, ye tell me the truth." Then he turned to Simeon the thief and asked: "Well, Simeon, canst thou go to the thrice-ninth land, to the thirtieth kingdom, and steal for me Yelena the Beautiful? I am strongly in love with her, and if thou canst steal her for me I 'll give thee a great reward."

" Stealing is my art, your Majesty," anwered the seventh Simeon, " and I will steal her for you; only give the command."

" Not only do I give the command, but I beg thee

to do it; and delay no longer at my court, but take for thyself troops and money, whatever is needed."

" Neither troops nor treasure do I need," answered he. " Let all of us brothers go together, and I will get Tsarevna Yelena the Beautiful."

The Tsar did not like to part with all the Simeons; still, though he regretted it, he was obliged to let them all go together. Meanwhile the forge was built in the court, and the eldest Simeon forged an iron pillar to the very sky; the second Simeon climbed on that pillar to the top, and looked in the direction in which was the kingdom of the father of Yelena the Beautiful. After he had looked he cried from the top of the pillar: " Your Majesty, I see Yelena the Beautiful sitting beyond the thrice-ninth land in the thirtieth kingdom under a window; her marrow flows from bone to bone."

Now the Tsar was still more enticed by her beauty, and said to the Simeons in a loud voice: " My friends, start on your journey at once, for I cannot live without Yelena, the beautiful Tsarevna."

The eldest Simeon made an axe for the third, and for the fifth he made a gun; and after that they took bread for the journey, and Simeon the Thief took a cat, and they went their way. Simeon the Thief had made the cat so used to him that she ran after him everywhere like a dog; and if he stopped on the road, or in any other place, the cat stood on her hind legs, rubbed against him, and purred. So the brothers went

their way for some time, and at last came to the sea,
which they had to cross, and there was nothing to
cross upon. They walked along the shore and looked
for a tree of some kind to make a vessel, and they
found a very large oak. The third Simeon took his
axe and cut the oak at the very root, and then with
one stroke and another he made straightway a ship,
which was rigged, and in the ship were various costly
goods. All the Simeons sat on that ship and sailed
on their journey.

In a few months they arrived safely at the place
where it was necessary for them to go. When they
entered the harbor they cast anchor at once. On the
following day Simeon the Thief took his cat and
went into the town, and coming to the Tsar's palace he
stood opposite the window of Yelena the Beautiful.
At that moment the cat stood on her hind legs and
began to rub against him and to purr. It is necessary
to say that in that kingdom they knew nothing of cats,
and had not heard what kind of beast the cat is.

Tsarevna Yelena the Beautiful was sitting at the
window; and seeing the cat, sent straightway her
nurses and maidens to ask Simeon what kind of
beast that was, would he not sell it, and what price
would he take. The maidens and nurses ran out in
the street and asked Simeon what kind of beast that
was, and would he not sell it?

Simeon answered: " My ladies, be pleased to relate
to her Highness, Yelena the Beautiful, that this little

beast is called a cat, that I will not sell it, but if she wishes to have it I will give it to her without price."

The maidens and nurses ran straight to the palace and told what they had heard from Simeon.

Tsarevna Yelena the Beautiful was rejoiced beyond measure, ran out herself, and asked Simeon would he not sell the cat.

Simeon said: "Your Highness, I will not sell the cat; but if you like her, then I make you a present of her."

The Tsarevna took the cat in her arms and went to the palace, and Simeon she commanded to follow. When she came to the palace the Tsarevna went to her father, and showed him the cat, explaining that a certain foreigner had given it to her as a present.

The Tsar, seeing such a wonderful little beast, was greatly delighted, and gave orders to call Simeon the Thief; and when he came, the Tsar wished to reward him with money for the cat; but as Simeon would not take it, he said: "My friend, live for the time in my house, and meanwhile, in your presence, the cat will become better used to my daughter."

To this Simeon did not agree, and said to the Tsar: "Your Majesty, I could live with great delight in your house if I had not the ship on which I came to your kingdom, and which I cannot commit to any one; but if you command, me I will come every day and teach the cat to know your daughter."

The Tsar commanded Simeon to come every day.
Simeon began to visit Tsarevna Yelena the Beautiful.
One day he said to her: " Gracious lady, often have I
come here; I see that you are not pleased to walk
anywhere; you might come to my ship, and I would
show you such costly brocades as you have never
seen till this day."

The Tsarevna went straightway to her father and
began to beg permission to go to the ship-wharf.
The Tsar permitted her, and told her to take nurses
and maidens, and go with Simeon.

As soon as they came to the wharf Simeon invited
her to his ship, and when she entered the ship Simeon
and his brothers began to show the Tsarevna various
rich brocades.   Then Simeon the Thief said to Yelena
the Beautiful: " Now be pleased to tell your nurses
and maidens to leave the ship, because I wish to show
you things so costly that they should not see them."

The Tsarevna commanded her maidens and nurses
to leave the ship.   As soon as they had gone, Simeon
the Thief ordered his brothers in silence to cut off
the anchor and go to sea with all sail; meanwhile
he showed the Tsarevna rich goods and made her
presents of some.   About two hours had passed while
he was showing the stuffs.   At last she said it was time
for her to go home, the Tsar her father would expect
her to dinner.   Then she went out of the cabin and
saw that the ship was under sail and land no longer
in sight.

She struck herself on the breast, turned into a swan, and flew off. The fifth Simeon took his gun that minute and wounded the swan; the sixth Simeon did not let her fall to the water, but brought her back to the ship, where she became a maiden as before.

The nurses and maidens who were at the wharf, seeing the ship move away from the shore with the Tsarevna, ran straight to the Tsar and told him of Simeon's deceit. Then the Tsar sent a whole fleet in pursuit. When this fleet coming up was very near the ship of the Simeons, the fourth Simeon seized the prow and conducted the ship to the underground kingdom. When the ship had become entirely invisible, the commanders of the fleet thought it was lost, with the Tsarevna; therefore they returned, and reported to the Tsar that Simeon's ship had gone to the bottom with Yelena the Beautiful.

The Simeons arrived at their own kingdom successfully, delivered Yelena the Beautiful to Tsar Ador, who for such a mighty service of the Simeons gave liberty to them all, and plenty of gold, silver, and precious stones, married Yelena the Beautiful himself, and lived with her many years.

THE ENCHANTED PRINCESS.

IN a certain kingdom a soldier served in the mounted guard of the king. He served twenty-five years in faithfulness and truth; and for his good conduct the king gave orders to discharge him with honor, and give him as reward the same horse on which he had ridden in the regiment, with all the caparison.

The soldier took farewell of his comrades and set out for his native place. He travelled a day, a second, and a third. Behold, a whole week had gone; a second and third week! The soldier had no money; he had nothing to eat himself, nothing to give his horse, and his home was far, far away. He saw that the affair was a very bad one; he wanted terribly to eat, began to look in one direction and another, and saw on one side a great castle. "Well," thought he, "better go there; maybe they will take me even for a time to serve, — I'll earn something."

He turned to the castle, rode into the court, put his horse in the stable, gave him hay, and entered the castle. In the castle a table was set with food and wine, — with everything that the soul could wish for.

The soldier ate and drank. "Now," thought he, "I may sleep."

All at once a bear came in. " Fear me not, brave hero; thou hast come in good time. I am not a savage bear, but a fair maiden, an enchanted princess. If thou canst endure and pass three nights in this place, the enchantment will be broken, I shall be a princess as before, and will marry thee."

The soldier consented. Now, there fell upon him such a sadness that he could not look on the world, and every moment the sadness increased; if there had been no wine he could not have held out a single night, as it seemed. The second night it went so far that the soldier resolved to leave everything and run away; but no matter how he struggled, no matter how he tried, he found no way out of the castle. There was no help for it, he had to stay in spite of himself.

He passed the third night. In the morning there stood before him a princess of unspeakable beauty. She thanked him for his service, and told him to make ready for the crown (marriage). Straightway they had the wedding, and began to live together without care or trouble. After a time the soldier remembered his native place; he wanted to spend some time there. The princess tried to dissuade him.

" Remain, stay here, my friend, go not away. What is lacking to thee?"

No, she could not dissuade him. She took farewell of her husband, gave him a sack filled with seeds, and said: " On whatever road thou mayest travel, throw these seeds on both sides. Wherever they fall, that moment trees will spring up; on the trees precious fruit will be hanging in beauty, various birds will sing songs, and tom-cats from over the sea will tell tales."

The good hero sat on his horse of service and went his way. Wherever he journeyed he cast seeds on both sides, and after him forests were rising, just creeping out of the damp earth. He rode one day, he rode a second, a third, and saw in the open field a caravan. On the grass merchants were sitting playing cards, near them a great kettle was hanging, and, though there was no fire under the kettle, it was boiling like a fountain within the pot. " What a wonder! " thought the soldier; " there is no fire to be seen, and in the kettle it is boiling like a fountain, — let me look at it more closely." He turned his horse to the place and rode up to the merchants.

" Hail, honorable gentlemen! " He had no suspicion that these were not merchants, but all unclean. "That is a good trick of yours, — a kettle boiling without fire; but I have a better one."

He took out a seed and threw it on the ground, — that moment a full-grown tree came up; on the tree were precious fruits in their beauty, various birds were singing songs, and tom-cats from over the sea were telling tales. From this boast the unclean knew him.

"Ah," said they among themselves, "this is the man who liberated the princess! Come, brothers, let us drug him with a weed, and let him sleep half a year."

They went to entertaining him, and drugged him with the magic weed. The soldier dropped on the grass and fell into deep sleep from which he could not be roused. The merchants, the caravan, and the kettle vanished in a twinkle.

Soon after the princess went out in her garden and saw that the tops of all the trees had begun to wither. "This is not for good," thought she; "it is evident that evil has come to my husband."

Three months passed. It was time for his return, and there was nothing of him, nothing. The princess made ready and went to search for him. She went by that road along which he had travelled, — on both sides forests were growing, birds were singing, and tom-cats from over the sea were purring their tales. She reached the spot where there were no more trees, the road wound out into the open field; she thought, "Where has he gone to? Of course he has not sunk through the earth."

She looked, aside by itself was one of the wonderful trees, and under it her dear husband. She ran to him, pushed, and tried to rouse him. No, he did not wake. She pinched him, stuck pins in his side, pricked and pricked him. He did not feel even the pain, — lay like a corpse without motion.

16

The princess grew angry, and in her anger pronounced the spell: "Mayest thou be caught by the stormy whirlwind, thou good-for-nothing sleepy head, and be borne to places unknown!"

She had barely uttered these words when the wind began to whistle, to sound, and in one flash the soldier was caught up by a boisterous whirlwind and borne away from the eyes of the princess. She saw too late that she had spoken an evil speech. She shed bitter tears, went home, lived alone and lonely.

The poor soldier was borne by the whirlwind far, far away beyond the thrice-ninth land, to the thirtieth kingdom, and thrown on a point between two seas; he fell on the very narrowest little wedge. If the sleeping man were to turn to the right, or roll to the left, that moment he would tumble into the sea, and then remember his name.

The good hero slept out his half year, — moved not a finger; and when he woke he sprang straight to his feet, looked on both sides. The waves are rolling; no end can be seen to the broad sea. He stands in doubt, asking himself, "By what miracle have I come to this place? Who dragged me hither?" He turned back from the point and came out on an island; on that island was a mountain steep and lofty, touching the clouds with its peak, and on the mountain a great stone. He came near this mountain and saw three devils fighting; blood was just flowing from them, and bits of flesh flying.

" Stop, ye outcasts! What are ye fighting for?"

" But seest thou our father died three days ago and left three wonderful things, — a flying carpet, swift-moving boots, and a cap of invisibility; and we cannot divide them."

" Oh, ye cursed fellows, to fight for such trifles! If ye wish I 'll divide them between you, and ye shall be satisfied; I 'll offend no one."

" Well then, countryman, divide between us if it please thee."

" Very good. Run quickly through the pine woods and gather one hundred poods of pitch, and bring it here."

The devils rushed through the pine woods, collected three hundred poods of pitch, and brought it to the soldier.

" Now bring me from your own kingdom the very largest kettle that is in it." The devils brought the very largest kettle, — one holding forty barrels, — and put the pitch into it. The soldier made a fire, and when the pitch was boiling he ordered the devils to take it on the mountain and pour it out from the top to the bottom. The devils did this in a flash. " Now," said the soldier, " push that stone there; let it roll from the mountain, and follow it. Whoever comes up with it first may take any of the three things; whoever comes up second will choose from the two remaining ones whichever he likes; and the last wonder will go to the third." The devils pushed the stone, and it rolled from the mountain quickly, quickly. One devil caught up, seized the stone, the stone turned, and in a flash put him under it, crushed him into the pitch. The second devil caught up, and then the third; and with them it happened as with the first, — they were driven firmly into the pitch.

The soldier took under his arm the swift boots and the cap of invisibility, sat on the flying carpet, and flew off to look for his own country. Whether it was long or short, he came to a hut, went in. In the hut was sitting a Baba-Yaga, bone-leg, old and toothless. "Greetings to thee, grandmother! Tell how I am to find my fair princess."

" I have not seen her with sight, I have not heard of her with hearing; but pass over so many seas and so many lands, and there lives my second sister. She knows more than I do; mayhap she can tell thee."

The soldier sat on his carpet and flew away. He had to wander long over the white world. Whenever he wanted to eat or drink, he put on the cap of invisibility, let himself down, entered a shop, and took what his heart desired; then to the carpet and off on his journey. He came to the second hut, entered; inside was sitting Baba-Yaga, bone-leg, old and toothless. "Greeting to thee, grandmother! Dost thou know how I can find my fair princess?"

"No, my dove, I do not know."

" Ah, thou old hag! how many years art thou living

in the world? All thy teeth are out, and thou knowest no good."

He sat on the flying carpet and flew toward the eldest sister. Long did he wander, many seas and many lands did he see. At last he flew to the end of the world, where there was a hut and no road beyond, — nothing but outer darkness, nothing to be seen.

" Well," thought he, " if I can get no account here, there is nowhere else to fly to." He went into the hut; there a Baba-Yaga was sitting, gray, toothless.

" Greeting to thee, grandmother! Tell me where must I seek my princess."

" Wait a little; I will call all my winds together and ask them. They blow over all the world, so they must know where she is living at present."

The old woman went out on the porch, cried with a loud voice, whistled with a hero's whistle. Straightway the stormy winds rose and blew from every side; the hut just quivered.

" Quieter, quieter!" cried Baba-Yaga; and as soon as the winds had assembled, she said: " My stormy winds, ye blow through all the world. Have ye seen the beautiful princess anywhere? "

" We have not seen her anywhere," answered the winds in one voice.

" But are ye all here? "

" All but South Wind."

After waiting a little, South Wind flew up. The old

woman asked: "Where hast thou been lost to this moment? I could hardly wait for thee."

"Pardon, grandmother; I went into a new kingdom, where the beautiful princess is living. Her husband has vanished without tidings, so now various Tsars and Tsars' sons, kings and kings' sons are paying court to her."

"And how far is it to the new kingdom?"

"For a man on foot thirty-five years, ten years on wings; but if I blow I can put a man there in three hours."

The soldier implored South Wind tearfully to take him and bear him to the new kingdom.

"I will, if it please thee," said South Wind, "provided thou wilt let me run around in thy kingdom three days and three nights as I like."

"Frolic three weeks if thou choosest."

"Well, I will rest for two or three days, collect my forces and my strength, and then for the road!"

South Wind rested, collected his strength, and said to the soldier: "Well, brother, make ready, we'll go straightway; but look out, have no fear, thou wilt arrive in safety."

All at once a mighty whirlwind whistled and roared, caught the soldier into the air, and bore him over mountains and seas up to the very clouds; and in three hours exactly he was in the new kingdom, where his beautiful princess was living. South Wind said, —

" Farewell, good hero; out of compassion for thee I will not frolic in thy kingdom."

" Why is that? "

" Because if I frolic, not one house will be standing in the town, not one tree in the gardens; I should put everything bottom upward."

" Farewell then; God save thee ! " said the soldier, who put on his cap of invisibility and went to the white-walled castle. Behold, while he was absent from the kingdom all the trees in the garden had stood with withered tops, and the moment he appeared they came to life and began to bloom. He entered the great hall; there were sitting at the table various Tsars and Tsars' sons, kings and kings' sons who had come to pay court to the beautiful princess. They were sitting and entertaining themselves with sweet wines. Whoever filled a glass and raised it to his lips, the soldier that moment struck it with his fist and knocked it from his hand. All the guests wondered at this; but the beautiful princess understood in a moment the reason.

" Surely," thought she, " my friend is here." She looked through the window; all the tree-tops in the garden had come to life, and she gave a riddle to the guests. " I had a home-made casket with a golden key; I lost this key, and did not think to find it: but now this key has found itself. Who guesses the riddle, him will I marry."

The Tsars and Tsars' sons, the kings and kings'

sons were long breaking their wise heads over this riddle, and could not solve it in any way.

The princess said: " Show thyself, dear friend."

The soldier removed his cap of invisibility, took her by the white hand, and began to kiss her on the sweet mouth.

" Here is the riddle for you," said the fair princess: " I am the home-made casket, and the golden key is my faithful husband."

The wooers had to turn their wagon-shafts around. They all drove home, and the princess began to live with her husband, to live and win wealth.

VASSILISSA THE CUNNING AND THE TSAR OF THE SEA.

A PEASANT sowed rye, and the Lord gave him a wonderful harvest. He could barely bring it in from the field. He drew the bundles home, threshed the grain, and poured it into bins; his granary was full to the brim. When he was pouring it in, he thought, " Now I shall live without trouble."

A mouse and a sparrow used to visit that peasant's barn; every one of God's days they came about five times, ate all they could, and then went out. The mouse would spring into her hole, and the sparrow fly away to his nest. They lived together in this way in friendship for three whole years, ate up all the grain; there remained only a mere trifle, about eight bushels, not more.

The mouse saw that the supply was drawing to an end, and began to contrive how to deceive the sparrow and get possession of all that was left. And the mouse succeeded. She came in the dark night-time, gnawed a great hole in a plank, and let all the rye down through the floor to the last grain. Next morning the sparrow came to the granary to have breakfast; looked, there was nothing! The poor fellow flew out hungry, and thought to himself, " Oh, the cursed creature, she has deceived me! I will fly now to her sovereign, the lion, and present a petition against the mouse; let the lion pass judgment on us in justice."

So he started and flew to the lion. " Lion, Tsar of beasts," said the sparrow, beating to him with the forehead, " I lived with one of thy beasts, the strong-toothed mouse. We lived for three years in one barn and had no dispute. But when the supply began to come to an end, she went to playing tricks, gnawed a hole through the floor, and let all the grain down to herself, — left me, poor fellow, to be hungry. Judge us in truth; if not, I will fly to seek justice and reparation from my own Tsar, the eagle."

" Well, fly off, with God!" said the lion.

The sparrow rushed with his petition to the eagle, related the whole offence, how the mouse had stolen and the lion had upheld her. The eagle grew fiercely angry, and sent a swift courier to the lion straightway: " Come to-morrow with thy army of beasts to such and such a field; I will assemble all the birds and give battle."

Nothing to be done, the lion made a great call and summoned the beasts to battle. There were assembled of them seen and unseen. As soon as they came to the open field, the eagle flew upon them with his winged warriors like a cloud from heaven. A great battle began. They fought for three hours and three minutes, and the eagle Tsar conquered; he covered the whole field with bodies of beasts. Then he sent his birds to their homes, and flew himself to a slumbering forest, sat on a lofty oak, bruised and wounded, and began to think seriously how to regain his former strength.

This was a long time ago. There lived then a merchant with his wife, and they had not a single child. The merchant rose up one morning and said to his wife: "I have had a bad dream. I thought that a great bird fastened on me, — one that eats a whole ox at a meal and drinks a pailful; and it was impossible to get rid of the bird, impossible not to feed it. I'll go to the forest; mayhap the walk will cheer me."

He took his gun and went to the forest. Whether he wandered long or short in that forest, he wandered till he came to an oak-tree, saw an eagle, and was going to shoot it.

"Kill me not, good hero," said the eagle, in a human voice. "If thou kill me, small will be thy profit. Better take me home, feed me for three years, three months, and three days. I shall recover at thy house, shall let my wings grow, regain my strength, and repay thee with good."

"What pay can one expect from an eagle?" thought the merchant, and aimed a second time. The eagle spoke as at first. The merchant aimed a third time, and again the eagle begged, —

"Kill me not, good hero! Feed me three years, three months, and three days; when I have recovered, when my wings have grown, and I have regained my strength, I'll repay thee with good."

The merchant took pity on the eagle, carried him home, killed an ox, and poured out a pailful of mead. "This will serve the eagle for a long time," thought he; but the eagle ate and drank all at one meal. A bad time to the merchant; from the unbidden guest utter ruin.

The eagle saw the merchant's loss and said: "Hear me, my host! Go to the open field. Thou wilt find there many beasts killed and wounded. Take their rich furs, bear them to the town to sell. Get food for thyself and me, and there will be some left for a supply."

The merchant went into the open field and saw many animals lying there, some slain and some wounded. He took the dearest furs, carried them to town to sell, and sold them for much money.

A year passed. The eagle said: "Bear me to that place where the lofty oaks are standing."

The merchant got his wagon ready and took him to that place. The eagle rose above the clouds, and when he swooped down, he struck a tree with his breast, the oak was split in two. "Well, merchant, good hero," said the eagle, "I have not regained my former strength; feed me another round year."

Another year passed. Again the eagle rose be-

yond the dark clouds, shot down from above, struck
the tree with his breast, split the oak into small
pieces. "Merchant, good hero, thou must feed me
another whole year; I have not regained my former
strength!"

When three years, three months, and three days
had passed, the eagle said to the merchant: "Take
me again to the same place, — to the lofty oaks."
The merchant carried him to the lofty oaks. The
eagle soared higher than before; like a mighty whirl
wind he struck from above the largest oak, broke it
into small bits from the top to the root, — indeed, the
forest was reeling all around. "God save thee, merchant, good hero!" said the eagle; "now all my
former strength is with me. Leave thy horse, sit on
my wings; I will bear thee to my own land, and pay
thee for all the good thou hast done." The merchant
sat on his wings, the eagle bore him out on the blue
sea, and he rose high, high. "Look now," said he,
"on the blue sea. Is it wide?"

"As a cart-wheel," answered the merchant.

The eagle shook his wings and threw the merchant, let him fall, gave him to feel mortal terror,
and caught him before he had reached the water, —
caught him, and rose still higher. "Look on the
blue sea. Is it great?"

"As a hen's egg."

The eagle shook his wings, threw the merchant,
let him fall, but did not let him reach the water,

caught him, and rose up higher than ever. " Look on the blue sea. Is it great?"

"As a poppy seed."

A third time the eagle shook his wings and threw the merchant from under the heavens; still he did n't let him reach the water, caught him, and asked: " Well, merchant, good hero, hast thou felt what mortal terror is?"

" I have," said the merchant; "and I thought I was lost forever."

" And so did I when thou wert pointing thy gun at me."

The eagle flew with the merchant beyond the sea, straight to the copper kingdom. " Behold, my eldest sister lives here!" said the eagle. " When we shall be guests with her, and she brings presents, take nothing, but ask for the copper casket." The eagle said this, struck the damp earth, turned into a gallant hero.

They went through the broad court. The sister saw him, and was delighted. " Oh, my own brother, how has God brought thee? I have not seen thee for three years and more; I thought thou wert lost forever. How can I entertain thee? How can I feast thee?"

" Entertain not me, my dear sister, I am at home in thy house; but entreat and entertain this good hero. He gave me meat and drink for three years, — did not let me die of hunger."

She seated them at the oaken table, at the spread cloth; she feasted and entertained them, then led them to her treasure-chambers, showed treasures incalculable, and said to the merchant: " Good hero, here are gold, silver, and precious stones; take what thy soul desires."

The merchant gave answer: " I need neither gold, silver, nor precious stones. Give me the copper casket."

" Thou 'lt not get it; that is not the boot for thy foot."

The brother was angry at his sister's words; he turned into an eagle, — a swift bird, — caught the merchant, and flew away.

" Oh, my own brother, come back!" cried the sister. " I 'll not stand for the casket."

" Thou art late, sister!"

The eagle flew through the air. " Look, merchant, good hero, what is behind us and what before?"

" Behind, a fire is in sight; before us flowers are blooming."

" That is the copper kingdom in flames, and the flowers are blooming in the silver kingdom of my second sister. When we are her guests, and she offers gifts, take nothing, but ask for the silver casket." The eagle came, struck the damp earth, and become a good hero.

" Oh, my own brother," said his sister, " whence hast come; where wert thou lost; why hast thou been so long without visiting me; with what can I serve thee?"

"Entreat me not, entertain me not, my dear sister, I am at home with thee; but entreat and entertain this good hero, who gave me meat and drink for three years, and did not let me die of hunger."

She seated them at the oaken tables at spread cloths, entertained and feasted them, then led them to treasure-chambers. "Here are gold and silver and precious stones; take, merchant, what thy soul desires."

"I want neither gold, silver, nor precious stones. Give me only the silver casket."

"No, good hero, thy desire is not for the right morsel; thou mightest choke thyself."

The eagle brother was angry, caught up the merchant, and flew away.

"Oh, my own brother, come back! I will not stand for the casket."

"Thou art late, sister!"

Again the eagle flew under the heavens. "See, merchant, good hero, what is behind us, what is before?"

"Behind us a fire is blazing; before us are flowers in bloom."

"That is the silver kingdom in flames; but the flowers are blooming in the golden kingdom of my youngest sister. When we are her guests, and she offers gifts, take nothing; ask only the golden casket."

The eagle came to the golden kingdom and turned into a good hero.

"Oh, my own brother," said the sister, "whence hast thou come? Where hast thou vanished so long that thou hast not visited me? With what shall I feast thee?"

"Entreat me not, feast me not, I am at home; but entreat and feast this merchant, good hero. He gave me meat and drink for three years, — saved me from hunger."

She seated them at the oaken table, at the spread cloth, entertained them, feasted them, led the merchant to her treasure-chambers, offered him gold, silver, and precious stones.

"I need nothing; give me only the golden casket."

"Take it for thy happiness. Thou didst give meat and drink to my brother for three years, and didst save him from hunger; I regret nothing that is spent on my brother."

So the merchant lived and feasted a while in the golden kingdom, till the time came for parting, for taking the road.

"Farewell," said the eagle; "think not on me with harsh feeling, but see that the casket is not opened till thou art at home."

The merchant journeyed homeward. Whether it was long or short, he grew tired and wished to rest. He stopped in a strange meadow on the land of the Tsar of the Sea; he looked and looked at the golden casket, could n't endure, opened it. That moment, wherever it came from, there stood before him a great castle all painted, a multitude of servants appeared, inquiring: "What dost thou wish for; what dost thou want?" The merchant, good hero, ate his fill, drank enough, and lay down to sleep. The Tsar of the Sea saw that there was a great castle on his land, and he sent messengers: "Go see what sort of an insolent fellow has come and built a castle on my land without leave; let him go off at once in health and safety."

When such a threatening word came to the merchant he began to think and conjecture how to put the castle into the casket as before; he thought and thought,—no, he could do nothing. "I should be glad to go away," said he, "but how, I can't think myself."

The messengers returned, and reported all to the Tsar of the Sea. "Let him give me what he has at home but knows it not; I will put his palace in the golden casket."

There was no other way, and so the merchant promised with an oath to give what he had at home but knew it not. The Tsar of the Sea put the palace in the golden casket at once. The merchant took the casket and went his way. Whether it was long or short, he came home, his wife met him. "Oh, be thou hearty, my world. Where wert thou lost?"

"Well, where I was I am not now."

"But while thou wert gone the Lord gave us a son."

" Ah! that is what was at home and I knew it not,"
thought the merchant; and he grew very sad and
sorrowful.

" What is the matter? Art thou not glad to be
here?" insisted his wife.

" Not that," said the merchant; and he told her all
that had happened to him, and they grieved and wept
together. But people of course cannot cry all their
lives. The merchant opened his golden casket, and
before them stood a great castle cunningly adorned,
and he began to live with his wife and son and gain
wealth.

Ten years passed and more; the merchant's son
grew up, became wise, fine-looking, a splendid fellow.
One morning he rose up in sadness and said to his
father: " My father, I had a bad dream last night.
I dreamed of the Tsar of the Sea; he commanded
me to come to him. ' I am waiting long,' said he;
' it is time to know thy honor.' "

The father and mother shed tears, gave him their
parental blessing, and let him go to a strange land.
He went along the road, along the broad road; he
walked over clear fields and wide steppes, and came
to a dreamy forest. It was empty all around, not a
soul to be seen; but there stood a small cabin by
itself, with front to the forest and back to Ivan.
" Cabin, cabin," said he, " turn thy back to the forest,
thy front to me." The cabin obeyed, and turned its
back to the forest, its front to Ivan. He entered the

cabin, inside was Baba-Yaga, bone-leg, lying from corner to corner. Baba-Yaga saw him and said: "Before now, nothing of Russia was heard with hearing or seen with sight, but now Russia runs to our eyes. Whence dost thou come, good hero, and where dost thou bear thy way?"

"Oh, thou old hag, thou hast given neither meat nor drink to a wayfaring man, and art asking for news!"

Baba-Yaga put drink on the table and various meats; she fed him, she gave him to drink, and put him to rest. Early next morning she roused him, and then she put questions. Ivan the merchant's son told the whole secret, and said: "Teach me, grandmother, how to go to the Tsar of the Sea."

"It is well that thou hast come to me; hadst thou not, thou wouldst have lost thy life, for the Tsar of the Sea is terribly angry because thou didst not go to him long ago. Listen to me: go by this path; thou wilt come to a lake, hide behind a tree and wait a while. Three beautiful doves, maidens, will fly there, — they are the daughters of the Tsar of the Sea; they will loose their wings, undress, and bathe in the lake. One will have many-colored wings: watch the moment, seize the wings, and do not give them up till she consents to marry thee; then all will be right."

Ivan the merchant's son took farewell of Baba-Yaga and travelled the path she had shown, walked and walked, saw the lake, hid himself behind a thick tree. After a time three doves came flying, one with many-colored wings; they struck the earth, turned into beautiful maidens, removed their wings, and took off their dresses. Ivan the merchant's son kept his eyes open; he crept up in silence and took the many-colored wings. He watched to see what would happen. The fair maidens bathed, came out of the water, two of them dressed straightway, put on their wings, turned into doves, and flew away. The third remained to find her wings. She searched, singing the while: "Tell who thou art, thou who hast taken my wings! If an old man, thou wilt be a father to me; if of middle years, my uncle dear; if a good youth, I will marry thee."

Ivan the merchant's son came from behind the tree. "Here are thy wings!"

"Now tell me, good youth, betrothed husband, of what stock or race art thou, and whither dost thou bear thy way?"

"I am Ivan the merchant's son, and I am going to thy own father, to the Tsar of the Sea."

"And my name is Vassilissa the Cunning."

Now, Vassilissa was the favorite daughter of the Tsar, and was first in mind and beauty. She showed her bridegroom how to go to the Tsar of the Sea, sprang away as a dove, and flew after her sisters.

Ivan the merchant's son came to the Tsar of the Sea, who made him serve in the kitchen, cut wood, and draw water. Chumichka, the cook, did not like him, and told lies to the Tsar. " Your Majesty," said he, " Ivan the merchant's son boasts that in one night he can cut down a great dense forest, pile the logs in heaps, dig out the roots, plough the land, sow it with wheat, reap that wheat, thresh it, grind it into flour, make cakes of the flour, and give these cakes to your Majesty at breakfast next morning."

" Well," said the Tsar, "call him to me."

Ivan the merchant's son came.

" Why art thou boasting that in one night thou canst cut down a thick forest, plough the land just like a clean field, sow it with wheat, reap the wheat, thresh it, and make it into flour, the flour into cakes for my breakfast next morning? See that by to-morrow morning this is all done; if not, I have a sword, and thy head leaves thy shoulders."

No matter how Ivan protested, it was no use; the order was given, it had to be carried out. He went away from the Tsar, and hung his stormy head from grief. Vassilissa the Cunning, the daughter of the Tsar, saw him, and asked: " Why art thou grieved? "

" What is the use in telling thee? Thou couldst not cure my sorrow! "

" How knowest? Maybe I can."

Ivan the merchant's son told her what task the Tsar had put on him.

" What task is that! That is a pleasure, — the task is ahead. Go thy way; pray to God and lie down to rest; the morning is wiser than the evening; toward daylight all will be ready."

Just at midnight Vassilissa the Cunning went out on the great porch and cried in a piercing voice. In one moment laborers ran together from every side, — myriads of them; one was felling a tree, another digging out roots, another ploughing the land. In one place they were sowing, in another reaping and threshing; a pillar of dust went up to the sky, and at daybreak the grain was ground, the cakes baked. Ivan took the cakes to the breakfast of the Tsar.

"Spendid fellow!" said the Tsar; and he gave command to reward him from his own treasure.

Chumichka the cook was angrier than ever at Ivan, began to talk against him again. "Your Majesty, Ivan the merchant's son boasts that in one night he can make a ship that will fly through the air."

"Well, call him hither."

They called Ivan the merchant's son.

"Why boast to my servants that in one night thou canst make a wonderful ship that will fly through the air, and say nothing to me? See this ship is ready by morning; if not, I have a sword, and thy head leaves thy shoulders."

Ivan the merchant's son from sorrow hung his stormy head lower than his shoulders, and went from the Tsar beside himself. Vassilissa the Cunning said to him: "Of what art thou grieving; why art thou sad?"

"Why should I not be sad? The Tsar of the Sea has commanded me to build in one night a ship that will fly through the air."

"What sort of task is that? That is not a task, but a pleasure; the task is ahead. Go thy way; lie down and rest: the morning is wiser than the evening; at daybreak all will be done."

At midnight Vassilissa the Cunning went out on the great porch, cried in a piercing voice. In a moment carpenters ran together from every side; they began to pound with their axes, and the work was seething quickly. Toward morning all was ready.

"A hero!" said the Tsar. "Come, now we will take a trip."

They sat on the ship together, and took as a third companion Chumichka the cook; and they flew through the air. When they were flying over the place of wild beasts the cook bent over the side to look out. Ivan the merchant's son pushed him from the ship that moment. The savage beasts tore him into little bits. "Oh," cried Ivan the merchant's son, "Chumichka has fallen off!"

"The devil be with him," said the Tsar of the Sea; "to a dog, a dog's death!" They came back to the palace. "Thou art skilful, Ivan," said the Tsar; "here is a third task for thee. Break my unridden stallion so that he will go under a rider. If thou wilt break him I will give thee my daughter in marriage; if not, I have a sword, and thy head leaves thy shoulders."

"Now that is an easy task," thought Ivan the merchant's son. He went away from the Tsar laughing. Vassilissa the Cunning saw him and asked about everything; he told her.

"Thou art not wise, Ivan," said she; "now a difficult task is given thee,—no easy labor. That stallion will be the Tsar himself: he will carry thee through the air above the standing forest, below the passing cloud, and scatter thy bones over the open field. Go quickly to the blacksmiths, order them to make for thee an iron hammer three poods in weight, and when thou art sitting on the stallion hold firmly and beat him on the head with the iron hammer."

Next day the grooms brought out the unridden stallion. They were barely able to hold him; he snorted, rushed, and reared. The moment Ivan sat on him he rose above the standing forest, below the passing cloud, flew through the air more swiftly than strong wind. The rider held firmly, beating him all the time on the head with the hammer. The stallion struggled beyond his power, and dropped to the damp earth. Ivan the merchant's son gave the stallion to the grooms, drew breath himself, and went to the palace. The Tsar of the Sea met him with bound head.

"I have ridden the horse, your Majesty."

" Well, come to-morrow to choose thy bride; but now my head aches."

Next morning Vassilissa the Cunning said to Ivan the merchant's son, "There are three sisters of us with our father; he will turn us into mares, and make thee select. Be careful, take notice; on my bridle one of the spangles will be dim. Then he will let us out as doves; my sisters will pick buckwheat very quietly, but I will not, — I will clap my wings. The third time he will bring us out as three maidens, one like the other in face, in stature, and hair. I will shake my handkerchief; by that thou mayest know me."

The Tsar brought out the three mares, one just like the other, put them in a row. " Take the one that pleases thee," said the Tsar.

Ivan the merchant's son examined them carefully. He saw that on one bridle a spangle had grown dim; he caught that bridle and said, " This is my bride."

" Thou hast taken a bad one; thou mayest choose a better."

" No use, this will do for me."

" Choose a second time."

The Tsar let out three doves just alike, and scattered buckwheat before them. Ivan saw that one of them was shaking her wings all the time. He caught her by the wing and said, " This is my bride."

" Thou hast not taken the right piece; thou wilt choke thyself. Choose a third time."

He brought out three maidens, one like the other in face, in stature, and hair. Ivan the merchant's son saw that one waved her handkerchief; he seized her by the hand, "This is my bride."

There was nothing to be done. The Tsar could not help himself, gave Vassilissa the Cunning to Ivan, and they had a joyous wedding.

Not much nor little time had passed when Ivan thought of escaping to his own country with Vassilissa the Cunning. They saddled their horses and rode away in the dark night. In the morning the Tsar discovered their flight and sent a pursuing party.

"Drop down to the damp earth," said Vassilissa the Cunning to her husband; "perhaps thou wilt hear something."

He dropped to the earth, listened, and answered: "I hear the neighing of horses."

Vassilissa turned him into a garden, and herself into a head of cabbage. The pursuers returned to the Tsar empty-handed. "Your Majesty, there is nothing to be seen in the open country; we saw only a garden, and in the garden a head of cabbage."

"Go on, bring me that head of cabbage; that is their tricks."

Again the pursuers galloped on; again Ivan dropped down to the damp earth. "I hear," said he, "the neighing of horses." Vassilissa the Cunning made herself a well, and turned Ivan into a bright falcon; the falcon was sitting on the brink, drinking water. The pursuers came to the well; there was no road beyond, and they turned back.

" Your Majesty, there is nothing to be seen in the open country; we saw only a well, and a bright falcon was drinking water out of that well."

The Tsar himself galloped a long time to overtake them.

" Drop down to the damp earth; perhaps thou wilt hear something," said Vassilissa the Cunning to her husband.

" There is a hammering and thundering greater than before."

" That is my father chasing us. I know not, I cannot think what to do."

Vassilissa the Cunning had three things, — a brush, a comb, and a towel. She remembered them, and said: " God is yet merciful; I have still defence before the Tsar." She threw the brush behind her: it became a great drowsy forest; a man could not put his hand through, could not ride around it in three years. Behold, the Tsar of the Sea gnawed and gnawed the drowsy forest, made a path for himself, burst through it, and was again in pursuit. He is drawing near them, has only to seize them with his hand. Vassilissa threw her comb behind, and it became such a great lofty mountain that a man could neither pass over it nor go around it.

The Tsar of the Sea dug and dug in the mountain, made a path, and again chased after them. Then

Vassilissa the Cunning threw the towel behind her, and it became a great, great sea. The Tsar galloped up to the sea, saw the road was stopped, and turned homeward.

Ivan the merchant's son was near home, and said to Vassilissa the Cunning: "I will go ahead, tell my father and mother about thee, and do thou wait here."

"See to it," said Vassilissa the Cunning, "when thou art home, kiss all but thy godmother; if thou kiss her thou 'lt forget me."

Ivan came home, kissed all in delight, kissed his godmother, and forgot Vassilissa. She stood there, poor thing, on the road, waited and waited; Ivan did not come for her. She went to the town and hired to do work for an old woman.

Ivan thought of marrying; he found a bride, and arranged a feast for the whole world (*mir*[1]).

Vassilissa heard this, dressed herself as a beggar, and came to the merchant's house to beg alms.

"Wait," said the merchant's wife; "I 'll bake thee a small cake instead of cutting the big one."

"God save thee for that, mother!" said Vassilissa.

But the great cake got burnt, and the small one came out nicely. The merchant's wife gave Vassilissa the burnt cake and put the small one on the table. They cut that cake, and immediately two pigeons flew out.

[1] *Mir* means in Russian the "world," the "universe;" and also the "commune," or village society.

"Kiss me," said the cock-pigeon to the cther.

"No, thou wilt forget me, as Ivan the merchant's son forgot Vassilissa the Cunning."

And the second and the third time he asked, "Kiss me."

"No, thou 'lt forget me, as Ivan the merchant's son forgot Vassilissa the Cunning."

Ivan remembered then; he knew who the beggar was, and said to his father and mother: "This is my wife."

"Well, if thou hast a wife, then live with her."

They gave rich presents to the new bride, and let her go home; but Ivan the merchant's son lived with Vassilissa the Cunning, gained wealth, and shunned trouble.

CHEKH MYTHS AND FOLK-TALES.

BOYISLAV, YOUNGEST OF TWELVE.

ONCE there was a king who groaned many a day; doctors came from far and near, but they could not cure him. At last his condition was such that one day all thought he must die. The following night he had a marvellous dream. It seemed to him that he was on Black Island, had freed three princesses, and straightway recovered. When he woke he felt a certain relief, but had almost forgotten the dream. The next night he had the same dream, and again on waking felt easier, but did not ascribe the relief to his dream. The third night he had no dream, but a vision, in which the three princesses appeared to him and said: " Free us, and thou wilt recover; if not, thou wilt die." Then they vanished, and the terrified king felt such pain that he could barely wait till morning. He summoned his twelve sons in haste, and when he had told them of his vision he said in a sad voice: " But how can I, poor man, go on a long journey to Black Island, of which I have never even heard? "

" I will go instead of thee," said Boyislav, the youngest son, with decision.

" We will all go," said the others, looking angrily at Boyislav, whom they hated with all their hearts, because he was his father's favorite.

" Ye cannot all leave me ; and thou, Boyislav, surely not," said the king, shaking his head. " Who would there be to reign in my place?"

" Let Boyislav stay at home," said the eldest; " besides, he would be merely a hindrance to us on the road."

" I a hindrance!" said Boyislav, flushing up with anger and pity. " Let me go, father; I will free the princesses alone."

His brothers began to laugh at him and then to dispute as to who should go to Black Island. Since they could not decide, the king said: "I know that ye would all gladly serve me, but since some of you must stay at home, I will make six blank lots and six written ones; whoever draws a written one will go, whoever a blank will remain."

The princes were satisfied and drew lots. They were angry when Boyislav drew a prize, and the king was sad; but he had given his word and could not withdraw it. That very day the princes set out and Boyislav with them. While on dry land they were prosperous; it was worse when they entered a boat and knew not whither to turn. Boyislav said that they ought to go north, but his brothers laughed at him. When they had sailed many weeks in one direction and another without finding Black Island, they were glad to follow his advice; and the third day they arrived at the place, but so terrible was it that no one dared to land save Boyislav. He took provisions and sprang on shore, telling his brothers to await his return. While light lasted he ran up and down on the island, but saw nothing except black rocks. He was forced to pass the night on a bare stone, but rose early, completely refreshed by sleep, and examined farther.

One day passed, and a second; the third day appeared, and still he found nothing. At last, in the evening, he came to a large stone, which seemed to him hewn out by men's hands. He lifted with all his might, turned it over, and found a great dark opening, from which a pleasant odor arose. He went down without delay, and soon found himself in a glorious garden, in which were three golden castles at a great distance. He gazed with astonishment; though there were things there without number such as he had never seen before, still his attention was attracted first by three horses, which rushed around him three times in a wild gallop, and then vanished in the twinkle of an eye. Boyislav looked after them, and heard a voice saying: " I welcome thee, Boyislav, youngest of twelve! "

He looked on every side, but could see no one. The voice cried out the second time: " I welcome thee, Boyislav, youngest of twelve! "

Now he knew where the voice came from; but though he went in that direction and examined everything very carefully, he could see no one. Only after the voice had called much louder than the first and second time, " I welcome thee, Boyislav, youngest of twelve ! " did he see behind a rock a famished little horse, so poor that he could count all its ribs.

" What dost thou want of me ? " asked Boyislav, not a little astonished that the horse knew him.

" 'T is thy wish to free the three princesses," answered the horse ; " then listen to what I advise : In the first castle thou wilt find the first princess, who will greet thee with kindness beyond measure, and offer thee food and drink. Eat with relish, but let not the princess eat with thee or kiss thee. Take what is left of the food when thou hast eaten, and go to the second castle ; there the second princess will greet thee with still greater kindness, and offer food and drink. Eat with relish, but for no reason let her eat with thee or kiss thee. Take what is left after eating, and go to the third castle, where the third princess will give thee the most kindly reception of all, and place food and drink before thee ; eat freely, but let not the princess eat with thee or kiss thee. Take what is left, and come here to me."

" Is nothing more needed to gain their freedom ? " asked Boyislav.

" Nothing," answered the horse ; " but thou must not speak a word all this time."

" That is very easy," thought Boyislav.

But the horse said with great emphasis : " Have a care ; for to thee 't is a question of life or death."

Boyislav went with quick step to the first castle,

where a princess of wonderful beauty ran forth toward him. " I welcome thee, Boyislav, youngest of twelve ! " cried she, with glad voice. " How art thou here? Come to my chamber ; let me give thee good cheer. What is thy father doing? How are thy brothers? "

Then she took his hand and seated him at the table, to which she brought the most savory food and drink, continually speaking of his home. But he gave no regard ; and when she wished to eat with him, he thrust her aside without mercy. Then he seized what was left of the food and hurried away. The princess gave him the sweetest of names, and stretched her hands toward him, but he acted as if he neither saw her nor heard her.

At the second castle a still more beautiful princess ran toward him, greeted him with still greater gladness, led him into a chamber, seated him at a table, and brought the most savory food and drink, talking continually. She moved toward him, wishing to kiss him ; but he thrust her aside very rudely, so that she fell to the floor. Before she could rise he had taken what was left of the food, and was gone.

He had barely reached the third castle when a princess ran out to meet him. She was far more beautiful than the other two, and wished to fall on his neck straightway. He was amazed at her beauty ; but keeping in mind the words of the horse, he thrust her away. But still she led him into the castle, seated him at a table in the loftiest chamber, and entertained him with the best food and drink. Boyislav ate and drank heartily, but when the princess wished to eat, he pushed her aside so rudely that, after staggering a few steps, she fell to the floor. Then, quickly gathering the remnants of food, he ran off, though the princess called him with heart-rending voice.

When he came to the horse he spread on the rock the remnants of food, which the horse devoured eagerly. "What now?" asked Boyislav.

"Go for the three princesses, and bring them to thy brothers in the boat; they are free, for they are the horses which thou hast seen running around thee. A wicked sorceress enchanted them, so that twelve hours they were horses and twelve hours princesses. Then come for me, or thou wilt suffer."

Boyislav did as the horse desired, and brought to his brothers the three princesses, who, with tearful eyes, thanked him for their liberation. Then he returned to the horse, which said, with sad voice: "Too bad! too bad!"

"What has happened?" asked Boyislav.

"Thou art unfortunate," answered the horse; "thy departure from home was unfortunate, for know that thy brothers have gone."

"Then I must perish here!" cried Boyislav.

"Now thou wilt not perish; but hadst thou gone on the boat thy death would be sure, for thy brothers had conspired to kill thee."

" Oh, the thankless wretches ! " cried Boyislav. " What shall I do now ? "

" If thou wilt obey me," said the horse, " thou wilt gain thy object in time. Go now to the garden of the first castle, and pluck four golden apples, but only four."

Boyislav went, and for the first time noticed the beauty of the whole garden; he went back and forth, and would have soon forgotten the apples had he not heard the neighing of the horse. Now he saw the tree with golden apples, and plucked four. Since they were so beautiful, he wanted more, but the horse neighed so fiercely that the whole castle trembled; his arm, which was stretched to the apples, dropped of itself, and he returned to the horse, which said, " Now sit on me."

Boyislav did so, and the horse bore him soon to the shore of the sea, and said, " Throw an apple in the sea."

" But it is a pity to lose it ! " said Boyislav.

" Throw it in ! " repeated the horse, with stern voice ; and Boyislav obeyed. That moment a road five hundred miles long rose out of the sea. The horse stepped on the road, and hurried along night and day. When the domes of a great city were seen in the distance, he said to Boyislav : " Now we are going to Red Island, to a king who has a very ugly daughter ; but have no fear in the world of her. When she casts eyes on thee, say that thou art seeking a bride, but before choosing thou must consult thy father. Then the king will offer thee a present; take nothing but a piece of rope for my bridle."

Boyislav promised obedience. When they came to Red Island, the road sank in the sea, and the horse hurried on. Boyislav left him on the meadow outside the city, and went straight to the king's castle, where he was courteously received. "Where art thou going, noble prince?" asked the king.

"In search of a bride," answered Boyislav; and the king led him to his daughter. She was so ugly that Boyislav was frightened.

"Does she not please thee?" asked the king.

"Oh, she pleases me," said Boyislav, — "pleases me greatly; but first I must talk with my father." The king smiled, and led his guest to the supper-chamber, where he was entertained in king's fashion. Boyislav wished to go very soon, but the king took him first to his treasury, and offered him much gold and silver.

"Thanks to thy Grace!" answered Boyislav. "My father has great treasures also; but if thou wilt make me some present, give me a piece of rope to repair my horse's bridle."

"Oh, I will give thee a splendid bridle and saddle!" said the king.

But Boyislav answered: "I wish no rich outfit on the road; it is an enticement to robbers."

The king tried to persuade him, but could not; then he had a rope brought which was very slender, but very long, so that Boyislav was hardly able to bear it away. After a kindly farewell to the king and the princess, he hastened outside the town, where the horse called from a distance: " Thou hast done well; now wind that rope round my body."

Boyislav opened the bundle, and a whole hour passed before he could wind the rope around the horse. When he had finished, they hurried to the sea, where the horse said, " Throw a second apple in the sea."

" But it would be an eternal pity! " said Boyislav.

" I tell thee to throw the second apple in the sea! " repeated the horse, with stern voice. Boyislav obeyed. That moment five hundred miles of road rose from the waves of the sea, along which the horse rushed like the wind, night and day. When the domes of a great city were visible in the distance, he said to Boyislav: " Now we are coming to Green Island, ruled by a king who has a daughter, not beautiful and not ugly; thou wilt say that thou art looking for a bride, but before choosing thou must consult thy father. When thou art taking leave, the king will offer all kinds of jewels as a gift; accept nothing, but ask for the cloth of the table from which thou hast eaten."

Boyislav promised this. When they had come to Green Island, the road sank in the sea, and the horse hurried toward the city. The horse remained in a meadow outside the gates. Boyislav went to the palace, where he was welcomed by the king, and presented to the princess.

"What brought thee to me?" asked the king.

"I am in search of a bride," answered Boyislav, looking at the princess, who seemed pleased at his words.

"And hast thou found one?" asked the king.

"Not yet," replied Boyislav.

"Does my daughter not please thee?" The princess blushed.

"Oh, she pleases me greatly," said Boyislav, "but first I must talk with my father."

The king frowned at these words, and the princess was flushed with anger; but Boyislav changed not, and was so courteous that the king grew ashamed, and conducted him to the supper-chamber, where there was a small table covered with a poor-looking cloth, but upon which stood the choicest food and drink. Boyislav ate with relish. When he had finished, the king took him to his treasure-chamber, where he offered him the richest presents; but Boyislav said: "My father has many treasures, and I prefer to travel unburdened." When the king insisted on his taking something as a keepsake, even if of the smallest value, Boyislav said: "Give me the cloth of the table on which I was entertained by thee."

"Oh, I should be ashamed to give such a thing,"

said the king. " I will give thee another very skil-
fully woven."

" I want no other," answered Boyislav, making
ready to go.

" Then take it," said the king, giving the cloth with
evident reluctance.

Boyislav parted with him and the princess, and
hastened to the horse, which called out from afar:
" Thou hast done well; now sit on my back, we'll
fare farther." Boyislav sprang on the horse, and he
raced over Green Island till he came to the sea.

" Throw the third apple in the sea," said the horse.

" But 't is a pity forever to lose it," said Boyislav.

" Throw the third apple in the sea, I say," commanded the horse, sternly ; and Boyislav obeyed.

That moment a road five hundred miles long rose
from the waves of the sea. The horse ran like a flash,
day and night, till they saw in the distance the domes
of a great city.

" Now we are nearing White Island," said the horse,
" where a king reigns who has the most beautiful
daughter under the sun. All the people on the island
are asleep; for in the king's palace a taper is burning
which never burns out, and till some one quenches it
they must all sleep. Go to the palace, look at the
princess as much as may please thee, then take the
taper, but be careful that it does not go out on a sudden; if it is quenched, run to me with all speed or
thou wilt have trouble."

Boyislav promised to obey faithfully. When they came to White Island the road sank in the sea. Boyislav, leaving his horse before the gates of the city, hastened to the palace. The most luxuriant trees were growing all over the island, and beautiful flowers were in bloom; the city was splendid, the palace of silver and gold, but nowhere was a living creature to be seen. Boyislav moved on carefully through the empty streets as if afraid of waking some person. When he entered the palace he was amazed at its matchless beauty, but all was as nothing in comparison with the beauty of the princess who was sleeping on a dark purple couch in the last chamber. She was clothed in a light garment, white as new-fallen snow, her dark hair fell on her white, slightly moving bosom, her lips were half open, her teeth shone like pearls, and her whole figure was so full of charm that Boyislav held his breath. With head inclined, with crossed hands, he looked at her long, — forgot the horse, the taper, and the whole world, not thinking whether he was living; he only felt that the princess was beautiful. When he had waited a long time he remembered the taper, looked around the room, saw it on the table, and saw on two couches the king and queen. He stepped quickly to the table to quench the taper and rouse the princess, when all at once he heard the horse neigh so fiercely that the palace trembled to its foundation; his hand dropped of itself, and he muttered: "Thanks to thee, oh horse!

Had I quenched the taper all would have risen, and who knows what might have come to me?"

He took the taper quickly and turned away, but when passing through the door he could not refrain from looking at the princess again; she seemed still more beautiful. He put the taper on the table, knelt and kissed her hand; with that her face became ruddy as a rose, and around her mouth appeared a smile. He sprang up; and as dark night had come, he thought of his return, seized the taper quickly, looked at the princess, wrote on the table, "Boyislav, youngest of twelve," and went from the palace, taking care that the taper should not be quenched. He reached the gate of the city, but there the taper was blown out by the wind. That moment was heard in the city a shout, which grew louder the longer it lasted; but the trusty steed appeared and bore him in a flash to the shore of the sea.

"Throw in the last apple," said the horse.

Boyislav obeyed without a murmur. That moment there rose from the waves a road which reached to firm land, and as dawn was appearing they came to the shore. Then the road sank in the sea.

"Now come down," said the horse; "let me rest, and do thou rest, too."

The horse went to the green meadow, and Boyislav lay on the grass and mused on the princess of White Island. Since he was wearied greatly, he fell asleep, but thought of the princess so that he sighed from sorrow when the horse roused him and said, "Let us go."

Boyislav mounted in silence. They travelled till they saw the domes of a great city. "What city is this?" inquired Boyislav.

"Seest not," asked the horse, "that is thy birth-place?"

"Sure enough! Go quickly, dear horse, that I may embrace my father."

"Hurry not," said the horse; "for it would be better for thee not to go."

"Why?" asked Boyislav with wonder.

"Because thy father has uttered sentence of death against thee."

"I do not believe that," replied Boyislav, shaking his head; and the horse was silent.

Boyislav's heart beat with joy when he entered the gates of his native place, but his joy was short-lived. He had scarcely passed one street when people began to gather around him, till at last an officer of the king's army seized the bridle of his horse, and ordered the people who were standing around to seize his arms. All rushed like hungry birds of prey on the terrified Boyislav.

"What art thou doing!" cried he, when at length he recovered himself. "Do ye not know that I am your prince?"

"Prince or not," cried all, "we know thee well enough to know that to-morrow thou wilt dance in the air." They took the unfortunate Boyislav to the castle, where, by command of the king, he was cast into a dark dungeon, and his horse, which they all laughed at, was shut up in a pen. The officer who brought Boyislav to the palace got a great reward, and went in high glee to the nearest inn to drink with his comrades.

Why was the king enraged with his favorite son? Because shameless lies had been told by his other sons. When Boyislav brought the three princesses of Black Island to the boat and returned for his horse, his brothers weighed anchor at once and sailed off. On the way they forced the unfortunate princesses to promise on oath to tell the king that they were the liberators, and to say that Boyislav on Black Island had attached himself to a worthless woman, and made sport of his old father.

Meanwhile they agreed to cast lots for the princesses. When the brothers declared their wish, the princesses said that they would not break their oaths, but could never be the wives of such men. The brothers paid small heed to this, for their hearts were hard. They were satisfied with having got rid of Boyislav. They ordered the oarsmen to press on. As a favorable wind blew without stopping, they soon arrived safely on firm land, where they hired horses and hurried to their native place.

The king, who had recovered as soon as the princesses on Black Island were freed, welcomed his sons and the princesses with tears in his eyes. But how he flushed up with anger when they told the story to which they had been forced by oath! He ordered the death of Boyislav at once, and offered a great reward for his capture. The wicked brothers rubbed their hands with glee, but the princesses withdrew to the chambers given them by the king, and passed their time in silent grief.

The king was astonished at this, and wished to know what prince they loved; he would give his blessing at once, and the proper income. But the princesses only shook their heads, and the king asked his sons the reason of the princesses' sorrow. The young men evaded the question, saying that perhaps the princesses were homesick. At last they led the conversation to Boyislav. The king flushed up with anger, which was all his sons wanted, so as to avoid speaking of the princesses of Black Island, for they knew nothing about them.

And now, when Boyislav was in prison, they continued to excite the king to give an order forbidding any one to ask mercy for him under pain of death. "Why should I endanger my life?" thought every one; "the king of course knows why he puts his son to death." Many pitied the prince, but only one man shed tears. He was an old warrior who had once commanded the king's armies, and was retained as a friend of the king; he did not believe that Boyislav deserved death, and resolved to ask pardon for him.

" Well," thought he, " I shall not live till spring, and it is all the same whether I die a day earlier or later. I have been in danger of death times without number and have never been even wounded; perhaps I shall escape now."

He went bravely to the king, who greeted him very kindly, as was his wont. " What dost thou wish? " asked he of the old man, who was silent.

" I ask mercy for Boyislav," said he.

" How darest thou slight my order? " asked the king, angrily. " Knowest not thou art doomed to death? "

" I know," answered the old man with dignity; " but I fear not death. I mean to say that thou art disgracing thyself by giving thy own blood to the hangman."

The king was struck with these words, and walked up and down the room with bowed head.

" Who knows whether Boyislav is really guilty or not? " said the old man, " for the conduct of the princesses from Black Island is strange."

" Thou art right, and I will not give him to the hangman; but still he must die. I shall have him confined with the lions. Let them tear him."

The old man made further effort, but the king would not be persuaded. When night came Boyislav was taken secretly from prison and shut in with the lions. But the brothers were not satisfied yet ; they told the king that Boyislav could easily escape, and advised him to wall up the doors. The king consented, and the next day the doors were walled up, there remaining only a small opening on the other side. This was fortunate, for otherwise Boyislav must have perished for want of air. He looked at the. lions without fear; they did not harm him. Then he took out the taper and the tablecloth, which he kept in his bosom, lighted the taper, laid the cloth on the ground, and asked for the choicest food; it appeared. He fed the lions first, then ate and drank himself. The lions lay at his feet in thankfulness; he lay on them and fell asleep. When awake he played with the lions, — who in a few days were tame, — or thought of the princess on White Island. In this way his days passed quickly, and before he knew it a whole year had gone.

Meanwhile the princess of White Island travelled over the world with an army in search of her liberator; she had already visited many kings, but in no royal family had she found twelve sons. At last she came to the dominions of the old king and learned that he had twelve sons. Her heart jumped for joy, and she marched night and day till she appeared before the capital. Straightway she sent messengers to the king, asking him to send her that prince who had freed her and her whole kingdom.

The king called the five princes who went with Boyislav, and asked if they had been on White Island.

" Of course ! " answered the truthless princes; and the eldest one shamelessly added that he had freed its princess.

" Then hurry to her," said the king.   He went.

" Where is the taper? " asked the princess when he came; but he knew nothing of it.   Thereupon the princess became so angry that she drew her sword and cut off his head with a blow.

Again she sent the messenger with the announcement that if her liberator were not sent, she would turn the city into dust and ashes.

" I freed her," said the second prince to the frightened king.

" Then go to her."

When she asked the second prince about the taper, he could give no answer, and lost his life.   The messenger returned to the king, and told him what had happened to the two princes; the three remaining ones were so terrified that they confessed the truth.

The old man, Boyislav's savior, now said to the king, " I told thee Boyislav was innocent; thou wouldst not believe me.   Now see how thou hast saved thy city from destruction, for the princess will surely carry out her threat unless Boyislav is delivered up."

" But how can I deliver him up when he is dead? " asked the king.

" He is not dead," replied the old man, joyfully, " for there is still a little opening in the lions' den, and there is light there night and day."

The king sprang up joyfully, hastened to the den, and had the walled-up doors opened. Boyislav looked on this carelessly; and when the king implored him with tenderness to come out, that he forgave him all, he shook his head saying: "I will not go, it is good enough for me here."

"But the princess will destroy my city," said the king.

"What princess?" asked Boyislav with curiosity.

"The princess from White Island."

In silence, but with gladness in his eyes, Boyislav quenched the taper, folded the tablecloth, and taking both with him walked out. When he went with the messenger to the princess, his heart beat with anxiety so that he could not raise his eyes when he stood before her.

"Thou art the man!" exclaimed the princess, joyfully. But when Boyislav knew not what to answer, she said reproachfully: "Has the ardor with which thou didst kiss me grown cold?"

"It has not," murmured Boyislav, wishing to kiss the golden hem of her robe.

The princess raised him up, and kissing him, said: "This is the earnest of our betrothal."

Boyislav was glad to respond; and now all returned to the castle, where feasting began, which was to be closed by the wedding of the princess and Boyislav. All were rejoiced except the princesses of Black Island, who were as sad as ever. The three princes who had gone to Black Island were in deathly terror. Boyislav in the middle of the feast grew sad, and when asked the reason, he inquired: " Where is my trusty horse? "

No one could answer him, till at last one of the servants remembered that the horse had been shut up in a pen. To the great astonishment of all, Boyislav ran out to him, fell upon his neck, and shed tears of joy.

" Thou hast done well to come," said the horse, sadly, " or I should have perished with hunger; for the cord brought from Red Island is eaten. Every span of it became a bundle of hay. But now thou hast attained thy object, and I am needed no longer; cut off my head."

" I cut off thy head! " exclaimed Boyislav.

" Then thou dost not wish to free me," said the horse, with chiding voice.

Boyislav drew his sword and cut off the horse's head at one blow. The horse disappeared in an instant, but in his stead appeared a beautiful prince, who fell on Boyislav's neck and shed tears of joy.

" What is this? " asked Boyislav, full of astonishment.

" Come to supper," said the prince; " I will explain it all." Both hurried to supper; scarcely were they at the door, when the youngest princess from Black Island fell into his arms, and the other two pressed his hands. When they had recovered from the first surprise, the prince said: "I am the only son of a powerful king, whose dominions are not far from Black Island. I would not marry the daughter of a queen who was a witch, and she enchanted me; and the princesses of Black Island — the youngest of whom is my bride — were turned into horses twelve hours of each day. Boyislav freed the princesses first, and now has freed me. The moment I regained my form, the spell was removed from Black Island."

All were delighted with Boyislav; but the king was thoughtful, and seemed to ponder over important things. At last he summoned the three princes who went with Boyislav to Black Island, and gave command to throw them to the lions; the lions tore them to pieces in an instant.

Now came new festivities; and when all was finished, Boyislav went with his wife to White Island; and the liberated prince, with his wife and sisters, went to Black Island, where they celebrated at once their wedding and their liberation.

THE TABLE, THE PACK, AND THE BAG.

BEFORE times long past, there lived in a little cottage an old father, with his three sons. The eldest son was called Martin; the second, Mihal; and the third, Yanek.

"Martin," the father used to say often, as they were sitting in the evening at a bowl of skimmed milk, "I shall not be long alive; I feel it in my body. When I die, the cottage will come to thee; but do not cheat thy old mother and thy brothers."

Martin always promised; but while the others were listening to their father, he looked sharply at the food, and picked out every piece of bread from the milk. Mihal saw this with astonishment; but Yanek was always grieved from his father's talk, and did not even think of eating.

The father spoke the truth. In no long time he groaned his last; but when he saw his death-hour, he had all summoned for the parting. He reminded Martin again that he was never to let the cottage go out of his possession; and then turning to Yanek, whom he loved most, he said: "Yanichek, thou art simple, 't is true; but what the Lord has kept from thee in wit, he has added in heart. Only be ever as kind as thou hast been, and obey thy brothers;" with that he coughed, and was no more.

Martin and Mihal gave themselves up to lamentation, but Yanek was silent; he stood by his father's bedside as if without sense. Only after a long time did he go out, sit in the garden under a tree, and cry like a little child.

After the funeral, Martin and Mihal decided to go out in the world, and leave Yanek with his mother. "The world is wide," said they; "there fortune may meet us quickly, while in this little cottage we should never come to anything as long as we lived."

It was all one to Yanek; but his mother who was still in good strength, did not like to have Yanek lose his fortune, and talked with his brothers so long that they took him with them. This was not agreeable to Martin and Mihal, but they reverenced their mother, and obeyed her.

All three made ready; Martin and Mihal put food in bags for themselves, and went out into the world. On the road Yanek said to his brothers, "I shall be glad to see if that fortune meets us soon."

"Thou mayest run to meet it," snapped the brothers, "since thou hast nothing to carry." They were angry that Yanek had taken nothing, while they must carry heavy bags on their backs.

They walked on a whole half-day; the sun was burning, and the brothers were tired and hungry.

They sat down at the roadside under a tree, in the shade, took out provisions, and began to eat, — that is, Martin and Mihal; but Yanek sat by himself and began to cry, either because he remembered his father's death or was hungry. His brothers ridiculed him and said: "See now, thou wilt not be so lazy another time, and then thou wilt not be hungry."

Yanek brushed away his tears with his sleeve, and said: "Ye might have a little shame. Ye are going out into the world so as to be able to support your mother when ye go home; but now ye have taken from her everything!"

Such an answer the brothers did not expect from simple Yanek. They were silent; and after a while, as if moved from kindness, they asked Yanek to eat with them; but they did not do it from compassion or brotherly love, but to lessen their fault. When they had eaten, they rose and went on their way. In the evening they came to a cottage and asked for lodgings. The cottager took them under his roof, and asked them to sup. Martin thanked him with a certain boastfulness, saying that he had provisions enough of his own.

The man sat down to supper with his wife. Yanek sat with downcast face alone in a corner. The woman went to the kitchen, and when returning, saw that Yanek had nothing to eat. "Oh, little boy, come and eat with us!" said she kindly. Turning to Martin she asked if that was their servant.

"What servant!" said Martin. "He is our brother, but such a lazy fellow, he would not bring anything for himself."

Yanek did not wish to go to the table, but consented at last. Martin squinted at the dish; and when he saw soup, he hated Yanek. Soup was his favorite dish, and now he must look on and see how Yanek enjoyed it, and must be satisfied with dry bread and a bit of cheese. Full of hatred he went to bed in the place which the cottager showed him, with his brothers. For a long time he lay awake, and when he fell asleep he saw in a dream, Yanek eating soup. In the morning the brothers rose before breakfast, because they wanted Yanek to have nothing to eat. Martin went through the nearest forest, hoping that they would find no house all day, and so Yanek would have no food.

The whole forenoon they walked through the thick forest, and Martin wished to eat his dinner; but the forest began to grow thin and soon they came to an open country. They looked for a road, went on a small hill, and then saw in the valley a great castle as high as ten houses placed one on the other. Yanek laughed, but Martin was not pleased: "We have lost the road," said he; "we must go back."

"But, foolish fellow," said Mihal, who was tired, "we are going out in the world, what difference does it make; it is all the same whether we go one way or another."

Without saying a word or looking at his brothers, Yanek went straight toward the castle. That started off Martin, and soon he caught up with Yanek. "Walk behind," said he, " I 'm the eldest; I must go ahead."

They soon came to the castle, but did not see a living thing; they were greatly afraid. Martin wished to run away; but when he saw Yanek open the door, he followed him. They entered a splendid hall. How astonished were they! On the floor was a pile of copper money five ells high. Martin and Mihal, blinded by the glitter of the money, threw out their remaining provisions, filled their bags, and wanted to run away; but Yanek opened the next door, through which the brothers saw in another hall a still greater pile of money, but silver. They emptied their bags of the copper money with all speed, and filled them with silver. They had barely done this when Yanek opened a third door, and cried out with wonder, — a thing which he seldom did, — " Ai ! " The brothers threw their bags on the floor, rushed to the door, but had to cover their eyes with their hands, for it was as bright as the sun in the next chamber. They saw this was gold. Still more quickly than before, they threw the silver out of their bags, and panting for breath, filled them with gold pieces.

" Now let us go," cried Martin; " some one may come, and then we shall suffer." They started from the castle as fast as they could. Yanek went too, and took as he was going only one piece of money

from each heap, and in the third room the remnants
of food which his brothers had thrown out. The
brothers escaped with the money successfully, meeting no one. Yanek followed at his leisure, eating
the provisions which his brothers had thrown away.
When they came to the forest, the two brothers
crawled into the thicket, threw their bags on the
ground, and began to rest. Yanek also lay down
after he had put the last bit of bread in his mouth.
Here Martin remembered the provisions, but he had
only ducats in his bag.

"Yanek," said he, "run back to the castle and
bring us from the first chamber the provisions which
we forgot there."

But Yanek answered bluntly, "I will not go."

"Why not?" asked Martin in anger.

"Because they might catch me, and I should have
to suffer instead of you; besides, there is no food
there, for when you threw it away I picked it up and
ate it."

"Monster!" screamed Martin in rage, "I'll teach
thee to obey thy eldest brother. Mihal, give him
here to me."

Mihal did not wait to be spoken to twice. They
took poor Yanek between them and put so many
blows on him that he was soon lying as if dead on
the ground; then they took their bags on their backs
and hurried home through the woods.

"That lazy-bones!" growled Martin, "let him go

wherever he likes; he will not dare to teach us again."
They got out of the forest quickly, and in the evening
came to an inn where they refreshed themselves.
Next morning they set out for home. In the neighboring town, where the king dwelt, they bought a
house, brought their mother to it, and began to live
like great lords.

Yanek, poor fellow, lay for a long time unconscious
in the forest. At last he woke from his trance, rested
his head against a tree, and fell to thinking of his condition. "Oh, cruel brothers, ye have left the forest!
Who knows whether I shall find the way home? I
am weak; I cannot walk far; I will go back to the
castle, no matter what meets me; I will take money,
too, and live like a lord."

Many a one will wonder that Yanek changed all at
once; but a beating has brought many a man to new
ways. So Yanek made ready and went to the castle.
In the castle there was not a living soul. Yanek
took off his coat, tied the sleeves at the wrist, and
began to rake gold into them. He had almost finished when he heard noises at a distance like bursts
of thunder. These noises grew louder and louder
till at last they were so loud that the castle trembled.
All at once a voice as if a fifteen-year-old bull were
bellowing, called, "Hu! hu! I smell the flesh of a
man!" and before Yanek could gather his wits after
the fright, he saw two giants standing at the door.

"Oh, worm of the earth, thou art the one who is

stealing our treasures!" howled one of the giants. "Ha, thou wilt be a nice roast for supper," added he, smacking his lips so that Yanek lost his senses. But the second giant whispered something in the ear of the first, who nodded, and said to Yanek: "Listen, worm of the earth, I grant thee life, but henceforth thou wilt watch our treasures when we are from home."

Yanek wanted to kiss the giant's hand, but he could barely reach to his knee. "Only watch well, worm of the earth," said the giant, graciously; "but so that thou shouldst not be hungry, strike on this little table three times with thy fist and call, 'Food for a king!' and thou wilt have food to thy liking."

Yanek promised everything, and from that time forth he led a very pleasant life, — he did nothing, no living soul ever came to the castle, the table was always obedient. But at last he grew tired of all this. "Watch your own treasures, lord giants," said he one day when the giants had gone out; "and thou, my good little table, come! — we will go home."

Yanek put the table on his back, stole away from the castle, and soon found himself in the forest. He strolled leisurely through the forest, and after no long time was in the open field. Here an old grandfather met him, and asked if he had not something to eat. "'Tis long since I have had a bit in my mouth," lamented the grandfather.

"Then I will help thee," said Yanek; "come with me to that tree over there." They sat under the tree; Yanek put his table on the ground, and striking on it three times with his fist, said: "Food for a king!" The table was covered with the daintiest dishes.

The grandfather ate his fill, and said: "Indeed this is a very beautiful thing! But, my lad, if thou wouldst give me this little table, I would give thee something better in place of it. This pack has the virtue that at command an army will spring out of it as numerous as ever thou carest to wish."

Yanek was greedy, but only from the time that he got a beating from his brothers; he took the pack, gave the grandfather the table, and they parted. But Yanek soon felt hungry; he was in the open field, and nowhere a house to be seen. Now he was angry at himself for having given away the table so frivolously; and besides he wished to know if what the grandfather said of the pack was true. He opened the pack and commanded "two hundred hussars to the field." He had barely spoken when horses were neighing, arms rattling, and sooner than he could think, two hundred hussars stood in line before him. The officers saluted Yanek, and asked with respect what he wanted.

"About five thousand yards from here, under that tree, an old man took a table from me; ride after him, take the table, and bring it to me."

He had barely finished speaking when the hussars rode off at a wild gallop, in no long time they returned, and their leader gave Yanek the table. Yanek opened his pack and said: "Two hundred hussars in here." In a twinkle the hussars were in the pack, from the first man and horse to the last. "That is not a bad thing," said Yanek to himself as he sat at the table, struck three times with his fist, and commanded, "Food for a king."

When he had eaten to his content he took his table and his pack and went on. It was inclining toward evening, and Yanek had to look for a night's lodging. But this made him small trouble; it was warm enough, he laid himself under a tree, put the pack under his head, held the table in his hand, and so fell asleep. Next morning he ate like a king and went on. This time he met a grandfather as he had the day before, and he too asked for food. Yanek commanded the table, and the grandfather ate his fill. "My lad," said he, "here is a bag; give me thy table for it."

"Oh, grandfather," said Yanek, with a laugh, "nothing can come of that."

"This is no laughing matter, my lad; the bag is worth getting, for it has this virtue, — that wherever and whenever thou hast the wish, thou canst call out of it as many castles as may please thee."

Yanek fell to thinking, and then said with a smile, "Let it be so."

The grandfather took the table, Yanek the bag; then they parted. But barely had the grandfather vanished from sight when Yanek opened the pack and commanded: " Three hundred Uhlans to the field!" Scarce had he spoken when three hundred Uhlans were standing in line before him. " Go now to the right on the road; at the ditch a man took my table: take that table and bring it to me."

The Uhlans flashed away, and a man could scarcely have counted ten before Yanek had the table. Then he opened the pack and commanded: " Three hundred Uhlans this way!" and the Uhlans vanished in the pack. Yanek was beside himself with gladness when he took the table, the pack, and the bag, and continued his way.

In the evening he came to the capital town, and there he learned that his brothers had become great lords. He went before the town, tore his clothes purposely, then lay in the dust and rolled several times. He did this so that he might seem out and out ragged and poor. Then he went to his brothers and implored them to take pity on him. They would not even recognize him; but his mother fell on his neck and begged for him. The brothers gave way, and granted him lodging, but in the stable. Yanek was satisfied; he lay on the bed which was given him, — that is, a bundle of straw, — and waited till all were asleep. Then he sprang over the fence to the garden, opened the bag, and commanded: " One castle out of the bag!" and that moment there stood in the garden the most beautiful castle. Then he opened the pack and commanded: " Fifty infantry come out !'" and fifty foot-soldiers stood before him.

" Ye," said he to them, " will be all night on guard here in my castle; but when in the morning the cock crows the second time, rouse me."

The warriors saluted and took their places on guard. Yanek took the table which he had secreted, as well as the pack and bag, and went into the castle. There he selected the most beautiful chamber, commanded the table, and supped. After supper he lay down and slept till the guards roused him. He rose, ate, and before any one was awake in the house of his brothers he commanded the warriors into the pack, the castle into the bag, then crawled over the fence, and lay on his straw in the stable. This he did night after night. But it was a wonder to his brothers how he was alive; for though they had two bags of ducats, they never gave him a morsel to eat. Therefore they pressed Yanek to tell them if he had gathered much coin in the castle; they thought he had money, but did not wish to show it before them.

" Simpleton ! I was glad to get out of there alive; for that castle belongs to giants," answered Yanek. " But I have something else, and it is better than your gold pieces."

Then he brought the table, struck it three times with his fist, and said : " Food for a king !"

Martin and Mihal stood like apparitions, they

could not believe their eyes; but when they began to eat they believed their tongues.

The story of the wonderful table was spread through the town, and soon came to the king. He was eager for the food of the table, and sent his chamberlain to Yanek to borrow the table for three days.

" Agreed," said Yanek; " here it is. But if it is not returned to me at the end of three days I will declare war against the king."

The chamberlain bowed, took the table, and told the king, with a smile, that Yanek would declare war against him unless the table was returned. The table pleased the king beyond measure, but still more the food; therefore he meditated how to deceive Yanek. He summoned all the joiners, carvers, and turners in the town, and ordered them to make exactly such a table as Yanek's. They went to work, and before the third day had passed there were two tables, and the king himself could not tell which was the right one. Soon he made sure of it, and then he sent the counterfeit table by the chamberlain to Yanek.

Yanek struck the table three times with his fist and ordered: "Food for a king!" The table trembled, but nothing more. "Food for a king!" shouted Yanek, full of anger; but he soon discovered that the king had deceived him, and he pounded the table till he pounded it to pieces.

" Take this and carry it to the king," said he to

the chamberlain, " and tell him that I 'll smash down his castle to-morrow as I have broken this table ! "

The chamberlain collected the fragments, took them to the king, and told him what Yanek had said. The king only smiled haughtily, and thought that he had finished with Yanek. In the night, however, he had wonderful dreams, and early next morning he ordered his army to be placed before the castle and be ready for battle.

Now Yanek came with his pack, counted the royal troops, and still once more asked the king to return his table; but the king only laughed. Then Yanek opened the pack and commanded: "A thousand times a thousand infantry out; a thousand times a thousand cavalry out." From the pack there was the rush of an avalanche. Soon the whole country in front of the castle was filled with the finest of armies. The king and his troops were as if before a vision; but when Yanek raised his hand as a signal for attack, the king raised a white flag and went to Yanek.

" Thou seest," said the king, almost imploringly, " I was mistaken; but I wish to correct my mistake. I will return the table, and besides I will give thee my daughter in marriage."

" Then peace," said Yanek. " But first bring thy princess; let me see her."

The princess soon came with her ladies, raised her veil, and stood before Yanek.

"The wedding will be to-day!" ordered Yanek,

and kissed the princess on the forehead. She was not angry; nay, it may be said she was glad. Then Yanek commanded: "A thousand times a thousand infantry in; a thousand times a thousand cavalry in," and closed the pack.

The royal army withdrew to the fortress, and now quick preparations were made for the marriage. At midday Yanek and the princess belonged to each other. Then they feasted, and the table gave meat and drink till the evening.

When all were in bed Yanek went out to the king's garden with his bag, opened it, and commanded: "Let the most beautiful castle that can be in the world come out of this bag!" And that was such a castle that Yanek himself was astonished.

Then he went to the old castle to the king, who had already prepared chambers to which he wished to conduct him and the princess; but Yanek answered that he had his own household, and the king had such faith in him that he believed. Yanek conducted his bride to the new castle, and she could not admire its splendor sufficiently.

In the morning people hurried to the king and told him that there was a new castle in the garden. The sun was just rising, and casting its rays on the castle, the castle was blazing with gold, silver, and precious stones. The king now respected Yanek still more, and gave him all that he could, even his kingdom.

So Yanek became king, and a great king who could

give battle to the whole world. On the boundaries he put castles everywhere out of the bag, and from the pack he garrisoned them with troops. The table gave him the best of food; what more could he want?

He reigned long, and was a real father to his subjects. As a punishment to his brothers he did not let them come near him; but his mother he cared for so well that she reached a great age. In the most beautiful chamber of the castle, on a golden throne, were the pack and the bag, and near them the table.

When King Yanek died he was mourned by all; he left his children the mightiest kingdom on earth. His eldest son succeeded him; but accustomed to splendor and luxury, he did not govern the kingdom so well as his father. After his death it was still worse. The succeeding kings were ashamed of their peasant stock; and so that no man might discover the real foundation of their power and turn them into ridicule, they took the table, the pack, and the bag, and cast them into a dark, damp cellar.

And will ye ask what became of such a mighty kingdom? The table rotted, the bag rotted, the mice gnawed the pack; and then it was all over with that kingdom.

In after times, when he was in straits, the king ran to the cellar, struck on the table, looked for the pack and the bag. But the table fell to pieces at the first blow, of the pack there remained but a few little straps, and of the bag a few threads.

THE KING OF THE TOADS.

MANY and many a year ago there was a cottage by the sea, and in this cottage lived a fisherman who caught fish in the sea. By the king's command he was allowed to take fish, not when he liked, but only once a week, and that on Mondays. He was anxious, therefore, to catch many on that day. Fish, of course, are not so crafty as men, but still they know enough to see that there is no fun in being caught. What is to be done with them afterwards they don't know; still, they must suspect that it can hardly be for their amusement. It is no wonder then that they did not crowd into the fisherman's net.

The fisherman worked every Monday till the sweat streamed down his face; and this all the more, since, come what might, he was obliged to bring fish to the king's kitchen each Monday. Once he worked the whole forenoon without catching even a white fish. "I will try once more," thought the tired fisherman; "I will throw everything into the water, and jump around to frighten the fish, they are so stubborn."

He threw the net deeply, and when he pulled it was very heavy. "Now there will be fish," thought he, joyfully; but what was his astonishment when, instead of fish, he drew out a great copper kettle.

The kettle was so well fastened that the fisherman had to work long before he could take off the cover. But how he was frightened! Scarcely had he removed the cover when out of the kettle rushed black smoke, which grew thicker and thicker, till at last it changed to a fiery man.

"Thou hast helped me, and I will help thee," said he to the terrified fisherman; "but in my own way I will destroy thee."

The fisherman lost his head, but soon recovering said: "Oh, I don't care, I am already tired of this world; still thou must do something for me, since I freed thee. I can't understand how thou wert able to live in such a small place, and under the water too, and then change so quickly."

"I'll show thee in a moment," said the fiery man ; and he began to turn into black smoke, and in no long time he was packed into the kettle again.

"Dost see me?" inquired he of the fisherman.

"I see thee," answered the fisherman, laughing ; "I see thee, but thou 'lt not see me any more."

The cover was already on the kettle and fastened firmly. The fiery man by no means expected to find such cunning among people, and considering his condition in the kettle, began to beg of the fisherman: "Let me out and I will reward thee."

"Swear that thou wilt never destroy me," said the fisherman.

The spirit answered with a solemn voice, " I swear."

The fisherman removed the cover, and black smoke rolled out, growing thicker and thicker, till at last it turned into a fiery man.

" Follow me," said he to the fisherman; and the latter followed without thinking.

In a short time they came to a high cliff in which steps were cut in the stone. The fiery man bent to the earth, plucked an herb, and giving it to the fisherman said: " Keep this with thee always. Put thy foot on this step; immediately after thou wilt be on a high mountain, from which thou wilt see a great lake. In the lake is a wealth of fish, and thou hast the right to catch as many of them as may please thee, but only once a week, on Mondays. When thou hast the wish to come down, climb to the top, and soon thou wilt be at the bottom."

Thereupon the fiery man vanished, but the fisherman went on the steps cut in the rock; in one moment a mighty wind caught him, and in a twinkle he was on a high mountain, from which he saw an altogether unknown country covered with dark forests, in the midst of which was a broad lake; only here and there was a grass-plot to be seen, there were neither hills nor the dwellings of men.

The fisherman went down from the mountain, and when he had reached the lake he found a boat with all the fishing-tackle, as if made ready for him. He went to work willingly, threw in the net, and drew out nothing; he threw it in a second time, drew out as much as before. " That fiery man has fooled me," thought he, " but the third throw is always the best." He cast his net again and drew out three fish; when he saw them in the net, he said bitterly: " Well, this is a wealth of fish! If it goes on in this way I 'll soon leave the place; besides, I don't like travelling by wind." But when he looked at the fish more carefully, and took them in his hand, he found that in all his life he had never seen anything like them. " These are not for me," muttered he, " I must give them to the king; he will soon try them." With that he left the boat, went to the mountain, and had barely touched the summit when a mighty wind seized him, and placed him on level land. He set out for home, and it was time; for his wife had already cooked the dinner and was waiting. As soon as he saw her before the door, he hurried his steps; and when she was in the cottage he began to run. And why did he run, because he feared her? Not at all. He cared nothing for her, as he said himself; but he loved domestic peace, and did everything his wife wanted, but always did it in such fashion that she might not know what he was doing; this was to preserve his own importance in her eyes. He went into the house slowly, and said at the door: " Well, my dear, I have caught a few fish to-day; but I had much trouble, or I should have been home long ago."

"Time for thee," snapped his wife; "if thou art late again I'll eat alone, leave nothing, and thou wilt find out that I am not thy slave to wait and suffer hunger."

"Oh well, things are not so bad to-day," said the fisherman; "better come and see these wonderful fish."

"They are just like any other fish," cried the woman, "only they look a little different, that's all."

"And for that very reason thou wilt take them to the king. He will pay us well for them; we should not be able to use them."

"Oh, thou couldst soon do away with them," replied his wife, "but that's why I'll take them to the king; besides, we are up to our ears in fish."

After dinner the fisherman's wife hurried to the king with the fish. When she came to the palace, she asked the first man she met where the king was, but got as answer: "I don't keep the king!" She went farther, making confusion everywhere until all the servants came together, but no one said anything to her. At last she reached the guard who stood before the king's chamber; she wanted to go without ceremony to his Kingly Grace. The guard pushed her back sharply, but the fishwoman did not retreat so easily; she tried once more to break through the guards, but this time she was repulsed. One of the guards, as firm as a rock, and with as much hair on his face as a bear, caught her by the hand and pulled her so roughly that she almost fell to the floor. She screamed that they were killing her, and roused the whole palace; even the king came. She turned straight to him and cried out over the heads of the men: "Royal Grace, I am bringing fish, and these bears won't let me in."

The king, who was in good humor that day, beckoned her to come. "What kind of fish, and how many?" asked he when she approached.

"Royal Grace, only three, but so wonderful that I have not seen such as long as I live." With that she took a fish from the basket and handed it to the king.

"Wonderful, indeed," said the king, "but give them not to me, give them to my cook; and here is to thee for the road," giving her a handful of gold-pieces.

The fishwoman, when she saw so much money, fell at the king's feet, and came near throwing him down; but he did n't mind. Then she took the fish to the kitchen, and ran headlong home.

After she had gone the king went to the kitchen, looked at one of the fish, and said to the cook: "Thou must dress these fish in a special manner, and answer with thy head for the cooking."

"Royal Grace, in what manner?" asked the cook, trembling with terror when he heard of his head; for though he was a great hero at cutting off heads, he trembled like an aspen when his own head was in question.

" That's thy affair," replied the king; " I will send my chamberlain to thee to look after the fish."

The king went away, and presently the chamberlain appeared. The cook did not know how to prepare the fish, and lost his wits, — but that was his luck, for he did everything without knowing it, and altogether different from his wont. At last when they had the fish on the pan, and began to butter them, the whole palace trembled. Then followed a terrible shock; and before the cook or the chamberlain could think what it meant, they received each such a slap on the face from an invisible hand that they fell senseless to the floor. And while they were lying in such concord on the floor, they knew not that one of the fish stood on his tail in the pan, and said to the other two: " Will ye serve me or be food for the king."

" Serve thee," said both in one voice. With that all three of them vanished, and to this day no man knows whither they went.

The cook woke up from his involuntary slumber sooner than the chamberlain; he did not rise, however, but waited for the other. Then he rose, groaned heavily, complained, and both hurried to the fish; but they were gone. " The devil take the fish!" said the cook; " but what will the king say?"

It was no great joy for the chamberlain that the fish were gone; still he went to the king and told him of all that had happened in the kitchen.

"I cannot believe it," said the king; "but if thou canst get more fish like these, thou wilt be forgiven this time. Now go to the fisherman and tell him to get other fish like these."

The chamberlain hurried away with light heart, rejoiced at his easy escape. The fisherman said that he could catch fish only on Mondays. The chamberlain told this to the king; the king was very angry. But what could he gain by that?

There was joy in the fisherman's cottage by reason of so much money, and the fisherman's wife could hardly wait till Monday. She roused her husband early Monday morning, got him a holiday breakfast, and almost pushed him out of the house, so as to bring those strange fish with all speed. The fisherman obeyed, not his wife, however, but the king, and hastened to the cliff with the wonderful herb in his bosom. He had barely stood on the step, when he was carried to the mountain; and from there he rushed to the lake, where he found a boat waiting for him as before. The first and second time he caught nothing; but the third time he drew out three fish. "Now my wife will be glad," thought he, and hurried up the mountain; from there he was taken to the valley in an instant, and ran home. His wife pulled the fish out of his hands, threw them into a basket, and ran to the king's palace. The guard was ordered to let her pass; and she went straight to the king, who came out to meet her, and looking at

the fish, to see if they were the same, gave her another handful of gold for her trouble. The fishwoman thanked him, took the fish to the kitchen,
and went home leisurely, for she counted the money
to see if there was the same as before; there was still
more. Now there was joy in the cottage; and the
fisherman was thankful in his heart to the fiery man,
by whose action he had gained such peace in his
household.

New orders were issued by the king to the cook,
who was trembling with terror, thinking what would
come of the fish. But the king, who did not believe
even the chamberlain, sent his eldest son to watch
both the chamberlain and the cook, lest they should
eat the fish themselves. They all stood in great
expectation around the pan in which the butter was
melting under the fish; but as soon as they began to
butter the fish, the castle was shaken more violently
than before, a still louder shock followed, and the
cook, chamberlain, and even the prince himself, received such slaps from an unseen hand that all three
fell senseless to the floor. And while they were lying
there, they did not know that one of the fish stood
on its tail in the pan, and said to the other two:
"Will ye be food for the king, or serve me?"

"Serve thee," answered the two in one voice; then
all three vanished in an instant, and to this day no
man knows whither.

The cook came to his senses first; but seeing the

chamberlain and the prince still on the floor, he stayed where he was. The chamberlain followed his example; at last the prince jumped up and roused both. For a while they acted as if they had lost their wits, then rose to their feet slowly, and complained. When they looked in the pan they found it empty. The prince told all carefully to his father. The king was raging, and threatened them all with death. At last he was pacified, and sent the prince to the fisherman. The prince gave the king's order, but the fisherman said that he could catch those fish only on Mondays. When the king heard this he fell into a towering passion, though he knew himself that the fish could be caught only on Mondays. At last he grew calm, but resolved to be present next time they cooked these most wonderful fish.

On Monday the fisherman's wife pushed her husband out of the house at the dawn of day. The fisherman came to the top of the mountain as before, then hastened to the lake, where on the third cast of the net he drew out three fish. He hurried to the top of the mountain; next moment he was in the valley, and ran home as fast as his breath would let him. His wife shortened the journey for him: she ran to meet him, and pulling the fish out of his hands, rushed off to the palace like a crazy woman. The king was waiting; and ran out the moment he saw her. When he looked at the fish he gave her two handfuls of gold. She took the fish to the kitchen,

and hurried away. When she came to the field she
sat down and counted the money ten times.

In the king's kitchen the king, the prince, and the
chamberlain watched the cook while he was preparing the fish. Because the king was present, great
attention was paid to everything. This was done
partly to make the king tired of being there; but he
gave them to understand that he would wait till the
fish were ready. After long preparation they got
them on the pan; but as soon as the cook began to
butter them the palace shook as in a tempest. Then
came a shock as from a lightning-stroke, and in an
instant all present received such slaps on the face
that they fell senseless to the floor. While lying
there without distinction of persons none of them
knew, not even the king, that one of the fish stood
on its tail in the pan and said to the other two:
"Will ye serve me or be food for the king?"

"Serve thee!" answered both in one voice; and
all three vanished.

After a long time the cook woke from his trance,
and seeing the king prostrate, remained as he was.
In like manner acted the chamberlain and the prince
when they recovered. At last the king rose, walked
around the pan quickly, saw no fish, wondered greatly,
and went to his chambers in silence. When the king
had gone, the prince, the chamberlain, and the cook
sprang from the floor and shook themselves.

The king pondered long over these fish, weighed

everything duly, and then sent for the fisherman. The fisherman came straightway; but how he wondered when he heard what had happened at the buttering of the fish! The king said: "Take me to that lake; I will examine everything carefully myself." The fisherman of course consented. The king took his body-guard, and all moved toward the cliff, with the fisherman at the head. When they arrived there the fisherman gave the king some of the herb which he had received from the fiery man, took him by the hand, and stood on the stone step. In an instant a mighty wind seized them; the king and the fisherman flew through the air, but the body-guard stood, as if fallen from heaven. They waited long; but when nothing came of it, they returned to the palace, and told the terrified people what they had seen.

In due time the king with the fisherman appeared on the summit of the mountain, from whence he saw the whole country. Although there was no palace, nor even a cottage, still it pleased him greatly at first sight.

"There," said the fisherman to the king, "is the lake where I catch the wonderful fish; I have n't gone farther yet in any direction."

"Very well," said the king, "let us go down."

On reaching the lake the king told the fisherman to catch the fish; but he went on himself to examine the place. The farther he went the thicker the grass, till at last he had hard work to get through; still he advanced till he came to a beautiful green meadow, having on one side the forest, and on the other the lake. Near the shore in a boat sat an old grandfather, whose head was as white as an apple-tree in blossom.

" Wilt thou row me over, grandfather? " asked the king.

" Why should I not, since that is what I am here for? "

The king took a seat in the boat. The old man rowed without hurrying; but the boat moved lightly over the smooth water, like a fly through the blue sky. When they reached the middle of the lake the old man turned to one side. Then the king saw a grand castle half hidden in the dark forest.

" Oh, what a beautiful castle! Who reigns there? " asked the king.

" Thou wilt learn if thou enter," replied the old man. When they touched the shore he gave the king a green twig, and said: " Take this twig; it will be of use to thee. Good-by, for thou wilt not see me again."

" But who will take me back ? "

" No one. Thou wilt go back on dry land; " and turning aside, he disappeared.

The king went straight to the palace; and if he wondered at the words of the old man, he was still more astonished when he entered the principal gate and saw no living soul. Thoughtfully he ascended the broad steps, went through one chamber, then another, a third, and a fourth; but nowhere did he find a living creature. "This is some enchanted castle," thought the king to himself. "Who knows how I shall escape? But I will see all, and then find the way home." He examined the chambers further till he came to the last, and there in the middle of the room sat an old man, bent to the floor. "I said this was an enchanted castle," thought the king; "here sits one man!"

The old man raised his head, and seeing the king, said: "Welcome; at last I see a human face!"

The king approached him and asked: "Who art thou, and what does this empty palace mean?"

"I am a king, but without subjects or power; another rules in my place," answered the old man, bitterly.

"What is the cause of this?"

"The treason of my own wife."

"And is there no rescue?"

"Well, the same as none; therefore be off at once, otherwise my wife will kill thee when she returns from the King of the Toads."

"I am not afraid of a woman," said the king. "I want to stand before her; we shall see if there is no escape."

"If there were escape I should not be sitting here confined by the King of the Toads!"

"Who is this King of the Toads?"

"Listen; I will tell thee my whole sad story. The sun is yet high, and until it sets my wife will not return: Once I ruled over a powerful nation; around my palace was a great city, and near it a beautiful garden. All is changed into a dark forest and a lake. The fish in the lake are my former subjects. I was once happy, and the more so because I obtained as wife a beautiful and kind princess; but the King of the Toads got into the place where the lake now is, and he turned my wife's heart from me. I remonstrated, begged, threatened my wife with death, but in vain. Every day she went to meet the King of the Toads, and listened to his wheedling speech. Once I came upon them in the summer-house, and heard with my own ears their whispering and kissing. At last the King of the Toads said: ' I will find the nest of the magic bird, will take its eggs, and give them thee to eat; thou wilt become immortal and ever young; then we shall be altogether happy.' ' Deceitful serpent!' I cried, springing from my hiding-place; and with a sharp sword I cut the King of the Toads in two. My wife fell upon him, weeping, and he grew together again. Looking at me with venomous eye he muttered words I could not understand, and that moment I felt my blood grow cold, and my veins stiffened so that I could not think of further struggle. I came home in misery and sat down on this chair to rest; but the King of the Toads froze me to my seat, and laid a spell upon the land. From that time I sit here, I know not how many years. My wife spends every day with her lover, and catches frogs for him out of the lake; in return, he promises her immortality and eternal youth. Now, thou canst see there is no aid for me; but escape thou before my wife kills thee."

"I will not flee," said the king, and drew his sword. "I'll cut off her head, — the traitorous soul!"

"Foolish man," said the old king; "the King of the Toads saves her, and will not let her be hurt."

"Let him guard her; I must avenge thee," answered the king, and sat on a chair waiting for the deceitful queen, paying no attention to the old man, who begged him by everything in the world to escape.

As the sun was going down the queen came, and was not a little astonished when she saw the stately knight with her husband. The king drew his sword and ran towards her, but the moment the sword touched her clothing it broke in two. It would have been bad for the king now, if he had not remembered the twig which the boatman gave him. He pulled it out quickly, and struck the queen three times. The third time he struck she dropped on a seat, and was unable to move an eye.

"Sit there, like thy husband," said the king, mockingly, and counselled with the old man what to do further.

"It would be better," said the old man, who gained

courage when he saw his wife frozen to the chair, "to persuade the King of the Toads to free the kingdom and me from enchantment."

"I will try," answered the king; and going to the adjoining chamber, where the queen's wardrobe was, he dressed in her garments and came back to the old man. "Now I will go to the King of the Toads and pretend to be his love, thy virtuous wife. Then I will beg him; and if he does not do what I want, I'll freeze him with this twig, and stroke him with my sword till his heart softens."

"But beg of him first," said the old man.

The king made his way in silence to the King of the Toads; but as it was night he could not find him, and was obliged to call out. He changed his voice, which deceived the King of the Toads, who came quickly and wished to embrace him, thinking that he was the queen.

"No, my dear," said the king; "first thou must do something to please me. What good is it for us to live together if my former husband is troubling me? Either kill him altogether or give him back his former condition, so that he may die; if thou wilt take the spell from him, he will fall to dust and ashes."

"Let it be as thou wishest," said he, drawing nearer.

But she moved away, and said: "I have one more favor to ask, but this concerns us alone. As soon as my former husband dies thou wilt take his place and we shall reign together, but what sort of a reign would it be if the whole country were enchanted; therefore give back its former shape to the kingdom, and I will marry thee before the world."

" So let it be," replied the King of the Toads, and embraced his supposed love, who refused no longer. Scarcely had he touched her when he was struck three times with the twig, in the dark night, and the King of the Toads was frozen to the earth.

" Serpent of hell! " cried the king with his powerful voice, " now I'll enchant thee for the eternal ages; " and with that he drew out his sword and cut him into countless pieces, which he threw into the water. Frogs rushed from every side with a terrible croaking, and greedily swallowed the bits of the body of their destroyer.

They had barely devoured him when the water began to run out of the lake; and the king saw by the light of the moon which had risen over the mountain summit, how the tree-tops were rising quickly from the water, higher and higher till the water disappeared altogether, and in the place of the lake was a splendid park, in which were multitudes of people who, praising the king, hurried to the castle. The king joined them, but before reaching the castle he had to pass through a large city; and only after travelling many streets did he arrive there. All the chambers were lighted up, and full of people, so that with difficulty did he find the old man, who was standing in the last chamber, and preventing the people from hewing the queen to pieces; but the king drew his sword and cut off her head. " She deserved it," said he to the old man, who dropped a few tears for his former wife.

Now universal rejoicings began, but the liberated king took no part in them. He called his deliverer and said: " My hours are numbered, I give the whole kingdom to thee; rule in my place."

The new king thanked the old one kindly, and when he rose in the morning, he heard that the old king was dead.

Our king mounted a fiery steed, rode to the city, and announced to the people the death and last will of their former ruler. They grieved for a moment, then with shouts of gladness greeted the new king.

After the burial of the old monarch, his successor examined the kingdom; and as everything pleased him greatly, he decided to stay there. Therefore he went to his former palace, but the road was far longer than when he had travelled it with the fisherman. He was obliged to ride several weeks before arriving there. No one knew him, for several years had passed while he was in the enchanted kingdom. At last an old grandfather came, who said: " I am one of the body-guard who went with thee to the cliff where thou didst leave us. Take me, I beg, into thy service again, for all my comrades are dead; I am alone."

The people believed quickly the grandfather's

words, gathered around the king and kissed the hem of his garment. The king sold his castle, put everything he could into wagons, and made ready for the road. Now he remembered the fisherman, asked how he was getting on, and when he had returned home.

" Only yesterday," was the reply.

" Send for him," commanded the king; and straightway the fisherman was there.

When the king asked about his adventures, the fisherman answered: " Royal Grace, I have no fish, and God alone knows what happened in that place. All at once the water disappeared under my boat and I was on dry land. I left everything and ran away; but trees began to grow under me, and so quickly that every second branches struck my face. Since it was in the night I might have lost my senses. In the morning I wondered when I saw instead of a forest an enormous city, with a great palace. I hurried from that magic country, thinking to see my cottage soon; but I travelled one day, I travelled two, a week, a month, and then a year — no sign of my cottage. I gave up for a time, and only yesterday I came home safely. My wife was dead; I am all alone now in this wide world."

" Do not cry," said the king; " thou hast me yet. Thou wilt stay with me."

The fisherman answered with tears, and all started off on their journey. They arrived safely at the new kingdom; and all lived happily till they died.

THE MOUSE–HOLE, AND THE UNDERGROUND KINGDOM.

BEFORE times long past there reigned a king somewhere, and he had three sons. When they had grown up, and were trained as befits princes, they came one day to their father and said: " Our kingly father, permit us to visit strange lands, since we know our own country well."

" Yes, it is proper," answered the king, wisely, " for royal princes to know more than any of my subjects; and I permit what ye ask, but on one condition. Ye are all of an age in which almost every man seeks the partner of his life; and as far as I know, ye also will do the same. I have no wish to tell you what princesses to fall in love with, but I ask this: Return before a year and a day, and bring me some gift — not costly, but valued — from your chosen ones."

The princes were astonished that their father had guessed their thoughts so well, and agreed without thinking. Then they took their crossbows and went to the open field. The eldest son let the bow-string go, and the arrow flew to the east. The second let the string go, and the arrow flew to the west.

" And where am I to aim ? " cried the youngest, whose name was Yarmil. That moment a mouse ran

near him to its hole; he let the string go, and the
arrow flew after the mouse.

"Oh, thoughtless fellow!" said the eldest prince
in rebuke; "now thou must go to the mouse-hole."

"It is settled," answered Yarmil, and shrugged his
shoulders.

They went home, prepared for the road, and next
day started; the eldest to the east, the second to the
west, and Yarmil to the mouse-hole. Up to that moment he had held it merely a jest; but how was he
astonished when on nearing the place the earth
opened so that he rode in conveniently, and sooner
than he could think was in an open country, in the
middle of which stood a white marble castle. Nowhere did he see a living soul; and he felt sure then
that he would find no one in the castle; but scarcely
had he entered the gate when a lady came forth to
meet him who had not only garments, but face, hair,
eyes, in short everything, white as newly fallen snow.
She held by the bridle a mettlesome white steed, and
without saying a word, indicated to Yarmil to de-
scend from his own horse and sit on the white one;
but he had barely mounted the white steed when it
rose with him through the air, and without heeding
the bit, went on till it brought him to the earth before
a splendid castle. Yarmil marvelled, for the castle
was so brilliant that he could not look at it, such was
the glitter of gold and precious stones. Around
about, wherever the eye could see, was a beautiful

garden, in which the most luxuriant trees were growing, the most beautiful flowers were in bloom, and birds of every color were singing.

When he had recovered from the first surprise, Yarmil dismounted and wished to lead the steed to the castle; but it tore away, rose through the air, and vanished like a white dove in the clouds.

Full of expectation Yarmil entered the castle. He struck on the gate; no answer, but it opened of itself. He went in on broad marble steps to the door of the first chamber. Again he knocked; no answer, but the door opened. He entered, but how did he wonder again! There was such splendor that he exclaimed, "My father is by far the richest king, but this chamber alone is worth more than his kingdom."

But if the first chamber was rich, the second was richer; and that splendor increased till he came to the eleventh, where there was a great crystal tub with golden hoops, into which, through a golden pipe, water still clearer than crystal was flowing. In the twelfth chamber were only four naked walls, an ordinary ceiling, and a common floor, but in the middle of the floor a diamond pan. When Yarmil examined more carefully, he saw written on it: "Whoever wishes to liberate me must carry me next to his body, and bathe me each day."

Urged by curiosity Yarmil removed a diamond, then a golden, and finally, with great effort, a silver,

cover. But how was he frightened when under it
appeared a great ugly toad! He wished to escape,
but at that moment such terror seized him that in
spite of himself he took the toad out of the pan and
put it in his bosom. The toad chilled him, but in a
moment he was as happy as if he had liberated some
one from death. Straightway he went to the eleventh
chamber, took the toad from his bosom, and washed it
carefully; but to his great affliction he saw that it was
a toad, and the more he washed the uglier it grew.
When he had grown tired he put it in his bosom
again and went to the garden to cheer himself.

A sight of the trees and the flowers hitherto unno-
ticed, the odor of them, and the singing of the birds
entertained him so that midday came before he knew
it. He went back to the castle, and there, to his
great surprise, saw in the first chamber a table covered with the most delicate dishes. He sat down
with appetite, and when he had eaten to his content,
and drunk of the wine which an unseen hand had
placed before him in a golden goblet, he confessed
that he had never tasted at his father's table, or at the
greatest festivals, such delicate dishes and such good
wine.

Now he looked the room through with more care;
the splendor did not charm him so much as at first,
but the many musical instruments, writing imple-
ments, and beautiful books pleased him beyond measure, for he was skilled in every good art.

After the supper, which was as good as the dinner, he lay on a soft bed and slept soundly till morning; then he ate a good meal, which was on the table, and spent the time as he had the day before. He was annoyed at his lonely life, but he soon drove away trouble. He was grieved because the more the toad was washed the uglier it grew; still he washed it with care, and carried it in his bosom.

Now the year was nearing its end, when he had to return to his father with a gift from his bride. He walked like one deprived of reason through the castle and the garden; nothing could comfort him, but still he did not forget to bathe the toad each day, and with greater care. When the last day of the year had come, he knew not what to begin; but while walking through the room he saw on his writing-table a sheet of paper not there before. He seized it quickly; and on it was written in black letters:

DEAR YARMIL, — I love thee unspeakably ; but be thou patient, as I am patient. A gift for thy father thou hast in the pan ; give it to him, but tarry not long at home. Put me back in the pan.

Yarmil hastened with joy to the twelfth chamber, took from the pan a rich casket set with diamonds, and put the toad in the pan ; then he ran out quickly, mounted the white steed which was waiting, and which rose in the air and flew regardless of bit, till it stopped before the white castle ; there the white lady gave Yarmil his horse, took the white steed, and led it away.

In a short time Yarmil came to the great gate, and when he had ridden through and looked, there was nothing behind but a mouse-hole. Putting spurs to his horse he rushed on at a gallop and came to the gate of his father's castle almost at the same moment as his brothers, so that all three were able to appear together before their father, and say: " Here we are, according to thy command."

" But have ye brought gifts from your princesses? " asked the king.

" Of course," cried the elder brothers, proudly. Yarmil answered, as it were, timidly, with a nod; for he knew not what was in that casket taken from the pan.

The king had invited a great number of guests to look at the gifts. All were in the banqueting-hall. The king led his sons thither, and when the feast was ended, he said to the eldest: " Now give me the gift from thy princess."

" My love is the daughter of a great king," said the prince, proudly; and he gave his father a casket containing a small mirror.

The king looked, and wondered not a little that he saw his whole person. Then he said: " Well, men's hands can do everything."

The second son gave him a still smaller mirror, but the king saw in it his whole person; still he only said: " Men's hands can do everything. But what has thy princess sent me?" asked he of Yarmil. In silence, and timidly, Yarmil gave him the casket. The king barely looked in it when he cried in amazement, "That princess of thine has wealth in abundance; these diamonds alone have more value than my kingdom." But he wondered when he took from the casket another such mirror, but smaller; and he was really frightened when in a twinkle a puppet sprang out and held the glass for him as soon as he looked at it, and the moment he stopped looking the puppet was gone.

"Oh," cried the king, "no hand of man could frame that;" and embracing Yarmil, he added with tenderness: "Thou hast brought me true joy, my son."

Yarmil called to mind the ugly toad, and had no regret now that he had spent a whole year with it; but his brothers and his mother, who was a witch and hated Yarmil, were enraged though they dissembled.

When the feast was over and the princes were parting with their father, he said: "Go now with rejoicing, but return in a year and a day, and bring me portraits of your princesses."

The elder brothers promised with joy, but Yarmil barely nodded, for he feared what his father would say should he bring the toad's portrait; still he went with his brothers beyond the town, where he parted with them, and galloped on to the mouse-hole. He was just drawing near when the ground opened to give a good entrance. At the white castle the white lady took his horse and gave him the white steed, which rose through the air, and regardless of bit, flew on till it reached the golden castle. Yarmil hurried to the twelfth chamber; the steed disappeared like a dove in the clouds.

In the castle nothing was changed, and the diamond pan was standing in the twelfth chamber. Yarmil removed the three covers, took out the toad and placed it in his bosom. Now he bathed it twice each day, but to his grief it grew uglier. How could he take the portrait of his princess to his father! He might paint the most beautiful lady, because he was very well skilled in painting, but he would not deceive his father. Only the hope that the toad would help him as before gave him strength to endure the dreary life.

At last the day was near in which he must return to his father. He looked continually on his writing-table till he saw to his great joy a sheet of paper on which was written in silver letters, —

DEAR YARMIL, — I love thee unspeakably; be patient, as I am patient. Thou hast my portrait in the pan; give it to thy father, but tarry not long. Put me back in the pan.

Yarmil hastened to the twelfth chamber, found in the pan a casket still richer than the first. He took it quickly, and put the toad in its place. Then he hur-

ried forth, sat on the white steed, which brought him
to the white castle, where the white lady gave him his
own horse. When he had ridden through the gate
and looked back, he saw nothing behind but a
mouse-hole. He put spurs to his horse, and rode to
the gate of his father's castle at the same time with
his brothers. They stood before their father and
said: " Here we are, as thou hast commanded."

" Do ye bring me portraits of your princesses? "
asked the king.

" Of course! " exclaimed the two elder brothers,
full of pride. But Yarmil only answered with a nod,
for he knew not what portrait the casket contained.

The king led them to the banqueting-hall, where
the guests were assembled. When the banquet was
over, he said to the eldest: " Now show me the portrait of thy princess."

The eldest brother gave a rich casket to his father.
He opened it, took out a portrait, and looking at it
from every side, said at last: " That is a beautiful
lady; she pleases me. Still there are fairer than she
in the world, but any man might love her." Then
he gave the portrait to the guests, and said to his
second son: " And the portrait of thy princess? "

The second son gave him promptly a richer casket,
and smiled with happiness. He thought doubtless
that his father must be astonished at the beauty of
his princess; but he looked on her with indifference
and said: " A beautiful lady too, but there are more

beautiful in the world; still any man might fall in love with her."

Then he nodded to Yarmil, who gave with trembling hand his diamond casket. Scarcely had the king looked at it when he exclaimed: "Thy princess must be rich beyond measure; thy casket is at any time worth twice my whole kingdom." But how was he astonished when he took out the portrait! He looked fixedly at it for a while, unable to utter a word. Then he said with the greatest enthusiasm, "No; such a lady cannot be found in the world."

All the guests crowded around the portrait, and in one voice agreed with the king. At last Yarmil drew near to look at his princess, unknown till that moment. Now he regretted no whit that he had spent two years in lone life and nursing a toad; but his brothers and his mother were raging, and envied him his princess.

Next day the princes were taking farewell, and the king said to them: "After this time I will not let you go again. In a year and a day I wish to see your princesses; then we will celebrate the weddings."

The two elder brothers were shouting with joy, but Yarmil answered no word. They took leave of their father and went together to the edge of the town, where they separated; the eldest went to the east, the second to the west, but Yarmil to the mouse-hole, which opened quickly to give him a convenient passage. At the white castle the white lady gave him

the white steed, which flew to the golden castle regardless of bit. There Yarmil descended, and the
steed vanished like a dove in the clouds.

Full of hope Yarmil hastened to the twelfth chamber, for he trusted to find there his wondrous fair
princess whose portrait he had taken to his father;
but he found in the pan the ugly toad, which he put
in his bosom, and now washed three times each day.
In vain was all his labor, for the more he bathed the
uglier grew the toad. Had it not been for the portrait he would have fled from the castle, and who
knows what he might have done? Every day his
strength decreased, and when the last day of the year
drew near it is a wonder that he did not despair; for
the toad had become now not only ugly beyond
measure, but all mangy, so that he shivered when he
looked at it. And now he must bring this to his
father as his chosen one.

" My father will kill me! " cried he with grief, and
threw himself on the couch. He thought what to
do, but could come to no resolve. At last he
reached to his bosom to look once more at the toad,
hoping that at sight of it a happy thought might
come; but a new surprise, — the toad was gone.
Now he began to lament. He ran through the whole
castle, searched every room, in the garden every tree
and bush, but no trace of the toad.

At last he remembered the dish in the twelfth
chamber, ran thither, but stopped on the threshold

as if thunderstruck; for that poor chamber had become a real paradise, and in tne middle of it stood a lady as beautiful, if not still more beautiful, than the portrait which he had carried to his father. In speechless amazement he looked at her, and who knows how long he might have stood there had she not turned to him and said: " My dear, thou hast suffered much; but I am not yet entirely free, and my people are not. Hurry now to the cellar; here is the key, and do to a hair what I command, or it will go ill with us. When the door is opened, thou wilt hear a terrible wailing; but listen to nothing, and speak not a word. Go down on the steps; below thou wilt find on a table twelve burning tapers, and before each taper one shirt. Roll up the shirts, quench the tapers, bring them all with thee."

Yarmil took the key. When he opened the door of the cellar he heard such wailing that it is a wonder his heart did not break; but mindful of what had been said by his bride, he went boldly, descended the steps, rolled up the twelve shirts, quenching at each one, one taper; then he took the shirts and the tapers and hurried back. But how did he wonder when he saw a man nailed to the door by his tongue! The man begged Yarmil by all things to set him free, so that there was a strange feeling in Yarmil's heart; but after short hesitation he mastered this feeling, and shut the door.

When he came to his bride and gave her the shirts,

with the tapers, she said: " These twelve shirts are my twelve skins, in which I was a toad; and these twelve tapers burned me continually. Now I am liberated, it is true; but it will be three years before I shall be completely free. Know that I am the daughter of a mighty king, whom that foul monster, who is nailed to the cellar door by the tongue, changed into a toad because I refused him my hand. He is a wizard; but there is a witch more powerful than he. To punish him, she nailed him to that door; I, too, am still in her power. Now promise that for three years thou wilt tell no living person into what creature I was enchanted; but especially tell not how many skins I had."

" Not even to my own mother! " exclaimed Yarmil, with excitement.

" It is just from thy own mother that thou must hide it most, for she is a witch, and hates thee; she knows long since that thou art three years with me, and most carefully will she try to learn from thee just what I have forbidden thee to tell."

Yarmil was greatly grieved, but the princess soon cheered him, especially when she said: " It is now high time to go, so as to come to thy father's at the right moment." Then she took him by the hand, and led him down the stairs. In front of the castle a carriage with four white horses was waiting; when they entered, the horses rushed off with such speed that soon they passed the white castle. Yarmil was going to ask who the white lady was, when the princess said: " That is my mother, who has aided in my liberation."

Soon they were at the great gate; and when they had passed it, and looked back, there was nothing but a mouse-hole. They arrived at the king's castle just in the same moment with the two elder brothers and their princesses. But no one looked at them, for the eyes of all were turned to Yarmil's bride.

The king was rejoiced most of all. He conducted the bride to the banqueting-hall, where there was a multitude of guests, and with tears of delight he exalted the happiness of his favorite son; but the elder princes and the queen were enraged, though they would not let it be known.

On the following day came the weddings of the three princes; though Yarmil and his bride were the last, still glory came only to them. At the banquet the guests drank continually to the health of his bride, so that the other princesses were purple from shame.

When Yarmil was almost reeling with delight, the queen drew near him, and praised with great flattery the beauty of his bride; but all at once she spoke of her origin, and in every way tried to discover whence she had come.

Yarmil at first evaded her questions; but when she urged him vehemently to tell from what land came his bride, he said: " Dear mother, I will do everything according to thy wish, but of this one thing ask me not."

"I know well whence she comes," smiled the queen; "I know, too, that thou didst not see her first in her present form."

"Of course not; but I am proud that I liberated her."

"Oh, my dear son!" exclaimed the queen, compassionately. "I pity thee greatly for letting thyself be so duped; but dost thou know that that beauty of hers is pure deceit?"

"Why?" asked Yarmil in fright.

"Because she is a witch," whispered the queen in his ear, with an anxious look. "There is still time," continued she, when she saw that Yarmil as it were believed, "to extricate thyself from her snares; and I wish to aid thee in every way. But thou must tell me what form she had before."

Yarmil said that he would not tell, but the queen did not abandon her plan. When she could not discover from him directly, she began to name every kind of beast, looking with exceeding quickness at his face. Yarmil shook his head unceasingly, but was confused when she said "toad."

"Then she was a toad before," cried in horror the queen. "Ah! dear son, it is ill, very ill with thee; but it may be well yet if only I know in how many skins she was living."

Again Yarmil answered decidedly that he would

not tell, but the queen tried so long that at last she discovered. Now she knew what she wanted, and went from Yarmil. It is a wonder that he was not suspicious, but he said nothing to the princess.

Next morning a number of guests went with the king and his sons to the chase, and stayed in the forest till evening; thus the queen could act freely.

While the three princesses and the remaining guests were walking in the garden, she stole into the chamber of Yarmil's bride, found the twelve shirts and the tapers, hid them in her own apartments, and in the evening, when the king had returned from the chase and all were sitting in the banqueting-hall at table, she went to the garden, where she burned the shirts and the tapers. At that moment Yarmil's bride felt great faintness, so that she went for fresh air in the garden.

Yarmil hurried after her, but he had scarcely gone through the door, when she cried: "Woe is me, Yarmil! Thou hast told what I forbade thee to tell. Forget me; I must now to the glass mountain, from which there is no liberation." Straightway she vanished in the darkness of night.

Yarmil remained a moment as if paralyzed; then he ran through the garden as if he had lost his wits, and called his bride by the most endearing names, but in vain. The guests ran out at the sound of his lamentation, and were greatly terrified when Yarmil told his misfortune. The queen also came quickly, and listened as if with terrified wonder to what had happened.

"That was a witch," said she; "and 't is well that other mishaps have not come."

But the king was grieved more than all, and put an end to the rejoicing. Next day the two elder brothers went away with their brides, and poor Yarmil stayed home alone. In vain did his father try to comfort him; in vain did he promise that he would go himself to seek another bride for him. Yarmil was not to be consoled; and when the first onrush of sorrow had passed, he resolved to go to the glass mountain for his bride.

"In what direction wilt thou go?" objected his father. "While I live no one has heard of a glass mountain."

"Still I will go," said Yarmil, firmly. "It will come to the same whether I perish on the road or at home; in any event I shall die of disappointment."

The king tried in all ways to dissuade him from going, but Yarmil would not let him talk. He mounted his horse, dropped the reins, and let him go whithersoever he would. He travelled long in this objectless way, hither and thither; but at last he saw that he must act differently if he meant to reach the glass mountain. But now came his real trouble; for wherever he asked about the glass mountain, people stared at him, and said that there was no such mountain in the world. Yarmil did not let himself be frightened; and now he galloped the more eagerly on his horse, and asked the more carefully everywhere. He had passed through towns without number, but still no one knew of a glass mountain. At last he heard the name.

In a certain town there was a juggler, — a showman with every kind of wonder. Yarmil was just going past him at the moment when he cried out: " The witch with her twelve daughters on the glass mountain! "

Yarmil called the juggler aside and said: " Here are ten goldpieces, tell me where the glass mountain is."

" I am a poor man," said the juggler, honestly, " and need these goldpieces greatly; but I know nothing of the glass mountain."

" Nor in what country it is? " asked Yarmil, impatiently.

"I know that," answered the man. " It is in the east, but they say it is very far off; and besides, they say that no one can go within twenty miles of it."

Yarmil threw the ten goldpieces into the juggler's cap, and putting spurs to his horse galloped off to the east. Many a time did the sun rise and set before he reached the glass mountain. But what good did it do him to go there? Around the mountain flowed an immensely great river, and on the bridge which was across it stood on guard three very fierce giants.

Yarmil's courage fell. That moment the white lady from the white castle appeared suddenly before him and said: "Bind thy horse's hoofs with thy coat, and go very carefully over the bridge. The giant who stands on watch will see thee only when thou art in front of him, and will start after thee; but throw behind this dust and nothing will harm thee. Do the same for the second and third giant." She gave him three packages of dust, and said: "Beyond the river is a mill in which they give a witch to grind. Ask the miller for a night's lodging; he will give it thee, and invite thee to supper. Towards the end of the supper the cook will bring him a roast cock, and to that he will not invite thee; he eats it all himself. The bones of it he leaves on the plate and the cook must throw them under the wheel; but tell her to hide them for thee. And when it will be midnight, go to the glass mountain and put the bones before thee; but be careful to save one till thou art on the summit, then throw that last one back over thy head."

The moment the lady had finished, she disappeared. Yarmil sprang from his horse, tore his coat into four pieces, and with them muffled the feet of his horse; then he mounted and rode cautiously to the bridge. The first giant was sitting with his back to him and dozing. Yarmil passed him safely; but that moment the giant woke, and howled with a terrible voice to him to come back. Here Yarmil threw the dust behind, and that moment there was such darkness that it hid the giant completely. The same happened with the second and third giant, and Yarmil crossed the river safely. Not far off was the mill, and the miller stood just on the threshold.

"What dost thou wish here?" growled he at Yarmil.

"Oh, grant me a night's lodging," said Yarmil; "I am a traveller from distant lands."

"I'll give thee nothing," answered the miller, roughly, "for if I did I should lose my place."

Yarmil begged again, and begged so long that the miller asked: "Whence art thou?" Yarmil told him; and the miller, meditating awhile, said: "Well, if thou art the son of so powerful a king, I will give thee a night's lodging; for we are from the same country, and I knew thy father very well."

Then he led him to a sitting-room; and since it was just dark, he asked him to supper. Yarmil watched continually to see if the cock would soon come to the table, and he had not long to wait. The miller grew sullen, and without speaking a word ate the cock. Yarmil went out, and pressing a few goldpieces into the hands of the cook, begged her to hide the bones of the cock for him. The moment the cook saw the goldpieces she was glad to agree.

When the miller had picked the cock he called the cook and ordered her strictly to throw the bones under the wheel. The cook took the plate and motioning as if she had thrown them into the water, put them very adroitly into her apron; when all were asleep she gave them to Yarmil. He waited quietly till the approach of midnight, then he went out cautiously and made for the glass mountain with his horse. Full of expectation he took out the first bone and put it on the mountain; and behold! in a moment a step was made so that he could walk comfortably on it, and so it happened with every bone. Yarmil was already at the summit and only one bone remained to him; this he threw with all his power over his head, and in a twinkle there was a pleasant highway along which his horse ran after him with ease.

All wearied, Yarmil fell down at the castle, in which lived the sorceress with the twelve princesses her daughters, and he soon fell asleep. When he woke the sun was high in the heavens; and before he could think what further to do, his own princess came to him.

"I told thee," said she, reproachfully, "to forget me; but thou didst not obey."

"Hide me somewhere quickly from the sorceress; in the night we will flee."

"Simple man!" said the princess smiling. "She knows long ago that thou art here; rather go to her, but be polite beyond measure. At dinner, rise after each dish and walk through the room, otherwise thou wilt stay here for the ages."

Yarmil had to obey. When he came to the sorceress he bowed low before her, and said: "Great mighty lady, I have come for my bride."

"I will give her to thee," smiled the sorceress, "but first thou must serve me three years."

" I am glad to do everything thou mayest desire,"
said Yarmil bowing; and the sorceress answered graciously, inviting him at once to the table, to which
just then one of the princesses brought the first dish.
Yarmil ate with a relish; but when he had finished,
he said to the sorceress: " Permit me, great mighty
lady, to walk a little. I have travelled so much that I
fear my legs will lose their power."

" Oh, walk if it please thee," answered the sorceress, but her eyes glittered with anger. And
Yarmil did the same after each dish, and the sorceress
was ready to split from rage. Next day she gave
him a wooden axe and saw, and said: " Thou must
clear all that forest over there, or be the son of
Death."

Yarmil took the axe and the saw, and went on. In
the forest he threw himself on the ground and
thought of death; for such a stretch of forest no
man could clear alone, still less with such tools. At
midday his princess brought him dinner.

" Ah!" scolded she, " thou art not working diligently."

"Why trouble myself for nothing? " sighed Yarmil.

" Only be of good courage," said the princess, comforting him. " It is not so bad to-day; it will be
worse to-morrow."

Then she gave him dinner; and when Yarmil had
eaten, he put his head on her lap and fell asleep
soundly. Then the princess took out of her bosom

some kind of powder, and muttering mysterious words she threw it in the air. And wonder of wonders! in the twinkle of an eye invisible hands began to fell the aged trees, cut, split, and pile, so that in a short time the whole forest was felled.

Now Yarmil woke up, and hurried with the princess to the castle. The sorceress praised him; she suppressed her rage with difficulty, and said: " Thou hast worked out thy first year in order."

Next day the sorceress gave him a spade and a wheelbarrow, and said: " Thou must carry away that mountain out there, or be the son of Death."

Yarmil went with his tools to the hill, but when there he threw himself on the ground, for a thousand men would not have been able to carry off the hill in ten years. At midday his princess brought him dinner, and said: " Oh, thou art working as diligently as yesterday!"

" I am," sighed Yarmil.

" Only be of good cheer," said the princess, comforting him. " To-day it is not so bad; it will be worse to-morrow."

When Yarmil had eaten, he put his head on her lap and fell asleep. The princess again threw into the air a powder of some kind, muttering mysterious words; and straightway unseen hands began to work so vigorously that in a short time the hill was carried away.

Then Yarmil woke up, and hurried to the sorceress

23

to tell her he had done what she had commanded. She flamed up in anger, but nevertheless said: " Thou hast worked the second year of thy service in order."

Next day she gave him a tailor's thimble, and said: " Thou must bail out that fish-pond, or be the son of Death."

Yarmil took the thimble and went. At the fish-pond, however, he threw himself on the ground and waited for the princess. She came sooner than usual; and when Yarmil, strengthened with food, had fallen asleep with his head on her lap, she threw powder in the air, muttering mysterious words. Soon the water began to disappear from the fish-pond. Now she roused Yarmil, and said to him: " Draw thy sword, and give good care. When all the water is gone from the pond the sorceress will take the shape of a rain-storm, and try to destroy us; but look well at the darkness, and where it is blackest strike there with thy sword."

Yarmil promised to do so, and had barely drawn his sword when a black darkness rushed from the castle, — but almost on the ground, so that Yarmil could strike the blackest spot with ease. At that moment the darkness turned into the sorceress, and Yarmil's sword stuck in her heart. With fearful cursing, she fell to the earth and died. Yarmil hurried to the castle with the princess, mounted his horse, and rushed off at a swift gallop.

He had to travel far before he came to his father's

castle; but to make up, there was joy unspeakable at the happy meeting. The queen was terrified when she saw them, and she had reason; for when Yarmil told all to his father the king gave her to be burned without mercy.

When the feasting was over Yarmil set out with his wife on the journey to their kingdom. When they came to the mouse-hole it was no longer a mouse-hole, but a magnificent gate leading to a great city, in the middle of which stood a golden castle on a hill; and in that city there were multitudes of people everywhere, and in the castle throngs of courtiers and servants, who greeted with mighty applause their master and mistress, thanking Yarmil at the same time for their liberation.

Now followed feasting, which lasted for eight whole days; and when the feasting was over they all lived happily beyond measure, because the royal pair were goodness itself.

THE CUIRASSIER AND THE HORNED
PRINCESS.

IN a certain town were encamped a regiment of
cuirassiers, and they had a very unpleasant life.
Twelve men of them agreed to desert, — three ser-
geants and nine from the ranks. They carried out
their plan; and when they had gone a good distance,
one said to the rest: "Let us look, brothers, and see
if we are not pursued." Another dismounted, and
climbed a high tree, — "Oh! they are searching;
but they will not overtake us, for we are far in advance of them." Then he came down, mounted his
horse, and all rode rapidly on, — rode till dusk.
Then the chief man said: "Where shall we go for
the night, brothers? Around here we see nothing
but mountains and forests."

One of them climbed a tree again to look for a
light. He saw one, and called to his comrades,
"Look out! We will ride in the direction in which
I throw this sword, for I see a light there."

All rode toward the light, and came to a very large
building in the wild mountains. At the first glance
they saw it was an enormous castle, which was open.
They entered the court, led their horses to the stable,
—where oats were ready for twelve horses,—and then

went themselves into a hall where a table was laid for twelve persons, so that all might sit down and eat; but there was not a living soul to be seen.

"Brothers," said one of them, "may we touch this food and drink?"

"Why not?" said the chief. "What if we have to pay a few ducats for the entertainment?"

They sat down, and ate with good relish. After they had eaten and drunk, an old sorceress slipped in and saluted them, saying: "Good evening, gentlemen. I greet you in this our famous castle. Did the supper taste well?"

"We ate with pleasure," answered one in the name of all, "only we were a little afraid how it would end."

"Fear not, fear not, I am glad ye are strengthened after the long ride," said the sorceress; and then she said further: "Now of course ye will need good beds, so as to refresh yourselves with grateful sleep. In the next chamber are twelve beds and twelve caskets. Lie on the beds prepared for you, but let no man dare, on pain of great punishment, to look at the caskets, which are unlocked."

All went to the next chamber; the sorceress gave them good-night and went out through the opposite door. In the morning when they rose everything was well prepared for them, — basins with water and towels, and food for each man. After breakfast they spoke of the good cheer which they had not expected to find in the castle. They spoke of various subjects till they came to the caskets, and the splendid things that must be therein. Some expressed great curiosity; some were heard to say that they could not refrain till evening from looking in the caskets; others warned their comrades not to do that which they might regret.

They had a pleasant time all day at the castle, an excellent dinner, a good lunch, a splendid supper. After supper they went to bed. The sun was shining brightly through the windows next morning, but no man was stirring.

The chief rose and called the others, saying, " It is time to be up." Only two gave answer; the rest did not move. These three went to the beds and found their comrades lifeless. All were terrified, and went to the stable to look at their horses. In the stable they found the nine dead horses, of the nine dead men.

" What shall we do? " asked one of them. " We must leave this place where our comrades have perished; nothing can comfort us again."

They returned to the hall where breakfast was ready for only three. They sat down and ate. After eating, the sorceress came again, and said: " Ye see, my friends, that sinful curiosity has cost those nine men their lives. They could withstand it no longer, rose at midnight, opened the caskets, and looked at the contents; scarcely had they lain down again when sudden death overtook them. Had they followed my advice, as ye have, all might have had a pleasant time, and lived joyously here a whole year. Now I see by your faces that nothing can comfort you here, and that ye would gladly go away."

"Yes," answered one, "we fear to remain longer in this place, where our comrades died a sudden death."

"There is nothing to fear," said the sorceress; "but since it is unpleasant for you, I will not keep you. Go where ye like, but before going each may look without fear or danger in his casket, and take the things inside to remember me by; they may be useful."

The men were afraid at first to open the caskets, having before their eyes the sad example of their comrades; but when the sorceress assured them again and again that they might open them without fear and take out the contents, they grew bold and opened them. The first took from his casket a cap, which the sorceress said had such power that whoever put it on his head no man could see him. The second drew from his casket a mantle, and whoever put it on, the sorceress said, could fly through the air as high as he wished. The third took a purse which had the power that whenever it was shaken ten ducats were in it.

The sorceress bade them good-by. They thanked her for the hospitality and useful presents, and saddling their horses, rode away from that castle with the Lord God.

They travelled long, and on the road kept telling what a good time they would have with their gifts. At last they came to a large town, took up their lodging at an inn, and asked what there was strange in the place. The innkeeper answered: "Nothing, unless it be that we have a princess immeasurably fond of playing cards, and who says that no one is able to play with her. She vanquishes every comer, and then has him flogged out of the castle."

The man who had the purse thought, "Wait a while, I 'll settle thy play." He made ready straightway, and went to the castle. He had himself announced, and declared that he wished to play with the princess. Meanwhile the other two ate and drank well in the inn.

The princess was glad to find some one again with whom to play cards and whom she might overcome. She had him brought in without delay. The game began. The man lost; but he did n't mind that, for whenever he lost he shook the purse and had ten ducats again. So he kept losing and shaking the purse till the princess was astonished, and thought to herself: "Where dost thou get all these ducats, good man? Thou hast not a treasury at thy side, and still thou hast plenty of money. How dost thou get it?"

She watched him and saw that he shook the purse on his knee, from which he took the ducats. She had already won a great bag of ducats, but still was not able to win all he had. She kept thinking how to get that magic purse. "Now let us rest a little," said she, and went to the next room, from which she brought two goblets of wine. One she gave him and drank the other herself, for they were tired and needed refreshment. Her wine was pure, but in his she put a sleeping-powder. She drank to his health, and he emptied his goblet at a draught. After a while he was so very drowsy that he slipped from the seat, dropped under the table, and fell soundly asleep. That was his misfortune. The princess took the magic purse and gave him one like it containing ten ducats.

When he woke up the princess said to him: "Now let us play again." They played while he had ducats. When the ducats were gone he shook and shook the purse, but in vain. The princess said: "Well, my dear man, since thou hast no money, go. But that disgrace which I have put on others I will not put on thee. I will not have thee flogged out of the castle because I have won much money from thee; go in peace."

He went to his friends in great trouble. They greeted him from afar, and called out: "Well, how didst thou prosper?"

"Oh, badly, very badly, brothers; I no longer have the purse; I lost that."

"Oh, comrade, that is bad; how shall we live

now? We are in debt for food and drink, and have nothing to pay with."

The one who had the magic mantle said : " Do ye know what, brothers? I 'll take a good vengeance on that wicked woman ! "

" But how? " was the question.

He answered, " This is how I 'll do it. Let me have thy cap so that no one may see me, and I 'll take my mantle. When the princess is going to church I 'll seize her, fly with her through the air to desert regions, so far away that she will never be able to come home again."

" Yes, that will be a just punishment for her," said the two others. The third one immediately took the cap, wrapped the mantle around him, and waited for the princess. As she was going along the street he seized her, flew far away with her to wild moun-tains, and let her down there on the ground near a pear-tree. On that tree were beautiful pears.

The princess begged the man to climb the tree and shake it, so that she might have some of the fruit to eat. " I 'll gratify thee just once," said he. But he was so cunning that he did not leave the cap or magic mantle on the ground, but took them up on the tree, hung them both on a limb, and shook the tree with all his might. The cap and the mantle fell to the ground before the pears. The princess put the cap on her head at once, wrapped the mantle around her, and was off in an instant, —

sooner than the man on the tree had recovered from his fright.

He was now alone in the wild mountains. What was he to do? He stood motionless as the tree at his side, as if senseless from a thunderbolt; he had no longer magic cap or magic mantle. "Oh, where shall I go?" groaned he, and walked around on the mountains. In his trouble and fright he picked up some pears and ate them. Then other terrible miseries came upon him, for he had barely eaten the pears when unheard of gigantic horns grew out of his head, so that he could not walk through the woods nor turn around; the horns stopped him everywhere; he could barely crawl forward.

With great care and much struggling, he dragged himself over a bit of road and came to a deep ravine, in which a hermit lived whose name was Wind.

"Oh, friend," said the man, "help me from the mountain, and take me home."

Said Wind, "I am not strong enough to bear thee to thy home, but go to my brother; he is the strongest of us. He will take thee home quickly."

"I should like to go to him, but I cannot move."

"He is not far from here, — there, on that side; but go as well as thou art able. He will rid thee of those horns."

The man pushed through as best he could, and came, covered with sweat, to another cave, in which the eldest Wind brother was living. He fell on his knees before Wind, and cried imploringly: "Be so kind as to bear me home!"

"I should like to help thee, my friend; but it is not so easy as may seem to thee. I must go to the Lord to ask with what force Wind may blow. If Wind may blow so trees will be torn out with their roots, thou canst reach home; if Wind blows but weakly, thou wilt not go there, for 't is far. Wait a while; I 'll come back soon."

Wind went to ask the Lord how hard he might blow, and the Lord commanded him to blow mightily.

When he returned, the man asked: "How is it?"

"Well," said Wind, "I must blow mightily; thou wilt reach home. But knowest thou there is an apple-tree over there? Climb it, pluck an apple, cut it into four parts, and eat; thy great horns will fall off."

The man was glad, climbed the apple-tree quickly, but the horns hindered him much. He plucked an apple and ate it; how soon was he free of the horns! He came down from the tree like a squirrel, and thought: "Oh, brother, thou 'lt get back thy things!" As he was coming down he took more apples and put them in his pocket; then went to the pear-tree and took pears. Soon Wind caught him up, bore him off swiftly, and in a short time put him down in front of the inn where his friends were waiting impatiently. They were all very glad.

"Where wert thou?" asked they.

" Oh, I was where ye will not be to your dying day, brothers ! "

" How didst thou prosper? "

" Badly, badly."

" Where hast thou the cap and the mantle?"

" Oh, that woman took them from me ! "

" Woe to us, — woe, passing woe ! Now we have neither the purse, the cap, nor the mantle. We are beggared beyond reckoning."

The innkeeper would not let them go because of their debt.

"What will become of us?" asked they in one voice.

The man whom Wind bore home said: "I have here noble and wonderful fruit which I brought from the wild mountains. One of you will take these pears to the street and sell them; but do not dare to sell them to any one save the princess when she is going home from church. For the people thou must put such a price that they will not buy; for the princess reduce the price so that she may buy."

One of the men put the pears in a clean basket, covered them with a neat cloth, and went to the square through which the princess was wont to go to church and return. Soon she was coming out of the church, her servant following some steps behind. She saw the uncommonly beautiful pears from a distance, came up herself, and asked: " How many dost thou give for a copper? "

" Oh, these pears are not sold for copper coin! They are so splendid, and have such a flavor, that I can give only three for a ducat."

The princess bought all, and gave them to her servant to carry; she had barely reached home, and sat near the table, when she took a golden knife, pared and ate with great relish a number of pears. She ate with such pleasure that she saw not how horns began to grow on her head after the first pear; and in a little while they had grown so much that she could not remain in the room. She went to the great supper-hall, but even there was forced to lie down on the floor, so broad and so lofty were her horns. She gave herself up to fearful lamentation and tears, so that all the servants and the king, her father, with the queen, her mother, ran in. All were horrified and wrung their hands, seeing the princess disfigured.

The king sent quickly for the doctors, who came in all haste from each corner and town. The servants ran to every place; each one in his excitement brought whomsoever he knew. The doctors met and shook their heads one after another; each said that in his life he had never seen nor had experience of such a case. They held a consultation, and at last decided to saw off the horns. They went to work, but in vain; they had barely sawed a piece, when it grew on again quickly, so that fright seized every one. The princess was so horrified and ashamed that she would have preferred to be out of the world; no man could help her. Then the king made proclamation that whoso would free the princess from the horns, would get her in marriage, and with her the whole kingdom.

Who was so glad now as the man with the apples? " Wait," thought he; " my little bird, thou 'lt sing as I whistle, — no man can help thee but me."

He had fine clothes brought, and dressed as a doctor had himself announced at the palace. He was soon admitted, and began to speak to the princess, saying: " You must have angered God greatly, must have committed grievous sins, for which you are punished in this way. I expect to give you real help; but first of all you must tell me sincerely what you have done, — my aid has to be rendered in view of that."

She confessed with weeping that she had been fond of playing cards; had outplayed all men, then had them flogged from the castle. The last time she had played with a stranger, from whom she had stolen a magic purse; and afterward she had stolen from another man a magic cap and mantle. No doubt the Lord had now punished her for that.

" Before we can think of a cure," said the unknown physician, " you must return the stolen property."

The princess had all the above-mentioned articles brought at once, and gave them gladly to the doctor, who promised to deliver them to the owners. " I will carry them away," said he. " and bring my medicine, through which you will be freed from the horns."

Half an hour later he returned, took her by the hand, looked at her tongue, and said: "Charming woman, you have eaten something, I suppose, from which these horns grew."

The princess answered: "I don't know that I have eaten anything harmful; I ate a few beautiful pears; with that exception I have never eaten any common food."

"You must have eaten something," said the doctor. "I have good medicine that will not fail; but I can only help you on condition that I receive the whole kingdom, with you in marriage, as our lord the king has proclaimed."

The king and princess promised then that the proclamation would be carried out if he would free her from the horns. After these words he set about the cure. He took from his pocket an apple, and cut it into four parts; he told her to lie down, and gave her the first fourth of the apple. She was not able however to lie with comfort by reason of the horns. When she had eaten all the four quarters of the apple, the horns fell off at a blow. Then there was mighty gladness throughout the whole castle; every one rejoiced that the princess, the only daughter of the king, was free of her horns.

The king had the marriage contract drawn up, and soon after they celebrated the wedding, at which the two friends of the young king were present; and he promised that while they lived they should remain at his court as the very first lords.

There was eating and drinking at the wedding; and among other things they ate bread made from rye. But, Mark tell thou no lie.

24

THE TREACHEROUS BROTHERS.

THERE was a king, and he had seven sons, —
young men strong and healthy as deer, except
the seventh, the youngest, whose name was Jalmir.
He was in his twentieth year, and still a nurse had to
care for him as for a little child. It was pitiful to
look at Jalmir; he was as shapely as a maiden, and
beautiful as a spring day, still could not walk from
weakness. How much the king had paid to doctors,
quacks, and every kind of old woman, to cure him,
but in vain! At last the afflicted father lost all hope
that his dearest son would ever grow strong.

For this reason there reigned in the king's palace
deep distress, which was in no way to the taste of
Jalmir's brothers, especially since they could not
hunt in the neighborhood. "What shall we do in
future?" asked the eldest one day when they were
resting in the forest after a hunt. "Let us go into
the world."

"Yes, yes!" answered all the others. They went
home and laid their wishes before their father.

"What am I to do?" objected the king. "Jalmir
is sickly; I shall be without aid in my old age."

The sons agreed with him in this, but wheedled
him so slyly that at last they received his consent

to go out in the world. They rushed with rejoicing to the stable, chose the best horses, took what money they could, and that same day rode away from their father's house at a gallop, without even saying good-by to their brother Jalmir. How strange was the feeling at the heart of the poor fellow when his nurse told him of this! He turned from her in silence; but under the pillow with which he covered his face he shed many tears. When it was growing dark the nurse hurried out of his chamber to chat with the servants. She began with the cook, and they talked till midnight was near before she knew it.

Meanwhile Jalmir was lying on his bed sadder than ever. This time he was not thinking of his bodily pain, but of his brothers who had left him without saying farewell; this troubled him most. He thought, "Shall I ever be well?" and some internal voice said that he would. Filled with hope he fell into a doze, and saw himself hunting on horseback, and hurling a spear at wild beasts as his brothers had done. All at once, and near midnight, a venerable man, with snow-white beard reaching to his waist, stood before the bed, and said: "Jalmir art thou sleeping?"

Jalmir started, opened his eyes, but saw no one. "That was a dream," thought he. He meditated a while, and again closed his eyes. After a short time the old man stood before him again, and asked:

" Jalmir art thou sleeping? " Jalmir opened his eyes quickly, but saw no one. "That was only a dream then," said he to himself, and again closed his eyes. But soon the old man stood before him and inquired a third time: " Jalmir art thou sleeping? "

" I am not," said Jalmir, and rubbing his eyes, saw the old man at his bed.

" Rise in the morning," said the old man, " provide thyself with everything for the road, and go through the southern gate. Outside the town thou wilt find under an old pear-tree a white horse; mount that horse and ride after thy brothers." Then the old man vanished in a twinkle.

Jalmir rubbed his eyes again, and looked around his chamber, but there was no old man anywhere. " It was only a dream," thought he. Again he lay down and slept soundly; but when he woke in the morning he felt so well that he sprang from his bed, and jumped around the chamber from gladness. His nurse returned at that moment; but when she saw that her weakly charge was well, she ran to the king, and before she had reached the door, cried: " Jalmir is well! "

The king went out, and asked in a sad voice: " Hast thou lost thy senses? "

"He is really well," said the nurse with greater rejoicing; but the king shook his head.

Meanwhile Jalmir recollected his supposed dream, and ascribed his recovery to that majestic old man.

" Since he has cured me, I must obey him," said he to himself. He dressed quickly and went to the king. When the king saw him he believed the nurse, and, thoroughly happy, fell on the young man's neck; but he was astonished still more when Jalmir said: " Now, father, let me go; I must follow my brothers."

"And thou wilt leave me ?" complained the father.

" I must," answered Jalmir seriously, and he told his dream. The king shook his head incredulously, and at first would not even hear of the departure of his favorite son; but at last he consented with tears. Jalmir made ready for the journey without delay.

The king gave him a carriage and four servants, he took money, and departed straightway. Outside the town he dismissed the servants, giving them the carriage and the horses, and walked on alone to the pear-tree, where a splendid white steed was waiting, stamping the ground impatiently. " Sit on me, quickly," said he with the voice of a man, " or we shall be late."

Jalmir sprang to his back and they went on, not on the ground though, but through the air. In a short time the white steed asked: " Dost thou see thy brothers ?"

" I do not see," answered Jalmir.

" But the hill on which they are ? "

" Neither do I see that."

" Thou wilt soon see it," said the steed, and hastened his course. "Dost thou see the hill now?" asked he after a time.

"I see," answered Jalmir, "and on it are six ants."

"Those are thy brothers," said the white steed. "But now listen; we shall soon come up with them, but do not make thyself known. We shall pass the night in an inn. Thy brothers will feast, but will not be able to pay, for they lost all their money foolishly yesterday. Pay for them; in the morning we shall go farther."

Jalmir promised to do this, and then the white steed came down to the earth. Soon they overtook the brothers, who did not know Jalmir; and indeed, how could they in that stately, fiery hero recognize their weakly brother. Jalmir bowed to them courteously, and asked permission to travel in their company.

"But where art thou going?" inquired one of the brothers.

"To see the world," answered Jalmir.

"We too," cried the others; "so thou must go with us."

Jalmir bowed to them, and in silence agreed with a nod. But his brothers all gave him their hands, and soon began to tell him how delightfully they had passed the previous day. Jalmir did not, however, find much that was pleasant in it, and frowned.

"Art sorry that thou wert not there?" asked one of the brothers. "Never mind, we can have such days yet without number."

With that they came to an inn. The innkeeper, seeing through the window so many lords, ran out and took the horses. When he took the white steed, Jalmir asked: "Hast thou a stable apart?"

"Yes; and such a one!" boasted the innkeeper.

"Then put my horse in it alone," said Jalmir, "for he is very vicious."

Then he followed his brothers to a room where they were already seated at a table, and calling with terrible uproar on the innkeeper for wine. In a short time the innkeeper brought all that he had, and the brothers drank, sang, shouted, and rioted till the inn trembled; but Jalmir barely drank for one, because he was sick from the action of his brothers. But how grieved was he when one of the brothers said: "This is a different life from being at home with that grumbling father and that sickly brother."

Gradually one after the other dropped under the table, overcome by wine. When all were asleep Jalmir said to the innkeeper: "Be careful that no harm comes to them; I will sleep a little too."

Then he was going to lie on a bench near the fire. "Do not," said the innkeeper; "I have a bed ready for thee. Come with me."

Jalmir, after useless refusals, followed him at last; but before he lay down he visited the white steed to see if he had plenty of oats and water.

When the brothers woke in the morning they looked for Jalmir with a great outcry: "It would

have been a nice thing if he had run away from us!"
cried one to another. "Who would pay? — for I
have no money."

Soon Jalmir came to the room and told them to
travel farther; all was settled.

"Thou art ours," said they. All embraced him, —
't is a wonder they did not suffocate him. Escaping
from the brothers, Jalmir went to his horse. The
brothers followed his example, and soon the inn was
far behind.

"Listen," said the white steed to Jalmir, when the
brothers had gone ahead. "In the evening we shall
come to a castle, in which lives a sorceress with her
seven daughters; they will take your horses, and lead
you to a chamber. The sorceress will bring you wine
after supper, but drink not. What will take place
later, thou wilt see."

"Why loiter so?" called one of the brothers
suddenly to Jalmir.

"I am coming," answered he; and the white steed
soon galloped so that in a few moments he was ahead
of the brothers.

"Slower or thou wilt leave us!" cried the brothers;
and the white steed waited for them of his own accord. Soon they entered a forest, rode and rode, but
there was no end to the forest; only in the evening
did they come out on a plain. In the middle of the
plain was a beautiful castle. "Oh, now we are in
luck," said the brothers, and they began to rejoice.

They galloped into the court of the castle, and were still more rejoiced when seven princesses came forth to meet them. They sprang from their horses in a moment to give a courteous salute; but how did they wonder when the princesses took their horses by the bridles and led them to the stable. Jalmir begged the youngest princess, who had taken his steed, to put the horse in a stable apart, for he was very vicious."

She did as he wished; he saw this, and only then did he go to the supper chamber, where his brothers and the six princesses were already sitting at a great table, covered with the daintiest dishes. He came to them with the youngest princess, but ate very little, though she urged him continually; but when the vile old woman who served them brought wine and poured it to each one in a golden goblet, Jalmir seized his goblet eagerly, but did not drink the wine. He poured it out on one side.

By degrees the brothers began to doze; at last one after another they fell asleep. Jalmir suspected that the old woman had drugged them, — which was true, — and that she had no good thoughts regarding them; therefore he feigned sleep so that in the hour of need he might aid his brothers. Soon after the old woman came and put away each brother with his partner on a couch, of which there were seven in the adjoining chamber; then she went out, but returned straightway with a great broom, and began to strike the brothers. First she struck the eldest, but he moved not; when she had finished with the six she came to Jalmir, and said to herself: "If six are asleep, so is the seventh." She went out, but soon returned with sulphur in her hand, and burned it under the nose of each brother. She began with the eldest, and as not one of them moved, she said when she reached Jalmir: "If six are asleep, so is the seventh."

She went out, but came back bringing pitch, which she burned on the breast of each brother. She began with the eldest, and as none of them sighed, she said when she reached Jalmir: "If six are asleep, so is the seventh; now I may cut off their heads without fear."

Jalmir quivered; and when the old woman went out, he sprang quickly from the couch, put each of his brothers in the place of a princess and did the same with himself. The old woman returned with a sword, but without a light, and cut off the heads of the seven princesses; then she went out. Jalmir sprang up in a moment and tried to rouse his brothers, but in vain. What anguish the poor fellow suffered; only towards morning did the brothers wake and look in terror at the dead bodies of the princesses. But Jalmir exclaimed in a voice of despair: "Let us flee!" and rushed forth; the brothers followed him. In the stable they untied their horses, and springing on them hurried in a wild chase from the castle and across the broad plain.

The sorceress soon saw their flight, and pursued;

but as they had crossed the boundary of her castle
lands she had power over them no longer, and with
work undone was forced to go home, where she cursed
herself above the dead bodies of her daughters. The
brothers rode without stopping, farther and farther,
till at last the castle disappeared from their sight;
then they made the first halt to rest and inquire of
Jalmir what had been done to them. When they
heard that he had saved them from certain death,
they fell upon his neck and cried: "Tell us who thou
art, since thou hast done so much for us."

"Who else but your brother Jalmir," answered he,
almost swimming in tears; and he pressed brother
after brother to his breast. But how astonished was
he when he saw that they were much colder to him
than they had been when they knew him not! Still,
they asked how he had recovered, why he had ridden
after them, and what their father was doing. But
gradually they grew silent and hung their heads.
Beyond doubt it was not to their liking that just the
youngest of them was so wise.

Jalmir also was silent, and his white steed dropped
behind of his own accord. When the brothers could
not hear him, he said to his master: "I told thee not
to discover thyself, but thou didst not obey me. The
results thou canst lay to thyself. In a few days we
shall come to a mighty king; thou and thy brothers
will enter his service. When in need come to me for
advice."

Jalmir stroked the white steed, and begged his forgiveness. From that time the brothers were no longer joyous as before, and kept noticeably aside from Jalmir. But since they had no money they wheedled him greatly whenever they saw an inn, since he always paid for them. After some days they came to a great city. Their first road, however, was to the inn, where they ate moderately but drank beyond measure; and now they began to do such senseless things that Jalmir went to his steed as quickly as possible to get consolation.

When the brothers were alone the eldest said: "I have had favors enough from that sickly brother; to-morrow we will go to the king of this country and serve him. What do ye think?"

"We will all go with thee," cried the others; but suddenly they were confused, for Jalmir had returned.

"Where are ye going?" inquired he, "I will go with you."

The brothers answered him sullenly, but Jalmir said he would go. Towards evening, when the brothers had had a good sleep, they went to the king, who made them men of his court without delay. Now they had a good living, large pay, and almost nothing to do; but as an offset they were still not at rest, for Jalmir was always a thorn in their eyes, especially since the friendship of the king for him increased every day.

Once when the brothers, from idleness, were examining the chambers of the king's castle, they came to one in which were all kinds of books, small and great, piled up to the ceiling. They fell to reading these books with great eagerness.

"Brothers," cried one of them suddenly, "I read here that the king has not a bird in his kingdom."

"Is this true?" exclaimed the others in wonder; "we have not noticed it."

"But know ye," asked the eldest, "to what use we may put this?" All shook their heads. "Listen," said he in a whisper; "we will tell the king that Jalmir knows about birds, and to send him for them."

"And the king will do so at once," said the brother who had read of the birds, "for here is written the great cost of the birds eaten on the king's table in a year."

They stopped reading at once and went straight to the king, to whom they told what they thought. "But, gracious king," said the eldest, "thou must sharply insist, or Jalmir will excuse himself, saying that he knows nothing of birds."

The king nodded graciously and sent for Jalmir. He came quickly, and the king said: "As thou knowest well I have no birds in my kingdom, therefore I command thee to bring them."

"I, gracious king," said Jalmir, in fright, "know nothing of birds."

"Whether thou knowest or knowest not," said the

king, in sudden anger, "thou 'lt get birds." With that he waved his hand, and poor Jalmir went out with drooping head. Whither can he go? Who can help him in peril? He went straight to the white steed and complained.

"Grieve not," said the steed; "at dusk we will go for the birds."

Jalmir thanked the horse, and could hardly wait till evening. The moment the sun had disappeared behind the woods he was ready for the road; and when the first star had appeared in the sky he led out the white steed, sprang on his back, and flew off like the wind. "But where are we going?" inquired Jalmir of his steed on the way.

"To that sorceress in whose castle thou didst save thy brothers from death," answered the horse.

"To that place!" cried Jalmir in fright.

"Have no fear," said the steed, comforting him; "only do to a hair what I tell thee."

The good steed now increased his speed so that he went like an arrow, and about an hour later he came to the ground at the castle of the sorceress. Jalmir sprang from him, and the steed said: "When thou art in the first chamber thou wilt see silver cages, and in them silver birds; in the second chamber will be golden cages with golden birds; in the third chamber diamond cages with diamond birds. Of all these touch nothing, or such a blow will fall that the whole castle will tremble, and the sorceress will seize thee to kill thee. But go to the fourth chamber; there take a wooden cage in which is a mean-looking bird, and hasten to me."

Jalmir entered the first chamber with courage, but cautiously, and looking at nothing, went to the second chamber; there the glitter of gold dazzled him somewhat. When he opened the door to the third chamber he stood almost blind on the threshold; but quickly recovering, he shaded his eyes, ran to the fourth chamber, and seizing the cage with the bird in an instant, rushed out swift as an arrow. He sprang on the horse, which rose with him through the air in a moment. The sorceress burst out of the castle, and cursing fearfully because she could not stop him, screamed: "But thou wilt come here again!"

When the white steed was beyond the boundary of the castle land, he said to Jalmir: "Open the cage and let the bird fly."

"But shall I not bring it to the king?"

"Only do what I ask," said the steed, with such a stern voice that Jalmir obeyed without thinking.

It was yet night when they reached home. Jalmir tied the horse in the stable and went to his room to strengthen himself with sleep, but he did not sleep long. The morning dawn had barely shown itself when in the king's garden was heard such a loud and cheerful singing of birds that all the

people were soon on their feet, and earlier than any
the king. At the first moment he was so astonished
that he asked whence these wonderful creatures had
come.

"Royal Grace," said one of the brothers, "thou
didst send Jalmir for them."

"True," said the king, as he bethought himself;
"but where is Jalmir?"

A courtier soon brought him, and the king fell on
his neck from very joy. He was now really dear
to the king; but for that reason was held in more
hatred by his brothers.

"How can we get rid of him?" asked the brothers
when they were alone.

"Maybe we can read something else," said one of
them.

"Very good," answered all, at once; and they hurried to the chamber in which so many books were
collected, and it was not long before one of the
brothers cried out: "The king has no beasts, and
they cost him more than the birds, since he uses
many more of them in a year."

"Then let Jalmir go for them," said the sixth
brother, smiling maliciously; and they went straight
to the king, to whom they told their minds. The king
nodded graciously; dismissed them, called Jalmir and
said: "I have no beasts in my kingdom; and since
they cost me much in a year, I command thee to get
me beasts."

"I, gracious king," said Jalmir in wonder, "know of none."

"Thou knowest well," said the king in anger, "for thy brothers told me."

"Did they?" said Jalmir in astonishment. "Well, I will try;" and he went to his white steed, to whom he told everything.

"Be not down-hearted," said the steed, comforting him. "Come to me in the evening; we will go for the beasts."

When it was dark the good steed was flying through the air. "But where shall we go?" asked Jalmir.

"To the sorceress from whom we got the birds," answered the steed.

"But I am afraid that she will catch me," said Jalmir.

"Fear not," said the steed; "only do to a hair what I tell thee." When he came to the ground in front of the castle, he said: "In the first chamber thou wilt see a beast with silver hair, tied with silver chains; in the second chamber a beast with golden hair and golden chains; in the third, one with pearl hair and pearl chains. Touch not any of these, or a blow will fall so that the whole castle will tremble, and the sorceress will seize thee to kill thee. But go to the fourth chamber; there seize an ugly dog that is tied with a ragged rope, and hurry to me."

Somewhat timidly, but all the more carefully, did

25

Jalmir pass the first, second, and third chamber, shading his eyes with his hands so the glitter of the silver, gold, and pearl might not blind him. When he entered the fourth chamber he broke the rope, seized the dog in his arms, rushed out, and swift as an arrow sprang on the horse, which rose in the air. And it was high time; for scarcely had he sat on the horse when the sorceress ran out after him. When she was unable to stop him, she cursed fearfully, and screamed: " But thou wilt come here again ! "

When the steed had sprung over the boundary of the castle land, he said: " Now let the dog go."

Jalmir obeyed at once, for he was sure the steed gave good counsel. When they came home, dawn was already appearing; still Jalmir lay on the bed, for he was greatly wearied. He did not sleep long, however; for barely had the dawn come when there was a noise in the castle, in the town, and outside the town, as if the earth were breaking. The king sprang in wonder to the window. But how astonished was he ! Right in the garden he saw deer, stags, rabbits; on the trees squirrels; on the ground under the trees mice; in short, such myriads of beasts that his eyes danced. In the king's garden it was pleasant for the beasts; but in the town and outside the town the people killed them, chased wildly after them, and threw stones at them. This displeased the king; and he issued an order that all beasts belonged to him, and that no man should dare to injure them. Then he went to Jalmir, thanked him cordially, and expressed his friendship with an ardent embrace.

The whole kingdom was pleased with the beasts, but Jalmir's brothers were not pleased.

"What shall we do with him?" asked the eldest of the others. "Instead of getting rid of him we have brought him into still greater favor with the king."

"But let us go and read again."

"Yes, yes," said a third; and all hurried off to the well-known room. They had read a long time when at last one cried out: "The king has no wine, and of course wine costs him money."

"Then let Jalmir go for it," answered the eldest, quietly; "and he must get luck from hell if he comes back."

They went straight to the king, and very insinuatingly they told him that Jalmir might easily supply him with wine.

"Then he will do it;" and dismissing them graciously he had Jalmir summoned, and told him his wish.

"Gracious king," answered Jalmir, "I know nothing of wine, but I will go and see."

The king was somewhat angry, thinking surely that Jalmir was unwilling, and thereupon said: "Thou wilt answer to me with thy head." Jalmir, bowing in silence, went out to the steed.

"Fear not," said the steed; "in the evening we

will go for the wine." The moment it was dark the kind steed shot away with Jalmir through the air.

"Where are we going this time?" asked Jalmir, a little frightened.

"To the sorceress from whom we got the birds and the beasts. But now pull a hair from my tail, and one from my mane; from the first make a rope three hundred yards long, from the other a net large enough to contain thee."

Jalmir did in silence according to the steed's words; and to his astonishment, before they came to the castle the rope and the net were finished.

"Now attend to my words," said the steed when he had come to the ground. "Tie one end of the rope to my foot and the other to the net, take the net with thee and put it on the door of the cellar, to which thou must go down on three hundred steps. In the cellar thou wilt see vessels with silver and gold and diamond hoops; pay no heed to them, or a blow will fall, and it will be ill with thee. Go to the farthest part of the cellar. There thou wilt see in a niche a little vessel with wooden hoops, take that quickly and hurry to me; but if thou art not able to come, just spring into the net and I will help thee."

Jalmir did everything according to the words of the steed. It was as clear as white day in the cellar from the silver, gold, and diamond hoops, so that he soon saw the little vessel in the niche; but when he caught it, it is a wonder that he did not fall under its weight. With a mighty effort he carried it to the steps; but there he struck his foot against a vessel, and such a blow fell that the castle trembled from its foundation to the highest points of its tower. Jalmir, however, did not grow weak; he sprang up like an arrow over the three hundred steps and jumped into the net.

Meanwhile, the sorceress flew out of the castle and sprang at the steed; but the steed got her down, and so thrashed her with his feet that he did not leave a sound bone in her body. At the same time he wound up the rope so nicely that in a little while he had drawn up the net containing Jalmir. "Sit quickly on me," said he. Jalmir mounted in a moment, keeping the vessel carefully in his arms. The steed rose in the air and flew like lightning, because the sorceress who had picked herself from the ground was chasing him. But soon they had the boundary of the castle land behind them, so that they had no further need to strain their powers.

When they reached home the steed was drooping wearily to the earth, so that Jalmir had to support him in going to the stable. Jalmir was barely able to go to his own room; but first, according to the command of the steed, he left the cask of wine at the door of the king's chamber, then he lay on his bed and was soon asleep.

When the king opened the door of his chamber in

the morning he saw the cask. " This must be wine," said the king, rejoicing; and taking off the head, he tried it. "It's wine; it's wine!" rejoiced he; and calling the people of the castle, he drank a health with them all.

" But what is this?" wondered they; " we have taken ten kegs of wine out already, and still it comes."

" This must be an enchanted cask," said the king, and began to laugh. Then he said in serious tones: " Little cask, I should like to have red wine." He drew some. And what a wonder! the wine was red. " I want yellow wine," said the king; and yellow wine flowed out.

" In real fact, it is an enchanted cask," said the king. " Oh, Jalmir," cried he in delight, " how can I reward thee!"

" I have only obeyed thy command, gracious king," answered Jalmir, who had just entered the room.

" Yes, thou hast done all that I commanded, and much more," said the king; " therefore I make thee my son, and proclaim thee viceroy."

All present broke out in tumultuous shouting, but Jalmir's brothers were silent; they bit their lips and clinched their fists. The king, altogether joyous and full of tenderness, from success and from wine, arranged to have a seven day's celebration in honor of the new viceroy. The people did not wait to have the order repeated, but began that very day, especially since they had plenty of food, and the wine which the enchanted cask gave them without stint. The new viceroy was greeted everywhere with shouts, and won at once the love of the people.

But his brothers were enraged all the more. Instead of going to the festivities they went to the room where the books were, and read as diligently as if they wished to become sages at once. This time, however, they were not able to find anything for a great while; but at last they read what they wanted.

" Now I have something for our darling viceroy ! " cried one. " In the sea is a golden castle, and in the castle a princess, the most beautiful under the heavens. If our king would take her in marriage, he would grow young and lengthen his life."

" Oh, that is splendid ! " said all, rejoicing. " The king will surely send him for the princess, and darling Jalmir will either be drowned in the sea or run home to his father."

When the feasting was over the brothers went to the king, who was, as it were, ill, —just the thing for them. " Gracious king," said the eldest, insinuatingly, " we are always trying to prepare some pleasure for thee."

" Indeed, I have need of it," said the king; " old age and disease are pressing me more and more every day."

"We have just found a remedy for those two evils," said the brothers.

" But what is it, —tell me ! " broke out the king, delighted. They told him what they had read.

" Well, Jalmir must take the road this very day,"
cried the king; and calling Jalmir he explained his
wish. Jalmir agreed in silence, but scarcely controll-
ing his tears, hastened to his steed and fell on his
neck, weeping.

" What is the matter now? " asked the steed. Jalmir told him all.

" Do not lose courage," said the horse. " Go to
the king, and ask him to give thee three hundred
loaves of bread, three hundred kegs of wine, and
three hundred beeves. Have all put into wagons, and
then we will go for the princess."

Jalmir went straightway to the king and asked for
these. The king had all provided quickly, and promised him mountains and valleys if he would bring the
princess. Jalmir took the road that very day, sitting
on his good white steed, which this time did not fly
through the air, but walked with slow step behind the
wagons on which the loaves, the wine, and the beeves
were carried. And many times did day and night
change places before they came to the sea. Now
they went along the shore; the white steed, going
ahead with Jalmir, showed the road to the wagons.

Jalmir saw a great fish on the beach which was
trying in vain to get back to the water. " Help it,"
said the steed; and Jalmir, springing to the ground,
helped the fish.

The fish sank under the water, but soon came to
the surface and said to Jalmir: " Wait, I must reward

thee. Take this whistle, and shouldst thou need aught from me, blow."

Jalmir took the whistle from the fish's lips, gave thanks, and sat again on his steed. After a time they heard as it were distant thunder. "What is that?" asked he of the horse.

"We shall soon be at the end of our journey," said the steed; "those are giants talking."

In a short time Jalmir saw three giants lying on the beach. When he came up they rose, and now he saw their stature. When he looked in their faces he had to bend back his head as if looking at the highest tower.

"What is the good word?" roared one of them, so that Jalmir had to cover his ears.

"I bring three hundred loaves of bread, three hundred kegs of wine, and three hundred slaughtered oxen," answered he.

"That is good of thee," said the giants, nodding their heads with satisfaction; and they rushed to the wagons in which the things were placed. They built a fire, and stuck the oxen on great spits to roast; then they went to the bread and wine, and soon had half inside themselves. A great eagle settled down near by, and looked wistfully at the beeves. Jalmir cut off a quarter and gave it to the eagle.

"Thank thee!" said the eagle. "I will help thee in time;" and she rose in the air with the quarter.

The giants did not leave the oxen very long over

the fire; and when they had finished, they said to Jalmir: "Now tell us thy wish; well do we know that ye little worms of the earth do nothing for nothing."

"I have no wish for myself," said Jalmir; "but my master has sent me to bring the princess from the golden castle which stands out in the sea."

"That one over there?" asked the other giant, pointing with his finger to the sea.

Jalmir looked around and saw for the first time a magnificent castle, which gleamed in the waves like the rising sun. "Yes," replied Jalmir.

"We will take thee to it," said the first giant; "but will the princess go with thee?"

"I will ask her," said Jalmir; "but how will ye take me there?"

"Thou wilt soon see," said the giants; and they took pieces of a cliff and hurled them into the sea. They went on breaking the cliff, and sooner than Jalmir expected there was a long stretch of dam in the sea. But the giants did not stop; they worked till the setting of the sun, so that in the evening they had one third of the dam finished, and on the third day it was possible to go with dry foot to the golden castle.

Jalmir thanked the giants heartily, and the morning of the fourth day he went to the princess. The castle was a wonder to look at; but he scarcely noticed it. He entered, and how surprised was he when in the first chamber he saw the princess. With downcast eyes he said: " My king and master has sent me to beg thee in his name to share his throne and crown."

" I will go," answered the princess, with a silvery voice; " but wilt thou remain at his court? "

" I must," said Jalmir. " I am the viceroy."

" Let us go, then," said the princess.

She mounted a splendid crow-black horse, Jalmir his white steed, and they galloped along the dam. On the way Jalmir took courage to look at the princess more closely, and thought that the king would grow younger, and lengthen his life, if the princess would marry him. At the same time he felt a certain agreeable straitening of the heart. He bent his head, and rode in silence at the side of the princess; and the nearer he came to the castle of the king, the more did trouble take hold of his heart. The more joyous, however, was the princess; and her eyes rested on him with a certain special delight. They arrived soon without great adventure.

The king went outside the town to meet them, and conducted them in solemn procession to the castle. " Art thou willing, honored princess, to become my spouse? " asked he of the princess when he had led her to the chambers prepared for her.

" First I must have my golden castle," replied the princess.

The king was amazed; but he bethought himself soon, and turned to Jalmir, gazing imploringly.

"I will go for it," said Jalmir, with decision, especially when the princess nodded graciously and smiled at him.

"Go, my dear Jalmir," said the king, with a soft voice. "I will reward thee in kings' fashion."

Jalmir went to the white steed for advice, and the steed said: "Tell the king to give thee three hundred loaves of bread, three hundred kegs of wine, and three hundred slaughtered oxen; then we will go for the golden castle."

Jalmir told the king his wishes, and the king gave him all. Everything was ready so soon that Jalmir was able to set out that very day. But it was a tedious journey; the wagons went slowly, and after them Jalmir still more slowly, and with drooping head, — why, he knew best himself. When they came to the giants, Jalmir gave them the loaves, the wine, and the meat, begging them urgently to bring the golden castle to the princess.

"Ah, little worm of the earth!" said the giants, laughing, "dost thou think that the castle is made of wood? but we will try," added they after they had looked at the three hundred loaves, at the kegs and the oxen.

They began eating, and when they had eaten heartily, they went to a neighboring forest, where they pulled up three of the strongest trees; and when they had played with them as men play with canes, they went along the dam to the golden castle. After

a short time they moved the castle from its founda-
tions, put it on the oak-trees, and then on to their
shoulders; and as if it were nothing they walked after
Jalmir without weariness till night, when they slept,
and next morning went farther. They worked in this
way till they drew near the king's castle; they did
not go to it, however, but waited till night. Then
they put the golden castle in the garden, bade farewell to Jalmir, and went home.

When the morning sun rose people shouted
"Fire!" in the castle. All ran to the garden to
put it out; but the princess standing in her window
cried, "Be quiet! That is my golden castle."

Soon after the king hurried in, and opening his
arms in delight, wished to embrace the princess,
calling out, "Now thou art mine!"

"Not yet," answered the princess. "What is my
golden castle to me if I have lost the key of it?"

The king was frightened; but soon he said, with
clear face: "My dear Jalmir will bring it to thee."
He wanted to go for him; but Jalmir came just then
to the princess to tell her that he had brought the
castle. The king told his wish; and Jalmir, gaining
pleasure and strength from a gracious smile of the
princess, departed. He took counsel of his steed,
who said: "The key is somewhere in the sea near
the dam." Jalmir mounted; they flew through the
air, and were soon on the island where the castle had
been.

"But how shall I find the key in the sea?" sighed Jalmir.

"Thou hast the whistle from the fish helped by thee into the water."

"Yes," rejoiced Jalmir; and he blew on the whistle.

That moment the fish swam to the surface, and asked, "What dost thou wish?"

"The princess has lost the key of her golden castle," answered Jalmir, who was about to ask the fish to find it; but the fish had already vanished to tell all fish to look for the key. Now there was life under water, — such gleaming of fish flying hither and thither, up and down! till at last after long swimming, one little fish brought the key to the chief fish. The chief fish gave it to Jalmir; Jalmir gave heartfelt thanks, and was soon flying through the air on his steed, so that he was home before night. When he had given the key to the king he went to his room and shut himself in. Why he did this he knew not himself; but he felt that it would have been better for him had he never seen that princess of the golden castle.

The king, perfectly happy, went with the key to the princess; he felt sure this time that she would make no objection. All the greater was his grief when she said: "I have the castle and the key to it; but what would life be in the castle without the water of death, the water of life, and the water of youth?"

"And where are they to be found?" asked the king.

" They are on my island," answered the princess so decidedly that the king went away in silence to think whom he should send. He had pity on Jalmir, and therefore he went to the brothers; but they spoke to him so convincingly that the king asked Jalmir again to go and do that last service for him. How could Jalmir refuse? Besides, what he had done he had done for her for whom he would have jumped into fire if need be. He went to his steed to ask aid once more, and for the last time. The steed reproached him for lack of courage, and said: " Sit on my back; we 'll go straight for the water." Jalmir did so with joy, and was soon going through the air to the island swifter than ever he had travelled before. In a short time the horse came down on the seashore and said: " Go to the island for the water of death, the water of life, and the water of youth; but hurry, or the waves will wash down the dam and thou wilt perish. I will eat grass here a while."

Jalmir went forward, but very slowly; for the image of the princess rose continually before his eyes. Except her, the whole world was as naught to him. He was perhaps half way on the dam when all at once the sea rose and bore it away. Jalmir screamed in terror and disappeared in the sea. The steed heard his screams, but did not run to help him, and hanging his head, went with slow step; he knew well that he could give no aid to Jalmir. Then came a terrible storm on the sea. The steed thought that Jalmir had perished; he rose in the air and shot away like a flash.

Not far from the dam — of which there was not a trace after the storm — was an eagle's nest high on the cliff, and in it five little eagles that stretched out their necks, without ceasing looking down eagerly, and crying meanwhile. "What do ye want?" called the old eagle, which sat near by on a cliff and looked down. But how quickly did she fly to the beach when she saw a body there! She recognized it at once; for though she was only a wild creature she remembered well that Jalmir had done her a kindness by giving her the quarter of beef for her young. She seized him now in her strong talons and bore him to the island where the golden castle had been; she plunged him into a spring, then placing him on the ground, sat near his side. Soon Jalmir began to breathe, — at first with difficulty and slowly, then more quickly and evenly, till at last he opened his eyes with a deep sigh. "Why not let me sleep longer? — I slept so lightly! I dreamed so sweetly!" said Jalmir, as if waking from slumber. When he looked around more attentively he called out in amazement, "What has been done to me?"

"Dost thou not know me?" asked the eagle, standing before him.

"I do not know thee," replied Jalmir, shaking his head.

"But I know thee well," cried the eagle. "Thou

didst give me a quarter of beef for my children. But what art thou looking for now?"

"The princess sent me to this island for the water of death, the water of life, and the water of youth," answered Jalmir.

"Then take them," said the eagle, and brought him to the three springs. Jalmir took three flasks from his bosom, and filled them with the three waters.

"But how shall I leave here?"

"I would gladly bear thee wherever thou wishest, but I cannot, for I have children; but I will go to my brother. He has no children." She flew off in a flash, soon returning, and with her her brother.

"But where has my white steed gone?" asked Jalmir suddenly.

"I will soon tell thee," answered the eagle, and she rose in the sky till she seemed to the eye of Jalmir as small as the point of a pine leaf. She remained motionless a moment, then came down like a bolt and said: "I saw thy steed under the old pear-tree which stands before the southern gate of the great town."

"Bear me to that place then," said Jalmir, with a voice of entreaty.

The eagle's brother caught him in his strong talons, and was soon flying with him high in the air; so high that Jalmir saw his native place, but it was as small as an ant-hill. He went farther, it became

26

greater, till at last the eagle came to the earth and put Jalmir down near the old pear-tree; then he parted with him, and soon vanished in the air.

The white steed was standing behind the pear-tree, with drooping head, and so gloomy that he did not notice his master.

"My very good steed!" cried Jalmir, and fell on his neck.

"Thou art alive and well?" asked the steed in amazement.

"Yes," answered Jalmir, and told him all that had happened.

"I am happy," said the steed; "but now sit quickly on me, we must go to the princess or we shall be late."

"What is the matter?" asked Jalmir in fright.

"The king wants the wedding to-day," answered the steed.

"Then let us hurry," said Jalmir, and he sprang on the steed, opened his arms toward the town, and cried: "Oh, my dear father!"

"Calm thyself," said the steed; "I know that thou wouldst embrace him; but vain is thy wish, for he died long ago." The steed rose in the air and flew so swiftly that his native place soon vanished from the tearful eyes of Jalmir. On the road the steed said: "When thou art king, judge justly, even if thy heart has to bleed."

Jalmir did not understand him; but when he came

to the town and heard how his brothers were laughing at their puny little Jalmir who had perished somewhere, an evil feeling seized him. Mastering himself however, he went to the princess to give her the three waters; and she hastened to the king to whom she said: " My dear bridegroom, so that our marriage be equal, thou must become young and beautiful as I am, and therefore I will rub thee with the water of death so that thy old age shall perish, then with the water of youth, and last with the water of life."

The king consented with gladness, and the princess rubbed him with the water of death; then he straightened himself on the couch so that the princess herself was terrified. Seizing quickly the water of youth; she rubbed him with it and the fresh color of youth shone on the face of the old king. " But still he is not so beautiful as Jalmir," sighed the princess, greatly grieved. With tearful eyes she reached for the water of life, but instead of it took the water of death and rubbed the king. Straightway the pallor of death spread over his face. The princess fell in a faint at his side and remained in it till Jalmir came by chance to the chamber, seized the water of life, and rubbed with it quickly the princess and the king. The princess stood up at once, but the king remained dead.

" Is there no help for him? " asked Jalmir with trembling voice.

" There is not," said the princess, shaking her head; " whoever is rubbed twice with the water of death can never live again."

" But what shall I do now? " muttered Jalmir, closing his eyes.

" Thou art king," answered the princess, " but I — "

" Queen! " cried Jalmir eagerly, and sank at her feet saying, " Forgive me, but I love thee more than myself."

The princess in place of an answer kissed him; and now they went to announce to the people that the old king was dead.

The people, who had already assembled in the square for the wedding of the king, were greatly distressed; but when the princess presented Jalmir as the new king, and herself as his wife, they broke out into mighty rejoicing, which had no end. But Jalmir's brothers were silent; and when the new king with his bride retired, they reported that these two had poisoned the old king. The people raised a tumult; but Jalmir went out among them and asked the cause. Some were silent, and others told him what his brothers had said. " Do ye believe this? " asked Jalmir.

" We do not believe," was shouted from every side.

" Very well," answered Jalmir, " but that ye may believe me I will tell how my brothers tried to kill me; " and he told them all.

"The wretches!" cried the people in a rage; and they caught all the six brothers. Before Jalmir could stop them the people had fired a stack of straw, and when it was blazing high they threw the six brothers into the flames.

"Now ye are all in one pile," laughed the people, "because hitherto ye were always setting fire."

Jalmir turned to the princess with tears in his eyes, but she soon consoled him. After the funeral of the old king they celebrated their betrothal; but when Jalmir, full of happiness, sat at the feast by the side of his bride, all at once he remembered his steed, ran to him, and fell on his neck thanking him as author of all his happiness.

"I have helped thee, do thou help me now," said the steed. "Lead me to the garden." Jalmir did as he desired; then the steed said: "Cut off my head."

"I cut off thy head!" cried Jalmir in fright.

"Wilt thou let me suffer one hundred years longer?" asked the steed in a sad voice.

In place of an answer Jalmir drew his sword, and with one blow cut off his friend's head. The head fell on the ground, but out of it flew a white dove which rose toward the sky. Jalmir turned in sorrow to the princess, but she soon drove the sadness away from his face. They lived happily together, and because they had the water of life, they lived so long that no one has memory of it.

MAGYAR MYTHS AND FOLK-TALES.

THE POOR MAN, AND THE KING OF
THE CROWS.

THERE was once a very poor man, and he had two lean cows. The two cows were to the poor man as their mother's breast to children; for not only did they give milk and butter, for which he got a few coppers to buy salt, but he tilled his patch of land with them.

Now, he was ploughing one day at the edge of the woods with the two cows, when, from wherever it came, a six-horse coach stood before him, and in it sat no other than the King of the Crows, who found this to say to the poor man, —

" Listen, poor man; I will tell thee one thing, and two will come of it. Sell me those lean cows; I'll give thee good money for them. I'll pay double price. My army has n't tasted a morsel for three days, and the soldiers will die of hunger and thirst unless thou wilt save them."

" If that's the case," said the poor man to the King of the Crows, " if it be that thy Highness's army has n't eaten anything for three days, I don't mind the difficulty. I'll let thee have the cows, not for money; let thy Highness return a cow for a cow."

" Very good, poor man, let it be as thou sayest. I will give thee a cow for a cow; more than that, for two thou wilt get four cows. For that purpose find me in my kingdom, for I am the King of the Crows. Thou hast but to look in the north for the black castle; thou 'lt be sure to find it."

With that the King of the Crows vanished as if he had never been there, — as if the earth had swallowed him. The poor man kept on ploughing with the two lean cows, till, all at once, the army of the King of the Crows appeared like a black cloud approaching through the air, with mighty cawing, and seizing the two cows tore them bit from bit. When•they had finished, the dark legions with tumultuous cawing moved on their way like a cloud. The poor man watched the direction in which they flew so that he might know the way.

Now he strolled home in great sadness, took leave of his two handsome sons and his dear wife, in the midst of bitter tears, and set out into the world to find the black castle. He travelled and journeyed over forty-nine kingdoms, beyond the Operentsia Sea and the glass mountains, and beyond that, where the little short-tailed pig roots, and beyond that, and still farther on, till he came to an ocean-great sand-plain.

Nowhere for gold was a town, a village, or a cabin to be seen where he might recline his head for a night's rest, or beg a morsel of bread or a cup of water. Food had long since left his bag, and he might have struck fire in the gourd[1] which hung at his side. What was he to do? Where could he save his life? Here he must perish of hunger and thirst in the midst of this ocean-great desert, and then at home let them wait for him till the day of Judgment. Here the poor man's power of walking decreased, and he floundered about like a dazed fish, like a man struck on the head. While stumbling along he sees on a sudden a shepherd's fire.

He moves towards the light, creeping on all fours. At last he arrives there with great difficulty, and sees that three or four men are lying around the fire, boiling kasha in a pot. He salutes them with, " God give you a good evening."

" God receive thee, poor man; how is it that thou art journeying in this strange land where even a bird does not go?"

" I am looking for the black castle in the north. Have ye heard nothing of it in your world-beautiful lives?"

" How not? Of course we have. Are we not the shepherds of that king, who rigorously and mercilessly enjoined that, if such and such a man, who sold him the two lean cows for his army, should find us, to treat him well with meat and drink, and then to show him the right road? Maybe thou art the man!"

" I am indeed."

---

[1] A pilgrim bottle made of a dried, long-necked gourd.

" Is it possible? "

" I am no one else."

" In that case sit here on the sheepskin; eat, drink, and enjoy thyself, for the kasha will be ready this minute."

As they said, he did. The poor man sat by the fire, ate, drank, and satisfied himself, then lay down and fell asleep. When he rose in the morning they gave him a round cheese, and drove the air out of his bottle; then they let him go his way, showing him the right road.

The poor man travelled and journeyed along the right road; and now, when he was hungry and dry, he had his bag, and his bottle too. Towards evening he sees again a shepherd's fire. He draws near the great fire, and sees the shepherds of the King of the Crows sitting around it cooking a meat stew. He wishes them, " God give you a good-day, my lords, the horseherds."

" God guard thee, poor man," said the chief herdsman; " where art thou going here in this strange land? "

" I am looking for the black castle of the King of the Crows. Hast thou never heard of it, brother, in thy world-beautiful life? "

" How not heard of it? Of course I have. Are we not the servants of him who commanded rigorously and unflinchingly that if such and such a poor man, who sold him two lean cows for his army, should wander along, to receive him kindly? Therefore, this is my word and speech to thee. Art thou, perchance, that man?"

"Of course I am."

"Is it possible?"

"I'm no one else."

"In that case sit down here by the fire, drink, and be filled."

The poor man sat down by the fire, ate, drank, and satisfied himself; then lying on the sheepskin, he fell asleep. When he rose in the morning the horseherds entertained the poor man again, wished him happiness, and showing the right road let him go his way; but they left neither his bag nor his bottle empty. Then he went along the right road. But why multiply words? — for there is an end even to a hundred words; it is enough to know that towards evening he came to the ground of the swineherds of the King of the Crows. He saluted them with, "God give you a good evening."

"God guard thee," said the reckoning swineherd.[1] "How is it thou art journeying in this strange land, where even a bird does not go?"

"I am looking for the black castle of the King of the Crows. Has my lord elder brother never heard of it in his world-beautiful life?"

"Haho, poor man! How not heard of it? Are we not the servants of the lord of that castle? But

[1] "The reckoning swineherd," — he who counts the pigs.

art not thou the poor man who sold his Highness the two lean cows?"

"Well, what's the use in delay or denial? I am, indeed, he."

"Art thou in truth?"

"I am no one else."

"But how wilt thou enter the black castle, since it is covered all around with a stone wall, and whirls unceasingly on a golden cock's foot? But make no account of that. Here is a shining axe. Just strike the wall with it so that sparks will fly, and thou wilt come upon the door, which will spring open. Then jump in. Have a care, though; for if thou slip and fall, neither God nor man can save thee. When thou art once inside, the King of the Crows will come forward and receive thee kindly. He won't put his soul on the palm of his hand at once; but when his Highness inquires what thy wish is, ask for nothing else but the salt-mill which stands in the corner."

Well, the talk ended there. In the morning the poor man moves on towards the black castle. When he arrives there, he saw that it whirled of itself on a golden cock's foot, like some infernal spindle; and nowhere can he see either window or door upon it, — nothing but the naked wall. He took the swineherd's axe and struck the wall, and sparks flew from the axe in such style that it could n't be better. After a time he came upon the door; it flew open, and he jumped in. If he had delayed but one flash of an eye the stone wall door would have crushed him; as it was, the edge of his trousers was carried off.

As soon as the poor man got in, he saw that the castle turned only on the outside. At this moment the King of the Crows was standing by the window, and saw the poor man coming for the price of the cows. He went to meet him, shook his hand, treated him as tenderly as an egg; then he led him into the most beautiful chamber, and seated him at his side on a golden couch. The poor man saw not a soul anywhere, although it was midday, the time of eating. All at once the table began to spread, and was soon bending under its load, so much food was on it. The poor man shook his head, — for, as I say, though no one was to be seen anywhere, neither cook nor kitchen-boy nor servant, still, was n't the table spread? It was surely witchcraft, surely some infernal art, but not the work of a good spirit, — maybe the salt-mill had something to do with it. That, however, did not come into the poor man's mind, though the mill stood there in the corner.

He was there three days, the guest of the King of the Crows, who received him with every kindness he could offer, so that no man's son could raise a complaint against his Highness. Morning, noon, and night the poor man's food appeared in proper form, but the roast and the wine had no taste for him; for it came to his mind that while he was feasting there, most likely his wife and children had not bread enough. I say it came to his mind; he began to be restless and uneasy. The King of the Crows noticed this, and said to him: "Well, poor man, I see that thou dost not wish to stay longer with me, because thy heart is at home, therefore I ask what dost thou wish for the two lean cows? — believe me, brother, thou didst save me from great trouble that time; if thou hadst not taken pity on me I should have lost my whole army from famine."

" I want nothing else," said the poor man, " but that salt-mill standing there in the corner."

" Oh, poor man, hast thou lost thy wits? Tell me, what good couldst thou get of the mill?"

" Oh, I could grind corn or a little wheat from time to time; if I did not some one else might, so there would be something to take to the kitchen."

"Ask for something else; ask for all the cattle which in coming hither thou didst see."

" What should I do with such a tremendous lot of cattle? If I should drive them home, people would think evil of me; besides, I have neither stable nor pasture."

" But I 'll give thee money. How much dost thou wish? Wouldst be content with three bags of it?"

"What could I do with such an ocean-great lot of money? My evil fate would use it to kill me; people would think that I stole the coin, or murdered some man for it; besides, I might be stopped with it on the road."

" But I 'll give thee a soldier as a guard."

" What good is one of thy Highness's soldiers?" asked the poor man, smiling; " a hen, I think, would drive him away."

" What! one of my soldiers?"

Here the King of the Crows blew a small whistle; straightway a crow appeared which shook itself, and became such a gallant young fellow that he was not only so, but just so. " That 's the kind of soldiers I have;" said the king and commanded the young man out of the room. The soldier shook himself, became a crow, and flew away.

" It 's all the same to me what kind of soldiers thy Highness has. Thy Highness promised to give me what I want, and I ask for nothing else but the salt-mill."

" I will not give it. Ask for all my herds, but not for that."

" I need not herds; all I want is the mill."

" Well, poor man, I have refused thee three times, and three times thou hast asked for the mill; now, whether I will or not, I must give it. But know that thou art not to grind corn or wheat with the mill; for it has this virtue, — that it accomplishes all wishes. Here it is, take it, though my heart bleeds after it. Thou didst me a good deed, therefore let it be thine."

The poor man put the mill on his back, took farewell of the King of the Crows, thanking him for his hospitality, and trudged home at his leisure. On the

27

way back he entertained the swineherds, the horse-herds, and the cowherds. All he did was to say, "Grind, my dear mill," and what food was dear to the eye, the mouth, and the taste appeared of itself; and if he said, "Draw up, my dear mill," all the food was as if the ground had swallowed it, — it vanished. Then he took leave of the good shepherds and continued his way.

As he travelled and journeyed, he came to a great wild wood; and having grown hungry, he said: "Grind, my dear mill." Straightway the table was spread, not for one, but for two persons. The mill knew at once that the poor man would have a guest; for that moment, wherever he came from, a great fat man appeared, who without saying a word, took his seat at the table. When they had enjoyed God's blessing, the great fat man spoke, and said:

"Listen, poor man. Give me that mill for this knotty club; for if thy mill has the power of accomplishing all thy desires [the fat man knew this already], my knotty club has this power, that thou hast need but to say, 'Strike, my club,' and the man thou hast in mind is the son of Death."

What was the poor man to do? Thinking if he did not give it of his free will the fat man would take it by force, he exchanged the mill for the knotty club; but when he had it once in his hand, he said in a low voice, for he was commanding the knotty club, "Strike, my dear club." And it so struck the fat man behind the ears that he gave forth not a sound; he did n't move his little finger. Then the poor man continued his journey homeward at his ease; and when seven years had passed he was able to say: " Here we are ! "

His wife who was weeping by the hearth, mourning over her dear lost lord and the two lean cows, scarcely knew the poor man, but still she knew him. His two sons had become large, and had grown out of their long clothes. When the poor man put his foot in his own house he set the mill down in the chimney-corner, loosed his mantle from his neck, hung it up on a nail, and only then did they know him.

" Well, father," said his wife, " thou hast come; God knows 't is time. I never expected to see thee again; but what didst thou get for Bimbo and Csako ? "

" This mill," answered he with many " see here's " and " see there's."

" If that 's the case, the palsy strike thy work," cried the woman; " better for thee to have stayed at home these seven years, and swung thy feet around here, than to have dragged that good-for-nothing mill from such a distant land, just as if thou hadst eaten the crazy-weed ! "

" Oh, my sweet wife, something is better than nothing; if we have no grain to grind for ourselves, we can grind for other people, if not in streams at least in drops."

" May a cancer eat thy mill!   I have n't a thing to put between my teeth, and still — "

" Well, my sweet wife, if thou hast nothing to put between thy teeth thou 'lt soon have.   Grind, my dear mill."

At these words, so much meat and drink appeared on the poor man's table that half of it would have been enough.   It was only then that the woman regretted her tongue rattling.   But a woman is a woman; beat her with a stone, only let her talk.

The poor man, his wife, and two sons sat down at the table, looking at the food like an army of locusts. They ate and drank to their hearts' content.   Whether from wine or some other cause, a desire to dance came to the two sons; and they jumped up and danced, so it was pure delight to look at them.   " Oh," said the elder one, " if we only had a gypsy! "   That moment a band of gypsies by the chimney struck up their music, and played away with such variations that the poor man too wished to dance, and so whirled his wife around that better could not be asked for.   The neighbors knew not what to think of the affair.   How was it that music was sounding in the poor man's house?

"What is this? " said they one to another, coming nearer and nearer, till they came up to the door and the windows.   Only then did they see that a band of gypsies were fiddling away with might and main, and the old man, his wife, and their two sons were dancing, while the table was bending under loads of rich meat and drink.

"Come in cousin! come in friend! come in brother-in-law, bring thy wife! come in brother!" and there was no end to the invitations of the poor man. Guests collected unceasingly, and still the table was spread. "'Pon my soul," said the poor man, "it's a pity my house is n't larger; for all these guests could scarcely find room in a palace." At these words, instead of the poor man's cabin such a magnificent palace appeared, with chambers, twelve in a row, that the king himself had n't the like of it.

A multitude of grand people with the king in the midst of them were out walking just at that time. "What's this? what's this?" asked they of one another. "There has always been a poor man's cabin here, now there's a king's palace, and besides, music is sounding, and gypsies are fiddling. Let's go and have a look."

The king went in front, and after him all the grand people, — counts, dukes, barons, and so on. The poor man came out and received the king with the great personages very kindly, and conducted them all to the head of the table as their fitting place. They ate, drank, and caroused, so that it was like a small wedding.

While they were enjoying themselves at the best, a great sealed letter came to the king. When he had read it, he turned yellow and blue, because it was written therein that the Turk-Tartar was nearing his kingdom with a great army, destroying everything with fire and sword, and sparing not the property of innocent, weeping people, whom he puts to the point of the sword; that the earth is drinking their blood; their flesh is devoured by dogs.

From great joy there was great sorrow.

Then the poor man stood forth and asked the king: " If 't is no offence, may I ask a question? "

" What may it be, poor man? "

" Would thy Highness tell me the contents of that great letter received just now? "

" Why ask, poor man? Thou couldst not mend the affair."

" But if I can? "

" Well, know then, and let the whole kingdom know, that the Turk-Tartar is moving on our country with a great army, with cruel intent; that he spares not the property of innocent, weeping people, puts them to the sword, so that the earth drinks their blood, and their flesh is devoured by dogs."

" And what will be the reward of him who drives the enemy out of the country? " asked the poor man.

" In truth," said the king, " great reward and honor await him; for if he should have two sons, I would give them my two daughters in marriage, with half the kingdom. After my death they would inherit the whole kingdom."

" Well, I 'll drive out the enemy all alone."

But the king did not place much confidence in the poor man's promise; he hurried together all his soldiers, and marched with them against the enemy. The two armies were looking at eaeh other with wolves' eyes, when the poor man went between the camps and commanded the club: " Strike, my dear club." And the club pommelled the Turk-Tartar army so that only one man was left to carry home the tidings.

The poor man gained half the kingdom and the two beautiful princesses, whom he married to his two stalwart sons. They celebrated a wedding which spoke to the seven worlds; and they are living now if they are not dead.

THE USELESS WAGONER.

THERE was once in the world a king, and he had
a Useless Wagoner who never and never did
anything but frolic in the tavern. The whole standing day and all the ocean-great night there was nothing for him but singing and dancing, eating and
drinking. The king had money of course.

But the king began to grow tired of this thing.
He called up the Useless Wagoner, and gave him a
terrible scolding. But 't is vain to seat a dog at table,
and when the Devil gets into a man he stays there;
so it was labor lost to drive the Useless Wagoner to
work, for he went his way, and frolicked as before.
At last the king resolved to take his life, and calling
him up, said, —

"Dost hear me, work-shunning Useless Wagoner!
I revile thy mother, if within the turn of four and
twenty hours thou dost not make for me a three-
hundred-gallon cask; and though one joint or seam is
not much, if it has that, I'll empale thee on a stake."

The Useless Wagoner said not a word to all this, but
put a hamper on his back, took a cutting-axe in his
hand, and strolled off to the forest to find a tree fit to
make a three-hundred-gallon cask.

When he came to the forest, being hungry and tired, he sat down under a large shady tree, opened his hamper, and began to eat lunch. He ate and ate, till all at once, from some corner or another, a little fox stood before him and begged food to eat.

" Of course I 'll give thee something. The food came here, 't will stay here ; " and with that he threw a slice of bread and a bit of sausage to the fox.

When the fox had finished eating she said: " Dost hear, Useless Wagoner? As thou hast taken pity on me, I will take pity on thee; in place of a good deed look for a good deed. Though thou hast not told me, still I know why thou hast come to this forest. I know, too, that the king is breaking his head to kill thee; but he 'll not be in time, for I will help thee out of thy trouble and make thee the three-hundred-gallon cask. And though one seam or joint is not much, even that will not be in it. Now lie down and rest."

And so it was. The Useless Wagoner lay down and rested. Meanwhile the little fox got such a three-hundred-gallon cask ready, that although a joint or seam is not much, even that was not to be seen in it.

When the cask was finished the Useless Wagoner took it home and gave it to the king, who, after looking at it, dropped his eyes and his lip like a sheep; for neither his father, his grandfather, nor his great-grandfather had ever seen such a cunningly made cask, for not a seam nor a joint could be seen in it for gold.

Well and good for the moment; but soon the king summoned the Useless Wagoner to his presence again, and cried out, —

" Dost thou hear me, work-shunning Useless Wagoner! I revile thy soul if within the turn of four and twenty hours thou dost not make for me a chariot which will go itself, without horses. I 'll break thee on a wheel ! "

The Useless Wagoner said nothing, but put his hamper on his back, took his cutting-axe in his hand, and wandered off to the forest to find a tree fit to make the chariot.

When he came to the forest he was hungry, and tired too ; therefore he sat down under a large, shady tree, opened his hamper, and began to eat lunch.

He ate and ate till all at once, from some corner or another, the little fox stood before him again, and begged food to eat.

" Of course, my dear little fox, I 'll give thee something. It came here, and 't will stay here."

With that he threw a piece of bread and a slice of ham to the little fox, who after she had eaten, said :

"Well, Useless Wagoner, in place of a good deed look for a good deed. Though thou hast not told me, still I know why thou art here. I know, too, that the king is breaking his head to kill thee ; but he won't, for I shall help thee out of trouble. I 'll make for thee the chariot which will go of itself, without horses ; but do thou lie down and rest."

And so it was. The Useless Wagoner reclined his head in rest; and meanwhile the little fox fashioned a chariot beautifully. When all was ready she roused the Useless Wagoner, and said, —

" Here is the chariot which runs of itself; thou hast but to step in and command it to stop in the king's court-yard. But I would tell thee this: Here is a whistle that will serve thee; shouldst thou fall into trouble, just blow, — it will help thee."

The Useless Wagoner thanked the fox for her kindness, and entered the chariot, which stopped not till it reached the king's court-yard.

When the king saw the chariot he said nothing, but shook his head, turned on the Useless Wagoner in a rage, and cried, —

" Useless Wagoner, I revile thy mother! In my stable there are a hundred hares; and if thou dost not herd them three days, if thou dost not drive them a-field in the morning and bring them back at night so that not one shall be missing from the hundred, I 'll strike off thy head."

What was the poor Useless Wagoner to do? Against his will, and of need, he let the hundred hares out of the stable and drove them a-field. They had barely touched the edge of the field when they ran in as many directions as there were hares. Who could bring them together again? The poor Useless Wagoner ran first after one and then after another hare; he chased the whole day, but could not bring back a single hare. It was already growing late, time to go home, but the hundred hares were in a hundred places; therefore the Useless Wagoner became terribly sad, and wished to make an end of his own life, — it was all the same whether he or the king took it; there was no salvation for him anyhow. So he put his hand in his bosom to take out his clasp-knife and strike himself in the heart, but instead of the knife he found the whistle which the little fox had given him. That was all he wanted; he drew out the whistle, sounded it, and, behold! all the hares ran up to him, — as tame as pet lambs fed from the palm of the hand.

When all the hares had come together he drove them home.

The king stood at the gate and let them in singly, counting, " One, two, three . . . ninety-nine, a hundred." Not one was missing.

Next day the Useless Wagoner drove the hares out again, and when they had barely touched the edge of the field they ran off in as many directions as there were hares.

But this time the Useless Wagoner took no thought of running and chasing after them; he thought to himself that he would take his whistle and blow, and they would come. So he lay down in a nice shady place, and slept to his liking.

But the king did not sleep; he was racking his brain to destroy the Useless Wagoner. So he called his only and dearly beloved daughter, and said to her, " My darling daughter, I have a great favor to ask of thee."

" What may it be, my father the king? "

" Of a truth nothing but this, — that thou dress in peasant's clothes, and go out to the field where the Useless Wagoner is herding the hundred hares, and beg one of him. If he gives it not for a good word, mayhap he will give it for a sweet kiss; but come not home to me without the hare, even if he asks a piece of thy body for it."

The princess granted her father's request. She gathered her wits about her, dressed up in peasant's clothes, and went in the field to the Useless Wagoner, who was sleeping at his leisure under a shady tree. The princess pushed him with her foot; he woke, and saw in a moment with whom he had to deal.

" God give thee a good-day, hareherd! "

" God save thee, king's daughter! What good dost thou bring the poor hareherd? "

" I have brought nothing but this, that I have come because I would like to get one little hare. Wouldst thou not give even one for good money ? "

" High princess, I will not give one for money; but if thou wilt give me three kisses, I can give them back. Then I don't mind; I 'll give thee a hare."

So the princess got a hare for three pairs of kisses, and ran home very joyfully; but just as she was touching the latch to open the gate, the hareherd sounded his whistle, the hare jumped like lightning from her bosom, and stopped not till it reached the flock.

The hareherd drove home his flock; the king was waiting for him at the gate, and let them in one by one, counting till he came to a hundred.

Next day the hareherd drove out his hares the third time, and left them to go their way.

The king now called his wife to the white chamber, and spoke thus to her: "My heart's beautiful love, I have a great favor to ask of thee."

"And what may it be, my dear husband?"

"Of a truth, nothing but this, — that thou dress in peasant's clothes, go to the hareherd in the field, and ask a hare of him. If he will not give it for fair words, he may for a sweet kiss; but come not home to me without a hare, even if he asks a piece of thy flesh."

Well, the queen yielded to her husband's request, put on a peasant's dress, and went to the field, where she found the Useless Wagoner sleeping in the shade. She roused him with her foot; he knew at once who was in the peasant's dress.

"God give thee a good-day, hareherd!"

"God save thee, kind queen! What good hast thou brought the poor hareherd? Why hast thou come, may I ask?"

"I have only come to ask if thou wilt give me a hare for good money."

" I will not give a hare for money, my queen; but if thou wilt give me three kisses, I will return them again. Then I don't mind; I'll risk my head, and let thee have a hare."

So the queen got a hare for three pairs of kisses, and took her way home joyously; but just as she was putting her hand on the latch to open the gate, the hareherd sounded the whistle, the hare jumped like a flash from the queen's bosom, and stopped not till it joined its companions.

When the hares were all together, the hareherd drove them home. The king was waiting for him at the gate, let each in singly, counting till he reached a hundred, — not one missing from the round number.

Next morning the hares were driven out as before; but the king now put on a peasant's dress, and went to the field himself. When he came to the hareherd he said: " God give thee good-day!"

" God save thee, poor man!" answered the hareherd. " What art thou looking for?"

" Well, what's the use in delay or denial? I have come to buy a little hare of thee for good money. Of course thou wilt part with one."

" I will not give one for money; but if I can wear out twelve rods on thy back, I don't mind; I'll risk my head on it."

What was the king to do? He stretched himself out with face and hands on the grass, and the hareherd flogged him as a corporal does a soldier; but he endured it all, gritting his teeth, and thinking to himself, "Wait a bit, thief of a Useless Wagoner, thou wilt have a dose when I get at thee!"

But all to no use, for when the king had reached home, and was just putting his hand on the latch to open the gate, the whistle sounded, and the hare sprang away from him like a flash, and ran till it joined the flock.

Then the Useless Wagoner drove home the hundred hares a fourth time. The king was standing at the little gate; he counted them one by one, but could find no fault, for they were all there.

The Useless Wagoner drove out the hares the fifth time to pasture; but the king mounted the chariot which went wherever the owner commanded, and drove to the Useless Wagoner, taking three empty bags with him. "Dost hear me, thou! — this-and-that-kind-of-work-shunning? Hareherd, I revile thy soul! If thou wilt not fill these three bags with truth, I will strike off thy head."

To all this the Useless Wagoner answered in words: "The king's daughter came out; I gave her, and she gave me. The queen came; I gave her, and she gave me. The king came; I gave him, and he — "

"Stop! stop!" cried the king, "the three bags are full; and I'd rather be in hell than hear thy words."

At this speech the chariot started off with the king,

and never stopped till it took him to the bottom of hell.

Then the Useless Wagoner went home, married the king's daughter, became king, and reigns yet with his queen, unless he is dead.

28

MIRKO, THE KING'S SON.

ONCE there was a king, and he had three sons. The king rejoiced in his three sons, and resolved to have them instructed in a befitting manner, so that he might leave good heirs to the kingdom. Therefore he sent his sons to school, where they got on well enough for a time, till at length they turned their backs on the school, went home, all three, and knew their studies no more.

The king grew fiercely angry at this, forbade his sons to stand before his face, and betook himself to live in the chamber of his palace next the rising sun, where he sat continually at the window and looked towards the east as if waiting for something; and with one eye he wept unceasingly, while with the other he laughed.

After the three princes had grown up to a good age, they agreed among themselves to inquire of the king why he was always sitting in the chamber next the rising sun, and why one of his eyes was always crying, while the other was always laughing. First the eldest son went in and put the question, saying, "My father the king, I have come to ask why one of thy eyes is always crying and the other always laughing, while thou art looking continually towards the east."

The king measured his son with his eyes from head to foot, said not a word, but took a sword which hung at the window and hurled it at him with such force that it sank into the door up to the hilt. The prince sprang through the door, thus escaping the blow aimed at him. When he came out his brothers asked what success he had had. He answered: "Try yourselves; then ye will know." The second brother tried, with the same result as the first. At last the youngest, who was called Mirko, went in and declared the cause of his coming. The king answered him not, but seized the sword in still greater anger, and hurled it at him so that it entered the stone wall up to the hilt. Mirko did not spring aside, but went to the sword, drew it out of the stone wall, took it to the king, his father, and placed it before him on the table.

Seeing this, the king opened his mouth and said to Mirko: "I see now, my son, that thou knowest somewhat better than thy two brothers what honor is; to thee then will I give answer. My one eye weeps unceasingly for sadness at your insignificance, not being fit to rule; but my other eye laughs because in the time of my youth I had a trusty comrade, the Hero of the Plain, who battled by my side, and he promised that if he should overpower his enemies he would come to dwell with me, that we might pass the days of our old age together. For this reason I sit ever by the window next the rising sun, because I await his coming; but every day there rise up against the Hero of the Plain, who dwells in the silken meadow, as many enemies as there are grass-blades on the field. Every day he unaided cuts them down; and until all his enemies have disappeared, he will not be able to come to me."

With that Mirko left his father's chamber, came out to his brothers, and told them the king's speech. They counselled together again, and agreed to ask leave of the king to try their fortune. First the eldest son went to his father and made known his wish. The king consented, and the eldest brother went to the royal stables where he chose a good steed, which he saddled next day, and set out on his journey. After he had been absent a whole year, behold he rides home, bearing on his shoulders the top of the copper bridge, which he threw down before the palace. He went in then, stood before the face of the king, and told him where he had been and what he had brought back.

The king heard his son's discourse to the end, and said: "Oh, my son, when I was of thy age the road to the copper bridge was a two hours' ride for me. Thou art a soft hero. Thou wilt never make vitriol. Go thy way."

With that, the eldest son left his father's chamber. After him the second brother went in, and asked leave of the king to try his fortune. Having received it, he went also to the stables and chose a good steed, which he saddled, mounted, and went his way. At the end of a year he came home, bringing the top of the silver bridge, which he threw down in front of the palace ; then he stood before the king, his father, and told him where he had been and what he had brought back.

" Oh," said the king, " when I was of thy age that was only a three hours' ride for me. Thou too art a soft hero; nothing at all will come of thee." With that he dismissed the second son.

At last Mirko appeared; he also asked to try his fortune. The king consented, and Mirko went to the stables to choose a steed. Finding nothing to his mind, he went out to the royal stud and examined it carefully, but could not decide which steed to take. Just then an old witch chanced to be passing that way, and asked what he wanted. Mirko told her. " Oh, my master," said she, " thou wilt not find a horse to thy wish here, but I will tell thee how to find one. Go to the king, thy father, and ask him for the horn with which in his youth he called together his golden-haired steeds. Sound this horn and the steeds will appear at once. Choose not among the golden-haired ones ; but last of all will come a shaggy-coated, crooked-legged old mare, — thou wilt know her by this, that when she strikes the pillars with her tail the whole palace will tremble from the blow. Choose her; try thy fortune with her."

Mirko took the old witch's advice, went straight-way to the king and said: "My father, I have come that thou mayest give me the horn with which in thy youth thou wert wont to call together thy golden-haired steeds."

The king asked: " Who told thee of this horn?"

" No man," answered Mirko.

"Well, my dear son, if no man told thee, thou art wise; but if some man told thee, he does not wish thee harm. I will tell thee where to find the horn; the rust has eaten it up, perhaps, by this time. In the seventh cellar it is enclosed in the wall; look for it, take it out, and make use of it if thou art able."

Mirko called a mason, went with him to the seventh cellar, found the hollow place in the wall, took out the horn, and carried it away. Then standing on the square before the palace, he sounded towards the east, the west, the south, and the north, and having waited a little, behold! he hears the golden horse bells ringing so that the whole city is full of the sound. The steeds came in, one more beautiful than the other in appearance and in breed. At a distance he saw the shaggy-haired, crooked-legged mare; and when she came to the gate, as true as I live, she struck the pillars with her tail so that the whole palace trembled.

When the steeds had stopped in the courtyard, Mirko went up to the mare, led her away to the stable, and then said that he had taken her to try his fortune. The magic mare answered: " That is well, my lord king's son; but first thou must feed me, for without that it will be hard to endure the long road."

"What kind of food dost thou wish? — for whatever my father has, I will give thee with a good heart."

"Very well, kind master; but a steed must be fed before starting, not while on the road."

"I know not what I can do," said Mirko, "except to give what I have with a good heart."

"Bring me straightway a measure of peas, and turn them into the manger."

Mirko obeyed, and when the peas were eaten, he brought a measure of beans; when these were eaten the mare turned to Mirko and said: "Now bring me half a measure of glowing coals."

The coals were brought; and when she had eaten the glowing coals, she became such a golden-haired steed as the Star of Dawn, and spoke further to Mirko. "Go now, my master, to the king, and ask of him that saddle which he used when he coursed the meadow with me in his youth."

Mirko went to the old king and asked for the saddle. The king answered that it was useless, for it had been thrown about a long time in the carriage-house, but if he could find it, he might take it. Mirko went to the carriage-house and found the saddle all befouled by the hens and turkeys. He took it, however, to his steed, which said that it was not proper for a king's son to sit on such a saddle. Mirko was about to carry it away and have a fresh cover put on, when she said: "Place it before me." He obeyed. Straightway she blew on it, and in an instant it became such a golden saddle that its like could not be found in seven kingdoms.

With this he saddled the magic mare, and she said: "Go now, my dear master, to thy father, and ask him for the weapons and the sword with which he fought when he journeyed with me."

Mirko asked his father; the old king said they were on the shelf if he wanted them. Mirko took them to the mare, who blew on them, and instantly they became the most beautiful gold-mounted sword and weapons. Mirko girded on the sword and took the weapons. Then the bridle was brought, and when blown upon became of the most beautiful gold.

Mirko bridled the mare, led her out of the stable, and wished to sit in the saddle, but she said: "Wait, my dear master; lead me out of the city first, and then sit on me." He hearkened to these words, and led her out of the city; then she stood still, and he sat in the saddle.

The magic steed now asked: "How shall I bear thee, dear master; with the speed of the fleet whirlwind, or of quick thought?"

"Carry me as may please thee," answered the prince; "only manage so that I shall endure the swift flight."

"Well, close thy eyes," said the steed, "and hold fast."

Mirko closed his eyes; the steed shot on like a rushing whirlwind, and after a short time struck the earth with her foot, and said to Mirko: "Open thy eyes! What dost thou see?"

"I see," said he, "a great river and a copper bridge."

"That, my dear master, is the bridge the top of which thy first brother brought home; but look for the open place."

"I see it," said Mirko; "but where are we going from here?"

"Only close thy eyes; I will take thee straight there."

With that she moved as quick as thought, and in a few moments struck the earth, stood still, and said to Mirko: "Open thy eyes! What dost thou see?"

"I see a great river, and across it a silver bridge."

"That is the bridge the top of which thy second brother took home; look for the open place."

"I see it," said Mirko; "but where do we go from here?"

"Only close thy eyes," said the steed; "I will take thee at once."

With that she moved on like lightning, and in a flash stamped on the ground, and said to the prince: "Open thy eyes! What dost thou see?"

"I see," said Mirko, "an enormously wide and

deep river, across it a golden bridge, and at both ends of the bridge, at this side and that, are four unmercifully large lions. Must we cross this bridge?"

"Never mind," said the steed, "I'll manage; only shut thy eyes."

The mare sped on like a swift falcon, and thus flew across the bridge. After a short time she struck the ground, and said: "Open thy eyes! What dost thou see?"

"I see," replied Mirko, "a summitless, high glass mountain, as steep as the side of a house."

"We must cross that very mountain, my master."

"That, I think, is impossible," said Mirko.

"Fear not," said the steed; "for I have on my feet the shoes which thy father fastened to me with diamond nails, seven hundred years ago. Only shut thy eyes and hold to me firmly."

Now the steed sprang up, and in an instant was on the glass mountain. She stamped, and said, "Open thy eyes! What dost thou see?"

"I see," said Mirko, "when I look behind, something dark, as large as a great plate."

"Oh, my master, that is the round of the earth. But what dost thou see before thee?"

"I see a narrow glass road, rising like a half circle. On both sides of it is emptiness of bottomless depth."

"My dear master, we must pass over that road; but the passage is so delicate that if one of my feet slip the least bit to one side or the other, there is an end to our lives. But trust thyself to me, and close thy eyes. Hold fast, I will manage."

With that she swept on, and in an instant stamped again. "Open thy eyes! What dost thou see?"

"I see behind me," said Mirko, "a faint light, in front of me is darkness so dense that when I hold my finger before my eyes I cannot see it."

"Well, we must go through that also; shut thy eyes and hold firmly."

She sped on anew, and again stamped. "Open thy eyes! What dost thou see now?"

"I see," said Mirko, "the most glorious, light, beautiful, snow-covered mountains, and in the midst of them a silken meadow; in the centre of the silken meadow something dark."

"This silken meadow," said the steed, "belongs to the Hero of the Plain; and the dark object in the middle is his tent, woven from black silk. Now close thy eyes or not as may please thee. We shall go there directly." Mirko spurred the steed, and they were at the tent in a twinkle.

Mirko sprang from his steed and left her at the tent by the side of that of the Hero of the Plain, and entered himself. Within lay a warrior stretched on the silken grass, sleeping; but a sword above him was cutting around in every direction, so that a fly could not light on his body. "Well," thought Mirko to himself, "though he be a good warrior I could slay him in slumber; but it would not be honorable to slay a sleeping man. I will wait till he rises." Then he went out and tied his steed fast to the tent, near the other, stretched himself on the silken grass, and called: "Sword out of thy sheath!" and the sword cut around above him, as his sword above the Hero of the Plain, so that a fly could not touch his body.

When the Hero of the Plain woke up and saw that a horse was tied near his own, he marvelled, and said: "What does this mean? I am here seven hundred years, and I have not seen a strange horse near mine before. Whose can this be?" He rose, went out, and saw Mirko sleeping near the tent with the sword cutting above him. "That," said he, "is an honest warrior; he has not slain me while sleeping. It would not become me to touch him now."

Then he pushed the foot of the sleeping hero with his own. Mirko jumped up straightway, and the Hero of the Plain asked: "Who art thou, and on what journey?" Mirko told whose son he was, and what his journey. "God has brought thee, dear younger brother," said the Hero; "thy father is my old friend, and thou, I see, art as good as thy father. But I have need of thee. This great silken meadow which thou seest, is every day filled with enemies, and every day I cut them down; but to-day as thou art with me, we shall not hurry. Come, let us eat and drink; let them crowd." Then the two went in, ate and drank till the enemy had so increased that they reached almost to the tent. The Hero of the Plain sprang then to his feet and said: " Up, my comrade, we 'll soon finish." Both leaped into their saddles and rushed to the centre of the enemy, crying out, " Sword from the sheath ! " The swords hewed off the heads of the countless multitude, so there was scarcely room to move for bodies. Twelve of the opposing warriors now flee from the rear, the Hero of the Plain and Mirko pursuing. They come to a glass mountain; the twelve warriors rushing ahead. Mirko pursues in hot haste. On the top of the mountain there is a nice, level space; he sees them running up it. He gallops after them; but all at once they are as if the ground had swallowed them. Mirko springs to the place where they disappear, finds a breach and a deep opening with winding steps. His steed rushes into the opening and down the stairs; they are soon in the lower world.

Mirko looks around the lower world and sees a shining diamond castle, which serves instead of the sun down there. The twelve fleeing warriors rush towards the castle, he after them, and ordering his sword out of the sheath, cuts off their heads in a moment. The next instant Mirko stands before the diamond castle. Within, there is such a clatter and pounding that the whole interior trembles and shivers. He dismounts and enters. Inside is an old witch weaving, and the racket is deafening. The building is full of armed men. The infernal old witch weaves them. When she throws her shuttle to the right, two hussars spring out on horseback; when she throws it to the left, two men on foot jump out armed.

Meanwhile Sword out of the Sheath cuts down the newly made soldiers, but the old witch weaves more. " Well," thinks Mirko to himself, " I shall never get out of here, at this rate;" but he commands the sword, and it cuts the old witch into small pieces. Then he carries the loom into the yard, where there is a pile. He throws everything on the pile and sets fire to it; but when all is burned one of the old witch's ribs springs out, begins to turn round in the dust, and she rises up again entire. Again Mirko is going to command the sword to cut her to pieces, but she speaks up, " Spare my life, Mirko, and await one good deed for another, if thou wilt let me go. Thou dost not know how to escape from here; I will give thee four diamond horse-shoe nails. Do as I say; thou wilt profit by it."

Mirko takes the nails and puts them away, but says to himself: " If I leave the old witch alive, she will put up her loom again, and the Hero of the Plain will never be able to free himself from his enemies." Again he orders his sword to cut the old witch in pieces; he throws the pieces into the fire, where they are consumed, so that she can never rise again. He mounts his steed and searches the underground world, but nowhere does he find a living soul.

Then he puts spurs to his steed, springs up the cir-

cular stairs, and issues forth into the upper world.
Straightway he comes down from the glass mountain,
and passing over the silken meadow, returns to the
Hero of the Plain, who thought Mirko had left him.
But when he saw his friend returning, he went out
to meet him with great joy, and took him into the
tent, where they feasted together gloriously. And
when the prince rose to go, he offered him his
silken meadow and all the royal domains; but
Mirko answered: "My dear elder brother, I have
finished thy enemies; they will never attack thy
kingdom again. I have this now to ask, that thou
come with me to my father the king, who has long
been waiting for thee."

Thereupon they mounted their steeds, and set out
for the realms of the old king. They went on easily
till they reached the glass mountain, where the Hero
of the Plain stopped, and said: "My dear younger
brother, I cannot go on, for the diamond nails are
long since worn from my horse's shoes, and his feet
have no grip."

Mirko called to mind that the cursed old witch
had given him the diamond nails, and said: "Grieve
not, elder brother, I have nails; I'll shoe thy horse
this minute."

So he took out the nails, and shod the Hero's
horse. Then they continued their journey over the
glass mountain with ease and comfort, like two jolly
comrades, and sped homeward as swiftly as thought.

At that time the old king was sitting at the window of his palace next the rising sun, and lo! he beholds two horsemen riding towards him. Straightway he takes his field-glass, and sees that it is his trusty old comrade, the Hero of the Plain, together with his son Mirko. He runs out, and from the tower commands that a twelve-year old ox be killed; and when Mirko and the Hero arrive, the great feast is ready. He receives them with joy, kisses and embraces them; this time both his eyes are laughing. Then they sat down to the feast, ate and drank with gladness. Meanwhile the Hero of the Plain spoke of Mirko's doings, and among other things said to the old king: "Well, comrade, thy son Mirko will be a better hero than we were; he is already a gallant youth. Thou hast cause to rejoice in him."

"Indeed, I begin to be satisfied with him," said the king, "especially since he has brought thee. But I do not think he would venture yet to measure strength with Doghead."

Mirko heard the conversation, but said nothing. After dinner, however, he spoke to the Hero of the Plain apart, and inquired who Doghead was, and in what direction he lived. The Hero of the Plain told him that Doghead lived in the north, and was such a hero that his like was not under the sun.

Mirko made preparations for his journey, took provisions, and next day set out for Doghead's.

According to his wont, he sat on his steed, held fast, and closed his eyes. The steed sped on, flying like the swift whirlwind. At length she stopped, struck the ground, and said to Mirko: " Open thy eyes! What dost thou see?"

" I see," said the prince, " a seven-story diamond castle, so bright that I can look on the sun, but not on it."

" Well, Doghead lives there; that is the royal castle."

Mirko sprang towards it, stopped right under the window, and called out in a loud voice: " Art thou here, Doghead? I have an account to settle with thee."

Doghead was not at home, but his daughter was, and such a beautiful princess that her like could not be found on the whole round of the earth. As she sat by the window embroidering, and heard the loud, piercing voice, she looked out so angrily with her wondrous black, beautiful eyes that Mirko and his horse were turned into stone in an instant from the flash. Then she thought: " Maybe this young man is a king's son." She went to look at him, was sorry she had turned him to stone so quickly, and approached, taking a golden rod, walked around the stone statue and struck it on all sides with the rod. The stone began to move, and in a moment Mirko and his horse stood alive before her. Then the maiden asked, " Who art thou, and on what journey?"

29

Mirko answered that he was a king's son, and had come to see Doghead's daughter.

The maiden was so displeased that she called out to her father very angrily; but presently she thought better of it, fell in love with Mirko, and led him up into the seven-story diamond palace, where she saw him with a good heart. During conversation at the table, Mirko confessed that he had come to try his strength with Doghead.

The maiden advised him not to do that, since there was no man on the round of the earth whom her father could not conquer. Seeing, however, that Mirko would not desist from his purpose, she took compassion on him, and told how her father might, perhaps, be overcome. "Go down," said she "into the seventh cellar of the castle. There thou wilt find an unsealed cask, in which my father keeps his strength. Here is a silver flask; fill it from the cask. Do not stop the flask, but keep it always hanging from thy neck uncorked; and when thy strength begins to fail, dip thy little finger in. Every time thou shalt do so, thy strength will be increased with the strength of five thousand men. Drink of the wine, for every drop contains the strength of five thousand men."

Mirko listened to her advice attentively, hung the flask upon his neck, went into the cellar, and found the wine. He took a good draught of it; then thinking that he had enough, and lest Doghead might make further use of the wine, he poured it all on the ground, to the last drop. There were six measures of wheat-flour in the cellar, which he sprinkled around to absorb the moisture. Having done this, he went up to Doghead's daughter, and declared that he was ready, and thanking her for the counsel, vowed to take her as wife for her kindness, and swore eternal fidelity.

The beautiful princess consented, making one condition, — that if Mirko should overcome her father, he would spare his life.

Mirko asked the maiden when her father might be expected to return, and from what quarter.

She answered that he was then in the realms of the setting sun, that he took delight in those regions, but would soon be home, for it was the hour of his coming. But it was easy to know it beforehand, for when he was forty miles distant, he was in the habit of hurling home a forty-hundred-pound club before him; and wherever it fell a fountain gushed out of the earth.

Mirko and the princess went on the balcony to wait for Doghead; all at once (the Lord save us!) the sky grew dark, and a forty-hundred-pound club fell in the court-yard. A stream rushed out of the earth as if from a force-pump.

Mirko ran down straightway to see how much his strength had increased. He picked up the club, whirled it around his head, and let it go so that it came down just in front of Doghead. Doghead's horse stumbled over the club, whereupon his master flew into a rage, and cried out: "May the wolves and dogs devour thee! Seven hundred years have I ridden thee, and to this day thou hast never stumbled. Why begin now?"

"Oh, dear master," answered the magic steed, "there is mighty trouble at home; for the club which thou hast sent ahead has been hurled back, and I stumbled over it."

"Oh, that's nothing!" said Doghead. "Seven hundred years ago I saw in a dream that I should have a struggle with Mirko, the king's son, some day. He is now at the castle; but what is he to me? There is more strength in my little finger than in his whole body." With that Doghead sped homeward and was soon there.

Mirko, the king's son, was waiting in the courtyard, and when Doghead saw the prince he made straight towards him and said: "Mirko, I know that thou art waiting for me. Well, here I am; what dost thou wish, that we should fight with swords or wrestle?"

"I care not," answered Mirko; "any way that may please thee."

"Well, let us try it first with swords," said Doghead.

He got off his horse; they stood face to face, and both commanded: "Sword out of the sheath."

The swords sprang out in fighting, and so cut above the heads of the two that the whole place was rattling with their blows. Sparks flew so thickly from their fierce slashing that fire covered the ground, and it was impossible to stand long in one place.

Then Doghead said: " Let us not spoil our swords, but put them up and try wrestling."

They laid aside the swords and began to wrestle. Doghead seized Mirko by the body, raised him up in the air, and so planted him on the ground that he sank in it up to the girdle. Mirko, frightened at this, thrust his little finger into the flask, and became so strong that he sprang out of the earth in a moment, rushed at Doghead, and so stretched him on the ground that he lay there like a flattened frog. Then, seizing him by the hair, he dragged him toward the castle, where a golden bridge was built across a bottomless lake. Having brought him to the middle of the bridge, he held his head above the water and commanded the sword to cut. The head fell into the bottomless lake, and Mirko threw the body after.

Doghead's daughter saw all this, and was powerfully angry at Mirko, the king's son. When he came before her she turned her face away and would not come to speech with him. But Mirko explained that he could not have done otherwise, for if he had spared Doghead's life, he would have lost his own; but as he had pledged his faith to the princess, he held to his word, and would marry her. The princess approved this, and they agreed to make ready and set out for Mirko's kingdom. The horses were brought, — Doghead's magic steed for the princess. They mounted the horses, but when ready to start, Mirko became very sorrowful.

" Why art thou sad Mirko? " inquired the princess.

"Because," said he, " I wish greatly to go home, but it is hard to leave this glorious, seven-story diamond castle here, which was thy father's, for there is none like it in our kingdom."

" Oh, my dear," said the princess, " I will turn it at once into a golden apple. I will sit in the middle of the apple; thou mayst put it in thy pocket, and thus carry home the castle and me. There thou canst change it back again whenever the wish comes."

The beautiful princess came down from her horse, gave the reins to Mirko, and taking out a diamond rod walked around the building and struck it on the sides with the rod. The castle began to shrink together, and became smaller and smaller until it was the size of a watchman's booth. Then she jumped in and it became a golden apple, but the diamond rod remained on the ground outside. Mirko, the king's son, picked up the golden apple and the diamond rod, put them in his pocket, sat on his steed, and leading Doghead's horse by the bridle, travelled home comfortably.

When Mirko had come home and seen his horses

in the stable he went to the palace, where he found the old king with the Hero of the Plain, satisfied and amused. He told them that he had conquered Doghead and put him to death; but the old king and the Hero of the Plain shook their heads.

Mirko, taking them both by the hands, said: "Come with me, and I will show you, so that ye may see with your own eyes that I have beaten Doghead; for not only have I brought his seven-story diamond castle with me, but his loveliest daughter with the castle, as proof of my work."

The old king and the Hero of the Plain marvelled at Mirko's speech, and were in doubt; but they went with him, and he led them to the flowery garden of the palace, in the middle of which Mirko took a beautiful spacious place for the diamond castle, where he put down the golden apple. He began to turn and strike it on the sides with the diamond rod. The apple swelled out and began to extend with four corners, and grew greater and greater, till it became a seven-story diamond castle as high as the trees.

Then taking them by the hands he led them up the diamond staircase and entered the halls of the castle, where the world-renowned beautiful princess met and received them with a good heart. Then she sent for the old king's other sons and the chief men of his court. In the dining-hall was a great horse-shoe table. She commanded it; the table opened of itself, and every kind of precious meat and drink appeared

upon it. Then the assembled guests feasted joyously. The old king was satisfied at last with his
son. He gave Mirko his kingdom and all his posses-
sions, but he withdrew himself to quiet private life,
with the Hero of the Plain, and many a pleasant day
the old comrades had together; and the old king's
two eyes were always laughing. The royal pair lived
happily, and had beautiful children. They are still
alive if they are not dead.

THE REED MAIDEN.

THERE was once a king, and he had two sons. The king sent his eldest son to marry. He went, and chose the elder sister of the Reed Maiden. When he brought home his wife the king was satisfied with the choice. After that the king sent his younger son to marry, and he answered that he would not take any poor skeleton of a thing, but that his wife must be the most beautiful flower on the whole round of the earth, — the most lovely, world-beautiful maiden.

Once the king's two sons went to hunt; on the way home the younger said to the elder: "My dear elder brother, I would beg of thee a favor."

"And what may it be, younger brother?"

"In truth, no other than this: When we come home, ask thy wife if there is any one more beautiful than she."

"If that's thy trouble, it is no great matter, for my wife is just coming to meet us. — Well, my heart's gold-enclosed ruby, wilt thou answer one question? Thou art for me the most beautiful, but is there one still more beautiful in the world?"

Now the princess all at once acted like one hard of hearing; she answered nothing, but stopped them with a nod, and commanded with her eye, " Silence! not a word more."

It stopped there. The younger brother, whatever he did not do, he stole into his brother's bed-chamber quietly. In the evening, when the elder brother and his wife came in, the husband said: " Tell me, my heart's heart, why didst thou not answer my question a little while ago?"

" I did not answer, dear husband, because thou didst ask me before thy brother. It would not have been well for him to know that I have a younger sister who is the most beautiful maiden on the whole round of the earth, but she is hidden in the middle one of three reeds; for this reason she is known as the world-beautiful Reed Maiden. The other two reeds are her waiting-maids."

" But thou hast not told me, my dear, in what corner of the world she is hidden."

" Oh, my dear husband, it is far from here, — as far as from here there and from there back; but as thou hast asked I will tell thee. Hast thou heard of the fame of the Black Sea?"

" I have not, indeed."

" Well, if thou hast not, then hear now. In the seventy-seventh island of the Black Sea, right in the middle, are hidden three reeds, but no mortal could go to them unless by some magic power or infernal art; but if by a miracle he should get there, he would not be able to bring away anything, — First, because

there is such darkness on the islands of the Black Sea
that a spoon might stand up in it; second, because
the world-beautiful Reed Maiden is guarded by a
witch whose life will end when the reeds are cut
down; therefore she guards them as the light of her
two eyes, or still more carefully. But if any man
could bring the maiden away, he would be the happi-
est person in the wide world; for the islands would be
lighted up, and he would gain a wife whom the starry
heavens would gaze upon with smiles."

When the king's younger son had heard all this
from root to branch, he went out of the room by the
same way he had entered. Then saddling his best
and favorite steed, he put provisions in his bag
and moved out into the wide world in search of the
beautiful Reed Maiden. He journeyed and travelled
over forty-nine kingdoms and beyond the Operentsia
Sea till he came to a hut; in the hut an old woman
was living: "God give thee good-day, dear old
mother."

"If thou hadst not called me old mother, I should
have eaten thee on the spot. But whither art thou
journeying in this strange land, where even a bird
does not go?"

"I am looking for the world-beautiful Reed Maiden,
who is blooming in the seventy-seventh island of the
Black Sea. Hast thou not heard of her, dear old
mother?"

"What's the use in denying, my son? I have not

heard. Why should I evade, since it can neither harm nor profit me? But here in the neighboring valley, over the mountain, straight ahead, near a round forest on the top of a hill, lives my elder sister; if she knows nothing about it, then no one in the world knows. Here, Mitsi, come out! Conduct the king's son to my elder sister."

The king's son followed Mitsi, who was no other than a large-whiskered little mouse. When they came to a cross-road Mitsi squeaked once, showed the middle of the road, and ran home. The king's son went along the right road, and arrived at the hut in which the second sister lived. She received him in like manner as the first, and sent her servant, Pitsi, to show him the road to her eldest sister. Pitsi was no other than a dove-white squirrel, with a long bushy tail. When the king's son came to the third hut, where the eldest sister lived, he said: "God give thee a good-day, dear old mother."

" If thou hadst not called me old mother, I should have eaten thee on the spot. Whither art thou wandering in this strange land, where even a bird does not go? "

" I am in search of the world-beautiful Reed Maiden, who is blooming in the seventy-seventh island of the Black Sea. Hast thou not heard of her, dear old mother? "

" Oh, king's son, thou wouldst wear off thy horse's legs to the knees, and wear out twelve pairs of iron

boots on thy own feet, before thou couldst reach
that place, for it is only possible to go there on a
steed that has sucked dragon's milk, eaten glowing
coals, and drunk the fiery flame; but thou hast in
thy head three golden hairs, grown from one root, of
which thou hast known nothing to this moment.
Come hither; let me cut them out."

The king's son bent down his head. The old
woman cut out the three golden hairs. "See, my
son, these three hairs have wondrous power. A fairy
gave them to thy father, with whom, as he was a
beautiful man, she fell in love, and thou hast inherited
them. Here they are; I give them to thee with this
latch-string. Go up on this terribly high mountain,
which in front of my hut supports the heavens.
When thou shalt come to the top, strike the three
golden hairs with the latch-string three times; at
once will stand before thee a magic steed that has
grown up on the silken meadow, sucked dragon's
milk, eaten glowing coals, and drunk fiery flames."

The king's son gave heartfelt thanks for the kindness shown him, then went up on the great unclimb-
able mountain that supported the heavens. When
he had reached the top he took out the three golden
hairs and struck them three times with the old latch-
string. Behold, a fiery cloud rushed towards him like
a shot arrow, with a fearful rumbling and cracking,
as if a whole stud of horses were before it, and then
stood still above his head. All at once he heard

from the fiery cloud a triple neighing, at the sound of which, as of a bell, the earth trembled three times. The magic steed rushed out, and like a flood, like a cloud-burst, plunged down by his side, blowing from its nostrils varied flames, — red, blue, and green. The latch-string became such a saddle that for the fur and diamond buttons, and silver and gold embroidery, the earth could not be seen.

" Hip, hop ! here am I, dear master ! That there be no delay in thy affair, wilt thou not sit on my back that I may be off with thee? Shall I go like the swiftest whirlwind, or like thought, or as a bird can fly ? "

" Go, my dear steed, in such fashion that there may be no fault in thee or me."

" But before we set out on the long road," said the magic steed, " I wish to say this: Since such dense darkness reigns in the islands that a spoon might stand straight in it, we must first go to the bright antechamber of the Sun, and take thence one burning ray."

When the steed had thus ended the speech, he rose in the airy heavens. They journeyed and travelled across forty-nine kingdoms till they came to the portals of the earth, where two bearded wolves stood on guard. These wolves stood on the road and demanded toll. The toll was no other than two pounds of flesh from the good steed. Now, if two pounds of flesh were taken from the steed, it

would be but half magic, and so would never reach
the end of the road. Whatever the king's son did
not do, he took his gleaming clasp-knife and cut out
two pounds of his own flesh; then he threw it to the
bearded wolves, and only on this condition did they
let him pass.

The king's son pursued his way till he came to
the Sun's bright antechamber, where he tied his
steed to a diamond pillar; then he bathed in the
fire-bath, and rubbed with fire-towels; looking at
himself from head to foot in the shining wall of
the antechamber as in a mirror, he combed his hair
with a golden comb. Here, 'pon my soul, what
came of the affair, or what did not, a subject-spirit in
the service of the Sun became enraged in good earnest (for his eyebrows struggled with each other), — no
doubt it was at the king's son, — and with a single
breath, which the son of the hurricane could not
withstand, blew straight ahead, so that the king's son
did not feel the ground under his feet for seventy-
seven miles. Then he fell into a terribly dark opening, and groped along in this cavern, feeling his way
like a blind man. If he made a step, he trod on a
serpent; if he felt with his hand, he grasped a warty
toad; if he looked around, he saw only red-eyed
worms, — creeping, crawling things. He went on and
on till he heard the plash of seething water. The
beating of iron hammers struck his ear-drum, and so
struck as almost to break it. This is the place where

thunderbolts are made.   He went on till he came to
a great iron gate, standing open just then; but a tremendous, cursed, hundred-headed dragon, who let no
one pass, kept guard there.   What could the king's
son take hold of ?   What could he do with his life?
Here, upon my soul! what he did, or what he did
not do, he took out a sweet-speaking, magic flute,
and blew on it so sadly that his tears rolled down.
Such touching notes did he draw from the flute
that the great powerful beast — the hundred-headed
dragon — became as a lamb, lowered his bloody
crest; his bristling scales dropped smoothly, one on
the other; he stretched on the ground, and cowered,
whining like a dog when he beholds his master after
an absence.   Seeing this, the king's son grew bold,
and going straight to the dragon, stepped upon him,
walked on his back, and the terrible wild beast did
not mind it; he only licked his foot, wagged his tail,
and let the king's son pass over.

After he had gone through the gate the darkness
began to part; and no wonder, for a charm-given,
lovely maiden, in a purple velvet robe, stepped before him.   She was no other than Dawn, the dearest
and best-beloved daughter of the Sun.   Now, the
splendid young prince pleased this flower of the skies.
She placed him by her side on her winged steed, and
flew across the vault of heaven, and they swept on till
they reached the razor bridge.   When they touched
the bridge, their horse became as if he were not; and

they crossed so that the horse's feet were not injured, and the razor's edge was not dented. Having passed the razor bridge they came to the copper forest, where were working at that moment the woodcutters of the Sun, who on iron wagons were taking wood to the kitchen, with a terrible rattling and pounding. Thence they rode to the silver forest, where silver-white birds cheered every wanderer. Two of the birds came and sang the sweetest notes. The silver-trees inclined thrice to the daughter of the Sun. Next they reached the golden forest, where sweet-voiced, golden-yellow birds enlivened the visitors, and threw down golden nuts here and there from the trees. The golden forest bent thrice to the daughter of the Sun.

In the middle of the golden forest was Dawn's garden; in the garden her copper-roofed mansion. When the Beauty of the Skies came home the pearly flowers shook their bells, and began to sound. On hearing this, the stars swept forth like a swarm, and glittered round about. The maiden nodded but once, and behold! purple clouds swam before her like so many sky-sacks, which serve on the extended firmament as boats. Dawn took her seat, but first she spread her mantle and seated the king's son at her side. Lest his part of the boat might be heavier, she drew him nearer to her with an embrace; but he dared not embrace in return.

They sailed and sailed through the airy heavens till they were weary; then they tied their boat to the tree with diamond blossoms, silver leaves, and golden apples. They sat on a golden bench under the tree, and were there but a moment, when at a nod from the Sun's daughter a golden butterfly appeared more quickly than a spoken word, and brought fresh-gathered honey of the skies on a rose-leaf. When they had eaten, thirst seized the king's son; then a modest star came bringing a goblet on a silver tray, in the goblet a charm-drink, and when the king's son had drunk from the golden goblet his thirst fell away as if it had been cut in two.

When their hunger and thirst were gone, at the Sun's daughter's nod the modest stars brought a cithara. Dawn then played on its golden chords with silver feathers, and sounded such notes that a man hearing them would spring up and whirl in the dance, even if his own father were lying dead on the table. After that came the hour of rest; the king's son was led across seventy-seven chambers to the bath-room. In the middle of the room stood a great golden cask filled with dew, and on a boxwood table lay lathery soap. The king's son bathed in the dew-water, washed himself with the lathery soap, and wiped with a towel of gold.

When he rose next morning, Dawn gave him a burning ray which she wound up like a ribbon, put in a box, and hung with a golden hair on the neck of the king's son. After that they parted amidst tear-shedding. The Sun's daughter sped across the vault of heaven on her winged steed, and the king's son continued his journey.

As I say, he had a ray to light up the island. The king's son journeyed and travelled till the steed spoke, saying: " Listen, dear master."

" What is thy command, dear horse? "

" Gird thyself well, for thou must cut the three reeds at a blow; a second blow would lose thee thy head. If at one blow thou succeed, the island will be lighted up. The world-beautiful maiden and her two attendants will be thine, but only on condition that thou cut not open the reeds before coming to water; for if thou dost, they will die a fearful death in a moment."

The king's son promised by heaven and earth that he would act as told. On the seventh day they came to the island of the Black Sea, where there was such darkness that a spoon would have stood up in it; but the king's son drew out the box hanging by the golden hair and removed the cover. All at once the way was lighted, but so strangely that it gave light only to him; he could see everything, but not a created soul could see him. When he came to where the three reeds were growing, they bent before him and bowed to the earth. They continued to bow; at the best moment the king's son drew his sword and with a blow all three reeds fell upon his breast. But from the three reed-stumps black blood sprang forth, and a bitter wail was heard as if a naked sword had been thrust into some one's heart. It had been thrust into the heart of the witch; for the black blood was hers, and the bitter wail was her death-sigh. She could only live while the three reeds stood. As soon as the old witch had breathed out her soul, the burning ray flew out of the silver box as if it had been shot from a gun, and the whole island was in light.

Then the king's son sat on his good steed and journeyed over forty-nine kingdoms as swiftly as the most fleet-winged bird could go. Once curiosity rose in him to know if there was indeed something in the reeds, and what it could be like. I say, curiosity rose up in him, and bored his side as if with an iron auger, so that what he did or did not do, he took out his gleaming knife and split the smallest reed, in which was the youngest attendant of the world-beautiful Reed Maiden. No sooner had he split the reed than a beauteous, pearl-given, lovely girl fell upon his breast; and her first word was: "Water! Only as much water as a little swallow takes in her beak when she gives drink to her young, or I die!"

But the king's son had it not. One drop of water is not much, but he could not give that much. The beautiful maiden, like a broken flower, began to wither, grew paler and paler, till at last the pallor of death seized her head, and bending to the breast of the king's son, she died.

The king's son was so sorry for his fault that if it had been possible, he would have atoned for it with his blood; but that was not possible. Therefore he came down from his good steed, dug a grave with his sword, and buried the maiden; as a grave-mark he planted the split reed, and from it a black rose sprang, which as mourning, bloomed in black.

A bitter weeping wail, a bitter woe-cry was heard from the two reeds that were not split yet, as if some one were bewailing a brother. Great sadness seized the king's son too, who thought, " I caused the death of this maiden. I broke this flower and planted it in the bosom of death." But if he had wept out his soul, it would have been useless; therefore he mounted his steed and rode farther. He travelled and journeyed till curiosity rose in his breast, and bored his side as with an iron auger. " Is there in the second reed another such maiden; and will she go like the first? "

At last he could resist the devil's boring no longer; so he took his gleaming clasp-knife, and split the second reed also. Behold, the elder attendant of the Reed Maiden, came out, saying: " Water, water, or I shall die a fearful death! " But the king's son had not one drop of water; the maiden grew paler and paler, till she dropped her head on the breast of the king's son, and died. The king's son came to the earth, dug a grave with his sword, and buried the maiden. At the head of the grave he placed the split reed; from it a beautiful rose-bush sprang up, which bloomed in black, as mourning.

A bitter weeping wail, a bitter woe-cry of pain was

heard from the unsplit reed, in which the world-beautiful maiden herself was hidden; and no less grief seized the king's son. He had killed two; with his own strength he had broken two beautiful flowers, and put them in the bosom of death. Grief covered him with black wing. His good steed went as a bird of swiftest flight till curiosity rose up in the breast of the king's son, bored his side as with an iron auger. "What sort of person is his future bride? who is the world-beautiful Reed Maiden?"

Since he could not resist this devil's boring, this mighty curiosity, he took out the third and last reed to split it; but the magic steed reached back, and taking the reed from the king's son, did not return it till they came to the shore of a lake.

At the water the king's son split the last reed, and there came forth such a maiden that her like was not born since the world began, nor before, nor after. Her first word was: "Water! Only as much water as a little swallow takes in her beak when she gives drink to her young, or I shall die in a moment!"

The king's son gave her to drink; she felt better. Then they embraced, and kissed, saying, "I am thine, thou art mine."

"Listen, my beautiful love," said the king's son, "while I ride home for a carriage of glass and gold do thou hide in this willow; but till I see thee, though one word is not much, speak not that much to any one."

The king's son rode for the glass and golden carriage; the maiden climbed the willow where she hid. Now, what came of the affair, and what did not, while the king's son was gone a crawfish-gathering gypsy girl happened under the willow-tree, and looking in the water she saw the quivering image of the charming maiden. Putting her hand on her hip she said: "What a beautiful shadow I have, quite worthy of a princess."

"It's thine of course! I'll tell whose it is," said a golden bird from the tree, in a golden voice.

The gypsy looked into the tree, where she saw the world-beautiful princess, for the sight of whom the sun would have stood still in heaven. The girl said nothing, but in a twinkle she dragged the maiden from the tree by her white foot, pulled off her purple velvet robe, and threw her into the water. The maiden did not sink, but shaking herself, turned into a golden-feathered duck and swam on the lake. The gypsy then, ill or well, put on the purple velvet robe, which sat on her as if it had been put on with a fork and rake; then she sat with great importance on the tree. But she did not sit long; for seeing the golden duck, she jumped down and began to throw stones at her. She threw and threw so many that her arm grew tired, but she could not hit, for the golden duck dived into the water the moment a stone flew over her. At last the gypsy was tired, climbed into the willow-tree and waited for fortune.

She had not long to wait, for soon the king's son came with a gold and glass carriage to take home the golden bird; but the gypsy had her mind, for she would not come down from the tree — at least she said so — till he should shoot the golden duck on the lake, so she might drink its red blood, and eat its tender flesh.

The king's son took his arrow, aimed to kill the golden duck; but the gypsy will not drink its red blood, will not eat its tender flesh, for the arrow never went with its point to the duck, but always turned towards her the feathered end. If it had found her, it would not have been her death. The king's son had shot away all his arrows, and besides it was evening; he had to leave the amusement and turn his wagon-tongue homeward.

At home he had told how beautiful a wife he was bringing; all the greater was the surprise when he led in the bride with raised veil. The king's son had praised the world-beautiful Reed Maiden, and now before the wedding assembly stands a leather-cheeked gypsy girl. The guests know not whether to laugh or to be angry.

Now, the queen — the former gypsy — thought that it could not remain thus, without the world-beautiful Reed Maiden visiting her husband in the night; therefore she put a sleeping-powder into his drink every God-given evening, from which the king's son slept like a shepherd's coat.

The world-beautiful Reed Maiden shook herself, turned into a little bird, and at midnight she came to the king's son's window. She knocked with her little beak, the window opened of itself, and she flew in; then the little bird shook herself, turned into a princess such as had not been born before, nor since, nor after that. She went to the king's son, spoke to him fondling words, but he did not hear; roused him, but he did not wake; bent over him, and at last cried long, but he did not feel the hot tears which burned his cheek, — he lay there motionless as a block.

Then she said: " Oh, king's son, youth of my soul, thy dear lips are dumb; open them for one, two words, to cheer thy beautiful love, thy tender violet. I will come yet twice, then never again."

But the king's son did not wake. When the clock struck one after midnight the maiden shook herself, turned into a bird, and flew out through the window; the window closed after her of itself.

The servant of the king's son heard all these words clearly, for he was awake; but in the morning when he woke he thought it was all a dream, therefore he did not tell the king's son what he had seen, but resolved that he would wait for the coming night, and if the maiden would appear again in the form of a bird, then surely it was not a dream, and he would tell the king's son.

The next evening also his wife gave the king's son a sleeping-powder, and he slept like a shepherd's coat. When the clock struck twelve the little bird rapped with her beak, the window opened before her, and closed behind.

The little bird shook herself and became the beautiful Reed Maiden. She went to the bed of the sleeping king's son, spoke to him, strove to rouse him, and cried as the evening before; but he was motionless as a block. When the clock struck one the maiden shook herself, was a bird, and flew out through the window, which closed behind her. The servant of the king's son heard all this clearly, for he had not slept, and was now sure that it was no dream. He said to his master next morning: "I would say something to thy Highness if I were not afraid."

"Oh, good Yanchi, thou wilt have no trouble, only speak."

"Well, the night before last, at midnight, a little bird flew to the window, struck and beat it with her beak ; the window opened before her. She flew in, shook herself, and became such a beautiful maiden that I looked on her as an altar image ; and I was afraid that she would bewitch me. The beautiful maiden then bent over thy Highness, spoke to thee, but thou didst not wake ; she cried a long time, but thou didst not feel her hot tears. At last she said, with a bird's tongue: 'Oh, king's son, youth of my soul, thy dear lips are dumb ; open them for one, two words, to cheer thy beautiful love, thy tender violet. I will come yet twice, then never again.' This was

repeated last night, but thy Highness spoke not a
word, and lay there like a block. And thy Highness
may believe that she was so beautiful that if I had
been lying dead on the table, I should have risen."

" Is that true, Yanchi?"

" As true as that the bright sun is shining in the
sky."

"Well, Yanchi, couldst thou take a slap on the
cheek for a hundred florins?"

" Not for the money, but gladly for thy Highness,
— even a hundred of them."

" If thou wilt, then take it when my wife gives me
the sleeping-powder again; for her dog soul gives it
so that I should not wake. Knock down the light as
though from awkwardness, then I will pour the sleep-
ing-draught quietly into the bath; the woman will
think that I have drunk it."

When bath-time came Yanchi took the candle as
if he wished to snuff it, and put it out. The king's
son, meanwhile, poured the sleeping-powder and wine
into the bath quietly. The gypsy queen thought that
he had drunk it, but she gave such a cuff to poor
Yanchi that his eyes saw stars; but Yanchi, for the
sake of his master, took the cuff as if a pretty girl
had kissed him.

As the clock struck twelve, the king's son feigned
sleep; but he was just as much awake as good
myself. I say, the clock struck twelve. The little
bird came to the window, knocked with her beak,

the window opened before and closed behind her; she shook herself and became such a maiden as neither before that, nor since, was born, so that the starry heavens would have looked at her with smiles. She bent over the king's son; when at last she cried, the king's son put his arm around her and drew her to him, that she might not become a little bird again; that she might not fly away any more.

He assembled, next day, all the dukes and counts in the kingdom, and all the doers of good, and taking before them the hand of the world-beautiful Reed Maiden, he asked, —

"What does that person deserve who tries to separate from each other a couple?"

Because the gypsy thought that the question was in favor of her own leathery face, she called out in an instant: "That person, my royal husband, deserves to be put in a cask, with spikes driven inward from the outside all through it, and rolled from the highest mountain in the kingdom."

"Oh, dog-given wretch, thou hast pronounced thy own sentence!"

And they took by the neck the queen, once a gypsy, and put her in a cask like that, with spikes driven in, and let the cask roll from the highest mountain in the kingdom.

KISS MIKLOS, AND THE GREEN DAUGHTER OF THE GREEN KING.

THERE was once a poor man, and he had three sons. When the poor man was on his death-bed, he called his three sons, and this was his word and speech to them: " My dear sons, if I do not tell, still mayhap ye know why our kingdom is in mourn-ing, in unbroken darkness, such that a spoon might stand up in it; but if ye know not, then I will tell. My sons, this unbroken darkness is here because they have stolen the sun and the moon from our bright heavens. But I will tell one thing, and two will come of it; a wizard foretold that among my three sons was one (which one I with firm trust cannot say) who would bring back the sun and the moon. There-fore, my sons, I leave you this: that after my death ye will go out to seek the sun and the moon, and not come home till ye bring back the sources of light."

With that the poor man turned to the wall, wan-dered forth from this world of shadows, and was buried with honor.

But here, my lord's son, what comes of the affair or what does not, I saw it as I see now; I was in the place where they were talking. The report ran through the whole kingdom of what the poor man had left in his will to his three sons, so that even the king heard it, and he summoned straightway to his presence the three brothers. And when the three brothers appeared before the king, he said: " My dear young men, I hear that your father — may God give him rest — on his death-bed left this to you: that after his death ye would go out into the wide, great world to look for the sun and the moon. Therefore, my sons, this is my word and speech to you: that whoso brings back the sun and the moon will be king after my death, and whoso will assist him in everything, this one I will make viceroy. Now go to my stable and to my armory and choose for yourselves horses and swords; I will give in a sealed letter to you the order that wherever ye go men shall give you in all places, hay, oats, food, and drink free of cost."

Here the three young men entered the king's stable, and the two elder chose the most beautiful golden-haired steeds; but the youngest, somewhere off by the wall in a hidden corner, among cobwebs and dirt, picked out for himself a wretched, shaggy haired, plucked colt. The two elder brothers laughed at the youngest because he intended to go on that ragged, nasty colt that was hardly able to stand on its feet; but the youngest brother thought nothing of this, and did not give ear to the talk of his brothers.

Now they went to the king's armory, where the elder brothers chose for themselves two beautiful

gold-mounted swords; but the youngest brother, who
had more wit, picked out a rusty steel sword. This
rusty sword now jumped out of the sheath, now
sprang in again, — played unceasingly. The two
elder brothers laughed at the youngest again, but
he put this as well as their former ridicule quietly in
his pocket, thinking to himself that he laughs truly
who laughs last; for the nasty colt, as surely as I live
and as ye live — I was present where they were talking, I saw as I do now, and I was looking as I am
now — was a magic six-legged steed, conceived of the
Wind, and eating live coals; and the rusty sword had
this kind of virtue that a man had only to say, " Cut,
my dear sword," and it cut down whatever he wished.
But the two elder brothers knew nothing of all this,
for they did not understand wood-work.

Now the three brothers moved on their way
through the kingdom, to look for the sun and the
moon. They travelled and journeyed over forty-
nine kingdoms, beyond the Operentsia Sea, beyond
the glass mountains, and beyond that, to where the
little short-tailed pig roots, and farther than that, and
still farther, till they came to the silver bridge. When
they came to the silver bridge the youngest brother,
speaking a word, said to his two brothers: " My dear
brothers, let us go under the bridge, for soon the
steed of the moon will be here, and the twelve-headed
dragon, from whose saddle-bow the bright moon is
dangling."

Now, the two brothers had barely hidden when the steed of the moon was on the bridge, and on the steed the twelve-headed dragon, from whose saddle-bow the bright moon was dangling. The milk-white steed of the moon stumbled on the bridge. Then the twelve-headed dragon was enraged, and said this to the steed of the moon, —

" Ah, may the crow eat thy eye, may the dog eat thy flesh, may the earth drink thy blood! From forest to forest I have ridden thee, from mountain to mountain I have sprung with thee, and thou hast never stumbled, but now on the even road thou hast stumbled. Well, in my world-beautiful life I have always heard the fame of Kiss Miklos; if he were here now, I would like to have a struggle with him."

At this word our Kiss Miklos — for let it be said, meanwhile, this was the name of the youngest brother — sprang out from beneath to the silver bridge on his golden-haired magic steed, and closed with the twelve-headed dragon. Long did they struggle, the one with the other, but Kiss Miklos said to the rusty sword: " Cut, my dear sword!" and with that it cut three heads off the dragon, and in the same order till all the twelve heads were hewn off, so that the twelve-headed dragon drew his shortest breath. Then Kiss Miklos took by the halter the milk-white haired, black-maned steed of the moon, on whose saddle-bow was dangling the bright moon, and gave him to the care of his second brother. Then they passed over the silver bridge, which sounded like most beautiful music from the golden shoes of the magic steed.

They travelled and journeyed then through forty-nine kingdoms, beyond the Operentsia Sea and the glass mountains, beyond that, where the little short-tailed pig roots, beyond that, and farther, till they came to the golden bridge.

Then Kiss Miklos spoke, and said this to his two brothers, speaking speech: " My dear brothers, let us hide under the bridge, for soon will the steed of the sun be here, and on him the twenty-four-headed dragon, from whose saddle-bow the shining sun is dangling. He will call me out at once to the keen sword, and I will measure with him strength with strength. He will not be able to conquer me, nor I him; then he and I will turn into flames. He will be a red and I a blue flame, but even then we shall not be able to conquer one the other, for we shall be of equal strength. But here is a sulphur stone; when the red flame springs highest toward the sky to press down the blue flame, that is me, strike the sulphur stone on the red flame."

Our Kiss Miklos had barely finished his speech when the steed of the sun was on the bridge, bearing the twenty-four-headed dragon and the shining sun. The steed of the sun stumbled on the golden bridge. The twenty-four-headed dragon was enraged at him, and said, —

" Ah, may the crow eat thy eye, may the dog eat

31

thy flesh, may the earth drink thy blood! I have ridden from forest to forest on thee, I have leaped thee from mountain to mountain, and never hast thou stumbled; but now on the even road thou hast stumbled. In my world-beautiful life I have heard always the fame of Kiss Miklos — may the dog devour him! — and if he were here now I would like to have a struggle with him."

At this word our Kiss Miklos sprang out on to the golden bridge, and closed with the twenty-four-headed dragon. But Kiss Miklos commanded, saying: "Cut, my dear sword!" and that instant it cut the twenty-four heads off the dragon; but, wonder of the world! when all the twenty-four heads were off, in the twinkle of an eye new ones grew out which the leaping sword could not cut. In vain Kiss Miklos said: "Cut, my dear sword!" for it could not cut these heads. Well, Kiss Miklos took the sword in his hand and whirled it like lightning; but he did nothing with it, for the dragon had power of the same kind as he.

When the dragon saw that he could not succeed against Kiss Miklos, he spoke in this way: "Listen to me, Kiss Miklos! I wish thou hadst perished with thy mother, for I see that I can do nothing with thee, nor thou with me. Let us make one trial. Turn thou into a blue flame, and I will turn into a red one, and whichever can put the other out, his will be the steed of the sun and the shining sun upon him."

That is what was done. Kiss Miklos turned to a blue flame, and the twenty-four-headed dragon to a red one. The two flames fought the one with the other, but neither was able to put out the other. Happily the two brothers threw the sulphur stone on the red flame, and then the blue flame put out the red one; and when it was quenched altogether, the twenty-four-headed dragon ceased to live.

Kiss Miklos gave the steed of the sun to his elder brother, and told his two brothers to go home quietly, for he had work of his own; and with that he took farewell of them. Miklos then shook himself, turned into a little gray cat, ran along the highroad, and all at once sprang into a cabin. In the cabin was the mother of the dragons and their two wives.

The younger dragon's wife saw the little gray cat; she took it on her lap, stroked it, and found this to say to the mother of the dragons: " Well, if I knew that that cursed Kiss Miklos had killed my lord, I would turn into such a spring of water that if he and his two brothers were to drink not more than one drop of it, they would die a fearful death on the spot."

With this the little gray cat sprang from the lap of the younger dragon's wife, and rubbed up to the skirt of the wife of the elder dragon, who took it on to her lap, stroked it, and found this to say: " Ah! if I knew that that cursed Kiss Miklos had killed my lord, I would change into such a pear-tree that if he and his two brothers were to eat no more than one morsel of a pear of mine, they would die a fearful death."

With this the little gray cat sprang from the lap of the elder dragon's wife, and rubbed on the skirt of the old woman, who took it on her lap, fondled it, and found this to say to her two daughters-in-law: " My dear girls, just prop up my two eyes with that iron bar, which weighs twelve hundred pounds, so that I may look around."

Her two daughters-in-law then took the twelve-hundred-pound iron bar and opened the old woman's eyes; then she spoke thuswise: " If that cursed Kiss Miklos has killed my two sons, I will turn into a mouth, one jaw of which will be on the earth and the other I will throw to the sky, so as to catch that cursed villain and his two brothers, and grind them as mill-stones grind wheat."

When the little gray cat had heard all this exactly, it shot away in a flash out of the cabin, sprang along, and never stopped till it came to the good magic steed. The old woman threw the twelve-hundred-pound bar after the cat, but she failed in her cast, for that moment her eyelids fell; she was not able to keep them open unless they were propped, for she was old. So Kiss Miklos escaped the twelve-hundred-pound bar, — certain death. I say that he escaped, for he came to his good magic steed, shook himself, and from a little gray cat became a young man as before. Then he sat on the good steed, which sprang once, jumped twice, and straightway Miklos was with his two brothers; then they fared homeward in quiet comfort.

The second brother grew thirsty, and found this to say: " Oh, but I am dry! My throat is burning! "

" If that is thy only trouble," said Miklos, " I will soon bring thee water. Out there a spring is bubbling up."

With that Kiss Miklos put spurs to his good magic steed, which sprang once, jumped twice, and was at the spring; but here, instead of filling the gourd that hung at his side, he drew his sharp sword, and thrust it three times into the bubbling water. In a moment from the spring blood gushed forth, and a word of bitter pain was heard. That was the blood of the younger dragon's wife, and the word of pain was her death-groan. The blood made all the water red, and when the two brothers came up they had no wish to drink a drop from the spring.

Well, they travelled and journeyed till the elder brother said: " Oh, but I am hungry! "

" If that is thy trouble," said Kiss Miklos, " we can easily cure it, for there near the dam is a pear-tree, and on it so much ripe fruit that the limbs are breaking. Wait, I will bring thee a pear directly; but lead thou the steed of the sun there."

Here Kiss Miklos put spurs to his steed, which

sprang once, jumped twice, and stood before the pear-tree. Miklos drew his sharp sword and stabbed the pear-tree in the trunk three times; from the trunk blood gushed forth, and a bitter word of pain was heard. The red blood was the blood of the elder dragon's wife, and the bitter word of pain was her death-groan. With that the pears fell, so that when the two elder brothers reached the tree, not only would they not eat the pears, but the desire of eating had gone from them.

Now they journeyed and travelled through forty-nine kingdoms, till at last Miklos saw from a distance that an unmercifully great mouth, one jaw of which was on earth and the other thrown up to the heavens, was nearing them like the swiftest storm, so that they had barely time left to run into the door of the Lead Friend's house. And a thousand-fold was their luck that they got in; for the unmercifully great mouth stood before the threshold of the Lead Friend, so that whoever should go out would fall into it, and be swallowed that minute.

"Hei! good Lead-Melting Friend," said Miklos, "hast thou much molten lead? I will pay thee for it in honest coin."

"Haho! my friend Kiss Miklos, I know thee; in my world-beautiful life I have ever heard thy fame. Long have I been waiting for thee. It is well that thou art here, — that thou hast entered my door, — for thou wilt never go a step farther from me."

" Oh! for God's sake," said Kiss Miklos, " do not pass thy own threshold, for straightway the mother of the dragons will swallow thee with her great mouth."

The Lead-Melting Friend went out of his chamber, saw the great mouth of the mother of the dragons, and went back in terror to his chamber, where he said this to Kiss Miklos: " Oh, my good friend Kiss Miklos, give counsel. What are we to do?"

" Hast thou much molten lead?"

" Not much, only eighteen tons; it is out there in the caldron boiling.

Knowest thou what? I will say one thing and two will come of it. Let us take the handles of that great caldron and pour its contents into the great mouth of the mother of the dragons."

Here, 'pon my soul! the Lead-Melting Friend put one handle on his shoulder, Kiss Miklos the other on his, brought the unmercifully great caldron to the threshold, and poured the eighteen tons of boiling lead into the old witch's mouth. The boiling lead burned up the stomach of the mother of the dragons, and straightway she breathed out her cursed soul.

So Kiss Miklos was freed from the mother of the dragons ; but, poor fellow, he was like one that goes from the pail into the barrel, for the Lead-Melting Friend caught his Grace by the neck and took him, as he would a straw, to the chamber, where he found this to say, —

"Look here, my good friend Kiss Miklos, in my world-beautiful life I have ever heard thy fame; therefore let us struggle now and see who is stronger, thou or I." With that the Lead Friend put only his little finger on Kiss Miklos; from that he began to sink, and went down through the lead floor of the chamber the distance of an ell.

"Kiss Miklos, my friend, dost thou wish to fight with me?" asked the Lead Friend. "Thou sayest nothing, so I see that thou dost not; therefore this is my word and speech: I will keep thee in endless slavery unless thou bring me the Green Daughter of the Green King. But ye," and he turned to the two brothers, "ye may go home in gentle quietness, and take with you the steeds of the moon and the sun, on which are the bright moon and the shining sun, for of them I have no need."

Here our Miklos, in the midst of bitter tear-shedding, took farewell of his dear brothers. They held on their way homeward, and arrived there in health. Great was the rejoicing in the kingdom that the poor man's sons, as their father had bequeathed them on his death-bed, brought home the bright moon and the shining sun. Therefore the king assembled all that were in his dominions of dukes, counts, barons, lords, lord's sons, chosen gypsies, and broad-brimmed, country-dressed Slovaks; of these he sought council and asked, "What do brothers deserve who have brought home the bright moon and the shining sun?"

To this question then they answered, " Our high lord, the one who has brought back the steed of the sun, and on it the bright shining sun, deserves to be king of the country, and he who has brought home the steed of the bright moon, and on it the fair moon, to be viceroy; and each one of them should receive as wife a daughter of thy Highness."

So it was done. The poor man's eldest son became king, and the second son viceroy; and each one of them got a maiden princess as wife. Then they let out the steed of the bright moon and the steed of the shining sun on the highway of the heavens, but both the moon and the sun shone sadly. For this reason they shone sadly: that he was without merited reward who had really freed them from the dragons, for Kiss Miklos was now in never-ending slavery to the Lead Friend.

Once the Lead Friend called Miklos and found this to tell him : " Well, Miklos, if thou wilt bring me the Green Daughter of the Green King, I will let thee go free, and I will strike from thee the three-hundred-pound ring and the twelve-hundred-pound chain. Therefore, good friend Miklos, I advise thee to start in the morning with the bright shining sun, and bring to me my heart's desire."

Now our Miklos moved on the road again, and a long one too; whether there will be an end to it, only the good God knows. And as he travelled and journeyed across forty-nine kingdoms, and beyond that, and still farther, at the foot of a great mountain was a little hill, and as a shot arrow, as the swiftest whirlwind, ran towards him a man who was always crying, "Out of my way! out of my way!" This was Swift Runner, who stood still in a moment, like a pillar, before Miklos, and asked, "Whither, whither, Kiss Miklos? for in my world-beautiful life I have ever heard thy fame."

"Haho! Swift Runner, better thou hadst not asked. I am going for the Green Daughter of the Green King. Hast thou ever heard of her?"

"I have not heard. I speak not of that, but of this: take me with thee, for thou wilt get good of me somewhere."

"Well, come on thy own legs, if it please thee."

They travelled and journeyed after that, two of them, till they came to the sea-shore, and saw a man who was drinking the sea to the last drop, just as I would drink a cup of water; and then he cried out unceasingly: "Oh, I'm thirsty! Oh, I'm thirsty!" This was Great Drinker who, when he saw Miklos, went to him and said: "God's good-day, famous Kiss Miklos; for in my world-beautiful life I have ever heard thy fame."

"God keep thee, Great Drinker!"

"On what journey art thou, renowned Kiss Miklos?"

"On what journey? Haho! better thou hadst not asked. I am going for the Green Daughter of the Green King. Hast thou heard of her?"

"I have not, in truth," answered Great Drinker; "I speak not of that, but of this: take me with thee, for mayhap thou 'lt get good of me."

"Well, come on thy own legs, if it please thee."

So there were three of them, and they travelled and journeyed after that till they saw a man running on the plain towards cattle, and he thrust the beautiful bullocks one by one into his mouth as I would a piece of bread, and swallowed them, hide and horns, one after the other; and even when he had swallowed all the standing herd of three hundred and sixty-six bullocks, he called out unceasingly: "Oh, I am hungry! Oh, I am hungry!" This was Great Eater who, when he saw Miklos, went to him and said: "God give thee a good-day, renowned Kiss Miklos; for in my world-beautiful life I have ever heard thy fame."

"God keep thee, Great Eater!"

"What journey art thou on, renowned Kiss Miklos?"

"Better thou hadst not asked. I am going for the Green Daughter of the Green King. Hast thou heard of her?"

"I have not heard, in truth," answered Great Eater; "but take me with thee, mayhap thou 'lt get good of me."

"Well, come on thy own legs, if it please thee."

Now there were four of them, and they travelled and journeyed till one day they struck upon a man whose bolster was the glowing coals, whose pillow was the burning fire, and whose blanket was the flaming blaze; he had nine pairs of boots on his feet, nine pairs of drawers and nine shirts on his body, nine neckcloths on his neck, nine sheep-skin caps on his head, nine pairs of trousers, nine vests on his body, and nine sheepskin overcoats hung from his shoulders, but even then he did nothing but cry out unceasingly: "Oh, I'm freezing! Oh, I'm freezing!" When he saw Kiss Miklos, he stood before him and said: "God give thee a good-day, renowned Kiss Miklos; for in my world-beautiful life I have ever heard thy fame."

"God guard thee, Great Freezer!"

"What journey art thou on, renowned Kiss Miklos?"

"Ah, comrade, thou shouldst not have asked. Hast thou heard of the fame of the Green Daughter of the Green King?"

"I have not heard of it."

"Well, if thou hast not, hear now; for I am going to her as a wooer."

"Take me with thee, mayhap thou wilt get good of me."

"Well, come on thy own legs, if it please thee."

There were five of them now. They journeyed and travelled after that till they came upon a man who was looking around unceasingly. In one twinkle, in the turn of an eye, he saw the round earth, and in an-

other turn of the eye he looked through the deep sea;
and he saw Miklos and his comrades thirty-five miles
off.

This was Far Seer, who stood before Miklos and
said: "God give thee a good-day, renowned Kiss
Miklos."

"God keep thee, Far Seer!"

"On what journey art thou, renowned Kiss Miklos?"

"Haho! good friend Far Seer, perhaps thou hast
heard of the Green Daughter of the Green King."

"I have not."

"Well then, hear now, for I am going to woo
her."

"Take me with thee, mayhap thou 'lt get good of
me."

Now there were six of them, and they journeyed
and travelled after that, across forty-nine kingdoms and
farther, till they came upon a man who threw a seven-
hundred-pound iron club thirty-five miles as easily as
I could throw a small stone a few yards   This was
Far Caster, who, when he saw Kiss Miklos and his
comrades, came and said: "God give thee a good-
day, renowned Kiss Miklos; for in my world-beautiful
life I have ever heard thy fame."

"God guard thee, Far Caster!"

"What journey art thou on?"

"Better thou hadst not asked.   Hast thou heard
of the Green King?"

"I have not."

" Well, I am going to woo his daughter."

" Take me with thee, mayhap thou 'lt get good of me."

" Come on thy own legs, if it please thee."

Like the seven deadly sins, they were seven now. They journeyed and travelled till they came to the castle of the Green King. Kiss Miklos stood before the king and said: " God give a good-day to thy Highness."

" God keep thee, renowned Kiss Miklos; for in my world-beautiful life I have ever heard thy fame. What journey art thou on? "

" In my journeys and travels I have heard that thy Highness has a charming, love-pervaded, beautiful flower-stalk. What is the use in delay and denial? I have come for her."

" Haho! my good friend, the Green Daughter of the Green King is not so easily taken, for there are three tests before thee; if thou stand these tests, I will give thee my most beloved, my truly one and only daughter. The first test will be this: Thou hast a swift runner and so have I. They are making for my daughter at present a wedding dress at Pluto's, or perhaps it 's ready this moment. If thy swift runner will bring that dress here, all right, — I care not: let the Green Daughter of the Green King be thine. My swift runner and thine will start to-morrow about four o'clock in the morning. But if I have not told thee, know now the thick end of the business, I will bring you all to the stake, if thy swift runner comes second."

But the Green King deceived; for that evening after sunset he sent off his swift runner, who was no other than his own old mother, who, let it be said meanwhile, was a witch, and a big one at that. Next morning at four o'clock, as had been agreed, Miklos started his own swift runner on the road so as to bring the wedding dress.

Swift Runner moved on, and he saw that the old mother of the Green King was a good way ahead, for she was just on the point of going in at Pluto's gate. Nothing more was needed. He rushed at her and she saw trouble soon, for he came up just as she had taken hold of the key; Swift Runner was not slow. He caught her by the jacket, hurled her back, ran in at the gate himself, and did not stop till he stood before his Highness, Pluto, told why he had come, and asked for the wedding dress. The dainty dress was nicely packed already in a box, and they gave it to him. Swift Runner hurried homeward, but the old mother of the Green King waited for him, and said: "Hear me, Swift Runner! Now thou art the victor, run not so fast; let us go home in pleasant quiet together."

Swift Runner stopped at the old woman's words, and they went on together, — went on till they came to a nice shady place, where the old woman found this to say: "Let us sit down in this shady place; let us rest. It is all the same. Thou art the winner. I will look in thy head."

Here Swift Runner sat down in the shady place; the old woman bent his head to her lap and began to search in it, and she searched and searched till Swift Runner fell asleep and was sunk in slumber. When Swift Runner was snoring away at his best, the old woman put a horse-skull under his head, — from that he would not have waked till the day of judgment; then she took the box from him and raced off as if she had been shot from a gun.

It was near four o'clock in the afternoon and Swift Runner had not come yet, though he said he ought to be there at three o'clock. Miklos therefore began to be uneasy, — his nose was itching, it was ringing in his right ear and jumping in his right eye, therefore he found this to say to his Far Seer: " Just look, canst thou see Swift Runner coming?"

Far Seer did not let this be repeated; in an instant he ran up on a hill, looked around, saw that Swift Runner was in a shady place, sleeping like a pumpkin, under a tree, with a horse-skull under his head.

" Oh, my good friend Kiss Miklos, the dog is in the garden! Swift Runner is sleeping in a nice shady place with a horse-skull under his head; the old woman is right here near the garden, and she has the wedding dress in a box."

" Here, good friend Far Caster," said Kiss Miklos, " stand forth and throw thy twelve-hundred-pound

club at that cursed horse-skull under the head of
Swift Runner; for as God is true, all seven of us will
see shame, and die a fearful death."

Far Caster was not slow; in an instant he hurled the
twelve-hundred-pound club and struck out luckily the
horse-skull from under Swift Runner's head.

Then, 'pon my soul! Swift Runner sprang up, rubbed
his eyes, looked around, saw that the old woman was
running near the garden, and bearing the wedding
robe. He was not slow. He rushed at her, but in truth
it hung from a hair that he did not see disgrace, for
the old woman had just taken the key of the Green
King's door when Swift Runner reached her. He
caught her by the jacket, took the box, and hurled
the old woman back to Pluto's in such fashion that
not her foot, nor even her little toe, touched ground
on the way. Then he gave the wedding dress to
Miklos, who took it that moment to the Green King,
and putting it on the boxwood table said: " High
lord, thy desire is accomplished; here is the dainty
wedding dress."

" Haho! renowned Kiss Miklos, this is but one
trial in which thou art the winner, there are two behind. The Green Daughter of the Green King will
not be thine till all of you, as many as there are,
spend one night in my iron furnace, which I have
heated with three hundred and sixty-six cords of
wood; if ye can endure that terrible heat, all right; if
not, ye will be roasted alive."

Here, 'pon my soul! what came of the affair or what did not, the Green King, as he had said, heated the iron furnace with three hundred and sixty-six cords of wood. The whole furnace was nothing but glowing fire, so that it was impossible to go near it. Now the question was, who should enter first, — who but Great Freezer? He was delighted with the pleasant amusement; he was shivering terribly because God's cold had then caught him, though he had nine pairs of boots on his feet, nine shirts and drawers on his body, nine neckcloths on his neck, nine sheep-skin caps on his head, nine sheep-skin overcoats on his back. I say, Great Freezer went first into the fiery furnace. He walked around in it, and straightway it became as cold as an ice-house; therefore he called out at the entrance: " Oh, I 'm freezing! Oh, I 'm freezing! " Then the others and Kiss Miklos went in, and they felt that the furnace was as cold as an ice-house, so that their teeth chattered. Kiss Miklos cried out at the entrance, saying, " Wood this way, or we shall freeze! "

The servants of the Green King threw an extra cord of wood into the furnace. With this Miklos and his companions made a fire, and gave earth no trouble. Next morning the Green King himself went to see the seven roasts, thinking they were burnt into dust. He opened the mouth of the furnace. He will fall on his back with horror, perhaps. Nothing of the sort; the seven good birds were sitting there alive in the furnace at the side of a fire, and not a dog's trouble had happened to a man of them.

Straightway the Green King called up Kiss Miklos and said to him: "Well, renowned Kiss Miklos, thou hast stood two trials, but the third still remains. If ye pass that unharmed, then I don't care; my daughter will be thine, for I shall see that thou art not inferior to thy fame. The third trial is not other than this: In the yard is a herd of cattle not less than three hundred and sixty-six in number, and also there are three hundred and sixty-six kegs of wine, and if ye do not eat the three hundred and sixty-six head of cattle and drink the three hundred and sixty-six kegs of wine by to-morrow, then I will have you all at the stake; but if ye eat and drink all, then as I say, I care not. Let my one and only most beloved daughter be thine."

In the evening after bedtime Miklos went with his comrades to the other yard where were the three hundred and sixty-six head of cattle and the three hundred and sixty-six kegs of wine; but now the question was who should eat that ocean-great lot of cattle and drink that thundering lot of wine. No one would take more delight in the cattle than Great Eater, and with the thundering lot of wine no one felt better than Great Drinker; they would take care of them if they were twice as great. Miklos and his comrades, except Great Eater, knocked one of the bullocks on the head, pulled off his jacket, cut up his flesh and roasted it. That was enough for them, but it was not enough for Great Eater; for he would not spoil the taste of his mouth with it. He ate that herd of beasts, one after another, as if the earth had swallowed them, — ate hair, hide, bones, and horns, so that he did n't leave a single thing as a novelty; and even then he cried out nothing but, " Oh, I 'm hungry! Oh, I 'm hungry!" Then he went to his comrades, ate what they had left of the roast, and pressed it down with the ox-hide for a dessert. Even then he cried without ceasing, " Oh, I 'm hungry! Oh, I 'm hungry!"

Then they began at the wine. Miklos and his comrades, except Great Drinker, rolled forth one keg of wine, knocked the bottom out, and went to drinking. That keg was enough for them, but not enough for Great Drinker; for him it was as much as one drop would be for me. He would not spoil the taste of his mouth with it, but fell to drinking from the rest in such Magyar-Mishka style that when he looked around he saw that the three hundred and sixty-five kegs were empty. Then he cried unceasingly, " Oh, I 'm thirsty! Oh, I 'm thirsty!" After that he came to his comrades, and what they had left he drank to the last drop; and cried: " Oh, I 'm thirsty! Oh, I 'm thirsty!"

Next morning the Green King went himself to the yard to see if Kiss Miklos and his comrades had endured the third trial, — had they eaten the cattle and

drunk the wine. It is a wonder that he did n't turn
into a pillar of salt he was so frightened when he saw
that there was not a horned beast left, nor a drop of
wine. Then he complained: "They have eaten
three hundred and sixty-six bullocks. Plague take it!
let them eat the cattle, but they might have left the
hides; those could at least have been sold to a Jew
for good money. — Well, renowned Kiss Miklos, thou
hast stood the three tests, now my only and most
dearly beloved daughter is thine; take her." With
that the Green King seated his Green Daughter in
a coach drawn by six black horses, and they drove
towards the dominions of the Lead Friend.

On the road the Green Daughter of the Green King
beckoned Miklos to her and asked him : "Hei! my
heart's beautiful love, renowned Kiss Miklos, tell me,
on thy true soul, art thou taking me for thyself or for
another? If thou art not taking me for thyself, I will
play tricks with thee."

"I am taking thee for myself; I am taking thee for
another," answered Kiss Miklos.

Well, no more was said. Once, when turning and
winding, they look in the coach; it is empty. The
beautiful girl is gone. In a moment they stop, search
the coach, but find her nowhere.

"Here, good friend Far Seer," said Kiss Miklos,
"look around ! Whither has our beautiful bird
flown?"

Far Seer did n't let that be said twice. In the

turn of an eye he surveyed the round earth, but he saw not the beautiful maiden.

" She is not on the dry earth," said Far Seer.

" Look into the sea," said Kiss Miklos.

Far Seer surveyed the deep sea, and saw her hidden in the belly of a three-pound whale, near the opposite shore of the sea.

" Ah, I see where she is ! "

" Where? " asked Miklos.

" Hidden in the belly of a three-pound whale."

" Here, good friend Great Drinker," said Miklos, " come hither, and drink up the water of this deep sea ! "

Great Drinker was not slow. He lay face under by the sea, and with three draughts drank up all the water. The three-pound whale was lying then in a bay near the opposite shore.

" Now, good brother Swift Runner," said Kiss Miklos, " step out and bring me that three-pound whale which is lying near the opposite shore."

Swift Runner rushed in a moment across the bottom of the sea, and brought back the three-pound whale. Miklos opened the whale, took out its stomach, cut it carefully, and out fell the Green Daughter of the Green King. Then he seated her in the coach, and they drove on.

They travelled and journeyed, and once the princess beckoned to Miklos, and asked: " My heart's beautiful love, renowned Kiss Miklos, tell me, on thy

true soul, art thou taking me for thyself, or for
another? If for thyself, very well; if not, I'll play
tricks with thee."

" I am taking thee for myself; I am taking thee for
another," answered Miklos.

No more was said. Once while turning and
winding, the beautiful maiden is gone, the coach is
empty. " Oh, the dog is in the garden!" They
stop, search the six-horse coach, but find no beautiful princess.

" Here, good friend Far Seer," said Miklos, "stand
forth, look around! Where is our beautiful bird?"

Far Seer surveyed the deep sea, but got no sight
of the princess. " She is not in the sea."

" If she is not in the sea, look on dry land."

Far Seer looked around again, and he saw that the
princess was at home, in the very middle of her
father's garden, on the highest top of a blooming
apple-tree, hidden in a ripe red apple. " I have
found her!" said Far Seer.

" Where is she?"

" At home, in the very centre of the garden, hidden on the highest top of an apple-tree, in the middle
of a ripe red apple."

" Here, Swift Runner, come forth!"

Swift Runner came forth, and stood like a pillar
before Miklos, waiting for command.

" Run in a twinkle to the garden of the Green
King, in the very middle of which is blooming an

apple-tree; climb the tree, and bring me the ripe red apple which is on its highest top."

Swift Runner rushed as a whirlwind, at horse-death speed, found the tree, climbed it, plucked the red apple, and then, as if shot from a cannon, came back to Miklos, and gave him the apple. Miklos cut the apple in two; the Green Daughter of the Green King fell out. He seated her again in the coach, and they fared farther.

They travelled and journeyed, and again the princess beckoned to Miklos, and said: "My heart's heart, renowned Kiss Miklos, tell me, on thy true soul, art thou taking me for thyself, or for another? If for thyself, very well; if not, I'll play tricks with thee."

"I am taking thee for myself; I am taking thee for another."

Well, they said no more. Once, while turning and winding, they look in the coach the maiden is gone; the coach is empty. "Oh, the dog is in the garden!" They stop, search the six-horse coach, but find not the maiden.

"Friend Far Seer," said Miklos, "look around! Where is our beautiful bird?"

Far Seer was not slow; in the turn of an eye he surveyed the round earth, but saw nowhere the Green Daughter of the Green King. "She is not on the round earth," said he.

"Well, look in the deep sea."

Far Seer looked again; in the turn of an eye he surveyed the deep sea, but saw not the princess. "She is not in the deep sea," said Far Seer.

"Well, if she is not in the deep sea, look in the cloudy heavens."

Far Seer looked around; in the turn of an eye he surveyed the broad sky and the cloudy heavens. He saw a cocoon hanging from a thread slender as a spider-web, and hidden in that cocoon the Green Daughter of the Green King. "I have found her!" said Far Seer.

"Where is she?" asked Kiss Miklos.

"Far, far away, near the round forest, from the cloudy heavens is hanging a silk thread, slender as a spider-web, and on the end dangles a cocoon; in that she is hidden."

"Now, Far Caster, come forth!" said Miklos.

Far Caster stood like a pillar before Kiss Miklos, only waiting for command; but he had not long to wait, for Miklos said: "Listen, good friend Far Caster. Seest thou that thin silk thread hanging from the cloudy sky near the round forest?"

"I see."

"Then cast it down; but only when Swift Runner reaches the place beneath, so that it may not fall on the earth, but into his hand. Therefore, Swift Runner, move thy wheels that way; catch the cocoon and bring it to us."

Swift Runner rushed at horse-death speed to the

place; Far Caster brought down the cocoon.   Swift
Runner caught it safely, and brought it to Miklos,
who with his bright knife cut it open, and out came
the princess.   Then he seated her a third time in the
coach; but they had arrived in the domains of the
Lead Friend, so the Green Daughter of the Green
King, having lost her power, could play no more
tricks.

Kiss Miklos took farewell of his good friends, thanking them kindly for their aid.   When they were alone
the Green Daughter of the Green King fell to crying,
and said: " My heart's beautiful love, I know thou art
taking me to that dog of a Lead Friend, and I would
rather be the bride of death than of him."

" Oh, my heart's golden bird," said Miklos, " I am
taking thee for myself; but thou canst not be mine
till I know where the strength of the Lead Friend
lies.   If we can discover that, it will be easy to destroy him."

" If that is thy grief, my heart's heart," said she, " I
will soon help thee; leave that to me.   Thou must
know I am a woman."

With that Miklos and the princess kissed each
other, and there was holy peace; they said: " I am
thine, thou art mine."

They travelled and journeyed across forty-nine
kingdoms, till Kiss Miklos could say, " We are at
home," — for they were at the Lead Friend's mansion,
— and could say to the princess, " Come out of thy

coach; it won't cost thee a copper." Here the Lead
Friend ran panting out of his mansion to the beautiful
princess, but she turned from him. This pleased not
the Lead Friend, and though one word is not much,
he uttered not that much, but brought her into the
lead mansion in silence.

Next day at sunrise the Lead Friend had to go to
his furnace, taking Kiss Miklos with him. The young
woman remained all alone. She took a lamp and
started to search through the lead house. From
chamber to chamber she went till she came to the
cellar, but that was closed against her with seven iron
doors. Now the question was to get into the cellar.
Another would not have been able to pass the first
door, but every iron door opened of itself before the
magic of the Green Daughter of the Green King.
She passed through the seven doors and entered the
cellar. She saw there seven leaden vats placed in a
row, and every one of them filled to the brim with
gold and silver. She took off her apron and filled it
with gold, went up, summoned the goldsmith, and
gilded the lead threshold a hand in thickness. The
Lead Friend was such a miser that he had not bread
enough to eat, and every little coin he turned seven
times between his teeth before he let it go once from
his hand.

Well, in the evening the Lead Friend came home
from his furnace, saw the housekeeping and what the
young woman had done. Then, 'pon my soul! he

plucked out his own lead beard and hair, trampled them like tow, and roared till the lead house was trembling.

"Who, in the name of a hundred thousand thunders, did this?" asked the Lead Friend.

"I did it," answered quite bravely the princess.

"How didst thou dare to do it without my knowledge, — without informing me?" With that the Lead Friend went to the Green Daughter of the Green King, and seized in his hand the golden hair which reached her heels. Twelve times did he drag her on the lead floor, and he wanted to take the lead flail to her. Kiss Miklos did not permit that, but took the maiden from his grasp and placed her on the silken bed. She was neither dead nor alive, but lay as a lifeless block of wood. But the Green Daughter of the Green King had no more pain than good myself; being a magic woman, seest thou, she had much in her power.

Now, what did she do? When the Lead Friend wound around his hand the golden hair reaching to her heels, she suddenly sprang out of her skin, and a devil jumped into it. And if the Lead Friend had struck him with the back of an axe, he would not have felt a dog's trouble; for the more he was beaten the more he would have laughed.

But the Lead Friend was troubled; ragged, with torn hair, crying and weeping he entered the white chamber, where the princess was lying without life.

He went to her; pushed her, but she waked not; talked to her, but she heard not; cried, but she listened not. At last he found this to say: "Wake, my heart's beautiful love; I will do all that may please thee, but stop the gilding."

Then the princess spoke up to the Lead Friend, " I'll stop the gilding, but tell where thy strength lies."

" Oh, my heart's beautiful love, I would rather part with life than tell that."

Well, things remained thus. Next day at sunrise the Lead Friend went to his furnace, taking Kiss Miklos with him, for he lived in the suspicion that Miklos and the Green Daughter of the Green King would plot together and strive for his destruction.

The bride remained alone; she took the lamp and turned straight to the cellar. The great iron doors opened before her and closed behind. When she had passed the seven iron doors and entered the cellar, she spread her silk apron, and filled it with gold. Three times she returned, and three times she bore away the same amount, so that the apron was almost torn under it. Straightway she called the goldsmith and had the lead thresholds of three chambers gilded to the thickness of a hand. And as I say, the Lead Friend was so stingy that he did not eat bread enough, and every little coin he put seven [1] times between his teeth before he let it out of his hand once.

[1] It is three in the text, but this is probably a mistake; so seven is put here to agree with p. 507.

The Lead Friend came home from his furnace towards evening, and saw the housekeeping, and saw also that now not one but three thresholds were gilded a hand's thickness.   Here, 'pon my soul! the Lead Friend fell into such rage that he tore his own lead beard and hair out, and trampled them as he would tow.   Then he roared so terribly that the lead house quivered, and turning to the princess he asked: "In the name of a hundred thousand devils, who did this?"

" I did it," answered the princess quite bravely.

" How didst thou dare to do this without my knowledge and consent? "

With that the Lead Friend seized the golden hair of the princess, which reached to her heels, and dragged her twelve times up and down the lead floor, twelve times did he hurl her against the floor, then he ran for the lead flail to kill her.   Kiss Miklos would not let him do that, but seized the maiden from his hands, and placed her on the silken bed.   The Green Daughter of the Green King was neither dead nor alive; she lay there still as a soulless block of wood. Still the princess felt no more pain than good myself. She knew witchcraft, and whatever she did or did not do, when the Lead Friend twisted her golden hair in his hand, she jumped out of her skin in a twinkle, and a devil got into it; if they had beaten him like a two-headed drum, or even more, he would have taken it as if they were fondling him.

Now the Lead Friend was terribly sorry; ragged,

with torn hair, he entered the white chamber weeping; he wept a long time; pushed the princess, who waked not; spoke to her, she heard not; at last he found this to say: " Wake up, my heart's beautiful love; all thy desires will be accomplished, only stop the gilding."

" I 'll stop the gilding, but tell where thy strength lies."

" Oh, my heart's beautiful love, I would rather part with my life than tell that."

Next day at sunrise the Lead Friend took Kiss Miklos to the furnace, lest while he was gone himself Miklos might go in secret and gather another man's hay. The bride was alone again, and wanted nothing better. Again she took the lamp and went straight to the cellar, where she opened her beautiful silk apron and filled it with gold, — took so much that the apron almost tore under it. She came seven times, and each time carried so much gold that her nose almost cut the earth, like the coulter of a plough. Then she called a goldsmith, and gilded to a hand's thickness the thresholds of seven rooms.

When the Lead Friend came home in the evening, he saw that not three but seven thresholds had a hand's thickness of gold on them. Then he fell into such a rage that he tore his leaden beard and hair, and trampled them as he would tow; but what good did that do him? — for he was trampling his own. Then he roared till the lead house rattled, and in his fury he asked: "A thousand million demons, who did this?"

"I did it," answered the princess all bravely.

"How didst thou dare to do this without my knowledge or command?"

With that he went in fury to the Green Daughter of the Green King, wound round his hand the golden hair which reached to her heels. Twelve times did he drag her over the leaden floor, twelve times did he dash her against it, twelve times did he raise her aloft, — and that was not enough; but he took out the lead flail, and began to thrash and beat the princess as if she were a bundle of wheat, so that she was swimming in blood. Kiss Miklos took her from his hands and placed her on the silken bed, where she lay, neither dead nor alive, still as a lifeless block.

Now the Lead Friend grew terribly sorry, and making himself squalid looking, he entered the white chamber, rushed to the princess, wept without ceasing, touched her but she woke not, spoke to her but she heard him not. At last he found this to say: "Wake up, my heart's beautiful love. I will tell where my strength lies. In the silken meadow under the seventh bush is a hare, under the tail of the hare an egg, in the egg a hornet, and in the hornet is hidden my strength, so that I live as long as the hornet lives; if the hornet dies, I die too."

The Green Daughter of the Green King heard all

these words clearly, but acted as if she were neither dead nor alive, — lay there like a soulless block.

Well, 'pon my soul! what came of the affair or what did not, the princess rose from her silken bed in the night-time, quietly, in one garment; but she threw a great shawl around her neck, slipped out of the gate, found Kiss Miklos, to whom her word and speech was this: " Wake up, my heart's beautiful love, renowned Kiss Miklos, I know now where the strength of the Lead Friend lies; but listen to my word. In the silken meadow under the seventh bush lies a hare, under the hare's tail is an egg, in the egg a hornet, in the hornet is the Lead Friend's strength. If thou kill the hornet, the Lead Friend will lose his strength."

Our Miklos wanted nought else. He turned himself at once into a hound, drove the hare from the seventh bush of the silken meadow. The hare began to run, but the hound was not slow; with a long stick he struck the egg from the hare's tail. The egg broke and the hornet flew out, but the hound was not slow; with a great jump he caught the hornet, and crushed it to bits in his teeth. Then the hound shook himself and turned into Kiss Miklos again.

At daylight the Lead Friend was sick. He had lost his strength, he could not move his hands or his feet, and lay groaning on his lead couch like a man who had been pressing a straw-bed for seven years; and when the sun rose he breathed out his cursed soul.

Who was more delighted at his death than our

33

Kiss Miklos and the Green Daughter of the Green King? Straightway they called a priest and a hangman and an iron cap. The priest joined them, the hangman thrashed around, God's arrow flashed, but no one was struck. There was soup plenty and to spare, lucky was the man who came with a spoon; the unhappy were happy; the gypsy fiddled, and the music spoke. When the feasting and the poppy week had passed, Kiss Miklos and his consort took a chariot of glass and gold, drawn by six black-haired steeds, and set out for Miklos's birthplace. Now, the shining sun had shone so sadly, and the bright moon had beamed so sadly that it could not be more so; but the moment they beheld Miklos and his wife in the chariot of glass and gold, the bright sun shone joyously, and so did the clear moon.

"What's this? what's this?" said to himself the old king, who still rejoiced in good health. He summoned the wise men and the skilled scribes of the kingdom to his palace and gave them the following question: "Explain to me this. It is seven years since the two sons of the poor man brought back the bright moon and the shining sun; these two sons are now ruling kings, — may God keep them in health! — but the clear moon and the shining sun gave us such sorrowful light, and now all at once both are radiant."

One old man skilled in letters, and so old that his white beard almost came to the earth, and he could not stand on his feet alone, but three men supported him, spoke the following words: " Haho! high lord, there is great reason for this. The clear moon and the shining sun were sad because the man who really freed them from the claws of the dragons was pinioned in bondage; and he is no other than the renowned Kiss Miklos, the poor man's youngest son, who even at this moment is driving to the king's palace with the Green Daughter of the Green King, in a chariot drawn by six horses."

That moment Kiss Miklos and his wife entered the white chamber together. Here the lords and those great wise men all rose before them, as did even the old king himself, who advancing embraced and kissed them, led them to his own purple velvet throne, seated them thereon, and turning to the wise men and the skilled scribes, asked them, " Who really deserves the kingdom, the elder brothers or Kiss Miklos? "

The council said: " Kiss Miklos."

Then Miklos rose and said to the old king and the council: " High king and worthy council, it is true that I deserve the kingdom, and I would take it were I not the heir of the far-famed Lead Friend, and were it not that the dominions of the Green King, after his death, — which from my heart I wish not, —will come to me. This being the case the worthy council can see, and thy Highness can see also, that I may not accept the kingdom. Let it remain as it is, — let my eldest brother be king, and my second brother be viceroy; they are, I think, honorable men, and worthy."

The lords, sages, and skilled scribes present, as well as the old king, rose up and confirmed the wise speech of the youthful Kiss Miklos.

Then the two brothers of Kiss Miklos — the king and the viceroy — entered; they embraced and kissed one another, and sacred was the peace. After that, Kiss Miklos and his wife returned to the domains of the Lead Friend, and after the death of the Green King, Kiss Miklos inherited his dominions. And so he ruled two kingdoms very happily; and he and the Green Daughter of the Green King are living yet, if they are not dead.

THE HEDGEHOG, THE MERCHANT, THE KING, AND THE POOR MAN.

WHERE there was, where there was not, it is enough that there was once a merchant, there were also a king, and a poor man.

One day the merchant went out to hunt, and he travelled and journeyed till, oh! my lord's son, he found himself in such a thick forest that he saw neither the sky nor the earth; he just groped around like a blindman. Here, 'pon my soul! whether the merchant tried to free himself by turning to the left or the right, he only went into a thicker place. When he was there five days, in hunger and thirst, stumbling about in the great wild wood without liberation, the merchant called out: —

"Oh, my God, if any one would take me out of this great wild thicket to the right road, I would give him the best of my three daughters, and as a wedding gift three sacks of coin."

"I'll lead thee out right away," said some one before him.

The merchant looked to the right, to the left, but not a soul did he see.

"Don't look around," said the certain one again, "look under thy feet."

The merchant then looked in front and saw that near his feet was a little hedgehog, and to him he directed then his word and speech. "Well, if thou wilt lead me out, I will give thee my best daughter and three sacks of coin; the first will be gold, the second silver, and the third copper."

The hedgehog went on ahead, the merchant walked after. Soon they came out of the great wild wood. Then the hedgehog went back, and the merchant turned his wagon-tongue homeward.

Now the king went to hunt, — went in the same way as the merchant; and he too was lost in the great wild wood. The king went to the right and the left, tried in every way to free himself; all he gained was that he came to a thicker and a darker place. He too stumbled around five days in the thick wood, without food or drink. On the sixth morning the king cried out: "Oh, my God! if any one would free me from this dense wood, even if a worm, I would give him the most beautiful of my daughters, and as a wedding gift three coaches full of coin."

"I'll lead thee out right away," said some one near him.

The king looked to the right, to the left, but saw not a soul.

"Why stare around? Look at thy feet; here I am."

The king then looked at his feet and saw a little hedgehog stretched out, and said to him: "Well, hedgehog, if thou wilt lead me forth, I'll give thee the fairest of my daughters and three coaches full of coin, — the first gold, the second silver, the third copper."

The hedgehog went ahead, the king followed, and in this way they soon came out of the great wild wood. The hedgehog went back to his own place; the king reached home in safety.

Very well, a poor man went out for dry branches. He went like the merchant and king, and he got astray, so that he wandered dry and hungry for five days in the great wild wood; and whether he turned to the right or the left he gained only this, that he went deeper into the denseness.

" My God," cried the poor man at last, " send me a liberator ! If he would lead me out of this place, as I have neither gold nor silver, I would take him as a son, and care for him as my own child."

"Well, my lord father, I'll lead thee out; only follow."

" Where art thou, dear son ? "

" Here, under thy feet; only look this way, my lord father."

The poor man looked near his feet, and saw a little hedgehog stretched out.

"Well, my dear son, lead me out and I 'll keep my promise."

The hedgehog went ahead, the poor man followed, and soon they came out of the great wild wood. The hedgehog then went back to his own place, and the poor man strolled home.

Well, things remained thus till once after bedtime there was a knocking at the poor man's door. "My lord father, rise up, open the door." The poor man, who was lying on the stove, heard only that some one was knocking at the door.

"My lord father, rise up, open the door."

The poor man heard, and heard that some one was knocking and as he thought calling out: "My lord father, rise up, open the door;" but in his world life he had never had a son. The third time he heard clearly, "My lord father, rise up, open the door."

The poor man did not take this as a joke. He rose up and opened the door. My lord's son, who came in to him? No one else than the little hedgehog.

"God give a good evening to my lord father and to my mother as well," said the hedgehog.

"God receive thee, my dear son. Hast thou come then?"

"I have indeed, as thou seest, my lord father ; but I am very tired, therefore wake up my mother and let her make a bed for me in my chamber."

What was the poor man to do? He woke up his wife ; she made a towering bed, and the hedgehog lay in it. In the morning the poor man and his wife sat down to breakfast. They did not wish to forget their adopted son, but gave him food on a wooden plate under a bench by the fire. The hedgehog did not touch it. "Well, my son," asked the poor man, "why not eat?"

"I do not eat, my lord father, because it is not proper to treat an adopted son like some orphan or another; therefore it beseems me not to eat all alone from a wooden plate under a bench at the fire. Seat me nicely at the table by thy side, put a tin plate before me, and place my food on it."

What was the poor man to do? He seated the Hedgehog at his side, put a tin plate before him, and measured out food on it; then the Hedgehog ate with his father and mother. When they had finished breakfast the Hedgehog spoke thuswise: "Well, my lord father, hast thou a couple of thalers?"

"I have."

"I suppose thou art keeping them to buy salt and wood with?"

"Yes, my son."

"I speak not of that, I am speaking of this: lend me the money; I will return it a thousand-fold. Se' not thy mind much on salt and wood now; but go, my lord father, to the market. In such and such a place an old woman has a black cock for sale; buy him of her. If she asks a small price, give her double; for that will be my steed. When thou hast bought the cock for two prices, in such and such a place is a saddler; go to him. In a corner of his shop is a cast-away, thrown-away, ragged, torn saddle; buy that for me, but give him two prices also. If he asks little, give him double."

The poor man put on his coat, put the two thalers in his pocket, went to the market, bought the black cock and the cast-away, thrown-away saddle for two prices; each one for two small bits of money.

The Hedgehog then saddled the black cock with the cast-away, thrown-away saddle, sat upon him, and went to the court of the rich merchant whom he had led out of the great wild wood; he knocked at the door and called: "Hei, father-in-law, open the gate, let me in!"

The rich merchant opened the gate in great wonder. Who was coming? No one other than our Hedgehog, riding on a black cock.

"Hear me, rich merchant," began the Hedgehog; "knowest thou thy promise? When I led thee out of the great wild wood, dost remember thy promise to give me the best of thy three daughters and three sacks of coin? Now I have come for the maid and the money."

What could the rich merchant do? He called his three daughters into the white chamber, and turned to the Hedgehog, saying: "Well, choose among the three the one who pleases thy eye, thy mouth, and thy heart."

The Hedgehog chose the second daughter, for she was the most beautiful of the three. The merchant then

measured out three sacks of coin, — in the first, as he
had said, there was gold, in the second silver, in the
third copper; then he put his daughter and the three
sacks of coin in a coach, to which four horses were
attached, and he sent on her way his most beautiful
daughter, with the Hedgehog. They travelled and
journeyed till the Hedgehog, who was riding at the
side of the coach on his black cock, came up, looked
in through the window, and saw that the bride was
in tears.

"Why dost thou cry, why dost thou weep, my
heart's beautiful love?" asked the Hedgehog of the
maiden.

"Why should I not cry, why should I not weep,
when God has punished me with such a nasty thing
as thee? — for I know not whether thou art a man
or a beast."

"If this is thy only trouble, my heart's beautiful
love, we can easily cure it; I'll keep the three sacks
of coin for myself, and thee I'll send back to thy
father, for I see that of me thou art not worthy."

Thus was it settled; the Hedgehog kept the three
sacks of coin, but the merchant's daughter he sent
back to her father. The Hedgehog then took the
coin to the poor man, who became so rich that I think
another could not be found like him in seven villages.

Now the Hedgehog plucked up courage, saddled his
black cock, sat on him, and rode away to the king,
stood before him, and spoke in this fashion: "Dost

thou remember, king, that when I brought thee out of the great wild wood, thou didst promise that if I would show the right road thou wouldst give me the most beautiful of thy three daughters and fill for me three coaches, the first with gold, the second with silver, and the third with copper coin? I am here so that thou mayest keep thy word."

The king called his three daughters to the white chamber and said: " I made a promise, and this is it: to give one of my three daughters to this Hedgehog as wife; I promised because the Hedgehog led me out of a great wild wood, in which I wandered for five days without food or drink, and he saved me from certain death. Therefore say, my dear daughters, which of you will agree to marry the Hedgehog."

The eldest daughter turned away, the second turned away also; but the youngest and fairest spoke thus: " If thou, my father the king, hast made such a promise, I will marry him. Let the will of God be done if he has appointed such a husband for me."

" Thou art my dearest and best daughter," said the king; and he kissed her again and again. Then the king measured out three coaches of coin, seated the princess in a chariot of gold and glass and started her on her journey, amid bitter tear-shedding, with the Hedgehog, who rode at the side of the chariot on his black cock. They travelled and journeyed across forty-nine kingdoms till the Hedgehog rode up to the chariot, opened the window, looked in, and saw that the princess was not weeping, but was in the best cheerful humor.

"Oh, my heart's beautiful love," said the princess, "why art thou riding on that black cock? Better come here and sit at my side on the velvet cushion."

"Thou art not afraid of me?"

"I am not afraid."

"Thou art not disgusted with me?"

"No; if God has given thee to me, then thou shouldst be mine."

"Thou art my only and most beloved wife!" said the Hedgehog; and with that he shook himself, and straightway turned into such a pearl-given, charming, twenty-four-years-old king's son that tongue could not tell, — golden-haired, golden-mouthed, golden-toothed. And the black cock shook himself three times, and became such a golden-haired magic steed that his equal would have to be sought for; the cast-away, thrown-away saddle became golden, everything on it was gold to the last buckle.

The king's son then picked out the most beautiful place in the kingdom; standing in the middle of this he thought once, and suddenly that instant there stood before him a copper-roofed marble palace, turning on a cock's foot, and in it every kind of the most varied and beautiful golden furniture, — everything and everything was of gold, beginning with the mirror-frame and ending with the cooking-spoon. The king's son conducted the beautiful golden bird

— the fair princess — into the pearl-given palace, where, like birds in a nest, they lived in quiet harmony. When the merchant's three daughters and the two elder princesses · heard of the happiness of the youngest princess, — how well she had married, — in their sorrow one of them jumped into a well, another drowned herself in a hemp-pond, and a third was drawn dead out of the river Tisza [Theiss]. In this way four of the maidens came to an evil end; but the second daughter of the merchant gritted her teeth venomously at the princess, and made a firm and merciless resolve that she would imbitter her life's happiness. She went therefore to the palace, and found service in the guise of an old woman. She, the devil-given, came at a critical time; for the Burkus king[1] had declared war against the king's son, and the princess, while her husband was in the field, was left to the care of the merchant's daughter, disguised as an old woman. Milk might as well be confided to a cat as the princess to that cockroach of the underground kingdom. While the king's son was gone, the Lord gave the princess two beautiful children. The old woman packed them into a basket, put them under a tree in the woods, then ran back to the princess, who, recovering from a faint into which she had fallen, asked the old woman to give her the children so that she might embrace and kiss them.

[1] The Prussian king, — King of Prussia.

"High queen," answered the old woman, "what is the use in delay or denial? They were two untimely, hairy monsters, and to save thee from terror at sight of them, I threw both into the river."

The two children slept quietly under the tree till a white deer burst with great noise through the thicket, went straight as if sent, and taking the basket hung it on his antlers; then the white deer disappeared in the forest, went on till he came to the bank of a stream, where he called three times. The Forest Maiden appeared as if by magic, took the basket with great delight, and ran panting into her own palace.

The two children were seven years with the Forest Maiden, who reared them as carefully as if they had been her own.

Here, 'pon my soul, what came of the affair, or what did not, the Forest Maiden once sent the little girl with a green jug for water, and enjoined on her rigorously to be careful not to break the jug.

The little girl did not let this be said twice; she was obedient and attentive. She took the jug, and was at the well in a moment. When she came, she saw a little golden bird flying around the well. Being a child, she wanted to catch the golden bird, therefore ran around with the jug in her hand till at last she saw that only the handle was left. The little girl, terrified, burst into tears, sat at the edge of the well, and cried there. The Forest Maiden waited and waited; but she could not wait longer, therefore she sent the little brother with a second jug, and told him sternly to be careful not to break the jug. The little brother went in the same way, for he also, like children of that age, barely saw the golden bird when he wanted to strike it with the jug, which he whirled around till only the handle remained in his hand; then he burst into tears, sat by his sister, and there the two were crying at the edge of the well.

Here, 'pon my soul, the golden bird pitied the children, and asked: " Why do ye cry? Why do ye weep, pretty children? "

" Oh, pretty bird," answered the boy, who had more sense than his sister, " why should we not cry? Why should we not weep? We shall be flogged for breaking the green jugs; our dear mother will whip us."

" Oh, my children, she is not your own mother! She is only your foster-mother. Your father and mother live far from here, — beyond those green mountains; so if ye will follow, I 'll lead you home."

The two children wanted nothing else. They went back no more to their foster-mother, for they would be flogged; but they followed the golden bird, which went always before them. And they travelled and journeyed till once in a forest they came upon a great heap of gold; near the gold was a number of dice, as if some one had been playing there. The little boy and girl each took a handful of gold, and went farther. They travelled and journeyed till they came to an inn; since they were wearied, and it was evening, they went in to ask lodging. In the inn three lords were playing dice; the two children at first merely noticed that they were playing. At last the boy took from his pocket the handful of gold, and began to play in such fashion that he won all the money of the three lords; and then one of them spoke thuswise: —

"Well, my dear son, I see that thou hast good luck. I have in a certain place a charming flower-garden; in the middle of the garden is a marble palace, and the palace has this peculiarity, — if it is struck on the side three times with this golden rod, it will turn into a golden apple; and thou mayest put down the marble palace and the flower-garden in any part of the world if thou wilt strike the golden apple with the small end of the golden rod. I will bet now this flower-garden and this marble palace; if thou canst win, they'll be thine."

The little boy agreed; and he won fortunately the flower-garden and the marble palace. The other then gave him the golden rod, and showed him where the garden and the palace were. Next morning the children sought out the garden and the palace, which the boy struck three times on the side, and it turned to a golden apple; he put the apple in his pocket, and strolled on homeward. The little golden bird flew always ahead of them. They travelled and journeyed till one time the golden bird stopped and said: —

"Well, dear children, now we are at home; put

34

down the golden apple on this spot and strike it three times with the rod, and ye will see what a beautiful marble palace and flowery garden there will be, speaking to the seven kingdoms. The report of the palace and garden will circulate immediately, and the king himself will come to look at them. Him ye must honor as your father, for thou my little boy art the king's son, and thou my little girl the king's daughter. Dear children, here in a golden frame is a picture which gives your arms and name. Hang in the palace this picture, in the best place; but lest it be seen, cover it with velvet, and show it to no man save your own father. When he asks what that picture is, draw the velvet from it, and the rest will follow."

So it happened; the two children hung up the picture in the best room of the marble palace, and covered it with velvet. Now, the report ran to distant parts of the kingdom that there was a charming and wonderful marble palace in such and such a place, and people hastened from the seventh province distant to look at it; so that the report came to the ears of the king himself. The king decided straightway to look at the flowery garden and marble palace; but he had hardly conceived the idea when the old woman gave him a drug. The king fell ill, and could not see the flowery garden and marble palace; and then the old woman, without invitation, stood before the king and said: "High king, if thou art so curious to see this flowery garden and marble palace, then I will go and see if they are as beautiful as report says, and tell the story to thy Highness."

The king in one way or another agreed, and the old woman went, not to see the garden, but to bring the two children to evil destruction; the wicked creature tried but succeeded not, for her weapons broke. Not to confound one word with another, I will tell the whole tale in order and accuracy.

The old witch had barely reached the famous flower-garden when the two children hurried before her and showed everything from root to top, and the old piece of leather began to talk thus: " It is true that the garden is beautiful, but it would be seven times more beautiful if ye would bring the world-sounding tree."

"What must be done to get that?" asked the little boy.

" Not other than this," answered the old skeleton: " In such and such a place, in an enchanted palace, is the world-sounding tree; but ye must go for it and bring it."

With that the old witch took farewell of the two children, and strolled home; but the boy had no peace from that hour. He wanted to go and bring the world-sounding tree; therefore taking farewell of his sister with bitter tear-shedding he set out for the tree. He was going and travelling across forty-nine king-doms till he came to a dark castle; this was the first enchanted castle. A big, lame, hairy devil stood there on guard with a fearful whip, so that no man might enter. The hairy devil shouted very angrily at our boy: "Stop! Who is there?"

"I," answered the little boy.

"Who is ' I ' ?"

"I."

"Art thou Yanoshka?" asked the devil.

"I am."

"What journey art thou on?"

"I am looking for the world-beautifully sounding tree. Hast thou not heard of it, my lord elder brother?"

"I have not heard of it; but in such and such a place my brother stands guard, and if he has not heard of it, then no one in the world has."

Yanoshka went forward on the right road in search of the world-sounding tree. He travelled and journeyed till he came to another enchanted dark castle; there a big, lame, hairy devil was standing on guard who shouted to our Yanoshka in great anger. Our Yanoshka was much braver now, for he knew he had nothing to fear.

"Who is it?" called out the devil.

"I."

"Art thou Yanoshka?"

"I am, at the service of my lord elder brother."

"Why art thou journeying here in this strange land, where even a bird does not go?"

"I am looking for the world-beautifully sounding tree. Hast thou not heard of it, my lord elder brother?"

"What is the use in delay or denial? I have not heard; but in such and such a place my eldest brother is on guard, and if he knows nothing of it, then no one in the world knows."

With this Yanoshka moved on towards the third enchanted castle; when he came, there was a big, lame, hairy devil on guard, who called out in great anger to Yanoshka: "Who is that?"

"I."

"Thou art Yanoshka?"

"I am."

"Why art thou journeying here in this strange land, where even a bird does not go?"

"I am looking for the world-beautifully sounding tree. Hast thou not heard of it, my lord elder brother?"

"Ho, ho, Yanoshka! of course I have; it is here in the garden of this enchanted palace. Thou mayest take it, but only if thou obey my words. If thou dost not value them or dost not observe them, thou wilt never see God's bright sky or the shining day again. I only want to say this: Here is a golden rod; strike the wall of the enchanted castle with it three times. Straightway a door will open before thee. In the very middle of the garden thou wilt find the world-beautifully sounding tree. Go around it three times and then hurry like a shot arrow, with the speed of a dog, or the stone wall will close, and thou wilt remain inside; and if thou art once shut in, God have mercy and pity on thee, for that instant thou wilt be turned to stone. This is my word and speech; if thou cling to it, thou wilt be lucky; if not, thou wilt be wretched forever."

The boy took the golden rod and struck the side of the enchanted castle with it. That instant the door opened before him. The king's son did not inquire much whether he might enter or not; in a moment he ran in through the door and straight to the garden. Every kind of singing and dancing maidens came to meet him, — some with citharas and harps; some played on cymbals and begged him to play and dance with them; some offered rich food and drink of every kind agreeable to the taste. But the king's son had no mind to eat or drink; he pushed aside the maidens and ran to the very centre of the garden, where the world-beautifully sounding tree was; then he went around it three times, turning toward the point whence he had come. That done he rushed from the garden, and a thousand times lucky was he. It was not the same for him to be a few minutes later, for the door closed and bit off the heel of his boot; but he did not care much about the heel of his boot. He ran home on the same road over which he had come; and when he arrived, the world-beautifully sounding tree was in the middle of the flowery gar-

den. Hitherto the flowery garden had been in good
fame, but now the fame was seven times greater, so
that people came from seven worlds to look at the
tree; and the report of it reached the king himself,
who determined in his mind if he had not seen it
yet he would now at least go to see it.

As soon as the old witch divined his thought she
put a powder in his coffee so that he became sick,
and was not able to leave the room; then she stood
before him without invitation, and said: "High king,
as thy Highness is sick, I will go to see if the world-
sounding tree is as beautiful as reported, and will soon
bring back word."

The king in one way or another agreed to the old
witch's proposal, and let her go to see the world-beautifully sounding tree. She had barely put foot in the
flowery garden when the two children ran out to her
to hear what the old woman would say this time.

"Beautiful children," said she, "beautiful is the
garden of itself, beautiful is the sounding tree, but
still seven times more beautiful would it be if the
world-sweetly speaking bird were to sing upon it."

"What must I do?" asked the little boy.

"Nothing else," answered the old witch, "than
this: In such and such a place is an enchanted
castle, and thence it would be necessary to bring
the world-sweetly speaking bird."

Then she went back; and from that hour the
king's son could not remain at home, but planned to

go for the world-sweetly speaking bird. Therefore, parting with his sister amidst bitter tear-shedding, he started through the kingdom and the world to bring home the sweetly speaking bird; but he enjoined on his sister that if the third day he were not at home, she should set out to seek him over a certain road, — and with that the king's son went his way.

He journeyed and travelled across forty-nine kingdoms to the first enchanted castle, where there stood on guard a big hairy devil, who had a terribly large whip in his hand, to kill, without pity or mercy, every man going up or down. Now, the hairy devil attacked Yanoshka sharply and roughly, thus: —

" Who art thou? "

" I, my lord elder brother."

" Who art thou? " asked the devil again.

" I."

" Art thou Yanoshka? "

" I am."

" Why art thou here in this strange land, where even a bird does not go? "

" I am going for the world-sweetly speaking bird. Hast thou heard of it, my lord elder brother? "

"What is the use in delay or denial? I have not indeed heard. But over there lives my elder brother; if he knows nothing of it, then no one in the world knows."

Now the king's son came to the second enchanted castle ; the second devil sent him to his eldest brother, the big lame devil.

When Yanoshka came to the third castle, the devil asked, " Why art thou here in this strange land, where even a bird does not go? "

" I am looking for the world-sweetly speaking bird. Hast thou not heard of it, lord elder brother, in thy world-beautiful life? "

" Of course I have; it is here in this enchanted castle. Thou mayest take it away if thou wilt listen to my word; if not, better thou hadst never been born. For if thou wilt not observe my words, thou wilt never see God's bright sun again. I only wish to say: Here is a golden rod; take it, and with it strike the wall of the enchanted castle three times. Straightway the door will open before thee; pass in, run to the end of the glass corridor and across eight chambers. In the ninth chamber is the world-sweetly speaking bird in a rusty cage. Thou wilt find there every kind of beautiful and more beautiful golden birds, but look not at them, listen not to them, take no one of them, but take the sweetly speaking bird sitting sadly in the rusty cage. Snatch the cage in an instant, and rush from the enchanted castle as if thou hadst been shot from a cannon."

The king's son took the golden rod and struck the wall of the enchanted castle with it three times, and in a twinkle the door opened before him. The king's son then asked few questions. Whether it was permitted or not he ran into the room in an instant. While he was running to the end of the glass corridor he was called by name, from the right to the left, to stop. It is true that he was frightened, but he paid no heed. He ran straight to the first chamber. Every kind of flowers, more and more beautiful, were in golden pots; but the king's son did not touch them. He ran to the second chamber. In that were all kinds of swords and guns, but he did not choose from them. He entered the third, fourth, fifth, and in this way till he came to the ninth chamber. The ninth chamber, as the devil had told him, was full of all kinds of golden and silver cages, and in them golden-feathered birds, more and more beautiful, were singing; but the world-sweetly speaking bird was drooping there sadly in a rusty cage, and was not singing.

As the world-sweetly speaking bird was not golden-feathered like the others, it did not please the king's son, and he did not take it, but chose from among the many golden-feathered birds the prettiest, and wished to take that; but as he reached towards it, suddenly, in the twinkle of an eye, he was turned to stone, and the door of the stone wall closed before him.

Now, the little princess every God-given day spread the table for her good brother, but he did not come. Every God-given evening she went out before the house and waited till nearly midnight; then she spread the bed for him, but he did not lie in it. So the first day passed, and the second, and the third, — day after day, but still the dear brother came not;

therefore the princess, crying and weeping, went out
to look for her brother. She journeyed and travelled
upon his trail till she came to the first enchanted castle, and the second, and at last the third. The devil
there stood on guard, with a great whip like a chain, so
as to strike on the head, without pity or mercy, every
one going up or down ; and he shouted angrily at the
little girl, " Who art thou ? "

" I."

" Thou art Marishka ? "   For meanwhile, let it be
said, this was the name of the king's son's sister.

" I am."

" Why art thou travelling in this strange land,
where not even a bird goes ? "

" I am looking for my brother. Hast thou not
heard of him, lord elder brother ? "

" Of course I have heard, — of course ! He is in
this enchanted castle, turned into stone ; he had to be,
for he would not obey me. Thou wilt go that way,
too, if thou wilt not hold to my word."

Now the little girl took the golden rod from the
devil, who told her what to do with it, and struck
the wall of the enchanted castle with it three times.
The door opened before her in a twinkle, the princess
ran in ; but she looked neither to the right nor the
left. She ran straight to the ninth chamber ; there
she took the rusty cage, struck her brother three
times on the side with the rod, then ran as if shot
from a cannon. And a thousand-fold was her luck

that she did not delay an eye-twinkle longer, for the
stone-wall door, as it was, cut the edge of her skirt
off when it closed.

The princess had barely come out of the enchanted
castle when she heard behind her frightful thundering, hammering and blowing, swearing and cursing,
with threats; they shouted after her: "Wait, thou! —
this-and-that-kind-of-wretch, it will soon be bitter for
thee!" But she did not turn to them; she ran like a
hunted deer till she reached home. Who was waiting
for her there? No one else but her dear brother.

The brother and sister then put up the sweetly
speaking bird on the world-beautifully sounding tree,
and the sweetly speaking bird spoke, sang more
sweetly than any cithara, so that whoever heard
it became ten years younger. If the flowery garden
had been famous before, it now stood in seven times
greater fame, so that from seven kingdoms the people came to look at it; and the king, hearing of
the fair fame of the flowery garden, resolved in
his mind that, though he had not gone yet, he would
go to see it now.

The old witch barely divined this intention of the
king when she gave him powders in black coffee,
from which the king became so sick that this time,
too, his visit to the beautiful garden came to nothing.
And then the old woman, without invitation, stood
before him, and said: " High king, thou hast such a
great desire to see the flowery garden, I will go at

once, and bring back word if its beauty is as great as its fame."

The king agreed, and the old woman went to see the flowery garden. She had barely put foot in it when the two children ran out to meet her, received her very cordially, and did not know where to seat her.

"Beautiful children," began the old sinner, "the marble palace is beautiful, the flowery garden is beautiful, the world-sweetly speaking bird is beautiful; but the flowery garden would be still more beautiful if the silver lake were flowing in it, and in the lake golden fish were playing."

"What must I do to get the lake?" asked the king's son.

"Only this," answered the old skeleton. "In a certain place, in an enchanted castle, is the world-silver lake, and in it the world-golden fish; it is only necessary to go for the silver lake, for the golden fish will come in it. All that is needed is to bring the lake."

Then the old woman took leave of the pair pleasantly, and went home. But the king's son from that day had no rest, so he took leave of his dear sister, and went out into the world for the silver lake. He travelled and journeyed across forty-nine kingdoms, and the Operentsia Sea, till he came to the first enchanted castle. A devil was guarding there, who sent him to his elder brother, and he to his eldest. The king's son arrived at the third enchanted palace. A devil stood guard there, with an enormous knotty club, to hit every man going up or down, without mercy or pity.

"God give thee good evening, my lord elder brother."

"God receive thee, Yanoshka; whither art thou faring in this strange land, where not even a bird goes?"

"I am looking for the world-silver lake. Hast thou not heard of it, lord elder brother?"

"Of course I have heard, — of course; it is here in this enchanted castle. But, my younger brother, thou wilt have to tie up thy drawers well if 't is thy wish to take that away; for if thou dost not obey my word, I tell thee, on my true soul, that thou wilt reach Pilate by supper-time. I wish to say this: Here is a golden rod; strike the side of the enchanted palace with it, and suddenly the door will open before thee, run in straight to the garden. Thou wilt hear thy name called, but listen not. Every kind of beautiful maiden will come before thee, offering meat and drink; but eat not, neither drink. Thou wilt find on the way every kind of rich thing, — gold, silver, diamonds, — but touch nothing. Then every kind of disgusting snake and toad will come out, but be not afraid; run straight to the silver lake, which flows in the garden, run around it three times towards home, and then run out as thou didst go in."

Well, the king's son took the golden rod, struck the side of the enchanted castle three times, and the door opened before him; scarcely had he put foot inside when maidens called him by name. "This way, this way, Yanoshka! Eat, drink, with relish, Yanoshka! This way, Yanoshka, my embracing two arms are open to thee, run no farther!"

The king's son, as if deaf, did not listen, but ran farther. Then maidens more and more beautiful came before him, — some sprang at him, dangled their golden hair in his face; the king's son did not stop, but struck at them rudely, rushing on. He had barely left the maidens when he fell on to piles of treasure thrown in his way: beaten gold was piled high, and milk-white silver coin, — here every kind of diamond ring, there swords set in diamonds; but the king's son touched nothing, and ran on. Then every kind of crawling, creeping thing swarmed around him, — here hissing snakes, there warty toads. Yanoshka looked not under his feet, but ran till he came to the silver lake, around which he rushed three times, and went out as he had come. A thousand-fold was his fortune, for had he been an instant later the stone wall would have closed before him; as it was it took the heel off his boot, but he cared nothing for that. He left his boots there and ran home barefoot; when he reached home the silver lake was already flowing through the flowery garden, and in it all kinds of precious golden fish were jumping.

Hitherto the marble palace and the flowery garden with the sounding tree and the sweetly speaking bird had been in fair fame, but now, when the silver lake was flowing through the garden, and golden fish playing in it, now I say their fame spoke to the seven worlds, and people came to look at them. When this reached the ears of the king he resolved that he would neither eat nor drink till he saw the marble palace with all its wonders. Though the old witch offered him black coffee repeatedly, the king did not take it; but sitting in the golden carriage with his wife, he drove to see the flowery garden.

Scarcely had the king and queen entered the flowery garden when the brother and sister ran out before them, panting, and kissed their hands.

" Oh, father, this little girl is like thee ! " cried the queen; " she is thy carved second ! "

" And the little boy looks like thee," answered the king.

Well, the king and the queen went around the garden in order, and they could not do justice to its beauty; when they saw the sounding tree and the sweetly speaking bird, they clapped their hands. The boy went up in a moment on the sounding tree, plucked from it a couple of golden apples, gave one to the king and the other to the queen, who could not praise sufficiently his kindness. Then the king and queen looked at the silver lake and the golden fish in it ; they visited the marble palace, and went from chamber to chamber till they had gone through seven in order.

The king and queen were unable to praise suffi-

ciently the beauty of the rooms; but when they came
to the most beautiful of all, the king found this to say,
speaking speech: "Well, my little servant, wilt thou
not answer a question of mine?"

"And what is it?" asked the prince.

"I should like to know why that picture is covered
with velvet, and what it depicts."

One word is not much, but the king's little son did
not say that much; speechless he drew the velvet
covering aside. The king and queen were amazed,
and knew their own children, whom they had never
seen before. One embraced one of them, and the
other the other; they could not speak, but they wept
and laughed, and then the world-sounding tree and
the sweetly speaking bird were heard.

Great was the rejoicing of every kind, but sad grew
the old sinner when the king seized her, made her fast
to a tree, and piled up beneath her a fire of sulphur.

NOTES.

————◆————

LETTERS in the Russian names and titles in this volume
have the following values : —

a	as	*a*	in hat
ai	"	*ai*	" bait
i accented	"	*ee*	" beet
j "	"		the French *J*
kh and h	"	*ch*	in the Gaelic *loch*
o accented	"	*o*	in bone
o unaccented	"	*u*	" full
u	"	*oo*	" moon

In this volume Russian names and titles without printed
accents are accented on the penult. Names and titles accented
on syllables other than the penult have the accents indicated
in the following list : —

Adór	Fedót	Kirbítyevna
Afrón	Goróh	Simeón
Andrónovich	Gosudár	Svaitozár
Baba-Yagá	Iván	Vóronovich
Bulát	Ivánushka	Yélena
Dolmát	Kirbít	

The few titles in the Russian tales are : —

Tsarevich,	*Tsar's son.*	
Tsarevna,	"	*daughter.*
Tsaritsa	"	*wife.*
Korolyevna,	*King's daughter, princess.*	

In Chekh and Magyar the accent is always on the first syllable.

In the Magyar consonantal combinations *cs* = *ch*, *gy* = *dy*, *s* = *sh*. Examples are Csako, pronounced Chako, — one of the cows sold by the poor man to the King of the Crows. This is a name given in Hungary to a cow with horns grown outward. Kiss Miklos, pronounced Kish Miklosh, means in English Nicholas Little. Magyar is pronounced Modyor, the unaccented *a* in Magyar being the equivalent, or nearly so, of our *o*.

The Russian myth-tales in this volume are all taken from Afanasyeff's[1] collection. At the end of each title are given, in parentheses, the part and page of the tale in the original work.

THE THREE KINGDOMS, — THE COPPER, THE SILVER, AND THE GOLDEN. Page 1. (Part vii. p. 97.)

The first name, that of the Tsar Bail Bailyanyin, is best translated as "White of White Land." There is in Russian mythology a lady of unspeakable beauty, Nastasya or Anastasya of the sea, who causes the sun to blush twice each day; she is perhaps the Nastasya, Golden Tress, of this story. Bail Bailyanyin, "White of White Land," may well be Bail Bog, the White God of pre-Christian Russians. And here a few words touching the persistence of myth-conceptions may not be out of place. In the tales of the Indians, and in fact of all men who have retained firm traces of primitive thought, the people of the myth-tellers are on the side of light and goodness, and their enemies on that of darkness and harm. This is parallel with the antithesis of day and night. The Russian phrases *baili dyen*, *baili svait*, "white day," "white world," are good examples of the old-time idea with which is connected, in all likelihood, the title Baili Tsar, "the White Tsar," still existent in Russia.

[1] The Russian title of Afanasyeff's work is, "Naródniya Rússkiya Skazki. A. N. Afanásieva, Moskvá." There are eight parts, usually bound in three volumes, and dated 1860–61–63.

IVAN TSAREVICH, THE FIRE-BIRD, AND THE GRAY
WOLF. Page 20. (Part vii. p 121.)

The variants of this tale among the Russians and other Slavs, as well as in Germany, are many, and would fill a volume of good size if collected and published. In some Russian variants Ivan Tsarevich retains Yelena the Beautiful, not through the art and friendship of the Wolf, but by his own craft and daring. When he has received the golden-maned steed in exchange for Yelena, and is going, he asks to take leave of the maiden ; the request is granted. He raises the beauty to the saddle-bow, puts spurs to the steed, rises in the air, shoots on above the standing forest, below the moving cloud, vanishes, holds on his way till he comes to the Tsar to whom he had promised to give the steed for the Fire-Bird. When the time comes for parting he asks to take a last ride on the steed, if only through the courtyard ; the Tsar agrees. Ivan mounts with the cage in his hand ; the steed rises as before, and he vanishes, comes to the place where he had left Yelena, and fares homeward with her till he meets his evil brothers.

IVAN THE PEASANT'S SON AND THE LITTLE MAN HIMSELF
ONE - FINGER TALL, HIS MUSTACHE SEVEN VERSTS IN
LENGTH. Page 37. (Part viii. p. 109.)

[Written down in the government of Saratoff, by Guskóff.]

In this tale we have Freezer and Great Eater, with powers exhibited on a smaller scale than those of the comrades of Kiss Miklos in the Magyar myth. The picture of the boat serving for the reality has its parallel quite frequently in Indian belief.

THE FEATHER OF BRIGHT FINIST THE FALCON.
Page 47. (Part viii. p. 1.)

Written down in the government of Vologda.

The Pig with Gold Bristles, the Deer with Golden Horns, and the Golden-Maned Steed with Golden Tail. Page 59. (Part ii. p. 268.)

Written down in the government of Voronej.

Water of Youth, Water of Life, and Water of Death. Page 72. (Part vii. p. 66.)

The sleeping maiden in this tale, with her slumbering host, reminds us at once of the Queen of Tubber Tintye in " The King of Erin and the Queen of Lonesome Island." See " Myths and Folk-lore of Ireland."

The Footless and Blind Champions. Page 82. (Part v. p. 164.)

This tale has many variants in Russian, and resembles the Brünhilde and Gunter story in the " Niebelungen Lied."

The Three Kingdoms. Page 97. (Part viii. p. 91.)

This story is remarkable for the change or metamorphosis of Raven, the great power, into a common raven after his defeat by Ivan Tsarevich and the surrender of the feather staff.

Raven is a great personage in American mythology, especially in that of the Modocs. Whenever he appeared and uttered his spell with an ominous laugh, everything was turned to stone. There are many rock groups of Eastern Oregon described in the myths as ancient mighty personages turned into stone by Raven. As soon as the body became stone, however, the spirit escaped, and took physical form in some other place. Over the spirit, Raven had no power.

Koshchéi Without-Death. Page 106. (Part vii. p. 72.)

[Written down in the government of Archangel.]

This name has been translated, but incorrectly, Koshchéi, the " Deathless " or " Immortal." Koshchéi was not deathless.

His death was in the world, but in a place apart from him, which is simply another way of saying that the source of his life was at a distance. We may find in this fact one very important clew to the discovery of the nature of personages like Koshchéi. No matter how they are cut up or slaughtered, where they act, they are alive and as strong as ever next instant ; it is as vain to try to kill them by attacking their bodies as it is to destroy winter by making bonfires in the open country, or destroy the summer by artificial cooling. There are two ways by which we may draw conclusions as to who these personages are, — one by discovering what or where their life or death is, the other by examining their acts. We do not know much at present about Koshchéi, from the fact that his death is in a duck's egg ; but if we could learn who the women are whom he carries away, that would throw light on his character. Let us take an American example. There is a personage, Winter, in a certain Indian myth whose heart is hidden away at a distance, and whose song brings frost and snow. The heart is found by the enemy of the Snow-maker; this enemy burns it, and the Snow-maker dies. In another Indian myth the hero's enemy is pounded to pieces, but comes to life, is killed repeatedly without result. At last the hero learns that his enemy's heart is in the sky, at the western side of the sun at midday; straightway he reaches up, gets the heart, crushes it, and his enemy dies. In this case the enemy is surely not a snow-maker.

Vassilissa Golden Tress, Bareheaded Beauty.
Page 124. (Part viii. p. 367.)

[Written down by Bronnitski.]

The name of the Tsar Svaitozar means "light-shining," "resplendent."

The wise blacksmith of the Savage Serpent receives a reward from Ivan Tsarevich similar to that given by Cucúlin to the Strong Smith in " Myths and Folk-lore of Ireland ; " he is made king.

THE RING WITH TWELVE SCREWS.
Page 137. (Part viii. p. 541.)

THE FOOTLESS AND THE BLIND. Page 149. (Part viii. p. 191.)

The struggle to the bitter end between Nikita and Yelena the Beautiful is well brought out in this tale.

KOSHCHÉI WITHOUT-DEATH. Page 165. (Part viii. p. 69.)

For an interesting parallel to this tale, see "Phakir Chand" in "Folk-tales of Bengal," by the Rev. Lal Behari Day.

GO TO THE VERGE OF DESTRUCTION AND BRING BACK SHMAT-RAZUM. Page 179. (Part vii. p. 38.)

In the original text the last task given by the king is to go "I know not where and bring back I know not what." Shmat-Razum is a variant.

MARYA MOREVNA. Page 203. (Part viii. p. 98.)

Morevna means "daughter of the sea."

This is a very fine tale, in which the ancient characters are well preserved. Koshchéi Without-Death, however, has his death with him this time.

YELENA THE WISE. Page 218. (Part vii. p. 304.)

THE SEVEN SIMEONS, FULL BROTHERS.
Page 228. (Part i. p. 370.)

The Simeons remind us at once of the brothers in "Fin Mac-Cumhail, the Seven Brothers, and the King of France." See "Myths and Folk-lore of Ireland."

THE ENCHANTED PRINCESS. Page 238. (Part viii. p. 138.)

This tale contains a good deal of myth material. Specially interesting is the withering of the trees when the soldier is put to sleep, and their budding forth when South Wind brings him back.

VASSILISSA THE CUNNING, AND THE TSAR OF THE
SEA. Page 249. (Part vi. p. 218.)

Vassilissa is written Vasilisa in Russian. I have doubled
the *s* to assist the reader, but regret now that I did not preserve
the Russian orthography and call attention to the pronunciation.

Tsar Unchristened Forehead is in the original text, and Tsar
of the Sea is given as a variant. I have taken the variant, which
is undoubtedly earlier than the name in the text. The battle
between beasts and birds in the beginning of the tale is very
curious. In Indian mythology struggles between beasts and
birds are common ; not, however, beasts and birds of the
present kind, but the beings who lived before men appeared,
and who fell from their former high places, becoming such
beasts and birds as those that we see now. The eagle in this
story corresponds in character to the mythologic birds before
their fall.

It is noteworthy that the struggles for superiority in Indian
myths are not carried on through fighting (the usual method in
Aryan myths), but through trials of skill, strength, dexterity,
— through playing ball, dice, foot-races, wrestling, and shooting.
The opponents always bet their heads, and the head of the
losing party is cut off without delay.

The "Chekh Myths and Folk-Tales," except " The Cuirassier
and the Horned Princess," are taken from a work in two parts
called, " Folk-Tales," by J. K. z. Radostova.[1] Prague, 1872.

BOYISLAV, YOUNGEST OF TWELVE. (Part ii. p. 241.)

THE TABLE, THE PACK, AND THE BAG. (Part i. p. 81.)

THE KING OF THE TOADS. (Part i. p. 133.)

THE MOUSE-HOLE, AND THE UNDERGROUND KINGDOM.
(In the original, " Mouse-Hole." Part ii. p. 361.)

[1] Národní Pohádky, od J. K. z. Radostova. V. Praze, 1872.

The Treacherous Brothers. (Part ii. p. 321.)

" The Cuirassier and the Horned Princess " (in the original, "Concerning a Cuirassier ") is taken from " Moravian Folk-Tales, Stories, Customs, and Beliefs," collected and written down by Benesh Method Kulda.[1] Prague, 1874. This work is in two parts.

The " Magyar Myths and Folk-Tales " are taken from the following sources, —

From "Original Folk-Tales of the Sayo Valley," collected by László Merényi.[2] (2 parts).

The Poor Man, and the King of the Crows.
(Part ii. p. 113.)

Kiss Miklos, and the Green Daughter of the Green King. (In the original, " The Lead Friend." Part i. p. 1.)

From "Original Folk-Tales," collected by László Merényi.[3] Pest, 1861. (2 parts).

The Reed Maiden. (Part ii. p. 35.)

From " Original Folk-Tales of the Danube Border," collected by László Merényi.[4] (2 parts).

The Useless Wagoner. (Part ii. p. 143.)

The Hedgehog, the Merchant, the King, and the Poor Man. (In the original, "The Hedgehog." Part ii. p. 5.)

---

[1] Moravské Národní Pohádky, Pověstí, Obyčeje a Pověry sebral a napsal. Beneš Method Kulda. V. Praze, 1874.

[2] Sajovölgyi Eredeti Népmesék Összegyüjtötte. Merényi László. Pest, 1862.

[3] Eredeti Népmesék Összegyüjtötte. Merényi László. Pest, 1861.

[4] Dunamelléki Eredeti Népmesék Összegyüjtötte. Merényi László. Pest, 1864.

From " Wild Roses. A Collection of the Mental Creations of the Sekler People," by Yanosh Kriza.[1] Klausenburg, 1863. (Volume I., all, I believe, that was published, contains ballads songs, and tales.)

MIRKO, THE KING'S SON. (Part i. p. 436.)

This beautiful tale was printed in the Keresturfiszek variety of Sekler Magyar, and has not been put into ordinary Magyar, so far as I know.

---

[1] Vadrószák, Székely Népköltési Gyüjtemény. Szerkeszti Kriza János. Kolozsvartt, 1863.